激情时刻

第57届美国总统竞选演讲和辩论实录

杜梦臻/袁 婧/编译

世界知识出版社

图书在版编目(CIP)数据

激情时刻：第57届美国总统竞选演讲和辩论实录：汉英对照 /
杜梦臻，袁婧编译.—北京：世界知识出版社，2012.12
ISBN 978-7-5012-4414-0

Ⅰ.①激… Ⅱ.①杜… ②袁… Ⅲ.①英语—汉语—对照读物
②演讲—美国—选集 Ⅳ.①H319.4：I

中国版本图书馆CIP数据核字（2013）第003258号

责任编辑	王晓娟
责任出版	赵 玥
责任校对	张 琨
封面设计	龚 磊

书 名	**激情时刻：第57届美国总统竞选演讲和辩论实录** Jiqing Shike: Di 57 Jie Meiguo Zongtong Jingxuan Yanjiang He Bianlun Shilu
主 编	杜梦臻 袁 婧
出版发行	世界知识出版社
地址邮编	北京市东城区干面胡同51号（100010）
网 址	www.wap1934.com
电子信箱	xjw_88@sohu.com
经 销	新华书店
电 话	010-85118128（编辑部） 010-65265923（发行）
印 刷	南阳印刷有限公司
开本印张	787×1092毫米 1/16 32¼印张
字 数	430千字
版次印次	2013年3月第一版 2013年3月第一次印刷
标准书号	ISBN 978-7-5012-4414-0
定 价	42.00元

目 录

目 录

Remarks by President Obama at Barnard College Commencement Ceremony

Thank you so much. Thank you. Please, please have a seat. Thank you.

Thank you, President Spar, trustees, President Bollinger. Hello, Class of 2012! Congratulations on reaching this day. Thank you for the honor of being able to be a part of it.

There are so many people who are proud of you – your parents, family, faculty, friends – all who share in this achievement. So please give them a big round of applause. To all the moms who are here today, you could not ask for a better Mother's Day gift than to see all of these folks graduate.

I have to say, though, whenever I come to these things, I start thinking about Malia and Sasha graduating, and I start tearing up and – it's terrible. I don't know how you guys are holding it together.

I will begin by telling a hard truth: I'm a Columbia college graduate. I know there can be a little bit of a sibling rivalry here. But I'm honored nevertheless to be your commencement speaker today – although I've got to say, you set a pretty high bar given the past three years. Hillary Clinton – Meryl Streep – Sheryl Sandberg – these are not easy acts to follow.

But I will point out Hillary is doing an extraordinary job as one of the finest Secretaries of State America has ever had. We gave Meryl the Presidential Medal of Arts and Humanities. Sheryl is not just a good friend; she's also one of our economic advisers. So it's like the old saying goes – keep your friends close, and your Barnard commencement speakers even closer. There's wisdom in that.

2

奥巴马在巴纳德学院毕业典礼上的演讲 ①

非常感谢大家。谢谢大家，请入座。谢谢大家。

谢谢你们，斯巴院长［译者注：中文名石德葆］、各位校董、伯林格校长。2012届毕业生，你们好！终于，你们迎来了这一天，祝贺你们！感谢你们让我有幸来参加这个活动。

有很多人为你们感到骄傲——你们的父母、家人、师长和朋友——都为取得这一成就作出贡献。因此，请为他们热烈鼓掌。今天在座的各位母亲们，见证所有孩子们毕业是最好的母亲节礼物。

但是我得说，每当我来到这种场合，就会想到玛莉娅和萨夏将来毕业的情景，我就会热泪盈眶——真不好意思。我不知道你们大家是怎么把持得住的。

首先，我要说明一个确凿的事实：我是一名哥伦比亚大学的毕业生。我知道可能会有一点同门弟子相争的劲儿。但我还是为能够在你们今天的毕业典礼上讲话而倍感荣幸——不过我得说，你们在过去的三年里树立了相当高的标准。希拉里·克林顿——梅丽尔·斯特里普——谢里尔·桑德伯格——在她们之后出场可不容易。

但我要指出，希拉里的工作不同凡响，她是美国有史以来最杰出的国务卿之一。我们已授予梅丽尔艺术与人文总统奖章。谢里尔不仅是一位好朋友；她还是我们的经济顾问之一。正如那句老话所说——亲近你的朋

① 巴纳德学院（Barnard College）是美国的一所私立女子高等学校，1889年于纽约市创办，以原哥伦比亚学院院长弗雷德里克·巴纳德的名字命名。1900年并入哥伦比亚大学，但仍保留独立的学校董事会和财政机构，有自己的教师、图书馆和与哥伦比亚大学共同享有的设施，但学士学位由哥伦比亚大学授予。课程涉及人文学、社会科学和自然科学，亦提供音乐、戏剧等方面的专门课程。学生可参加哥伦比亚大学的许多活动，亦可到哥伦比亚大学听课。

Now, the year I graduated – this area looks familiar – the year I graduated was 1983, the first year women were admitted to Columbia. Sally Ride was the first American woman in space. Music was all about Michael and the Moonwalk.

No Moonwalking. No Moonwalking today.

We had the Walkman, not iPods. Some of the streets around here were not quite so inviting. Times Square was not a family destination. So I know this is all ancient history. Nothing worse than commencement speakers droning on about bygone days. But for all the differences, the Class of 1983 actually had a lot in common with all of you. For we, too, were heading out into a world at a moment when our country was still recovering from a particularly severe economic recession. It was a time of change. It was a time of uncertainty. It was a time of passionate political debates.

You can relate to this because just as you were starting out finding your way around this campus, an economic crisis struck that would claim more than 5 million jobs before the end of your freshman year. Since then, some of you have probably seen parents put off retirement, friends struggle to find work. And you may be looking toward the future with that same sense of concern that my generation did when we were sitting where you are now.

Of course, as young women, you're also going to grapple with some unique challenges, like whether you'll be able to earn equal pay for equal work; whether you'll be able to balance the demands of your job and your family; whether you'll be able to fully control decisions about your own health.

And while opportunities for women have grown exponentially over the last 30 years, as young people, in many ways you have it even tougher than we did. This recession has been more brutal, the job losses steeper. Politics seems nastier. Congress more gridlocked than ever. Some folks in the financial world have not exactly been model corporate citizens.

No wonder that faith in our institutions has never been lower, particularly

友，但更要亲近在你们巴纳德学院毕业典礼上讲话的人。这话寓意深长。

我毕业那年——这个地方看着眼熟——我毕业于1983年，那一年哥伦比亚大学首次开始录取女生。当时萨莉·莱德成为第一位进入太空的美国女性。那时的音乐全是迈克尔和太空步。

不走太空步。今天不走太空步。

我们当时有"随身听"，没有iPods。这四周的一些街区没有现在这样诱人。时报广场不是适合全家人去的地方。我知道这一切都属陈年旧迹。毕业典礼演讲人絮叨旧事是再糟糕不过的。但是，尽管有种种差别，八三届毕业生其实与你们各位有许多共同之处。这是因为，当时我们踏入社会的时候，也正值国家从一场特别严重的经济衰退中恢复。那是一个变革的时期，一个充满未知的时期，一个政治辩论激情高涨的时期。

因为在你们刚开始熟悉这所校园的时候，经济危机降临，不等你们第一学年结束，它已经导致500多万人失业。所以，你们最能够体会到这一点。自那时起，你们或许目睹了一些父母将退休计划无奈延迟，一些朋友在求职之路上苦苦挣扎。面对未来，你们也许像当年坐在这个座位上的我们一样，忧心忡忡。

when good news doesn't get the same kind of ratings as bad news anymore. Every day you receive a steady stream of sensationalism and scandal and stories with a message that suggest change isn't possible; that you can't make a difference; that you won't be able to close that gap between life as it is and life as you want it to be.

My job today is to tell you don't believe it. Because as tough as things have been, I am convinced you are tougher. I've seen your passion and I've seen your service. I've seen you engage and I've seen you turn out in record numbers. I've heard your voices amplified by creativity and a digital fluency that those of us in older generations can barely comprehend. I've seen a generation eager, impatient even, to step into the rushing waters of history and change its course.

And that defiant, can-do spirit is what runs through the veins of American history. It's the lifeblood of all our progress. And it is that spirit which we need your generation to embrace and rekindle right now.

See, the question is not whether things will get better – they always do. The question is not whether we've got the solutions to our challenges – we've had them within our grasp for quite some time. We know, for example, that this country would be better off if more Americans were able to get the kind of education that you've received here at Barnard – if more people could get the specific skills and training that employers are looking for today.

We know that we'd all be better off if we invest in science and technology that sparks new businesses and medical breakthroughs; if we developed more clean energy so we could use less foreign oil and reduce the carbon pollution that's threatening our planet.

We know that we're better off when there are rules that stop big banks from making bad bets with other people's money and – when insurance companies aren't allowed to drop your coverage when you need it most or charge women differently from men. Indeed, we know we are better off when women are treated fairly and equally in every aspect of American life – whether it's the

当然，作为年轻女性，你们还将应对某些特殊的挑战，比如是否能够享有同工同酬的待遇；是否能够平衡工作和家庭的需要；是否能够对自身的健康享有完全的决定权。

虽然过去30年来女性的机会有了突飞猛进的增加，但作为年轻人，你们在很多方面面临着比我们当时更为严峻的挑战：经济衰退愈演愈烈，就业形势日趋严峻，政治争斗难以调和，国会决议僵持不下，一些金融界人士行为举止很难被称为模范企业公民。

因此，公众对我们体制的信任下滑也不足为奇，尤其是当好消息不如坏消息引人注意的时候。人们每天接到一连串耸人听闻的消息或者丑闻，其中传递的信息是：变革是竹篮子打水；努力亦无济于事；现实生活与理想生活之间的鸿沟，难以逾越。

我今天的任务就是要告诉你们，不要相信这些说法。因为尽管困难重重，但我坚信你们精明能干。我见证过你们的激情，我见证过你们的奉献。我见证过你们的投入，我看到过你们挺身而出，人数空前。我听到了你们的声音，创意和对数码技术的精通使得这种声音格外响亮，而我们这些年长的人几乎不得其解。我看到心情迫切、跃跃欲试的一代人正准备跻身于历史的激流中，扭转其方向。

这种蔑视困难、积极进取的精神贯穿于整个美国历史的进程，是我们一切进步的源泉。此时此刻，我们需要你们这一代继承和发扬光大的正是这种精神。

可以看出，问题并不在于事情是否会好转——情况总是会变好的。问题也不在于我们是否已经有了应对我们所面临的挑战的解决办法——我们一直掌握着这些解决办法，已有相当一段时间了。比如说，我们知道，如果有更多的美国人能得到你们在巴纳德接受的这样的教育——如果有更多的人能够获得今天的雇主所需要的那些特定的技能和训练，美国的情况会更好。

我们明白，如果我们投资于能够造就新的企业并带动医学突破的科学与技术，如果我们开发出更多的清洁能源以减少外国石油的进口并减少对我们的地球构成威胁的碳污染，我们大家的日子会过得更好。

我们明白，如果能出台一些规则，阻止大银行拿别人的钱去恶赌——

salary you earn or the health decisions you make.

We know these things to be true. We know that our challenges are eminently solvable. The question is whether together, we can muster the will – in our own lives, in our common institutions, in our politics – to bring about the changes we need. And I'm convinced your generation possesses that will. And I believe that the women of this generation – that all of you will help lead the way.

Now, I recognize that's a cheap applause line when you're giving a commencement at Barnard. It's the easy thing to say. But it's true. It is – in part, it is simple math. Today, women are not just half this country; you're half its workforce. More and more women are out-earning their husbands. You're more than half of our college graduates, and master's graduates, and PhDs. So you've got us outnumbered.

After decades of slow, steady, extraordinary progress, you are now poised to make this the century where women shape not only their own destiny but the destiny of this nation and of this world.

But how far your leadership takes this country, how far it takes this world – well, that will be up to you. You've got to want it. It will not be handed to you. And as someone who wants that future – that better future – for you, and for Malia and Sasha, as somebody who's had the good fortune of being the husband and the father and the son of some strong, remarkable women, allow me to offer just a few pieces of advice. That's obligatory. Bear with me.

My first piece of advice is this: Don't just get involved. Fight for your seat at the table. Better yet, fight for a seat at the head of the table.

It's been said that the most important role in our democracy is the role of citizen. And indeed, it was 225 years ago today that the Constitutional Convention opened in Philadelphia, and our founders, citizens all, began crafting an extraordinary document. Yes, it had its flaws – flaws that this nation has strived to perfect over time. Questions of race and gender were unresolved. No woman's signature graced the original document – although we can assume

如果在你最需要的时刻，不允许（禁止）保险公司取消你的保险资格，男女收费标准不一，我们的日子会过得更好。确实，我们都知道，如果妇女在国家生活的方方面面，——无论是薪酬所得还是健康决定权，都能得到公平与平等的对待，我们的日子会过得更好。

我们明白这些都是实实在在的道理。我们知道，很显然，我们所面临的挑战都会迎刃而解。问题是，我们是否能够拧成一股绳，拿出意志力——在我们自己的生活中，在我们共有的体制中，在我们的政治事务中——实现我们所需要的变革。我坚信，你们这一代具有这种意志力。我相信，新一代女性——在座的各位，都将会在这条道路上带头前行。

我承认，这句话，可以不费吹灰之力在巴纳德学院的毕业典礼上赢得掌声和喝彩。说这样的话很容易。但事实确实如此。在某种程度上，这是简单的数学题。今天，妇女不仅占这个国家总人口的一半，还是这个国家劳动力的半壁江山。越来越多的女性的收入超过了她们的丈夫。你们在我们的大学毕业生中，在拥有硕士学位和博士学位的毕业生中占了一半以上。所以，你们在人数上超过了我们。

妇女不仅能改变自己的命运，还能改变这个国家乃至这个世界的命运。在几十年来的缓慢、持续、不凡的进展之后，这样的发展目标即将在本世纪成为现实。

然而，你们能领导这个国家走多远、能使这个世界走多远，还要取决于你们自己。你们必须有这种愿望。进步不可能由别人拱手奉上。作为一个希望你们、希望（我的女儿）玛莉娅和萨夏拥有这一前途及更美好前途的人，作为一个有幸成为几位坚强杰出的女性的丈夫、父亲和儿子的人，请允许我贡献几条建议。这是义不容辞的。请容我慢慢道来。

我的第一条建议是，仅仅参与还不够，要为在决策中赢得一席之地而奋斗。能为坐上首席而奋斗就更好了。

有人说，我们民主中最重要的角色是公民角色。的确如此，225年前的今天，在费城召开了制宪大会，我们的开国元勋，我们所有的公民，着手起草了一项伟大的纲领。是的，该文件存在缺陷，后来国家为了完善它作出了努力。种族和性别问题当时还悬而未决，因此最初的文件上没有妇女的签名来为之增添光彩，但是我们可以想象，一些开国之母在开国之父

that there were founding mothers whispering smarter things in the ears of the founding fathers. I mean, that's almost certain.

What made this document special was that it provided the space – the possibility – for those who had been left out of our charter to fight their way in. It provided people the language to appeal to principles and ideals that broadened democracy's reach. It allowed for protest, and movements, and the dissemination of new ideas that would repeatedly, decade after decade, change the world – a constant forward movement that continues to this day.

Our founders understood that America does not stand still; we are dynamic, not static. We look forward, not back. And now that new doors have been opened for you, you've got an obligation to seize those opportunities.

You need to do this not just for yourself but for those who don't yet enjoy the choices that you've had, the choices you will have. And one reason many workplaces still have outdated policies is because women only account for 3 percent of the CEOs at Fortune 500 companies. One reason we're actually refighting long-settled battles over women's rights is because women occupy fewer than one in five seats in Congress.

Now, I'm not saying that the only way to achieve success is by climbing to the top of the corporate ladder or running for office – although, let's face it, Congress would get a lot more done if you did. That I think we're sure about. But if you decide not to sit yourself at the table, at the very least you've got to make sure you have a say in who does. It matters.

Before women like Barbara Mikulski and Olympia Snowe and others got to Congress, just to take one example, much of federally-funded research on diseases focused solely on their effects on men. It wasn't until women like Patsy Mink and Edith Green got to Congress and passed Title IX, 40 years ago this year, that we declared women, too, should be allowed to compete and win on America's playing fields. Until a woman named Lilly Ledbetter showed up at her office and had the courage to step up and say, you know what, this isn't

的耳旁轻声细语地指点过一些高招。我是说，几乎肯定如此。

这份文件的特别之处，在于它为那些没有被纳入我们宪法的人们提供了争取权利的空间和可能性。它为人民提供了借助于一些原则和理想拓展民主范围的语言。它允许发起抗议和运动，允许传播新思想，一代又一代地改变着世界，形成了一股永不休止的潮流，延续至今。

我们的开国元勋认识到，美国并非一成不变；我们充满活力，不会停滞不前。我们向前看，不回头。既然新的大门已经为你们敞开，你们就有义务去把握这些机会。

你们需要这么做，不仅是为了你们自己，也是为了那些没能得到你们已经拥有以及还将拥有的种种选择的人。许多工作场所仍在实行过时的政策，原因之一就是妇女只占财富500强公司首席行政官的百分之三。我们仍在为争取妇女权利而再次进行早已完成的抗争，原因之一就是妇女在国会中所占的席位还不到五分之一。

我不是说取得成功的唯一途径是晋升到公司的最高层，或是竞选公职，不过，请让我们面对这个事实：如果你们竞选公职，国会将能大有作为。我想大家对此是深信无疑的。但如果你们决定不亲自参政，至少也应

right, women weren't being treated fairly – we lacked some of the tools we needed to uphold the basic principle of equal pay for equal work.

So don't accept somebody else's construction of the way things ought to be. It's up to you to right wrongs. It's up to you to point out injustice. It's up to you to hold the system accountable and sometimes upend it entirely. It's up to you to stand up and to be heard, to write and to lobby, to march, to organize, to vote. Don't be content to just sit back and watch.

Those who oppose change, those who benefit from an unjust status quo, have always bet on the public's cynicism or the public's complacency. Throughout American history, though, they have lost that bet, and I believe they will this time as well. But ultimately, Class of 2012, that will depend on you. Don't wait for the person next to you to be the first to speak up for what's right. Because maybe, just maybe, they're waiting on you.

Which brings me to my second piece of advice: Never underestimate the power of your example. The very fact that you are graduating, let alone that more women now graduate from college than men, is only possible because earlier generations of women – your mothers, your grandmothers, your aunts – shattered the myth that you couldn't or shouldn't be where you are.

I think of a friend of mine who's the daughter of immigrants. When she was in high school, her guidance counselor told her, you know what, you're just not college material. You should think about becoming a secretary. Well, she was stubborn, so she went to college anyway. She got her master's. She ran for local office, won. She ran for state office, she won. She ran for Congress, she won. And lo and behold, Hilda Solis did end up becoming a secretary – she is America's Secretary of Labor.

So think about what that means to a young Latina girl when she sees a Cabinet secretary that looks like her. Think about what it means to a young girl in Iowa when she sees a presidential candidate who looks like her. Think about what it means to a young girl walking in Harlem right down the street when she

该确保自己享有选举权。这很重要。

例如，在像芭芭拉·米库尔斯基和奥林匹娅·斯诺及其他女性进入国会前，联邦政府资助的大部分疾病研究主要侧重于疾病对男性的影响。40年前的今天，帕齐·明克和伊迪丝·格林等女性进入国会并通过［《教育法》修正案（第九条）］，从而宣布女性也有资格在美国的运动场上参与竞赛并赢得胜利。一个名叫莉莉·莱德贝特的女性来到她的办公室，勇敢而明确地说：你们知道吗，这不对，女性没有得到公正待遇——我们缺乏一些必要的手段来捍卫同工同酬的基本原则。

所以不要接受别人对于事情理当如何的看法。应该由你来除奸革弊；应该由你来指出不公不义；应该由你来督促社会体制负起责任，有时需要全盘改变。你应当挺身而出，发表意见，撰文游说，游行示威，组织民众，投票表决。不要满足于袖手旁观。

那些反对变革、受益于不公平现状的人，总是赌定公众要不是愤世嫉俗就是洋洋自得。可是纵观美国历史，他们一再下错赌注，我相信这一次也不例外。可是说到底，2012届的同学们，这将取决于你们。不要等待你身旁的人成为第一个为正义发言的人。因为有可能，只是有此可能，他们正在等你带头。

这就涉及我的第二条建议：切勿低估以身作则的力量。你们即将毕业的事实，且不说目前大学毕业的女生人数超过男生，都是因为前辈女性——你们的母亲、祖母、姨婶——打破了你不能或者不应当身在此处的神话。

我想起一位朋友，她是移民的女儿。念中学时，她的指导老师告诉她，你不是念大学的材料，你应当考虑去当秘书。她很固执，所以还是念了大学，进而拿到硕士学位。她竞选地方公职，结果胜选。她竞选州政府公职，再度胜选。她竞选国会议员，又是胜选。请听好了，希尔达·索利斯最终的确成为一名秘书——她成为美国劳工部的"秘书"［译者注："秘书"和"部长"在英文中是同一个单词］。

所以想想看，当一名拉丁裔的小女孩看到一名长得像她的内阁部长，会作何感想。当一名衣阿华州的小女孩看到一名长得像她的总统候选人，会作何感想。当一名小女孩走在哈莱姆区的街上，看到一名长得像她的驻

sees a U.N. ambassador who looks like her. Do not underestimate the power of your example.

This diploma opens up new possibilities, so reach back, convince a young girl to earn one, too. If you earned your degree in areas where we need more women – like computer science or engineering – reach back and persuade another student to study it, too. If you're going into fields where we need more women, like construction or computer engineering – reach back, hire someone new. Be a mentor. Be a role model.

Until a girl can imagine herself, can picture herself as a computer programmer, or a combatant commander, she won't become one. Until there are women who tell her, ignore our pop culture obsession over beauty and fashion – and focus instead on studying and inventing and competing and leading, she'll think those are the only things that girls are supposed to care about. Now, Michelle will say, nothing wrong with caring about it a little bit. You can be stylish and powerful, too. That's Michelle's advice.

And never forget that the most important example a young girl will ever follow is that of a parent. Malia and Sasha are going to be outstanding women because Michelle and Marian Robinson are outstanding women. So understand your power, and use it wisely.

My last piece of advice – this is simple, but perhaps most important: Persevere. Persevere. Nothing worthwhile is easy. No one of achievement has avoided failure – sometimes catastrophic failures. But they keep at it. They learn from mistakes. They don't quit.

You know, when I first arrived on this campus, it was with little money, fewer options. But it was here that I tried to find my place in this world. I knew I wanted to make a difference, but it was vague how in fact I'd go about it. But I wanted to do my part to do my part, to shape a better world.

So even as I worked after graduation in a few unfulfilling jobs here in New York – I will not list them all – even as I went from motley apartment to motley

联合国大使，她会作何感想。不要低估了你们以身作则的力量。

这张文凭将会开辟新的可能性，因此，回过头去，说服另一个小女孩也去追求学业。如果你们学习的专业是需要更多女性投入的领域——比如计算机科学或者工程学——那就回头说服另一名学生加入你们的学习行列。如果你们进入的是需要更多女性加入的领域，如建筑施工或者计算机工程——那就回头聘一位新人。做一个指导者。做一个好榜样。

一名女孩要成为计算机程序员或者军事指挥官，她必须首先具备这样的理想。直到有其他女性告诉她，不要让我们的流行文化沉迷于美丽和时尚——而是专注于学习，发明创新，与人竞争，发挥领导作用，她就会一直在意这些事情。好，米歇尔会说，在意一点又何妨。你可以既时髦又有力量。那是米歇尔的建议。

永远不要忘记一个女孩仿效的最重要的榜样就是她的父母。玛莉娅和莎夏将会成为杰出的女性，因为米歇尔和玛丽安·鲁宾逊都是杰出的女性。所以，要认识到你们的力量，并且明智地加以运用。

我的最后一点建议，很简单，但可能是最重要的一点：坚持不懈。坚持不懈。有价值的事物得之不易。没有一个有成就的人能够避免失败——有时甚至是一败涂地。可是他们坚持不懈，从错误中学习。他们绝不放弃。

你们知道，我刚到这个校园时，没有多少钱，更没有多少选择。但正是在这里，我试图寻找我在这个世界上的立足之地。我知道我想有所作为，但却不清楚如何去做。可我想尽自己的一份力量去建设一个更美好的世界。

apartment, I reached out. I started to write letters to community organizations all across the country. And one day, a small group of churches on the South Side of Chicago answered, offering me work with people in neighborhoods hit hard by steel mills that were shutting down and communities where jobs were dying away.

The community had been plagued by gang violence, so once I arrived, one of the first things we tried to do was to mobilize a meeting with community leaders to deal with gangs. And I'd worked for weeks on this project. We invited the police; we made phone calls; we went to churches; we passed out flyers. The night of the meeting we arranged rows and rows of chairs in anticipation of this crowd. And we waited, and we waited. And finally, a group of older folks walked in to the hall and they sat down. And this little old lady raised her hand and asked, "Is this where the bingo game is?" It was a disaster. Nobody showed up. My first big community meeting – nobody showed up.

And later, the volunteers I worked with told me, that's it; we're quitting. They'd been doing this for two years even before I had arrived. They had nothing to show for it. And I'll be honest, I felt pretty discouraged as well. I didn't know what I was doing. I thought about quitting. And as we were talking, I looked outside and saw some young boys playing in a vacant lot across the street. And they were just throwing rocks up at a boarded building. They had nothing better to do – late at night, just throwing rocks. And I said to the volunteers, "Before you quit, answer one question. What will happen to those boys if you quit? Who will fight for them if we don't? Who will give them a fair shot if we leave?"

And one by one, the volunteers decided not to quit. We went back to those neighborhoods and we kept at it. We registered new voters, and we set up after-school programs, and we fought for new jobs, and helped people live lives with some measure of dignity. And we sustained ourselves with those small victories. We didn't set the world on fire. Some of those communities are still very poor.

因此，即使当我毕业后在纽约从事几份没有成就感的工作的时候——我不会一一列举——即使从一间杂乱的公寓又搬到另一间同样杂乱的公寓的时候，我也在努力求索。我开始给全国各地的社区组织写信。有一天，芝加哥南区的一个小型教会组织回了信，给了我一份为当地居民服务的工作，他们那里的钢厂停业使他们受到沉重打击，那里的就业机会也一天天消失。

　　当地社区一直被帮派暴力所扰，所以我一到那里，我们争取做的第一件事情就是与社区领袖开会商量应对帮派的对策。我为这项工作忙了好几个星期。我们邀请了警察；我们打了电话，我们去了教堂；我们散发了传单。要开会的那天晚上，我们排好了一排排椅子，以为会有一大群人到会。我们等啊等。最后，一群老人走进大厅，然后坐下来。有一位瘦小的老太太举起手，问道："宾果游戏是在这里吗？"真是糟糕透了。没有人来。我的第一个社区大会——无一人到场。

　　后来，和我一起工作的志愿者对我说，够了，我们不干了。他们在我来之前已经干了两年之久。他们觉得没有任何成就可言。说实话，我也感到相当的气馁。我不知道我在做什么。我考虑是不是不干了。当我们交谈的时候，我往外面看了看，看到一群年轻的男孩在马路对面的空地上玩耍。他们正对着一座用板子钉起来的建筑物投掷石块。他们百无聊赖——在深夜，扔石头玩。我对那些志愿者说："在你们退出之前，先回答一个问题。如果你们不干了那些男孩会怎么样？如果我们不为他们着想，还有谁会为他们奋斗呢？如果我们走了，还有谁会给他们一个公平的机会呢？"

　　志愿者们一个接一个地决定不放弃。我们回到那些街区，继续坚持工作。我们给新选民登记，我们安排课后活动，我们争取新的就业机会，并帮助人们活得更有尊严。我们用那些小小的胜利鼓励自己。我们并没有做什么惊天动地的事情。这些社区中有一些仍然很贫穷。那里仍然有很多的帮派出没。但我相信，就是这些小小的胜利帮助我在这三年半里作为总统赢得了更大的胜利。

There are still a lot of gangs out there. But I believe that it was those small victories that helped me win the bigger victories of my last three and a half years as President.

And I wish I could say that this perseverance came from some innate toughness in me. But the truth is, it was learned. I got it from watching the people who raised me. More specifically, I got it from watching the women who shaped my life.

I grew up as the son of a single mom who struggled to put herself through school and make ends meet. She had marriages that fell apart; even went on food stamps at one point to help us get by. But she didn't quit. And she earned her degree, and made sure that through scholarships and hard work, my sister and I earned ours. She used to wake me up when we were living overseas – wake me up before dawn to study my English lessons. And when I'd complain, she'd just look at me and say, "This is no picnic for me either, buster."

And my mom ended up dedicating herself to helping women around the world access the money they needed to start their own businesses – she was an early pioneer in microfinance. And that meant, though, that she was gone a lot, and she had her own struggles trying to figure out balancing motherhood and a career. And when she was gone, my grandmother stepped up to take care of me.

She only had a high school education. She got a job at a local bank. She hit the glass ceiling, and watched men she once trained promoted up the ladder ahead of her. But she didn't quit. Rather than grow hard or angry each time she got passed over, she kept doing her job as best as she knew how, and ultimately ended up being vice president at the bank. She didn't quit.

And later on, I met a woman who was assigned to advise me on my first summer job at a law firm. And she gave me such good advice that I married her. And Michelle and I gave everything we had to balance our careers and a young family. But let's face it, no matter how enlightened I must have thought myself to be, it often fell more on her shoulders when I was traveling, when I was

我希望我能说这种执着源于我与生俱来的某种毅力。但事实是，这是后天学到的。我是从养育我的人身上学到的。更具体地说，我是从影响了我的生活的那些女性身上学到的。

我是一个单身母亲的儿子，她含辛茹苦，在努力维持家庭生计的同时完成学业。她有过破碎的婚姻，甚至一度靠领取食品券勉强养家度日。但她没有放弃。她获得了学位，并确保我和我妹妹能依靠奖学金和辛勤努力来获得我们的学位。当我们在海外生活时，她常常叫我起床——天不亮就起床，学习英语课程。当我抱怨时，她就会看着我说："小子，这对我也并不轻松。"

我的母亲最终完全投入到帮助世界各地妇女获得创业所需资金的工作中——她是微型信贷的一个先驱。但这意味着她经常不在家，而且她有着自身的挣扎，要努力在做母亲和发展事业之间找到平衡。她不在家时，我的外祖母承担起照顾我的责任。

她仅受过高中教育。她在当地银行找到一份工作，她遇到了事业上的玻璃天花板，眼看着她曾经培训过的男人晋升到比她更高的级别。但她没有退却。她没有因一次次机会旁落而变得冷漠或愤怒，而是继续尽自己最大的努力做好工作，最终她成为银行的副总裁。她没有退却。

后来，我遇到一位女性，她被派来担任我在一家律师事务所从事的第一份暑期工作的指导。她对我的指导如此之好，以致于我娶了她。米歇尔和我竭尽全力在发展事业与照顾幼小的孩子之间找到平衡。但是说实话，不管我当时可能认为自己是多么开通，在我外出旅行时，在我不在家时，家事往往更多地落在她的肩上。我知道，在照顾我们的两个女儿时，她为没有在工作上付出足够的时间感到内疚；而当她上班时，又为没有给孩子足够的时间感到内疚。我们俩都唯愿我们有某种超人的能力，使我们能够两者兼顾。但我们坚持住了，我们的努力保证了婚姻的稳定。

away. I know that when she was with our girls, she'd feel guilty that she wasn't giving enough time to her work, and when she was at her work, she'd feel guilty she wasn't giving enough time to our girls. And both of us wished we had some superpower that would let us be in two places at once. But we persisted. We made that marriage work.

And the reason Michelle had the strength to juggle everything, and put up with me and eventually the public spotlight, was because she, too, came from a family of folks who didn't quit – because she saw her dad get up and go to work every day even though he never finished college, even though he had crippling MS. She saw her mother, even though she never finished college, in that school, that urban school, every day making sure Michelle and her brother were getting the education they deserved. Michelle saw how her parents never quit. They never indulged in self-pity, no matter how stacked the odds were against them. They didn't quit.

Those are the folks who inspire me. People ask me sometimes, who inspires you, Mr. President? Those quiet heroes all across this country – some of your parents and grandparents who are sitting here – no fanfare, no articles written about them, they just persevere. They just do their jobs. They meet their responsibilities. They don't quit. I'm only here because of them. They may not have set out to change the world, but in small, important ways, they did. They certainly changed mine.

So whether it's starting a business, or running for office, or raising an amazing family, remember that making your mark on the world is hard. It takes patience. It takes commitment. It comes with plenty of setbacks and it comes with plenty of failures.

But whenever you feel that creeping cynicism, whenever you hear those voices say you can't make a difference, whenever somebody tells you to set your sights lower – the trajectory of this country should give you hope. Previous generations should give you hope. What young generations have done before

　　米歇尔之所以能够坚强地招架一切并忍受我，而且最终忍受公众聚光，是因为她同样来自一个不轻易退却的家庭——因为她看到她的父亲每天一大早起来去上班，尽管他从未念完大学，尽管他患有影响行动的多发性硬化症。她看到，尽管她的母亲从未念完大学，但在那个学校，那个贫民区的学校，她每天都确保米歇尔和她的哥哥受到他们应该得到的教育。米歇尔看到她的父母从不放弃。他们从不顾影自怜，不管他们面临多么不利的境况，他们从不放弃。

　　正是这些人激励着我。有时人们问我，总统先生，是谁激励着你？是这个国家各地那些默默耕耘的英雄——今天在座的你们一些人的父母和祖父母——他们不露锋芒，他们不会在报纸、杂志上留下姓名，他们只是坚持不懈。他们只是尽忠职守。他们敢作敢当。他们坚韧不拔。正是因为有他们我才站到这里。他们或许并没有从一开始就要改变世界，但他们以一点一滴的重要方式，改变了世界。无可厚非，他们改变了我的世界。

　　因此，无论是创办一家企业、竞选公职、还是抚养一个美好的家庭，请记住：要在这个世界上留下你的足迹并不是一件轻而易举的事情。它需要耐心，需要投入，伴随而来的是大量挫折和无数次的失败。

　　但是，每当你感觉到那种迎面扑来的冷嘲热讽，每当你听到人们说你无法改变现状，每当有人告诉你要苟且偷生——这个国家走过的道路应该给你带来希望。前几代人的经历应该给你带来希望。在你之前的一代又一代年轻人做过的一切应该给你带来希望。无论是在塞尼卡福尔斯还是在塞尔玛或是在石墙，当时那些参加游行、动员起来、挺身而出、进行静坐的年轻人，他们不仅仅是为自己这样做，他们这样做是为了别人。

should give you hope. Young folks who marched and mobilized and stood up and sat in, from Seneca Falls to Selma to Stonewall, didn't just do it for themselves; they did it for other people.

That's how we achieved women's rights. That's how we achieved voting rights. That's how we achieved workers' rights. That's how we achieved gay rights. That's how we've made this Union more perfect.

And if you're willing to do your part now, if you're willing to reach up and close that gap between what America is and what America should be, I want you to know that I will be right there with you. If you are ready to fight for that brilliant, radically simple idea of America that no matter who you are or what you look like, no matter who you love or what God you worship, you can still pursue your own happiness, I will join you every step of the way.

Now more than ever – now more than ever, America needs what you, the Class of 2012, has to offer. America needs you to reach high and hope deeply. And if you fight for your seat at the table, and you set a better example, and you persevere in what you decide to do with your life, I have every faith not only that you will succeed, but that, through you, our nation will continue to be a beacon of light for men and women, boys and girls, in every corner of the globe.

So thank you. Congratulations. God bless you. God bless the United States of America.

Barnard College, Columbia University, New York, New York, May 14, 2012

就是这样，我们获得了妇女权利；就是这样，我们获得了选举权；就是这样，我们获得了工人权利；就是这样，我们获得了同性恋权利。就是这样，我们使我们的合众国更趋完美。

如果你们愿意现在就来尽你们的职责，如果你们愿意竭尽所能缩小美国的现状与理想之间的差距，我想让你们知道：我会与你们站在一起。不管你是谁、不管你的外貌如何、不管你爱的是谁或敬拜什么样的神，你仍然可以追求自己的幸福——如果你准备为美国实现这个十分简单却又非常美好的信念而奋斗，我会在前进的道路上与你并肩迈出每一步。

与以往任何时候相比——与以往任何时候相比，2012届的毕业生们，现在美国都更需要你们所能贡献的一切。美国需要你们高瞻远瞩、胸怀大志。如果你们为争取自己的发言权而奋斗，树立一个更好的榜样，坚持做你们一生中立志要做的事业，我坚信，不仅你们会取得成功，而且由于你们的努力，我们的国家将继续是为全球每一个角落的男人和女人、男孩和女孩照耀航程的灯塔。

因此，谢谢大家。向你们祝贺。上帝保佑你们。上帝保佑美利坚合众国。

（杜梦臻／译）

Remarks by President Obama at the University of Denver

Four years ago as I had the privilege to travel all across the country and meet Americans from all walks of life. I decided nobody else should have to endure the heartbreak of a broken health care system. No one in the wealthiest nation on earth should go because they get sick. Nobody should have to tell their daughters or sons the decisions they can and cannot make for themselves are constrained because of some politicians in Washington.

And thanks to you, we've made a difference in people's lives; Thanks to

奥巴马在丹佛大学的演讲

四年前，我有幸周游了全国，与各行各业的人萍水相遇。我暗下决心，决不让任何人因医疗系统的不健全而疾首痛心；在这个物阜民丰的国度，决不让任何人因疾病而穷困潦倒；决不让任何人需要告诉他们的子女，他们能做什么而不能做什么的决定，受制于华盛顿的某些政客。

幸好有你们，人们的生活才能日新月异；幸好有你们，让我今天遇到的很多人得以悉心照顾，病有所医。他们的人生能得以完整的充实，都离不开你们。

我们已经经历了那么多，我们现在不能犹豫和放弃。我们还要继续落实医疗改革，要创造就业机会，我们还有太多的事情要做：有太多的老师

you, there are folks that I meet today who have gotten care and their cancer's been caught. And they've got treatment. And they are living full lives and it happened because of you.

We've come too far to turn back now. We've got too much work to do to implement health care; We've got too much work to do to create good jobs; We've got too many teachers that we've got to hire; We've got too many schools that we've got to rebuild; We've got too many students who still need affordable higher education.

There's more homegrown energy to generate. There are more troops that we've got to bring home. There are more doors of opportunity we've got to open to anybody who is willing to work hard and walk through those doors. We've got to keep building an economy. Or no matter what you look like or where you come from, you can make it here if you try. And you can leave something behind for the next generation. That's what at stake right now in Colorado. That's why I'm running for President of the United States of America. That's why I'm asking for your vote.

I still believe in you. And if you still believe in me, and if you're willing to stand with me, and knock on some doors with me, and make some phone calls with me, and talk to your neighbors and friends about what's at stake, we will win this election. We will finish what we started. And we'll remind the world why America is the greatest nation on earth.

God bless you and God bless the United States of America.

Auraria Events Center, University of Denver, Denver, Colorado, August 08, 2012

等着我们去招募，有太多的学校需要我们去重建，有太多的学生需要让他们能够负担得起大学教育。

有太多的本土能源需要去发掘，有更多的军队需要归国，有更多的机会之门需要我们去开启，使那些任劳任怨的人们有机会获得成功。我们要继续振兴经济，做到无论种族，不问出身，一分耕耘即有一分收获，并造福于后代。这，就是我们在科罗拉多州要争夺的！这，就是为什么我要竞选美国总统！这，就是为什么我希望你们把神圣的一票投给我！

我依旧相信你们！如果你们依旧相信我，如果你们愿意支持我，和我一起去叩门拜访，和我一起拿起电话，告诉你的左邻右里和旧故新交，我们在为什么而战斗，那我们就能在这场竞选中胜券在握！我们就会像上次那样大获全胜！我们就会昭告天下，为什么美国是世界上最伟大的国家！

上帝护佑你，上帝护佑美利坚合众国。

（杜梦臻／译）

Remarks by President Obama at Iowa State University

Hello, Cyclones! Thank you. It is good to be back in Iowa. Please give Mischa a big round of applause for the great introduction.

Audience Member: We love you!

The President: I love you back, and I'm glad to be here. You guys look pretty cheerful being back at school. That's good to know. Yes, sort of?

Well, listen, before I begin, I think it's important to say that our thoughts are with our fellow Americans down on the Gulf. They're preparing for – the New Orleans guy right here. They're obviously preparing for a big storm, Hurricane Isaac.

And we've been getting ready for this storm for days. We've got response teams and supplies in place. America will be there to help folks recover no matter what this storm brings, because when disaster strikes we're not Democrats or Republicans first, we are Americans first. We are one family. We're one family and we help our neighbors in need.

It is great to be back in Ames. Class is in session. I didn't hear as many cheers – come on. Whew! Cyclones football kicks off at home this Saturday.

I won't pretend I can give a speech like Coach Rhoads can, but I'm going to try – because just over two months from now, for the first time in most of your lives, you will get a chance to pick a President. And the truth is you've got more at stake in this election than just about anybody. When you step into that voting booth, the choice you make in that one instant is going to shape your

28

奥巴马在衣阿华州立大学的演讲

你好，队友们！很高兴回到衣阿华，让我们对米莎精彩的介绍报以热烈的掌声。

我们爱你！

我也爱你们，很高兴来到这里，回到学校你们兴奋不已，我十分欣慰，嗯，是的，一丝欣慰。

好的，各位听好，在我开始讲话之前，我想有必要强调一件事，那就是，我们的心将和美国墨西哥湾的同胞紧密相连，他们为那里的新奥尔良人时刻准备着，显而易见，他们为大风暴艾萨克飓风时刻准备着。

country and your world for decades to come.

And I know that's a pretty heavy idea to lay on you on a Tuesday. But it's true. The decisions we make as a country on big issues like the economy and jobs and taxes and education and energy and war and climate change – all these decisions will directly affect your life in very personal ways. And I've got to say, this is something I'm acutely aware of when I make these decisions, because they're decisions that are going to affect Malia and Sasha, my daughters, as well.

It's the way it's always been – one generation makes decisions on behalf of the next. But here's the thing, Cyclones [1] – your generation chooses which path we take as a country. Your vote decides where we go from here. Will we make sure that more good jobs and opportunity take root not in China or India or Germany, but right here in Iowa and all across America, so you don't have to leave home to get those good-paying jobs?

Are we going to reward an honest day's work with the chance to buy a home of your own, with health care that's there for you when you get sick, with the ability to put a little away for your retirement?

Are we going to make it easier for you to afford your degree and pay off your student loan debt? Are we going to build more good schools and hire more good teachers, so that our kids are prepared to attend colleges like Iowa State, and prepared for the 21st century workforce?

Will this be a country that keeps moving away from foreign oil and towards renewable sources of energy like wind and solar and biofuels – energy that makes our economy more secure, but also makes our planet more secure?

Will this be a country that leads not just by the strength of our military, but the power of our diplomacy and the power of our example?

Will this be an America where no matter who you are, no matter what you look like, no matter where you come from, no matter who you love, you can

---

① 衣阿华州立大学的校队别名 Cyclone（旋风），其渊源可追溯到 1895 年。

　　为了应对这场风暴，我们已经做了数日的准备工作，我们的应急小组和物资已经准备就绪。不论这场暴风的损失多么惨重，美国都会毫不动摇地帮助灾民，这是因为，当灾难来临之时，我们首要的不是以民主党还是共和党来区分彼此，而是我们都是美国人，都是一家人，我们应该同舟共济，给那些需要帮助的邻居提供援助之手。

　　回到艾姆斯的感觉真好，学生们正在上课，我怎么没有听到欢呼声？来吧各位，一起欢呼吧，本周六校队足球比赛就要开赛啦！

　　我不敢保证我的演讲能像罗兹教练那样，但是我想试试——因为在接下来的两个月里，你们获得有生以来第一次选择总统的机会。事实是，你们在这次选举中举足轻重，当你们走进选举棚，作出决定的那一瞬间，你将影响到整个国家和世界未来几十年的发展。

　　我知道，在接下来的某个周二，落在你们身上的将是无比沉重的担子，但这是事实。在经济、就业、税赋、教育、能源、战争、气候变化这类重大议题上，我们代表国家所做的一切决定都与你们的个人生活息息相关。我要说，这就是我做决定时，会敏感地意识到的东西，因为这些决定也将对我们的女儿玛利亚和萨沙产生影响。

　　一直以来都是这样，前人代表后人做出抉择，但事情就是这样。队友们——你们这一代将决定国家的发展路线，你们的选票将决定我们国家未来的走向。衣阿华及全美国是否应该确保能够取代中国、印度和德国，为本国人民提供源源不断的工作机会呢？这样你们就不必背井离乡去寻求高薪工作。

　　我们是否应该让你们有机会购置自己的房屋，生病时为你们提供医疗保健，让你们退休时有能力来安顿自己以回报自己的辛勤工作呢？

　　我们是否应该让你们更加轻松地支付学费、偿还助学贷款呢？我们是不是应该兴办更多的学校并雇佣更多的优秀教师，好让我们的孩子能够进入贵校一样的学府并为21世纪人才作准备呢？

　　我们的国家是否能够从进口国外石油转向利用风能、太阳能、生物燃料等可再生能源，从而使我们的经济更加稳固，我们的星球更为安全呢？

　　我们的国家是否应该不单靠军事实力，而是靠外交手段和言行举止来引领世界呢？

pursue your own happiness and you can make it here in America if you try?

That's the question. That's what the last four years have been about. That's what this campaign is about. And that's why I'm running for a second term as President of the United States of America.

Now, listen, I know it's easy to get fed up with campaigns and politics. Sometimes it seems it's meaner and smaller and more gridlocked than ever. And every day, there's a steady stream of cynics who will tell you nothing really changes; you can't make a difference; you won't be able to close the gap between life as it is and life as you want it to be. Old folks will always tell you that – and I'm in that category now.

And, frankly, some folks, they make it their political strategy to try to make you feel discouraged. They'll tell you over and over again how bad everything is, and then, of course, they'll add that it's all Obama's fault. And they'll tell you that if you believed in change four years ago, your faith was foolish and you were being naïve. Last week, my opponent's campaign went so far as to write you off as a "lost generation" – that's you according to them.

And what they hope is that by telling you these things, you'll get discouraged and you'll just stay home this time.

But you can't believe it. I don't believe it. We knew that solving our biggest problems were going to take more than one year, or one term, or even one President. But we went ahead and we got started. We know we've still got a lot of work to do to get to where we need to be. But we are going to get there.

I believe that because I believe in you. As tough as times have been, you're tougher. I've seen your passion. I've seen your service. I've seen your generation eager and impatient to make a difference. And already, you've proved that you can.

Think about it, four years ago, you believed we could put a college education within the reach of all who were willing to work for it. So we created a college tax credit that's saving families up to $10,000 for college tuition over

我们的国家是否能够做到不论身份、相貌、籍贯、信仰，只要你努力尝试就能在美国拥有幸福、功成名就呢？

这些都是问题，都是我们在过去的四年里致力解决的问题，是我们这次竞选的主要议题，这也是我再次竞选美国总统的原因。

各位请注意，我知道你们很容易对竞选和政治产生抵触之心，他们似乎越来越卑鄙、狭隘、僵持不下，加上每天都有些愤世嫉俗之人不断地告诉你，什么改变也没发生，你也改变不了什么，理想生活和现实生活的巨大鸿沟永远无法填补。上了年纪的人经常会这么说——我感同身受。

坦白地讲，有些人的政治策略就是想让你感到灰心丧气，他们会不厌其烦地告诉你这个世界有多么糟糕，然后顺水推舟地把罪名强加于我。他们还会告诉你如果你相信四年以来发生了改变，那你就太愚昧、太幼稚了。上个星期，我的竞选对手的活动偏离了轨道，竟把你们贬低为"迷惘的一代"——这就是他们对你们的印象。

他们这么做，就是希望通过告诉你们这些，让你们心灰意冷，坐以待毙。

但是，你不能相信，我也不会相信。我们知道解决重大问题需要的不仅仅是一年、一任甚至一位总统的努力，但我们勇往直前，正在起航，我们知道要实现我们的目标还需要许多努力，但我们正一步步地向成功迈进。

我坚信成功是因为我相信你们。艰难时局，你们更要坚强，我看到了你们的激情澎湃，你们的奉献精神，以及你们青年一代想要改变世界的迫切心情。你们已经证明了你们可以做到！

想一想，四年前，你们相信我，能够给所有想上大学的人提供机会，因此我们建立了大学税务抵免系统，四年间给每个家庭节省一万美元学费，我们创建了助学贷款体系，让数之不尽的纳税人把钱投到大银行，我们要把钱直接交到学生手里，同时把百万学子的助学金额翻了一番。

four years. We took on a student loan system that was giving billions of taxpayer dollars to big banks, and we said let's give the money directly to students, and we doubled grant aid for millions of students.

We just won the fight to keep federal student loans from doubling for more than 7 million students. That would not have happened in Washington except for you. Your vote did that. You made that change. You helped millions of young people and maybe yourself get the kind of college education you deserve. Don't believe them when they tell you, you can't make a difference.

You believed four years ago that we could use less foreign oil and reduce the carbon pollution that threatens our planet. And in just four years, we've doubled – doubled – the generation of clean, renewable energy like wind and solar.

We developed new fuel standards so that your car will get nearly 55 miles per gallon by the middle of the next decade. That's going to save you money at the pump. That will reduce greenhouse gas emissions by a level roughly equivalent to a year's worth of emissions from all the cars in the world.

Today, America is less dependent on foreign oil than at any time in nearly 20 years. We're on track to emit fewer greenhouse gases this year than we have in nearly 20 years. You can keep those trends going. You believed in America, and that's what's brought about change.

You believed that nobody should go broke in America just because they get sick. I believe that, too. What the other side calls Obamacare – I've kind of grown to like the term Obamacare. I do care. I care about folks with preexisting conditions. I care about kids who don't have insurance. And so today, because of the new health care law, nearly 7 million young people, including some of you in this audience, have been able to stay on your parent's plan.

Your grandparents are saving money on their medicine. Women have gained access to free preventive care like mammograms and contraception. Your vote made that happen. You made that change.

我们刚刚为700万名学子成功地抑制了联邦学生贷款的翻倍上涨，多亏了你们，华盛顿才免遭劫难，是你们的选票发挥了作用，是你们改变了这一切，你们帮助你们自己及成千上百万的年轻人得到了你们应有的大学教育。当他们告诉你不会发生改变的时候，切勿相信他们。

四年前，你们相信，我们能够减少石油进口，降低威胁地球的碳污染。仅仅四年间，我们就使风能、太阳能一类的清洁、再生能源翻了一番。

我们制定了新燃料标准，使我们的轿车在未来的五六年可以实现每加仑行驶55英里，这将为你们节省汽油花销，并减少温室气体排放，这相当于将全世界所有汽车一年的排放量减半。

现在，美国依赖进口石油的程度达到了20年来的最低点，我们也正在努力使温室气体排放量也达到20年来的最低点，你们可以让这一趋势保持下去，你们曾经相信美国，这就是那份信任带来的变化。

你们曾经相信，没有人会只因看病而一贫如洗，我也相信。对手们所谓的"奥巴马医保"——我开始喜欢这个词了。我真的很在乎。我在意那些没有投保的民众，那些没有保险的儿童。由于新的医疗法案的出台，现在包括你们在座的各位在内，将近七百万年轻人能够继续父母的医疗保险计划。

你们的祖父母节省了医药费，女性也可以享受免费的预防保健服务，比如乳腺造影和避孕保健，是你们的选票让它成为现实，是你们让这一切改变得以实现。

It was young people like you that said we could end the war in Iraq. Today that war is over – as promised. More troops are home with their families, earning their educations through the Post-9/11 GI Bill, starting new businesses. And no one will ever again have to hide who they love in order to serve the country they love, because your vote ended "don't ask, don't tell" once and for all. You made that change.

So the point is, Ames, your vote matters. Your vote made a difference. Change was possible because of you. And now we've more work to do –- to grow this economy, create good jobs, to strengthen the middle class. And in November, your voice will matter more than it ever has before.

This week in Tampa, my opponents will offer you their agenda. It should be a pretty entertaining show. It will be. And I'm sure they'll have some wonderful things to say about me.

But what you won't hear from them is a path forward that meets the challenges of our time. Instead, it will be an economic plan that says if you just give folks making $3 million or more a year another $250,000 tax cut, then jobs and prosperity will magically rain down on everybody else.

Some of you guys are a little young, so you may not remember it, but we tried this for 10 years before I was elected. It didn't work out so well. It didn't work out then; it won't work now.

I don't want to pay for another millionaire's tax cut by raising taxes on the middle class. I don't want to pay for that tax cut by cutting financial aid on 10 million students. Our economic strength doesn't come from the top down; it comes from students and workers, and a growing, thriving middle class. That's how we grow an economy.

So in just over two months, you will make a choice about which path we take, and it's going to be a stark choice. You can choose whether we give massive new tax cuts to folks who've already made it, or whether we're going to keep taxes low for every American who's still trying to make it.

正是你们这样的年轻人曾经说过，我们会结束伊拉克战争，如今战争结束，诺言履行。更多的士兵凯旋归来与家人团聚，按照《后9/11军人安置法案》的规定，正在接受教育，开创新事业。没有人再会为了服役于挚爱的国家而隐姓埋名，因为你们的选票终结了曾经"不问不说"的现状，是你们让这一切得以改变。

因此，艾姆斯，你们的选票很关键，你们的选票将会起到重要作用，世界可能因你们而改变。现在，我们还要有很多任务要完成——加快经济增长、创造就业机会，并使中产阶级发展壮大。

本周，在坦帕，我的对手也会向你们提供他的议事日程，这将是一个很有戏剧性的演出，是的，我相信他们会谈到我的许多"光辉事迹"。

但是他们不会告诉你，在我们前进的道路上充满了挑战，相反，他们会提出这么一个经济计划——如果给年薪大于或等于300万的人减税25万美元，工作岗位和经济繁荣就会神奇地降临到每个人头上。

在座的各位有些年龄尚小，可能并不记得此事，但在我当选前的十年里，这种方法曾经被不断地尝试，不论是过去还是现在，但均无济于事。

我不想利用增加中产阶级的赋税、削减1000万学子的助学金来为百万富翁的减税计划买单。我们的经济实力并不是靠自上而下的模式，它依靠的是学生、工人和一群新兴的中产阶级，这才是我们经济的发展方式。

所以，在接下来的两个多月里，今后的道路，由你们各位来决定，这将是一个严酷的抉择。是给富人继续享受减税的福利，还是让每个事业刚起步的美国同胞保持较低的赋税，选择权在你们的手中。

I've cut taxes for the middle class, and for families, and for students. And I want to make sure that taxes aren't raised a dime on your family's first $250,000 of income. That means that 98 percent of Americans and 97 percent of small businesses wouldn't see an income tax increase. You can choose.

You can choose whether we're going to give up new jobs and new industries to China and India, or whether we're going to fight for those jobs by investing in the research of our scientists and the drive of our students and the innovation that harnesses new sources of energy, and brings the next generation of manufacturing to places like Ames and Milwaukee and Detroit and Pittsburgh. That's your choice.

You can decide whether the best way to make college affordable is to – as my opponent put it – hope your parents can just lend you the money. Or you can say, let's help more Americans earn the kind of education you receive here at Iowa State. Let's help more Americans go to community colleges to get the skills and trainings that employers are looking for right now.

Let's help more Iowans learn to be leaders at the Harkin Public Policy Institute that a Cyclone alum and your great Senator, Tom Harkin, is setting up. He's working along with your new president, Steven Leath – doing a great job.

And as Mischa mentioned, although I am getting gray, I still remember what it was like for you guys – because Michelle and I finished paying off our loans just eight years ago. We know what it's like. We shouldn't make it harder. We should make it easier. We shouldn't end the college tax credit we created; we should extend it. Because in America, higher education isn't a luxury – it's an economic necessity that every family should be able to afford. That's the choice in this election.

You can choose an energy plan written by and for big oil companies.

That's what my opponent is offering. Or you can choose an all-of-the-above energy strategy for America – renewable sources of energy. Governor Romney called those "imaginary". Congressman Ryan said they're a "fad".

　　我已经为中产阶级、家庭、学生减税，而且我想确保在你们的家庭收入首次达到25万美元之前，税率保持不变，那将意味着98%的美国同胞和97%的小企业主将不会增税，选择权在你们的手上。

　　是要放弃新岗位、新工业跑去中国和印度，还是通过投资科学研究，挖掘学生的潜能，促进新能源的开发，把下一代带到像艾姆斯、密尔沃基和底特律这样的生产基地来争取工作机会，选择权在你们的手上。

　　你们能够决定这负担大学学费的最佳方式——正如我的竞争对手说的——是伸手向父母借钱，还是帮助更多的美国同胞能像你们一样接受衣阿华州立大学这样的教育。让我们帮助更多的国人走进社区大学，获得雇主所需的技能，接受相应的训练。

　　让我们帮助更多的衣阿华学子，学着去做哈金公共政策学院的领袖，这个学院由伟大的参议院汤姆·哈金一手创办，他是你们的校友，与你们的新校长史蒂芬·里斯一道——作出巨大贡献。

　　正如米莎所说，虽然我已满头银丝，但你们的境况，我感同身受——因为我和米歇尔在八年前才还清我们的贷款，我们知道你们的感受，我们不会让你们更加艰辛，而只会让你们更加轻松。我们不会废止我们建立的大学税务抵免体系，反而还会大力发展它，因为美国的高等教育不应一种奢侈的享受——它应是每个家庭都能负担得起的必需品。

　　你们能够选择由石油公司一手操办的能源计划。

　　那也正是我的竞争对手的观点，或者，你也可以为美国选择最高的能源战略——可再生能源，罗姆尼州长称之为"虚无缥缈"，议员瑞恩则称为"奇思怪想"的新能源战略。

Let me tell you something – they need to come to Iowa because they're the future. They're worth fighting for.

Nearly 7,000 good Iowa jobs depend on the wind industry. It's time to stop giving $4 billion of taxpayer subsidies to oil companies that are making a profit every time you pump gas. Let's give it to homegrown energy sources that have never been more promising. That's good for jobs. It's good for the economy. It's good for the environment. That's the direction we need to go in.

But it's all up to you. It's up to you whether we go back to a health care system that let insurance companies decide who to cover and when. I think it might make sense for you to choose to keep moving forward with the new health care law that's already cutting costs and covering more people and saving lives.

Governor Romney promised that sometime between taking the Oval Office and going to the Inaugural Ball, he'd sit right down, grab a pen, and kick 7 million young people off their parent's plan by repealing health reform. Day one, that's what he says he's going to do.

Maybe we should call his plan "Romney Doesn't Care" – because I do care. I do care. And this law is here to stay. Now is not the time to refight the battles of the last four years. Now is the time for us to go ahead and move forward.

And I'll work with anybody who wants to make our health care system better, but I'm not going to stand by and let folks talk about how we should go back to the days when ordinary folks who are working really hard suddenly find themselves losing their home, losing their savings just because they get sick.

They can choose to refight the battles that were settled 10 years ago or 20 years ago or sometimes in the last century. I think women should be trusted to make their own health care decisions. That's a choice that you've got to make.

I think that students who are brought here by their parents as babies shouldn't be kicked out of the only country they know just because their parents were undocumented workers. That's my view. It's your choice.

听我说——这些能源就是未来的希望，衣阿华的发展需要这些能源，它们值得我们去争取。

衣阿华将近7000个工作岗位都和风能工业紧密相关，该是时候停止让纳税人自掏40亿美元养着那些石油公司了，要知道，每次你打开煤气阀门，他们都有利可图。让我们发展前景无限的本国能源，无论对就业、经济、环境来说都大有好处，这就是我们的前进方向。

但是，选择权在你们手中。要不要回到那个被保险公司随意宰割的医保系统，由你们决定。我想大家可能会明智地选择坚持新的医疗法，因为它已经节约了大量花销，覆盖群众广泛并挽救了无数生命。

罗姆尼州长曾许诺从就任总统到竞选活动这段时间，他将坐下来大笔一挥废除医疗改革，把700万人从他们父母的医疗计划中剥离出来，就职第一天，他就会兑现承诺。

也许我们应该把他的计划称为"罗姆尼不医改"①——因为我真的在乎你们，十分在乎，这个法案就证明了这一点。现在不是我们重温过去四年战争的时刻，现在是我们勇往直前迈向未来的时刻。

我将同愿意改善我们医疗系统的同仁一道努力，但对于那些口出狂言要回到旧体系的人，我绝不会坐视不管，因为那个体制，曾让众多辛苦工作的劳苦大众因为疾病而无家可归、倾家荡产。

他们选择重温我们过去十年前，二十年前甚至是上个世纪已经解决的斗争，我认为女性应被赋予医疗保健的选择权，那是你们自己的选择。

我认为从小跟随父母迁移过来的学生不应该被迫离开他们唯一熟识的地方，只因父母是无证工人。这就是我的立场。选择权，在你们的手里。

———————————

① 谐音：罗姆尼漠不关心。

41

I don't think we should write – rewrite the Constitution to prevent gay Americans from being able to marry the person they love. That's my view. It's your choice.

The strength of our character doesn't come from shoving anybody to the sidelines. It comes from hearing every voice, harnessing every talent, realizing that here in America we are greater together than we are on our own.

And this November, you get to decide – you get to decide the future of this war in Afghanistan. Governor Romney said ending the war was "tragic". He doesn't have a plan to bring home the 33,000 troops who will come home from Afghanistan next month.

I said we'd end the Iraq war. We did. I said we'd get bin Laden. We did. Today all of our troops are out of Iraq. We're bringing them home from Afghanistan. And as long as I'm Commander-in-Chief, we're going to make sure that we serve our veterans as well as they've served us – because nobody who fights for America should have to fight for a job when they come home. But these are your choices.

Governor Romney wants to pass a new $5 trillion tax cut targeted towards the wealthiest Americans. That's not going to cut our debt. Ignoring inequality doesn't make it go away. Denying climate change won't make it stop. These things won't make for a brighter future. They won't make your future stronger.

And so, in two months, you get to choose the path that will actually lead to a better future. You have the chance to prove the cynics wrong one more time.

And the other side is going to spend these next two months – they are going to spend more money than you've ever seen in your life. They will have an avalanche of attack ads and insults and distractions. And sometimes, they'll just – how do I put it – they will fib.

And they've got $10-million checks from wealthy donors who like things just the way they are. They're counting on you young people to just accept their version of the way things ought to be, to just kind of leave the questions that

我认为我们不应该撰写，或者重新撰写宪法来阻止美国同性恋者与爱人结婚，这是我的立场。选择权，在你们的手里。

我们品性的优点，并不是孤立他人，而是要集思广益，任人唯贤，认识到这一点：在美国，团结一致比孤军奋战的力量更加强大。

这个11月，你们的选择将会决定——决定阿富汗战争的未来，罗姆尼州长说过，结束战争是场"悲剧"，而且他无意让下个月本应从阿富汗返乡的33000名士兵真正回国。

我说过我们会结束伊拉克战争，我们做到了；我说过我们会干掉本·拉登，我们也做到了。现在我们所有的军队都撤离了伊拉克，我们正打算把阿富汗的战士们也接回家，只要我还是三军总司令，我就会保证安顿好我们的退伍军人，我们将像你们当时服务我们一样来为你们服务，任何一个曾为这个国家战斗过的人，都不应该再为养家糊口而抗争。选择权，在你们的手中。

罗姆尼州长想要通过一项新的法案为最富有的一些美国人再减少50000亿美元的税款，而我们，却不在减税的行列之内。对贫富差距、气候变化视而不见解决不了问题，我们未来不会因此而更加光明，更加美好。

所以，在两个月内，你们将选择一个能够真正引领美好未来的道路，你们有机会向愤世嫉俗者再次证明他们大错特错。

在接下来的两个月，对手们会花大价钱——下足血本，进行一连串的攻击广告，肆言詈辱，分散你们的注意。但是，他们只是——怎么说呢——只是在编造谎言。

affect your lives up to big oil and insurance companies; up to politicians that decide what a woman can or can't do when it comes to her own health. That's what they're counting on. That's their strategy.

I'm counting on something different. I'm counting on you. I'm counting on you. Those who oppose change, those who benefit from the status quo, they've always bet on cynicism. They always bet on complacency. But throughout America's history, they have lost that bet, and they're going to lose it this time, too. And that's because of you.

It depends on you registering to vote. It depends on you showing up to vote. It depends on you refusing to wait for the next person, or the person next to you in class, or the person in the next town, or the person in another state. It's going to depend on you to close that gap between what America is and what we know it can be.

Because let me tell you, everybody else is waiting on you. When they see you register, they'll register. When they see you vote, they'll vote.

And I'm asking you one more time to do what we did – what young people all across the state of Iowa did four years ago. I'm asking you to believe. I'm asking you to believe. Not in my ability to bring about the changes you want to see; I'm asking you to believe in your abilities. I'm asking you to believe in what you can accomplish.

We've come too far to turn back now. We've got more work to do. We've got more young people to send to college. We've got more good jobs to create. We've got more homegrown energy to generate. We've got more good teachers to hire and more good schools to build. We've got more troops we've got to bring home. We've got more veterans we've got to take care of. We've got more doors of opportunity that we have to open up to every single person who's willing to work hard and walk through those doors.

That's why I'm asking you for a second term. And if you're willing to stand with me and work with me, and knock on some doors with me – and make

他们已经从呼风唤雨的富有捐赠者手中得到1000万美元，他们仅指望你们年轻人接受他们的观点，把牵扯到你们未来的大事丢给大石油和保险公司，把女性健康选择权抛给政治家来决定。这正是他们所指望的，这就是他们的策略。

我则与他们迥然不同，我指望你们，把希望寄托于你们。那些反对改革，安于现状的人，他们总是愤世嫉俗，沾沾自喜，孤注一掷。但纵观美国历史，他们已经满盘皆输，这次他们也不会赢，因为有你们在。

这取决于你们登记投票，取决于你们出席投票，取决于你们不再等候，不论是下一个人、班上的某个人、另个城镇里的人或另一个州的人，立即投票，缩小美国现实与理想差距，要靠在座的各位。

让我来告诉你，因为其他人都在等着你们，你们登记，他们就会登记，你们投票，他们就会投票。

我想让你们再次重复我们所过的事——所有衣阿华州年轻人四年前做的事。我请各位相信，我请你们相信，并非相信我的能力才带给你们想要的改变，而是我让你们相信自己的能力，我要你们相信你们自己所取得的成就。

现在我们已经走得太远，无法回头，我们要作更多的努力，让更多的年轻人上大学，创造更多的工作机会，生产更多的本国制造能源，雇佣更多的老师，创办更多的好学校，让更多的士兵返乡，安顿好更多的退伍军人，为奋发图强的人开启更多机会之门并帮助他们渡过难关。

some phone calls with me – and if you're willing to vote for me in November, we will win Iowa. We will win this election. We will finish what we started. And we'll remind the world why the United States of America is the greatest nation on Earth.

Thank you, everybody. God bless you. God bless the United States of America.

Iowa State University, August 28, 2012

这就是我让你们为我的连任投下一票的原因，如果你们愿意支持我，和我一起同心协力，和我一起叩门拜访，和我一起拿起电话，如果你们愿意11月份为我投票，我们将赢得衣阿华，我们将赢得这场竞选！我们将会像上次那样大获全胜！我们将昭告天下，为什么美国是世界上最伟大的国家！

　　谢谢大家，上帝保佑你们，上帝保佑美利坚合众国。

（袁婧　杜梦臻／译）

Obama's Speech to
the Democratic National Convention 2012

Thank you. ... Thank you. Thank you. Thank you so much.

Thank you so much. Thank you. Thank you very much, everybody. Thank you.

Michelle, I love you so much. A few nights ago, everybody was reminded just what a lucky man I am. Malia and Sasha, we are so proud of you. And yes, you do have to go to school in the morning.

And Joe Biden, thank you for being the very best vice president I could have ever hoped for and being a strong and loyal friend.

Madam Chairwoman, delegates, I accept your nomination for President of the United States.

Now, the first time I addressed this convention, in 2004, I was a younger man – a Senate candidate from Illinois who spoke about hope, not blind optimism, not wishful thinking but hope in the face of difficulty, hope in the face of uncertainty, that dogged faith in the future which has pushed this nation forward even when the odds are great, even when the road is long.

Eight years later that hope has been tested by the cost of war, by one of the worst economic crises in history and by political gridlock that's left us wondering whether it's still even possible to tackle the challenges of our time.

I know campaigns can seem small, even silly sometimes. Trivial things become big distractions. Serious issues become sound bites. The truth gets buried under an avalanche of money and advertising. And if you're sick of

奥巴马接受2012年民主党总统候选人提名的演讲

谢谢，非常感谢大家，谢谢在座的各位。

米歇尔，我爱你！几天前的那个助选之夜，① 整个国家见证，我是一个无比幸运的男人。玛利亚和萨沙，你们是父母的骄傲！没错，明早你们还是得去上学。

感谢乔·拜登，你一直是我梦寐以求的副总统最佳人选，同时也是我最坚强和最忠诚的战友。

主席女士，各位代表，我接受你们的美国总统提名。

我第一次在民主党大会上演讲，还要追溯到2004年，那会儿我还年轻。身为伊利诺伊州议员候选人，我在演讲中谈到了希望。我说的希望不是盲目乐观，不是一厢情愿，而是要直面困难，直面无常，用坚定不移的信念，不断推动国家进步，即使前途未卜，即使长路漫漫！

八年转瞬即逝，通过战争的代价、历史上最为严重的经济危机，以及政治上的僵局，我所说的希望经受了考验。它甚至让我怀疑，这个希望是否还能够继续应对时代的挑战。

我自知，竞选有时显得琐碎，甚至无聊。鸡毛蒜皮的小事大大分散了注意力，重大问题却演变成语言的攻击。在金钱和广告的狂轰滥炸下，真相被掩盖了。如果你们听够了我的举证，相信我，我也烦。

然而说一千道一万，当你拿起那张选票去投票时，你会面临比这个时代任何时候都要明确的选择。未来几年，华盛顿将作出一系列重要决策，事关就业与经济、税收与赤字、能源与教育、战争与和平等问题，这些决策将在未来几十年内对我们以及我们孩子们的生活产生巨大的影响。

---

① 指9月4日米歇尔·奥巴马为丈夫助选之夜。

hearing me approve this message, believe me, so am I.

But when all is said and done, when you pick up that ballot to vote, you will face the clearest choice of any time in a generation. Over the next few years big decisions will be made in Washington on jobs, the economy, taxes and deficits, energy, education, war and peace – decisions that will have a huge impact on our lives and on our children's lives for decades to come.

And on every issue, the choice you face won't just be between two candidates or two parties. It will be a choice between two different paths for America, a choice between two fundamentally different visions for the future. Ours is a fight to restore the values that built the largest middle class and the strongest economy the world has ever known – the values my grandfather defended as a soldier in Patton's army, the values that drove my grandmother to work on a bomber assembly line while he was gone. They knew they were part of something larger – a nation that triumphed over fascism and depression, a nation where the most innovative businesses turn out the world's best products, and everyone shared in that pride and success from the corner office to the factory floor.

My grandparents were given the chance to go to college and buy their home – their own home and fulfill the basic bargain at the heart of America's story, the promise that hard work will pay off, that responsibility will be rewarded, that everyone gets a fair shot and everyone does their fair share and everyone plays by the same rules, from Main Street to Wall Street to Washington, D.C.

And I ran for president because I saw that basic bargain slipping away. I began my career helping people in the shadow of a shuttered steel mill at a time when too many good jobs were starting to move overseas. And by 2008 we had seen nearly a decade in which families struggled with costs that kept rising but paychecks that didn't, folks racking up more and more debt just to make the mortgage or pay tuition, put gas in the car or food on the table. And when the house of cards collapsed in the Great Recession, millions of innocent Americans

在每一个问题上，你所作的选择，不仅关乎两个政党或者两个候选人，而是关乎美国未来要走的两条截然不同的道路，关乎美国未来的两种截然不同的蓝图。民主党奋斗的价值观，就是要造就最为庞大的中产阶级和举世公认的经济强国。这也是我祖父作为巴顿将军麾下的士兵所要捍卫的价值观，也是我祖父奔赴战场后，驱动我祖母在轰炸机生产线上辛勤工作的价值观。我的祖父母知道，他们是这个国家伟大事业的一部分，这个国家曾经战胜了法西斯和大萧条，这个国家曾经拥有最具创新力的企业，制造出了全世界最好的产品。这个国家的每位公民，从办公室到工厂，人人都能分享荣耀与成就。

我的祖父母有机会上大学，购置了属于自己的房产，这就是美国梦的核心契约。这是一种公认的社会契约，那就是收获源于努力和付出，尽己之责必得回报，人人享有均等机会，人人得到合理份额，人人遵守相同规则，不论你是来自寻常大街小巷，还是来自华尔街，抑或华盛顿特区。

我之所以竞选总统，是因为我看到这种基本契约正在渐行渐远。我的职业生涯，开始于帮助钢铁厂那些无所凭借的失业工人，当时大量工作岗位移向海外。直到2008年的近十年间，我们目睹了无数家庭在持续上涨的物价与岿然不动的工资之中苦苦挣扎，人们债台高筑，只好去典当物品，或维持基本的生活费用。而当次贷危机来临，经济泡沫轰然破灭时，数百万无辜同胞失去了工作、住房和毕生的储蓄，这场悲剧带来的灾难，直到今日我们仍在奋力弥补。

lost their jobs, their homes, their life savings, a tragedy from which we're still fighting to recover.

Now, our friends down in Tampa at the Republican convention were more than happy to talk about everything they think is wrong with America. But they didn't have much to say about how they'd make it right. They want your vote, but they don't want you to know their plan. And that's because all they have to offer is the same prescriptions they've had for the last 30 years. Have a surplus? Try a tax cut. Deficit too high – try another. Feel a cold coming on? Take two tax cuts, roll back some regulations, and call us in the morning.

Now, I've cut taxes for those who need it – middle-class families, small businesses. But I don't believe that another round of tax breaks for millionaires will bring good jobs to our shores, or pay down our deficit. I don't believe that firing teachers or kicking students off financial aid will grow the economy – or help us compete with the scientists and engineers coming out of China. After all we've been through, I don't believe that rolling back regulations on Wall Street will help the small-businesswoman expand, or the laid-off construction worker keep his home.

We have been there, we've tried that, and we're not going back. We are moving forward, America.

Now, I won't pretend the path I'm offering is quick or easy. I never have. You didn't elect me to tell you what you wanted to hear. You elected me to tell you the truth. And the truth is, it will take more than a few years for us to solve challenges that have built up over decades. It'll require common effort, shared responsibility, and the kind of bold, persistent experimentation that Franklin Roosevelt pursued during the only crisis worse than this one. And by the way, those of us who carry on his party's legacy should remember that not every problem can be remedied with another government program or dictate from Washington.

But know this, America: Our problems can be solved. Our challenges

现如今，我们来坦帕出席共和党大会的朋友们上，正喜不自胜地批评美国的种种错误，但建设性意见却只字未提。他们只想要你们的选票，却不想让你们知道他们的计划，因为他们只会开出三十年前的老方子："有了盈余？试试减税吧。""出现赤字？试试另一个。""如果还行不通？双倍减税。如果还是行不通的话，明早再打电话。"

现在，我已经为那些需要的人减税，包括中产阶级家庭、小业主。但我不相信新一轮的为百万富翁减税会创造更多的就业机会，或者弥补财政赤字。我不相信解雇教师或者取消学生的助学津贴会有助于经济增长，会帮助我们与来自中国的科学家和工程师去竞争。毕竟我们已经尝试过了，我不相信最大限度地减少对华尔街的监管，会帮助女性小业主扩展生意，或帮助失业的建筑工人保住他们的住房。

我们是从那里走过来的，我们已经尝试过了，我们不能再走回头路。美国，我们将继续前进！

实际上，我不会假装我提议的道路是什么终极捷径，我也从未如此说过。大家选我当总统，不是让我整天甜言蜜语，大家选我当总统，是想让我告诉你们实情。而事实是，要解决几十年以来累积的问题，我们还要付出几年甚至更长的时间。这要求我们分担责任，同舟共济，用当年富兰克林·罗斯福战胜大萧条的方法，付出无畏而持久的探索精神。顺便说一句，作为罗斯福政党遗产的继承者，我们应当牢记，不是每个问题都能通过另立政府规划或者依靠华盛顿的一纸命令就能解决的。

can be met. The path we offer may be harder, but it leads to a better place, and I'm asking you to choose that future. I'm asking you to rally around a set of goals for your country, goals in manufacturing, energy, education, national security and the deficit, real, achievable plans that will lead to new jobs, more opportunity and rebuild this economy on a stronger foundation. That's what we can do in the next four years, and that is why I am running for a second term as president of the United States.

We can choose a future where we export more products and outsource fewer jobs. After a decade that was defined by what we bought and borrowed, we're getting back to basics and doing what America's always done best. We are making things again. I've met workers in Detroit and Toledo who feared – they'd never build another American car. And today they can't build them fast enough because we reinvented a dying auto industry that's back on the top of the world. I worked with business leaders who are bringing jobs back to America not because our workers make less pay, but because we make better products – because we work harder and smarter than anyone else. I've signed trade agreements that are helping our companies sell more goods to millions of new customers, goods that are stamped with three proud words: "Made in America."

And after a decade of decline, this country created over half a million manufacturing jobs in the last 2 1/2 years. And now you have a choice. We can give more tax breaks to corporations that shift jobs overseas – or we can start rewarding companies that open new plants and train new workers and create new jobs here in the United States of America. We can help big factories and small businesses double their exports. And if we choose this path, we can create a million new manufacturing jobs in the next four years. You can make that happen. You can choose that future.

You can choose the path where we control more of our own energy. After 30 years of inaction, we raised fuel standards so that by the middle of the next decade, cars and trucks will go twice as far on a gallon of gas. We have doubled

但是，也请同胞们谨记：我们的问题是能够解决的，我们的挑战是能够应对的！我们所选择的道路可能充满坎坷，但是，它能够把我们引向幸福美好之所在，因此，我恳请你们选择这样一个未来。我恳求你们为了自己的国家，为了共同的目标而凝聚在一起！美国现在面临一系列需要实现的目标，包括基础设施、能源、教育、国家安全与赤字。我们将创造更多的就业机会，谋求更多的经济发展机遇，在更强的基础上重振美国的经济雄风。这是今后四年我们要做的主要任务，也是我竞选连任的原因。

美国要选择一个出口更多产品，减少就业岗位外流的未来。十年产业外迁之后，美国应当回归到最擅长的领域——制造业。我见过不少底特律和托莱多的工人，他们曾害怕再也造不出一辆美国车。时过境迁，今天他们担心自己造得不够快，因为在经历彻底革新之后，我们即将消失的汽车工业又重新跃居世界领先地位。我和一些商业领袖共过事，他们让美国人重新就业，这不是因为我们的工人薪水要的少，而是他们做得更好，因为我们比其他人更努力、更聪明。我签署了贸易协定，帮助美国的企业把更多的商品卖给成千上万的新顾客，这些商品上都印有三个令人骄傲的字：美国制造！

十年经济衰退过后，美国在过去两年半的时间里，在制造业领域创造了超过50万个就业机会。现在，一个抉择摆在大家面前：是为在海外建立外包业务的企业减税，还是奖励在国内建设新工厂和培训新工人的企业呢？我们可以帮助国内的大工厂和小企业实现出口翻番。如果我们选择了这样的一条道路，我们就可以在未来四年内创造100万个制造业就业机会。你们能够让这一切发生，你们能够实现这样的未来！

our use of renewable energy, and thousands of Americans have jobs today building wind turbines and long-lasting batteries. In the last year alone, we cut oil imports by 1 million barrels a day, more than any administration in recent history. And today the United States of America is less dependent on foreign oil than at any time in the last two decades. So now you have a choice between a strategy that reverses this progress or one that builds on it.

We've opened millions of new acres for oil and gas exploration in the last three years, and we'll open more. But unlike my opponent, I will not let oil companies write this country's energy plan or endanger our coastlines or collect another $4 billion in corporate welfare from our taxpayers. We're offering a better path.

We're offering a better path where we – a future where we keep investing in wind and solar and clean coal, where farmers and scientists harness new biofuels to power our cars and trucks, where construction workers build homes and factories that waste less energy, where – where we develop a hundred-year supply of natural gas that's right beneath our feet. If you choose this path, we can cut our oil imports in half by 2020 and support more than 600,000 new jobs in natural gas alone. And yes, my plan will continue to reduce the carbon pollution that is heating our planet, because climate change is not a hoax. More droughts and floods and wildfires are not a joke. They are a threat to our children's future. And in this election, you can do something about it.

You can choose a future where more Americans have the chance to gain the skills they need to compete, no matter how old they are or how much money they have. Education was the gateway to opportunity for me. It was the gateway for Michelle. It was – it was the gateway for most of you. And now more than ever it is the gateway to a middle-class life. For the first time in a generation, nearly every state has answered our call to raise their standards for teaching and learning. Some of the worst schools in the country have made real gains in math and reading. Millions of students are paying less for college today because we

你们可以选择这样的道路，美国能够掌控更多的能源。历经30年的努力，我们提高了燃料标准，到下个十年中叶，汽车和卡车在相同的油耗下能行驶两倍的里程。我们实现了可再生能源的使用翻一番的目标，成千上万的美国人在风能涡轮机和高效能电池制造产业中找到了工作。仅仅是去年，我们每天减少的原油进口，一天就是100万桶，减少的幅度超过近期的任何一届政府。现在美国对进口原油的依赖程度处于近20年来的最低点。那么现在，大家有投票选择产业发展前景的权利，是选择逆势而为还是选择乘势而上呢？

过去三年里，我们开发了几百万英亩的油气田，还有更多的油气田等待开发。不同于我的对手，我不会让大公司绑架国家的能源政策，也不会让他们威胁到海岸，更不会通过征收我们纳税人另一个40亿美元，去增加大企业的福利。

我们会提供一条更好的路径。我们将持续增加对风能、太阳能和清洁煤产业的投资，用更多的生物能源驱动轿车和卡车，用更少的能源建造住房和工厂，开发能够供应上百年的本土天然气资源。如果你们选择了这条道路，到2020年，我们将会减少一半的石油进口，并且仅仅在天然气领域，就能增加60万个新的就业机会。同时，我的计划能够继续减少碳污染造成的温室效应，因为气候变化不是儿戏，日益增多的旱灾、洪水和野火不是玩笑，它们已经威胁到我们孩子们的未来。在这次选举中，大家可以为此做点什么。

你们可以选择这样的未来：不论你年龄多大，不论你是否富有，你的竞争力都会得到加强。教育对我来说是机遇之门，对于米歇尔如此，对大多数人来说都是如此。现在超越往昔，教育成为通向中产阶级生活的大门。百年难得一见，几乎每个州都响应了我们的号召，提升了教学质量，一些国内垫底的学校在培养学生算术和阅读方面取得了长足的进步。成千上万的大学生其学费支出正在减少，因为我们使用了新的纳税系统，通过征收银行和借贷人更多的税负来资助教育产业。

finally took on a system that wasted billions of taxpayer dollars on banks and lenders.

And now you have a choice. We can gut education, or we can decide that in the United States of America, no child should have her dreams deferred because of a crowded classroom or a crumbling school. No family should have to set aside a college acceptance letter because they don't have the money. No company should have to look for workers overseas because they couldn't find any with the right skills here at home. That's not our future. That is not our future. A government has a role in this. But teachers must inspire. Principals must lead. Parents must instill a thirst for learning. And students, you've got to do the work, and together.

I promise you we can out-educate and out-compete any nation on earth.

So help me. Help me recruit a hundred thousand math and science teachers within 10 years and improve early childhood education. Help give 2 million workers the chance to learn skills at their community college that will lead directly to a job. Help us work with colleges and universities to cut in half the growth of tuition costs over the next 10 years. We can meet that goal together. You can choose that future for America.

That's our future.

You know, in a world of new threats and new challenges, you can choose leadership that has been tested and proven. Four years ago I promised to end the war in Iraq. We did. I promised to refocus on the terrorists who actually attacked us on 9/11, and we have. We've blunted the Taliban's momentum in Afghanistan and in 2014, our longest war will be over. A new tower rises above the New York skyline, al- Qaida is on the path to defeat and Osama bin Laden is dead.

And tonight we pay tribute to the Americans who still serve in harm's way. We are forever in debt to a generation whose sacrifice has made this country safer and more respected. We will never forget you, and so long as I'm commander-in-chief, we will sustain the strongest military the world has ever

现在大家有一个选择，那就是加强美国的教育。不能让一个孩子因为教室太拥挤或者是学校过于破旧而耽搁他的读书梦，不能让一个家庭因为贫困而让子女失去读大学的机会，不能让一家企业因为在本土找不到训练有素的工人而被迫将工作外包。政府当然责无旁贷，但是老师亦须鼓励学生，校长亦须领导有方，父母亦须给孩子灌输学习的渴望，而学生们自己，也应该给力。

我向大家承诺，我们将会在教育方面与任何国家匹敌。

所以请大家向我伸出援助之手。请帮助我在10年内招募10万名理工科教师，以加强早期少儿教育。请帮助我让200万名工人在社区大学里获得技能培训，使之胜任相应工作。请帮助我与大学一起，在未来的十年里实现学费增长减半。我们携手并肩，一定能够达到这一目标。你们可以为美国选择这样的未来！

这是我们自己的未来！

众所周知，面对世界的新威胁和新挑战，民众所选择的领导者须是经受过考验和历练的。四年前，我们承诺结束伊拉克战争，承诺全力追捕制造"9·11事件"的恐怖分子，现如今我们已经做到。我们成功打击了阿富汗塔利班势力的嚣张气焰，到2014年，这场美国最旷日持久的战争也将结束。世贸大楼已在纽约重新拔地而起，基地组织正在走向衰亡，本·拉登也已被击毙。

今夜，我们要向那些仍置身战争一线、服务国家的美国公民致敬，他们的无私奉献使美国更加安全，更加令世人尊敬。我们永远不会忘记你们！只要我还是三军总司令，我就将保持美国在世界上最强大的军力。而当你们脱下戎装，我们将像你们当时服务我们一样来为你们服务，任何一位曾经为这个国家战斗过的人，都不应该再为养家糊口、容身之所或医疗保障而抗争。

known. When you take off the uniform, we will serve you as well as you've served us, because no one who fights for this country should have to fight for a job or a roof over their head or the care that they need when they come home.

Around the world, we've strengthened old alliances and forged new coalitions to stop the spread of nuclear weapons. We've reasserted our power across the Pacific and stood up to China on behalf of our workers. From Burma to Libya to South Sudan, we have advanced the rights and dignity of all human beings – men and women; Christians and Muslims and Jews.

But for all the progress that we've made, challenges remain. Terrorist plots must be disrupted. Europe's crisis must be contained. Our commitment to Israel's security must not waver, and neither must our pursuit of peace. The Iranian government must face a world that stays united against its nuclear ambitions. The historic change sweeping across the Arab world must be defined not by the iron fist of a dictator or the hate of extremists, but by the hopes and aspirations of ordinary people who are reaching for the same rights that we celebrate here today.

So now we have a choice. My opponent and his running mate are new to foreign policy. But from all that we've seen and heard, they want to take us back to an era of blustering and blundering that cost America so dearly. After all, you don't call Russia our number one enemy – not al- Qaida, Russia – unless you're still stuck in a Cold War mind warp. You might not be ready for diplomacy with Beijing if you can't visit the Olympics without insulting our closest ally.

My opponent – my opponent said that it was tragic to end the war in Iraq. And he won't tell us how he'll end the war in Afghanistan. Well, I have, and I will. And while my opponent would spend more money on military hardware that our Joint Chiefs don't even want, I will use the money we're no longer spending on war to pay down our debt and put more people back to work – rebuilding roads and bridges and schools and runways, because after two wars that have cost us thousands of lives and over a trillion dollars, it's time to do some nation building

环顾全球，我们不断巩固与老同盟的关系，加强与新盟友的联系，以遏制核武器的扩散。我们重申了美国在亚太地区的力量存在，并代表我们的工人，迎接中国的挑战。从缅甸、利比亚到南苏丹，我们推动了人权和尊严——无论是男性还是女性，是基督徒、穆斯林，还是犹太人。

虽然取得了这些进展，但挑战犹存：我们还必须破解恐怖主义的阴谋，解决欧洲的危机。我们对以色列安全的承诺不能动摇，对和平的追求不能动摇；伊朗政府必须面对一个一致反对其核计划的世界；横扫阿拉伯世界的历史性变革，不能靠独裁者的铁拳或极端分子的仇恨来诠释，而须依靠普通人的希望和抱负，他们和我们一样寻求同样的权利。

现在，我们面临一个选择。我的对手和他的竞选伙伴在外交政策方面是新手，据我们所见所闻，他们想要把美国带回那个狂暴而又浮躁的年代，而那个时代让美国付出了沉痛的代价。我们不能把俄罗斯称作头号敌人，除非你还是冷战时期的思想。如果你(罗姆尼)访问伦敦奥运会时还出言冒犯我们最亲密的盟友，那你可能还没有作好与北京打交道的准备。

曾经我的对手说结束伊拉克战争是场悲剧，当前他也尚未表示如何结束阿富汗战争。好吧，是我结束了伊拉克战争，未来终结阿富汗战争的，还是我。下一步，我的对手准备在军队硬件装备上撒大把的钱，其实这件事连参谋长联席会议都不愿染指。而我将在国内投入更多的资金，不再在战争上靡费金钱，以避免债务增加。我将致力于让更多的人回到工作岗位，重建公路、桥梁、学校和机场跑道。两场战争硝烟过后，美国损失了数千条生命和上万亿美元，现在到了好好建设我们美好家园的时候了！

right here at home.

You can choose a future where we reduce our deficit without sticking it to the middle class. Independent experts say that my plan would cut our deficit by $4 trillion. And last summer I worked with Republicans in Congress to cut a billion dollars in spending, because those of us who believe government can be a force for good should work harder than anyone to reform it so that it's leaner and more efficient and more responsive to the American people.

I want to reform the tax code so that it's simple, fair and asks the wealthiest households to pay higher taxes on incomes over $250,000 – the same rate we had when Bill Clinton was president, the same rate we had when our economy created nearly 23 million new jobs, the biggest surplus in history and a whole lot of millionaires to boot.

Now, I'm still eager to reach an agreement based on the principles of my bipartisan debt commission. No party has a monopoly on wisdom. No democracy works without compromise. I want to get this done, and we can get it done. But when Governor Romney and his friends in Congress tell us we can somehow lower our deficits by spending trillions more on new tax breaks for the wealthy, well – what'd Bill Clinton call it? You do the arithmetic. You do the math.

I refuse to go along with that, and as long as I'm president, I never will. I refuse to ask middle-class families to give up their deductions for owning a home or raising their kids just to pay for another millionaire's tax cut. I refuse to ask students to pay more for college or kick children out of Head Start programs to eliminate health insurance for millions of Americans who are poor and elderly or disabled all so those with the most can pay less. I'm not going along with that.

And I will never – I will never turn Medicare into a voucher. No American should ever have to spend their golden years at the mercy of insurance companies. They should retire with the care and the dignity that they have earned. Yes, we will reform and strengthen Medicare for the long haul, but we'll do it by reducing the cost of health care, not by asking seniors to pay thousands

　　大家可以选择一个减少赤字的未来，这样的一个赤字不应该成为中产阶级的负担。独立专家曾说过，我的计划将会削减财政赤字 4 万亿美元。去年夏天，我曾与共和党在国会一起削减了 10 亿美元的开支，因为我们认为，政府应该在锐意革新方面作出表率，这样政府会变得更精简、高效和负责任。

　　我希望修改税法，让它变得更加简单、公平、透明。通过修订税率，使收入超过 25 万美元的富人交纳更多的税金。这个税率将与比尔·克林顿担任总统时看齐，须记得那时我们提供了接近 2300 万个新就业机会，实现了美国历史上最多的财政盈余，造就了难以数计的百万富翁。

　　现在，我仍然热切地盼望，两党债务委员会在秉承原则的基础上，达成共识。没有哪个政党能够垄断智慧，没有哪个民主不是建立在协商之上。我希望达成此愿，我也相信我们能够达成此愿。但是罗姆尼州长和他国会的朋友们告诉我们，该给富人减税，如此这般才能减少赤字。哎，真不知道比尔·克林顿作何感想？我倒是想请罗姆尼先生先做做算术题。

　　我不会同意罗姆尼先生们的想法，只要我当一天总统，我将永远不会同意。我不愿看到，中产阶级家庭为富人减税而节衣缩食，从而放弃购置住房或抚养孩子的计划。我不愿看到，孩子们为了读大学而交纳更多的学费。我不愿看到，孩子们被请出启蒙计划。我更不愿看到，数百万的穷人、老人、残障人士需要付出更多的医疗保险成本。让穷人受苦，而让富人从中受益，我不同意这么做！

　　我也永远不会把老年保健医疗制变成一纸保单。美国人不应该在医疗保险公司的摆布下度过自己的流金岁月，你们应该在退休时拥有属于自己的关爱与尊严。是的，我们要着手改革长期的老年保健医疗制度，但是实现的途径是减少医疗保险的成本，而不是向年长者额外讨要数千美金。我们也会坚持社会保障的承诺，采取负责任的举措，而不是被华尔街所操纵。

of dollars more. And we will keep the promise of Social Security by taking the responsible steps to strengthen it, not by turning it over to Wall Street.

This is the choice we now face. This is what the election comes down to. Over and over, we've been told by our opponents that bigger tax cuts and fewer regulations are the only way, that since government can't do everything, it should do almost nothing. If you can't afford health insurance, hope that you don't get sick. If a company releases toxic pollution into the air your children breathe, well, that's the price of progress. If you can't afford to start a business or go to college, take my opponent's advice and borrow money from your parents.

You know what, that's not who we are. That's not what this country is about. As Americans, we believe we are endowed by our Creator with certain inalienable rights, rights that no man or government can take away. We insist on personal responsibility, and we celebrate individual initiative. We're not entitled to success. We have to earn it. We honor the strivers, the dreamers, the risk-takers, the entrepreneurs who have always been the driving force behind our free enterprise system, the greatest engine of growth and prosperity that the world's ever known.

But we also believe in something called citizenship – citizenship, a word at the very heart of our founding, a word at the very essence of our democracy, the idea that this country only works when we accept certain obligations to one another and to future generations.

We believe that when a CEO pays his autoworkers enough to buy the cars that they build, the whole company does better. We believe that when a family can no longer be tricked into signing a mortgage they can't afford, that family's protected, but so is the value of other people's homes – and so is the entire economy. We believe the little girl who's offered an escape from poverty by a great teacher or a grant for college could become the next Steve Jobs or the scientist who cures cancer or the president of the United States – and it is in our power to give her that chance.

这就是你我现在所面临的选择，这也是选举的最终意义之所在。我们的对手不厌其烦地告诉大家，更大规模的减税是唯一正途，其他皆可随其自然，政府无为而治就好了。那好吧，如果付不起医疗保险，那你就祈祷自己别生病。如果企业释放的毒气危及到你孩子的健康，那你只好认为这是社会发展进步的代价。如果你没钱创业或者没钱上大学，那么就接受我们对手的建议吧，找你父母借钱去。

你们知道吗？我们美国人压根就不应该是这个样子，这也不是美国价值之所在。身为美国公民，我们拥有上帝赋予的不可剥夺的权利，这些权利不是哪个人或者哪个政府想拿走就能拿走的。我们坚持公民责任，鼓励个人创造，告诉大家成功不是从天而降，而必须奋力博取。我们敬重奋斗者、梦想家、冒险家、企业家，他们推动着自由企业制度的发展，为社会的发展和繁荣提供了不竭的动力。

但是，我们对一种叫做"公民权"的东西深信不疑。它是美国建国之基的核心，它是民主要义的所在。它的理念是，只有民众同意互相负有义务，并且对下一代负有义务，我们的国家才能照常运转。

我们深信，如果一位首席执行官付给他的工人足够的薪水，让他们购买自己制造的汽车，那么这家公司就能够做的更棒。我们深信，当一个家庭可以不再被哄着签订他们难以承受的抵押合同，这个家庭就安全了，推而广之，其他家庭如此，整个经济体亦是如此。我们深信，一位出身卑微

We know that churches and charities can often make more of a difference than a poverty program alone. We don't want handouts for people who refuse to help themselves, and we certainly don't want bailouts for banks that break the rules. We don't think the government can solve all of our problems, but we don't think the government is the source of all of our problems – any more than our welfare recipients or corporations or unions or immigrants or gays or any other group we're told to blame for our troubles – because – because America, we understand that this democracy is ours.

We, the people – recognize that we have responsibilities as well as rights; that our destinies are bound together; that a freedom which asks only, what's in it for me, a freedom without a commitment to others, a freedom without love or charity or duty or patriotism, is unworthy of our founding ideals, and those who died in their defense. As citizens, we understand that America is not about what can be done for us. It's about what can be done by us, together – through the hard and frustrating but necessary work of self-government. That's what we believe. So you see, the election four years ago wasn't about me. It was about you. My fellow citizens – you were the change.

You're the reason there's a little girl with a heart disorder in Phoenix who'll get the surgery she needs because an insurance company can't limit her coverage. You did that.

You're the reason a young man in Colorado who never thought he'd be able to afford his dream of earning a medical degree is about to get that chance. You made that possible.

You're the reason a young immigrant who grew up here and went to school here and pledged allegiance to our flag will no longer be deported from the only country she's ever called home – why selfless soldiers won't be kicked out of the military because of who they are or who they love, why thousands of families have finally been able to say to the loved ones who served us so bravely, welcome home. Welcome home. You did that. You did that. You did that.

的小姑娘，如果在恩师的帮助下告别贫困，或者准许去大学读书，那么她有可能就是下一位史蒂夫·乔布斯，或者是攻克癌症的科学家，或者是美国总统，我们拥有赋予她光明未来的力量。

人所共知，教会和慈善机构常常扮演着与扶贫工作不太一致的角色。我们不想把救济品发放到那些已经放弃自救的人手中，同样，我们理所当然地不想救助那些公然违反规则的银行。政府不是万能的，但我们也不想让政府成为所有问题的肇事者，让福利受领人、企业、工会、移民、同性恋以及其他组织，都来责骂我们惹是生非。因为我们知道，民主掌握在我们手中。

美国的全体公民意识到权责一致，意识到使命共担，意识到一味索取的自由，只知享受的自由，没有仁爱之心、怜悯之心、责任之心和爱国之心的自由，不是我们的追索目标。美国公民深知，国家的概念不是意味着要为我们做什么，国家的概念意味着我们要万众一心，团结一致，通过历程坎坷但必不可少的自治，以达成我们的目标。这是我们坚信不疑的。所以你们看到，四年前的选举无关乎我本人，选举关乎美国全体民众。亲爱的同胞们，你们才是推动社会进步的伟大力量！

在菲尼克斯一有位患有心脏病的女孩，在保险公司足额险金的支撑下，将进行所需的手术治疗，这是你们的功劳，是你们现实了这一切。

在科罗拉多有一位小伙子，以前对攻读医学学位的学费望而却步，但现在却即将入学，这是你们的功劳，是你们帮助他梦想成真。

当一位年轻的移民，生于斯，长于斯，学于斯，她曾经对我们的国旗宣誓效忠，她唯一称之为祖国的国度再也不会将其驱离出境了。无私的美国大兵在军中服役，履职尽忠，当他们将不会被迫离开军队，成千上万的家庭最终能够对最可爱的人说一句："欢迎回家，欢迎回家！"这些全都是你们的功劳！

If you turn away now – if you turn away now, if you buy into the cynicism that the change we fought for isn't possible, well, change will not happen. If you give up on the idea that your voice can make a difference, then other voices will fill the void, the lobbyists and special interests, the people with the $10 million checks who are trying to buy this election and those who are trying to make it harder for you to vote, Washington politicians who want to decide who you can marry or control health care choices that women should be making for themselves. Only you can make sure that doesn't happen. Only you have the power to move us forward.

You know, I recognize that times have changed since I first spoke to this convention. Times have changed, and so have I. I'm no longer just a candidate. I'm the president. And – and that's – And that – and that means I know what it means to send young Americans into battle, for I've held in my arms the mothers and fathers of those who didn't return. I've shared the pain of families who've lost their homes, and the frustration of workers who've lost their jobs. If the critics are right that I've made all my decisions based on polls, then I must not be very good at reading them.

And while I'm proud of what we've achieved together – I'm far more mindful of my own failings, knowing exactly what Lincoln meant when he said, "I have been driven to my knees many times by the overwhelming conviction that I had no place else to go."

But as I stand here tonight, I have never been more hopeful about America. Not because I think I have all the answers. Not because I'm naive about the magnitude of our challenges.

I'm hopeful because of you.

The young woman I met at a science fair who won national recognition for her biology research while living with her family at a homeless shelter – she gives me hope.

The auto worker who won the lottery after his plant almost closed, but kept

　　如果你们此时转身不顾，如果你们听信了那些质疑变革的嘲讽，那么变革就无法到来。如果你们不再相信你们的声音可以改变一切，那么其他游说者和特殊利益群体的声音就会乘虚而入，他们会用千万美元去购买选票，会让你们的投票变得更加困难，华盛顿的政客会决定你该和什么样的人结婚，会剥夺本来属于女性自己的医疗决定权。只有你们才能阻止这一切，只有你们才有力量使国家继续前进！

　　跟我首次在大会上讲演时相比，已经时过境迁。时光在更迭，我也在改变。我已不再是个候选人，现在我是总统。我知道派遣年轻的士兵上战场，意味着什么，因为我亲自拥抱过那些牺牲者的父母。对失去家园者的痛苦和失业者的失望，我都苦同亲尝。批评者说我的抉择都是看着民调见风使舵，如果他们说的对，那我一定是体察民情的高手了。

　　尽管我对我们共创的事业骄傲不已，我更深知我的不足，深深领悟到林肯总统那句话的意思，他说："当我感到走投无路时，我总是要向上帝跪下呼求。"

　　但当我站在这里，我从未像今夜这般对美国满怀着希望，不是因为我有解决所有问题的灵丹妙药，也不是因为我天真地低估了挑战。

　　是你们给了我希望。

　　一位年轻的女性在科博会荣获了生物学研究国家级荣誉，可她和家人却生活在流民收容所，是她给了我希望。

coming to work every day, and bought flags for his whole town and one of the cars that he built to surprise his wife – he gives me hope.

The family business in Warroad, Minnesota, that didn't lay off a single one of their 4,000 employees when the recession hit – even when their competitors shut down dozens of plants, even when it meant the owner gave up some perks and some pay because they understood that their biggest asset was the community and the workers who had helped build that business – they give me hope.

I think about the young sailor I met at Walter Reed Hospital still recovering from a grenade attack that would cause him to have his leg amputated above the knee. And six months ago we would watch him walk into a White House dinner honoring those who served in Iran (sic; Iraq) – tall and 20 pounds heavier, dashing in his uniform, with a big grin on his face, sturdy on his new leg. And I remember how a few months after that I would watch him on a bicycle, racing with his fellow wounded warriors on a sparkling spring day, inspiring other heroes who had just begun the hard path he had traveled. He gives me hope. He gives me hope.

I don't know what party these men and women belong to. I don't know if they'll vote for me. But I know that their spirit defines us. They remind me, in the words of Scripture, that ours is a future filled with hope. And if you share that faith with me, if you share that hope with me, I ask you tonight for your vote. If you reject the notion that this nation's promise is reserved for the few, your voice must be heard in this election. If you reject the notion that our government is forever beholden to the highest bidder, you need to stand up in this election. If you believe that new plants and factories can dot our landscape, that new energy can power our future, that new schools can provide ladders of opportunity to this nation of dreamers, if you believe in a country where everyone gets a fair shot, and everyone does their fair share and everyone plays by the same rules, then I need you to vote this November.

America, I never said this journey would be easy, and I won't promise

一位汽车工人中了大奖，却在工厂几乎倒闭之时坚持每天上班，他给全镇的人都买了国旗，还买了自己参与制造的汽车给他妻子以惊喜，是他给了我希望。

在明尼苏达，一个家族企业在危机之时，从没有在4000多名员工中裁掉任何一个人，尽管他们的竞争对手关掉了几家工厂，尽管这意味着经营者要去承担这些损失，因为他们懂得，他们最大的财富是整个社区，以及帮助他们创业的人们，是他们给了我希望。

我又想起在沃尔特·里德医院遇到的年轻水兵，他被手雷所伤，膝盖以上需要截肢，目前正在康复之中，半年前见面那次，是白宫向伊战归国的将士们致敬的晚宴上，他仍很魁梧，重了20磅，戎装熠熠，笑容满面，换了假肢的他还是很结实。还记得又过了几个月，就见他蹬自行车了，在明媚的春日，和其他伤员战友们一起比赛，其他的重伤员在治疗伊始就充满了希望，是他给了我希望。

我不清楚以上这些人是哪个党的，也不知道他们是否会投票给我，但是他们的精神书写了美国，他们让我想起了石碑上的铭文："我们的未来充满希望。"如果你们和我拥有共同的信仰，如果你和我抱有共同的希望，那么我请你今夜为我投票。如果你们也不愿意接受美国只有少数人的应许之地，你们的呼声肯定会在大选中得到呼应。如果你们也不接受政府永远被竞价者所控制，那么你们一定要在大选中站稳立场。如果你们也相信新的工厂将出现在地平线上，新型能源可以给明天注入能量，如果你也相信新的校园能为怀抱梦想的民族提供机遇，如果你也相信一国之中应该机遇均等，责任共担，规则之下人人平等，那么，请在11月投我一票。

that now. Yes, our path is harder, but it leads to a better place. Yes, our road is longer, but we travel it together. We don't turn back. We leave no one behind. We pull each other up. We draw strength from our victories. And we learn from our mistakes. But we keep our eyes fixed on that distant horizon knowing that providence is with us and that we are surely blessed to be citizens of the greatest nation on earth.

Thank you, God bless you and God bless these United States.

Charlotte, North Carolina, September 6, 2012

同胞们，我从来没有说过这会是一条捷径，我也不会这样承诺。是的，这条路更加艰辛，但却是通往理想的正途，虽然长路漫漫，好在你我并肩同行。我们不抛弃，不放弃，彼此搀扶，我们从胜利中得到力量，在失误中汲取教训，我们注视着天边的极限，坚信上帝与你我同在。成为地球上最伟大国家的公民，必然是上帝对你我的恩泽。

谢谢大家！上帝保佑你们！上帝保佑美利坚合众国！

（杜梦臻/译）

Obama's Speech on the Anniversary of 9/11

This week, we mark the eleventh anniversary of the September 11th attacks. It's a time to remember the nearly 3,000 innocent men, women and children we lost, and the families they left behind. It's a chance to honor the courage of the first responders who risked their lives – on that day, and every day since. And it's an opportunity to give thanks for our men and women in uniform who have served and sacrificed, sometimes far from home, to keep our country safe.

This anniversary is about them. It's also a time to reflect on just how far we've come as a nation these past eleven years.

On that clear September morning, as America watched the towers fall, and the Pentagon burn, and the wreckage smoldering in a Pennsylvania field, we were filled with questions. Where had the attacks come from, and how would America respond? Would they fundamentally weaken the country we love? Would they change who we are?

The last decade has been a difficult one, but together, we have answered those questions and come back stronger as a nation.

We took the fight to al Qaeda, decimated their leadership, and put them on a path to defeat. And thanks to the courage and skill of our intelligence personnel and armed forces, Osama bin Laden will never threaten America again.

Instead of pulling back from the world, we've strengthened our alliances while improving our security here at home. As Americans, we refuse to live in

奥巴马纪念 "9·11" 袭击讲话

本周，我们纪念 "9·11" 遇袭事件11周年。此时此刻，我们追念那3000多名无辜遇害的男女老少，也向他们的家人表示慰问；此时此刻，我们向紧急救援人员表示敬意，那一天和此后的日日夜夜，他们挺身而出，舍己救人；此时此刻，我们感谢为国换上戎装、赴汤蹈火的军人，他们保家卫国，远离家乡。

这个纪念日，是为他们而设。这个纪念日，也是为了回顾这11载春秋，我们的国家取得了什么进步。

那一年，9月的一个晴朗的清晨，世贸大厦在众目睽睽之下，轰然倒塌，五角大楼燃烧起火，飞机残骸在宾夕法尼亚的田野中被焚毁，我们心中充满了疑问：这些袭击来自何方？美国应该如何应对？我们深爱的祖国是否会就此一蹶不振？我们是否会就此改变本色？

过去的10年充满了艰难险阻，但我们共克时艰，一一解答了这些问题，再次重振国之雄风。

我们向 "基地" 组织发起了反击，扫除了该组织的首恶分子，让他们走上了灭亡的道路。由于我国情报人员和军人的大智大勇，奥萨马·本·拉

fear. Today, a new tower rises above the New York skyline. And our country is stronger, safer and more respected in the world.

Instead of turning on each other, we've resisted the temptation to give in to mistrust and suspicion. I have always said that America is at war with al Qaeda and its affiliates – and we will never be at war with Islam or any other religion. We are the United States of America. Our freedom and diversity make us unique, and they will always be central to who we are as a nation.

Instead of changing who we are, the attacks have brought out the best in the American people. More than 5 million members of the 9/11 Generation have worn America's uniform over the past decade, and we've seen an outpouring of goodwill towards our military, veterans, and their families. Together, they've done everything we've asked of them. We've ended the war in Iraq and brought our troops home. We brought an end to the Taliban regime. We've trained Afghan Security Forces, and forged a partnership with a new Afghan Government. And by the end 2014, the transition in Afghanistan will be complete and our war there will be over.

And finally, instead of turning inward with grief, we've honored the memory of those we lost by giving back to our communities, serving those in need, and reaffirming the values at the heart of who we are as a people. That's why we mark September 11th as a National Day of Service and Remembrance. Because we are one American family, and we look out for each other – not just on the difficult days, but every day.

Eleven years later, that's the legacy of 9/11 – the ability to say with confidence that no adversary and no act of terrorism can change who we are. We are Americans, and we will protect and preserve this country we love. On this solemn anniversary, let's remember those we lost, let us reaffirm the values they stood for, and let us keep moving forward as one nation and one people.

the White House, Washington D. C., September 8, 2012

登无法再对美国造成威胁。

我们没有在世界上退守一隅。相反，我们加强了联盟的力量，同时改善了国内的安全。作为美国人，我们决不在恐惧中苟活。今天，一栋新的高楼在纽约地平线上升起。我国日益国强民安，更受世人尊重。

我们没有相互指责，决不受外界挑拨而互不信任、互为猜疑。我总说，美国在与"基地"组织及其附庸作战，我们决不以伊斯兰教和其他任何宗教为对立面。我们是美利坚合众国。自由和多样使我们独树一帜，而这些也始终是我们的立国之本。

我们没有丧失我们的本色。相反，面对这些袭击事件，美国人民展示了最优秀的品质。10年来，500多万"9·11一代人"换上戎装。我们看见军人、老兵及其家人处处受到真诚的拥戴。他们同心协力，履职尽忠，出色地完成了每项任务。我们结束了在伊拉克的战争，撤回了我们的军队。我们推翻了塔利班政权，为阿富汗安全部队提供训练，与阿富汗新政府建立伙伴关系。到2014年底，阿富汗将完成过渡，我们在那里的战事将彻底结束。

最后，我们没有陷入悲痛不能自拔。我们回馈社区，救困扶危，坚持我国人民的核心价值，以此缅怀逝者。正因为如此，我们确定每年9月11日为全国服务与纪念日。我们美国同胞是一家人，不仅在艰难的日子相互守望，而且每一天都相互扶持。

可以充满自信地说，11年来，任何敌人、任何恐怖主义行径都无法改变我们的本色，这就是9·11留下的宝贵遗产。作为美国人，我们将捍卫和维护我们热爱的祖国。在这隆重的纪念日到来之际，让我们铭记所失，让我们重拾逝者的遗愿，让我们的国家和人民继续奋勇向前！

（杜梦臻/译）

Remarks by Obama
to the 67th UN General Assembly

Mr. President, Mr. Secretary General, fellow delegates, ladies and gentleman:

I would like to begin today by telling you about an American named Chris Stevens.

Chris was born in a town called Grass Valley, California, the son of a lawyer and a musician. As a young man, Chris joined the Peace Corps, and taught English in Morocco. And he came to love and respect the people of North Africa and the Middle East. He would carry that commitment throughout his life. As a diplomat, he worked from Egypt to Syria, from Saudi Arabia to Libya. He was known for walking the streets of the cities where he worked – tasting the local food, meeting as many people as he could, speaking Arabic, listening with a broad smile.

Chris went to Benghazi in the early days of the Libyan revolution, arriving on a cargo ship. As America's representative, he helped the Libyan people as they coped with violent conflict, cared for the wounded, and crafted a vision for the future in which the rights of all Libyans would be respected. And after the revolution, he supported the birth of a new democracy, as Libyans held elections, and built new institutions, and began to move forward after decades of dictatorship.

Chris Stevens loved his work. He took pride in the country he served, and he saw dignity in the people that he met. And two weeks ago, he traveled to

奥巴马在第67届联合国大会上发表的演讲 ①

主席先生、秘书长先生、与会代表们、女士们先生们：

大家好，今天作为我演讲的开始，我首先想向诸位讲述一位美国人的故事，他的名字是克里斯·史蒂文斯。

克里斯出生在加利福尼亚州格拉斯山谷的一个小镇，父母是律师和音乐家。克里斯年轻时参加了和平志愿者队伍，在摩洛哥教英语期间，他与北非和中东人民结下了深厚的情谊和崇高的敬仰，他对当初的承诺恪守不渝。作为一名外交官，他的足迹遍及埃及、叙利亚、沙特阿拉伯、利比亚等国。在他工作城市的大街小巷，人们都知道他，经常可以看见他品尝美食，拜访居民，笑容可掬地用阿拉伯语交谈倾听的身影。

在利比亚革命初期，克里斯搭乘一艘货轮前往班加西工作。他作为美国的代表，帮助利比亚人民解决暴力冲突，为伤病员提供护理，同时为利比亚人民绘制蓝图：人民权利皆受尊重的国度。革命结束后，他拥护新诞生的民主政体，同利比亚人一道，举行了选举，努力建设新的体制，在摆脱数十年专制统治之后，开始奋勇向前。

克里斯热爱自己的工作。他为自己服务的国家深感骄傲。他在普通人身上看见了尊严。两周前，他前往班加西，考察有关新建文化中心和一所医院现代化改造的规划。正值此时，美国使团驻地遭到袭击。克里斯曾为保全这所城市鞠躬尽瘁，结果和其他3位同事却在这里惨遭毒手，时年52岁。

---

① 美国总统奥巴马当地时间25日在第67届联合国大会发表主旨演讲，在当天的演讲中，奥巴马的言辞完全集中在中东问题上，连崛起的中国和亚洲核心同盟国日本也没有言及。韩联社称，有观点认为，奥巴马之所以将重点放在中东问题，是因为今年11月总统选举中中东问题将是最为核心的问题。

Benghazi to review plans to establish a new cultural center and modernize a hospital. That's when America's compound came under attack. Along with three of his colleagues, Chris was killed in the city that he helped to save. He was 52 years old.

I tell you this story because Chris Stevens embodied the best of America. Like his fellow Foreign Service officers, he built bridges across oceans and cultures, and was deeply invested in the international cooperation that the United Nations represents. He acted with humility, but he also stood up for a set of principles – a belief that individuals should be free to determine their own destiny, and live with liberty, dignity, justice, and opportunity.

The attacks on the civilians in Benghazi were attacks on America. We are grateful for the assistance we received from the Libyan government and from the Libyan people. There should be no doubt that we will be relentless in tracking down the killers and bringing them to justice. And I also appreciate that in recent days, the leaders of other countries in the region – including Egypt, Tunisia and Yemen – have taken steps to secure our diplomatic facilities, and called for calm. And so have religious authorities around the globe.

But understand, the attacks of the last two weeks are not simply an assault on America. They are also an assault on the very ideals upon which the United Nations was founded – the notion that people can resolve their differences peacefully; that diplomacy can take the place of war; that in an interdependent world, all of us have a stake in working towards greater opportunity and security for our citizens.

If we are serious about upholding these ideals, it will not be enough to put more guards in front of an embassy, or to put out statements of regret and wait for the outrage to pass. If we are serious about these ideals, we must speak honestly about the deeper causes of the crisis – because we face a choice between the forces that would drive us apart and the hopes that we hold in common.

Today, we must reaffirm that our future will be determined by people like

　　我向诸位讲述这段经历，是因为克里斯·史蒂文斯体现了美国人最优秀的品质。他与其他外事服务人员一样，为各大洋不同文化之间架起沟通的桥梁，全身心地践行联合国的国际合作精神。他为人谦逊，但同时恪守不渝——坚信人人皆应自由主宰自己的命运，过上享有自由、尊严、公平和机会的生活。

　　对班加西平民的袭击就是对美国的袭击。我们感谢利比亚政府和利比亚人民给予的协助。毋庸置疑，我们将毫不留情地追查凶手，将他们绳之以法。最近该地区包括埃及、突尼斯和也门在内的其他国家的领导人采取行动保障我国外交人员和设施的安全，并呼吁人们保持冷静，对此我表示由衷的感谢。全球各地的宗教机构也同样如此。

　　然而，应该知道，过去两个星期发生的袭击不仅仅是针对美国，也公然践踏了联合国的创建理念：可以和平解决分歧；外交可以取代战争；在全球联系日益紧密的大环境下，努力为我们的公民带来更多的机遇和安全与我们所有人都休戚相关。

　　我们倘若真要坚持这些理想，那么在使馆门前增设警卫，发表哀悼声明，抑或静待民愤平息，这些都是远远不够的。我们倘若真要坚持这些理想，就必须坦诚布公地剖析这场危机更深层的原因，因为我们面临着抉择，一边是助长我们分裂的势力，另一边是我们共同拥有的希望。

Chris Stevens – and not by his killers. Today, we must declare that this violence and intolerance has no place among our United Nations.

It has been less than two years since a vendor in Tunisia set himself on fire to protest the oppressive corruption in his country, and sparked what became known as the Arab Spring. And since then, the world has been captivated by the transformation that's taken place, and the United States has supported the forces of change.

We were inspired by the Tunisian protests that toppled a dictator, because we recognized our own beliefs in the aspiration of men and women who took to the streets.

We insisted on change in Egypt, because our support for democracy ultimately put us on the side of the people.

We supported a transition of leadership in Yemen, because the interests of the people were no longer being served by a corrupt status quo.

We intervened in Libya alongside a broad coalition, and with the mandate of the United Nations Security Council, because we had the ability to stop the slaughter of innocents, and because we believed that the aspirations of the people were more powerful than a tyrant.

And as we meet here, we again declare that the regime of Bashar al-Assad must come to an end so that the suffering of the Syrian people can stop and a new dawn can begin.

We have taken these positions because we believe that freedom and self-determination are not unique to one culture. These are not simply American values or Western values – they are universal values. And even as there will be huge challenges to come with a transition to democracy, I am convinced that ultimately government of the people, by the people, and for the people is more likely to bring about the stability, prosperity, and individual opportunity that serve as a basis for peace in our world.

So let us remember that this is a season of progress. For the first time in

今天，我们必须重申，我们的未来必将由像克里斯·史蒂文斯这样的人民决定——而不应该被杀害他的元凶左右。今天，我们必须宣布，这种惨无人道和蛮横无理的行径在我们联合国决无立足之地！

两年前，突尼斯一位小贩为抗议本国蠹国害民的腐败燃火自焚，引发了"阿拉伯之春运动"。由此全世界转型之风方兴未艾，美国也一贯支持变革的力量。

突尼斯的示威活动推翻了专制统治者，可谓大快人心，因为走上街头的男女老少的心愿，与我们自己的信念不谋而合。

我们支持埃及发生的改革，因为我们对民主的支持最终使我们与人民同心同德。

我们支持也门的领导层过渡，因为腐朽的现状已与人们的利益背道而驰。

我们与同盟一道，在联合国安理会的授权下，对利比亚进行了干预，因为我们有能力制止对无辜百姓的屠杀，因为我们相信：民意，定能制暴！

借此会议举行之际，我们再一次宣布，巴沙尔·阿萨德政权必须下台，从而使叙利亚人民结束苦难，迎来新的曙光。

我们的立场是基于我们的信念，即自由和自决并不专属于某一种文化。这些并不专属于美国的价值观或西方的价值观——而是普世的价值观。即使向民主的过渡仍将面临巨大的挑战，我坚信只有"民有、民治、民享"的政府才更有可能最终创造稳定、繁荣和个人机会，为世界的和平奠定基础。

decades, Tunisians, Egyptians and Libyans voted for new leaders in elections that were credible, competitive, and fair. This democratic spirit has not been restricted to the Arab world. Over the past year, we've seen peaceful transitions of power in Malawi and Senegal, and a new President in Somalia. In Burma, a President has freed political prisoners and opened a closed society, a courageous dissident has been elected to parliament, and people look forward to further reform. Around the globe, people are making their voices heard, insisting on their innate dignity, and the right to determine their future.

And yet the turmoil of recent weeks reminds us that the path to democracy does not end with the casting of a ballot. Nelson Mandela once said: "To be free is not merely to cast off one's chains, but to live in a way that respects and enhances the freedom of others."

True democracy demands that citizens cannot be thrown in jail because of what they believe, and that businesses can be opened without paying a bribe. It depends on the freedom of citizens to speak their minds and assemble without fear, and on the rule of law and due process that guarantees the rights of all people.

In other words, true democracy – real freedom – is hard work. Those in power have to resist the temptation to crack down on dissidents. In hard economic times, countries must be tempted – may be tempted to rally the people around perceived enemies, at home and abroad, rather than focusing on the painstaking work of reform.

Moreover, there will always be those that reject human progress – dictators who cling to power, corrupt interests that depend on the status quo, and extremists who fan the flames of hate and division. From Northern Ireland to South Asia, from Africa to the Americas, from the Balkans to the Pacific Rim, we've witnessed convulsions that can accompany transitions to a new political order.

At time, the conflicts arise along the fault lines of race or tribe. And often they arise from the difficulties of reconciling tradition and faith with the diversity and interdependence of the modern world. In every country, there are

为此，请铭记，这是一个进步的时期。几十载春秋，突尼斯、埃及和利比亚第一次迎来一场可信度高、竞争激烈、秩序公平的选举，推选出了新的领导人。这种民主精神不应只限于阿拉伯世界。在过去的这一年，我们见证了马拉维和塞内加尔权力的和平转移，索马里有了一位新总统。在缅甸，总统释放了政治犯，将封闭的社会对外开放，一位勇敢的持不同政见者被选入议会，缅甸人民还期待未来更进一步的改革。放眼世界，人民正在发出自己的声音，坚决要求维护固有的尊严和决定自己未来的权利。

然而，最近几周的动荡局势再次提醒我们，通往民主之路并不止于选举投票。纳尔逊·曼德拉曾说："赢得自由并非仅仅要打破自身的枷锁，还要以尊重及增进他人自由的方式生活。"

真正的民主不允许公民因个人信仰而沦为阶下囚；真正的民主确保公司企业无需行贿就能开门营业。民主需要公民不怀恐惧地发表言论和自由集会，需要健全的法制和公正的程序。

换言之，真正的民主——真正的自由——要靠艰苦努力。当权者必须抵抗住镇压异见的诱惑。在经济困难的时期，有些国家会被糖衣炮弹所诱惑，不去励精图治地去从事改革工作，而是召集人民对抗国内及国外的

those who find different religious beliefs threatening; in every culture, those who love freedom for themselves must ask themselves how much they're willing to tolerate freedom for others.

That is what we saw play out in the last two weeks, as a crude and disgusting video sparked outrage throughout the Muslim world. Now, I have made it clear that the United States government had nothing to do with this video, and I believe its message must be rejected by all who respect our common humanity.

It is an insult not only to Muslims, but to America as well – for as the city outside these walls makes clear, we are a country that has welcomed people of every race and every faith. We are home to Muslims who worship across our country. We not only respect the freedom of religion, we have laws that protect individuals from being harmed because of how they look or what they believe. We understand why people take offense to this video because millions of our citizens are among them.

I know there are some who ask why we don't just ban such a video. And the answer is enshrined in our laws: Our Constitution protects the right to practice free speech.

Here in the United States, countless publications provoke offense. Like me, the majority of Americans are Christian, and yet we do not ban blasphemy against our most sacred beliefs. As President of our country and Commander-in-Chief of our military, I accept that people are going to call me awful things every day – and I will always defend their right to do so.

Americans have fought and died around the globe to protect the right of all people to express their views, even views that we profoundly disagree with. We do not do so because we support hateful speech, but because our founders understood that without such protections, the capacity of each individual to express their own views and practice their own faith may be threatened. We do so because in a diverse society, efforts to restrict speech can quickly become a

"假想敌"。

此外，总有一些人拒绝人类进步——那些抓住权力不放的独裁者，一味维系现状的腐败势力，以及煽动仇恨、制造隔阂的极端主义分子。从北爱尔兰到南亚、从非洲到美洲、从巴尔干半岛到环太平洋地区，我们目睹了伴随新政权过渡而出现的骚乱和动荡。

有时，冲突起源于不同种族或部族之间的不公分界线；还往往源起于传统、信仰和融合性相互调和的失败。在每个国家中，都有一些人认为不同的宗教信仰构成威胁；在每种文化中，都有一些追求自身自由的人必须扪心自问愿意在多大程度上容忍他人的自由。

我们在近两周看到，一段粗制滥造、令人厌恶的视频在整个穆斯林世界引发了强烈愤怒。现在我已明确表示，美国政府与这段视频没有任何关系，而且我坚信，所有尊重我们的共同人性的人都不会让有所企图的人得逞！

这不仅是对穆斯林的玷污，也是对美国的玷污——因为正如会场外面的这座城市所清楚展现的，我们是一个热情接纳不同种族和不同信仰的国度。穆斯林在美国可以虔诚礼拜，这里是他们的家园。我们不仅尊重宗教自由，还制定法律保护个人不因外表或信仰而受到伤害。我们理解为什么人民看到这段视频深感冒犯，因为我们百万子民，就在其中。

我知道有些人会问我们为什么不干脆禁止这样的视频。这个答案铭刻在我国的法律之中：即公民言论自由受宪法保护。

在美国，出言不逊的出版读物数不胜数。大多数美国人和我一样是基督教徒，但我们不禁止亵渎我们最神圣的信仰的言论。身为一国总统和三军统帅，对于人们对我的不逊之言、不敬之语，我坦然接受。而且我还会誓死捍卫他们这一权利。

放眼世界，无数美国人为捍卫公民言论自由而奋不顾身，哪怕有些观点与我们大相径庭。我们这样做并不是因为我们支持仇恨言论，而是因为我们的建国先贤明白，倘若没有这样的保障，每个人阐述自身观点，践行自身信仰的能力都有可能由此退化。我们这样做的原因是，在一个多样化的社会中，限制言论的做法可能很快就演变成压制异议及镇压少数派的手段。

tool to silence critics and oppress minorities.

We do so because given the power of faith in our lives, and the passion that religious differences can inflame, the strongest weapon against hateful speech is not repression; it is more speech – the voices of tolerance that rally against bigotry and blasphemy, and lift up the values of understanding and mutual respect.

Now, I know that not all countries in this body share this particular understanding of the protection of free speech. We recognize that. But in 2012, at a time when anyone with a cell phone can spread offensive views around the world with the click of a button, the notion that we can control the flow of information is obsolete. The question, then, is how do we respond?

And on this we must agree: There is no speech that justifies mindless violence. There are no words that excuse the killing of innocents. There's no video that justifies an attack on an embassy. There's no slander that provides an excuse for people to burn a restaurant in Lebanon, or destroy a school in Tunis, or cause death and destruction in Pakistan.

In this modern world with modern technologies, for us to respond in that way to hateful speech empowers any individual who engages in such speech to create chaos around the world. We empower the worst of us if that's how we respond.

More broadly, the events of the last two weeks also speak to the need for all of us to honestly address the tensions between the West and the Arab world that is moving towards democracy.

Now, let me be clear: Just as we cannot solve every problem in the world, the United States has not and will not seek to dictate the outcome of democratic transitions abroad. We do not expect other nations to agree with us on every issue, nor do we assume that the violence of the past weeks or the hateful speech by some individuals represent the views of the overwhelming majority of Muslims, any more than the views of the people who produced this video

我们这样做是因为，生活中信仰的威力不可小觑，宗教分歧有可能煽起强烈情绪，而遏制仇恨言论的最得力的武器不是镇压，而是各抒己见——用豁然大度之声来对抗偏执和亵渎，提倡理解与尊重的价值。

但我知道，并非所有与会国都认同和理解这种对自由言论的保护。我们承认这一点。但在2012年，在一个任何持有手机的人只要动一动手指就能将激进言论传遍世界的各个角落的时代，那种认为我们能够控制信息流动的观点早已经过时。而现在的问题便是，我们应如何予以回应？

关于这个问题的意见必须达成一致：任何言论都不能为滥用暴力开脱。任何言词都不能成为杀害无辜的借口。任何一段视频都不能成为袭击驻外使馆的理由。任何诽谤之词都不能成为一些人在黎巴嫩焚烧餐馆，在突尼斯砸毁学校，或在巴基斯坦造成物损人亡的托词。

现代世界，科技日新月异，我们若采用相同手段予以回击，就会使煽动言论的始作俑者借机在全世界制造混乱。我们若那样回应，就会让败类得逞。

广义而言，这两周发生的事件也提醒我们，所有人必须要坦诚地对待西方世界与正在向民主迈进的阿拉伯世界之间的紧张关系。

请允许我澄清：正如我们不能解决世界上的每道难题，美国没有也不会试图左右外国的民主过渡的结果。我们不期望其他国家事事都与我们观点一致，我们也不认为两周来的暴力行径或某些人的仇恨言论代表着绝大多数穆斯林的观点，正如制作这段视频的人的观点并不代表美国人民一样。但我坚持认为，每一个国家的每一位领导人都有义务对暴力和极端主义行为予以高声谴责。

represents those of Americans. However, I do believe that it is the obligation of all leaders in all countries to speak out forcefully against violence and extremism.

It is time to marginalize those who – even when not directly resorting to violence – use hatred of America, or the West, or Israel, as the central organizing principle of politics. For that only gives cover, and sometimes makes an excuse, for those who do resort to violence.

That brand of politics – one that pits East against West, and South against North, Muslims against Christians and Hindu and Jews – can't deliver on the promise of freedom. To the youth, it offers only false hope. Burning an American flag does nothing to provide a child an education. Smashing apart a restaurant does not fill an empty stomach. Attacking an embassy won't create a single job. That brand of politics only makes it harder to achieve what we must do together: educating our children, and creating the opportunities that they deserve; protecting human rights, and extending democracy's promise.

Understand America will never retreat from the world. We will bring justice to those who harm our citizens and our friends, and we will stand with our allies. We are willing to partner with countries around the world to deepen ties of trade and investment, and science and technology, energy and development – all efforts that can spark economic growth for all our people and stabilize democratic change.

But such efforts depend on a spirit of mutual interest and mutual respect. No government or company, no school or NGO will be confident working in a country where its people are endangered. For partnerships to be effective our citizens must be secure and our efforts must be welcomed.

A politics based only on anger – one based on dividing the world between "us" and "them" – not only sets back international cooperation, it ultimately undermines those who tolerate it. All of us have an interest in standing up to these forces.

现在必须孤立那些将对美国、西方或以色列的仇恨作为政治煽动的核心手段的人，即使他们没有直接采用暴力手段。因为这样的手段只会掩护恶徒的暴力行径，有时还会成为其借口。

那种让东方西方势不两立，南边北边不共戴天，穆斯林、基督徒、印度教徒、犹太人水火难容的政治，绝不可能实现真正的自由。它给年轻人带来的是希望的假象。焚烧美国国旗丝毫无助于让孩子受教育，捣毁餐馆不会给人以温饱，袭击大使馆更不会创造任何就业岗位。那种政治只能让那些必须通过众志成城才能达到的目标变得更加难以企及：比如让我们的孩子受教育，为他们创造就业机会；保护人权，扩大民主。

要知道，美国决不会退出国际社会。我们要将伤害我们的公民和朋友的凶手绳之以法，将与盟友同舟共济，愿与其他国家结为伙伴，深化我们在贸易投资、科学技术、能源发展等领域的合作——所有这些努力都能够刺激经济增长，造福子民，巩固民主成果。

但是，这些努力需要有互利互尊的精神方能卓有成效。没有任何政府或公司，也没有任何学校或非政府组织能够在人民安全受到威胁的国家中踏实地展开工作。要使合作关系产生效果，我们的公民必须得到安全保障，我们的努力必须是民意之所向。

建立在愤怒上的政治，让世界变得你我势不两立的政治，不仅会阻碍国际合作，而且最终也会伤害对这种政治一再容忍的无辜百姓。因此，抵制这种势力，符合我们所有人的利益。

Let us remember that Muslims have suffered the most at the hands of extremism. On the same day our civilians were killed in Benghazi, a Turkish police officer was murdered in Istanbul only days before his wedding; more than 10 Yemenis were killed in a car bomb in Sana'a; several Afghan children were mourned by their parents just days after they were killed by a suicide bomber in Kabul.

The impulse towards intolerance and violence may initially be focused on the West, but over time it cannot be contained. The same impulses toward extremism are used to justify war between Sunni and Shia, between tribes and clans. It leads not to strength and prosperity but to chaos. In less than two years, we have seen largely peaceful protests bring more change to Muslim-majority countries than a decade of violence. And extremists understand this. Because they have nothing to offer to improve the lives of people, violence is their only way to stay relevant. They don't build; they only destroy.

It is time to leave the call of violence and the politics of division behind. On so many issues, we face a choice between the promise of the future, or the prisons of the past. And we cannot afford to get it wrong. We must seize this moment. And America stands ready to work with all who are willing to embrace a better future.

The future must not belong to those who target Coptic Christians in Egypt – it must be claimed by those in Tahrir Square who chanted, "Muslims, Christians, we are one." The future must not belong to those who bully women – it must be shaped by girls who go to school, and those who stand for a world where our daughters can live their dreams just like our sons.

The future must not belong to those corrupt few who steal a country's resources – it must be won by the students and entrepreneurs, the workers and business owners who seek a broader prosperity for all people. Those are the women and men that America stands with; theirs is the vision we will support.

The future must not belong to those who slander the prophet of Islam. But

我们不能忘记，极端主义让穆斯林人民苦难深重。就在我们的文职人员在班加西遇害的同一天，一位几天后即将举行婚礼的土耳其警官在伊斯坦布尔遭到杀害；十几位也门人在萨那的汽车炸弹爆炸中丧生；好几名阿富汗儿童的父母痛悼几天前在喀布尔一起自杀炸弹爆炸中痛失爱子。

对褊狭和暴力行径的煽动，或许一开始只是针对西方，但它继而变得一发而不可收拾；同样，对极端主义的煽动，引发了逊尼派教徒和什叶派教徒、部落与宗族之间的交战。这些所带来的不是富强繁荣，而是动荡混乱。在不到两年的时间里，我们看到，大批和平的示威行动给穆斯林占主体的国家带来巨大变化，这种变革的效果，胜过十年动乱。极端主义者心知肚明，对于改善民生，他们无计可施。因此，暴力是他们维持自身存在价值的唯一手段。他们没有建树，只有破坏。

现在是时候将鼓吹暴力和分裂的政治模式抛在身后了！在许多问题上，我们都面临着抉择：是希冀着未来？还是囚禁于过去？输不起的我们，必须把握这一刻！美国已整装待发，愿同所有渴望拥抱美好未来的人们一道，共同努力！

未来决不能落入在埃及攻击科普特基督教徒的恶徒之手——它必须由那些曾在解放广场齐声高呼"穆斯林，基督徒，我们是一家人！"的人来掌握。未来决不能落入凌辱妇女的人之手——它必须由那些知书达理的女孩子，由那些让全世界所有女孩也能像男孩一样追求梦想的人士来缔造！

to be credible, those who condemn that slander must also condemn the hate we see in the images of Jesus Christ that are desecrated, or churches that are destroyed, or the Holocaust that is denied.

Let us condemn incitement against Sufi Muslims and Shiite pilgrims. It's time to heed the words of Gandhi: "Intolerance is itself a form of violence and an obstacle to the growth of a true democratic spirit." Together, we must work towards a world where we are strengthened by our differences, and not defined by them. That is what America embodies, that's the vision we will support.

Among Israelis and Palestinians, the future must not belong to those who turn their backs on a prospect of peace. Let us leave behind those who thrive on conflict, those who reject the right of Israel to exist. The road is hard, but the destination is clear – a secure, Jewish state of Israel and an independent, prosperous Palestine. Understanding that such a peace must come through a just agreement between the parties, America will walk alongside all who are prepared to make that journey.

In Syria, the future must not belong to a dictator who massacres his people. If there is a cause that cries out for protest in the world today, peaceful protest, it is a regime that tortures children and shoots rockets at apartment buildings. And we must remain engaged to assure that what began with citizens demanding their rights does not end in a cycle of sectarian violence.

Together, we must stand with those Syrians who believe in a different vision – a Syria that is united and inclusive, where children don't need to fear their own government, and all Syrians have a say in how they are governed – Sunnis and Alawites, Kurds and Christians. That's what America stands for. That is the outcome that we will work for – with sanctions and consequences for those who persecute, and assistance and support for those who work for this common good. Because we believe that the Syrians who embrace this vision will have the strength and the legitimacy to lead.

In Iran, we see where the path of a violent and unaccountable ideology

　　未来决不能落入盗窃国家资源的少数腐败徒之手——它必须让学生和实业家、工人和追求全民共富的工商业主当家做主。美国愿与这些人士同舟共济；他们的愿景就是我们支持的愿景。

　　未来决不能落入诽谤伊斯兰先知的人手中。我们不但谴责这一诽谤行径的人，同时对视频中亵渎耶稣基督像、捣毁教堂、或否认纳粹大屠杀的行径表示强烈愤慨，这才更有信服力。

　　让我们谴责煽动攻击苏菲派穆斯林和什叶派穆斯林朝圣者的行径。现在该是时候重温甘地的箴言了："不容忍本身即是一种暴力，是妨碍真正民主精神壮大的障碍。"我们齐心协力，共创一个世界，在这个世界中，我们不因差异而被禁锢，而因彼此间的不同而充满活力！美国体现着这一理想，我们支持这一理想。

　　对于以色列人和巴勒斯坦人来说，未来决不能属于拒绝和平前景的人。让我们抛开靠冲突得势之人，拒绝以色列存在的人。路漫漫其修远，但一个安全的以色列犹太国与一个独立繁荣的巴勒斯坦并存并立的目标，却清晰可见。美国理解，这样的和平必须是通过各方达成公正的协议而取得，因此，对于所有准备踏上这一征途的人，美国将伴你们同行。

　　在叙利亚，未来决不能属于屠杀自己人民的独裁者。倘若今日放眼世界，要为呐喊示威、和平抗议行为找一个原因，那就是因为有一个政权在折磨儿童，在炮轰民宅。我们必须不断努力，保证公民的维权行动不会最终沦为教派暴力循环。

　　我们必须齐心协力，站在坚信改变未来的叙利亚人一边，即一个团结的、包容的叙利亚，它的儿童不必惧怕政府，所有叙利亚人，包括逊尼派和阿拉维派、库尔德人和基督徒，都可以对国务政事发表己见，这是美国所支持的。这是我们将为之努力的结果——要让迫害者受到制裁、承担后果，要让为社稷而谋利益的人得到援助和支持。我们相信，有共同理想的利比亚人有能力，也有权利领导这个国家！

leads. The Iranian people have a remarkable and ancient history, and many Iranians wish to enjoy peace and prosperity alongside their neighbors. But just as it restricts the rights of its own people, the Iranian government continues to prop up a dictator in Damascus and supports terrorist groups abroad. Time and again, it has failed to take the opportunity to demonstrate that its nuclear program is peaceful, and to meet its obligations to the United Nations.

So let me be clear. America wants to resolve this issue through diplomacy, and we believe that there is still time and space to do so. But that time is not unlimited. We respect the right of nations to access peaceful nuclear power, but one of the purposes of the United Nations is to see that we harness that power for peace. And make no mistake, a nuclear-armed Iran is not a challenge that can be contained. It would threaten the elimination of Israel, the security of Gulf nations, and the stability of the global economy. It risks triggering a nuclear-arms race in the region, and the unraveling of the non-proliferation treaty. That's why a coalition of countries is holding the Iranian government accountable. And that's why the United States will do what we must to prevent Iran from obtaining a nuclear weapon.

We know from painful experience that the path to security and prosperity does not lie outside the boundaries of international law and respect for human rights. That's why this institution was established from the rubble of conflict. That is why liberty triumphed over tyranny in the Cold War. And that is the lesson of the last two decades as well.

History shows that peace and progress come to those who make the right choices. Nations in every part of the world have traveled this difficult path. Europe, the bloodiest battlefield of the 20th century, is united, free and at peace. From Brazil to South Africa, from Turkey to South Korea, from India to Indonesia, people of different races, religions, and traditions have lifted millions out of poverty, while respecting the rights of their citizens and meeting their responsibilities as nations.

在伊朗，我们目睹了横行无忌与不负责任的意识形态所带来的后果。伊朗人民有着非凡悠久的历史，许多伊朗人希望与邻人一道过上和平富足的生活。但是，伊朗政府在限制自己人民权利的同时，支持大马士革的独裁者，支持海外的恐怖主义组织。它一而再，再而三地浪费机会，拒绝向世人解释其核设施的和平用途，未能履行联合国赋予的义务。

因此，我明确表示：美国希望通过外交途径解决伊朗核问题，问题解决的时间和余地依然存在，然而，这个时间不是没有限度的。我们尊重各国以和平方式使用核能的权利，联合国的宗旨之一就是确保我们把核能用于和平目的。毫无疑问：如果伊朗拥有核武器，事态将难以控制。它将威胁到以色列的生存、海湾国家的安全和全球经济的稳定，可能在该地区触发核军备竞赛，破坏不扩散核武器条约的成果。这就是为何，多国联合阵线要求伊朗政府承担责任，也是为何，美国将采取必要行动防止伊朗取得核武器。

惨痛的经历告诉我们，不尊重国际法和人权，就不可能走上安全与繁荣的道路。联合国在战争的废墟上创建，正是基于这一原因。也正是这一原因，在冷战中，自由战胜了暴政。过去二十载，前车之鉴，历历在目。

历史表明，和平与进步青睐懂得如何选择的人。世界各地的国家都曾走过艰难的道路。欧洲曾经是20世纪最血腥的战场，如今却能团结一致，共享自由与和平。从巴西到南非，从土耳其到韩国，从印度到印尼，不同种族、宗教、传统的国家帮助亿万民众摆脱贫困，同时尊重公民的权利，履行作为国家应尽的责任。

And it is because of the progress that I've witnessed in my own lifetime, the progress that I've witnessed after nearly four years as President, that I remain ever hopeful about the world that we live in. The war in Iraq is over. American troops have come home. We've begun a transition in Afghanistan, and America and our allies will end our war on schedule in 2014. Al Qaeda has been weakened, and Osama bin Laden is no more. Nations have come together to lock down nuclear materials, and America and Russia are reducing our arsenals. We have seen hard choices made – from Naypyidaw to Cairo to Abidjan – to put more power in the hands of citizens.

At a time of economic challenge, the world has come together to broaden prosperity. Through the G20, we have partnered with emerging countries to keep the world on the path of recovery. America has pursued a development agenda that fuels growth and breaks dependency, and worked with African leaders to help them feed their nations. New partnerships have been forged to combat corruption and promote government that is open and transparent, and new commitments have been made through the Equal Futures Partnership to ensure that women and girls can fully participate in politics and pursue opportunity. And later today, I will discuss our efforts to combat the scourge of human trafficking.

All these things give me hope. But what gives me the most hope is not the actions of us, not the actions of leaders – it is the people that I've seen. The American troops who have risked their lives and sacrificed their limbs for strangers half a world away; the students in Jakarta or Seoul who are eager to use their knowledge to benefit mankind; the faces in a square in Prague or a parliament in Ghana who see democracy giving voice to their aspirations; the young people in the favelas of Rio and the schools of Mumbai whose eyes shine with promise. These men, women, and children of every race and every faith remind me that for every angry mob that gets shown on television, there are billions around the world who share similar hopes and dreams. They tell us that

正是由于我在这一生中所见证的进步，特别是在担任总统近四年后所见证的进步，让我对我们生活的世界充满希望。伊拉克的战事已经尘埃落定。美国军队业已返回家园。我们在阿富汗开始了过渡，我们和盟友将在2014年如期结束战争。"基地"组织已经被削弱，乌萨马·本·拉登已经命丧黄泉。各国协力同心，确保核设施的安全，美国和俄罗斯正在削减军备。从内比都到开罗到阿比让，我们看到艰难的抉择背后，是公民被赋予更大的权力。

面临经济挑战，世界各国齐心协力，增进繁荣。通过20国集团，我们与新兴国家合作，帮助世界经济持续复苏。美国实施了刺激增长、打破依赖的发展议程，与非洲领导人携手努力，帮助他们满足本国的食品供应。旨在打击腐败，促进政府开放透明的新型伙伴关系正在向前推进。[我们]通过"平等未来伙伴关系"作出了新承诺，确保女性能够充分参与政务，赢得机会。稍后，我将针对我们在打击人口贩卖的恶性事件中所作的努力，作简要介绍。

所有这一切都使我看到希望。但是，给我带来最大希望的不是我们的行动，不是领导人的行动——而是目力所及的平凡大众：是美国军人为了万里以外的陌生人甘冒伤残乃至生命的风险；是雅加达或汉城的学生充满热忱地用他们的知识造福人类；是布拉格广场上或加纳议会中一张张为追求民主理想而呼吁呐喊的面庞；是里约热内卢贫民窟中和孟买学校里闪烁着希望之光的青少年的双眸。这些不同种族、不同信仰的男女老幼，又让我不禁想起视频中的那群暴徒，与他们相比，世界上总有亿万民众怀揣同样的希望和梦想。他们告诉世人：人性是相通的。

there is a common heartbeat to humanity.

So much attention in our world turns to what divides us. That's what we see on the news. That's what consumes our political debates. But when you strip it all away, people everywhere long for the freedom to determine their destiny; the dignity that comes with work; the comfort that comes with faith; and the justice that exists when governments serve their people – and not the other way around.

The United States of America will always stand up for these aspirations, for our own people and for people all across the world. That was our founding purpose. That is what our history shows. That is what Chris Stevens worked for throughout his life.

And I promise you this: Long after the killers are brought to justice, Chris Stevens' legacy will live on in the lives that he touched – in the tens of thousands who marched against violence through the streets of Benghazi; in the Libyans who changed their Face book photo to one of Chris; in the signs that read, simply, "Chris Stevens was a friend to all Libyans."

They should give us hope. They should remind us that so long as we work for it, justice will be done, that history is on our side, and that a rising tide of liberty will never be reversed.

Thank you very much.

the Unite Nations Headquarters, New York, New York, September 25, 2012

当今世界，人们太过于关注我们的分歧。分歧，是我们在新闻报道中耳濡目染、在政治辩论中一再重复的中心话题。但是，倘若剥离其外壳，其实世界各地的人都渴望能有决定自己命运的自由、工作带来的尊严、信仰带来的安慰、服务于人民的政府——而非与之相反的现状。

美利坚合众国将永远支持这些理想，不仅为我们自己，也为了世界各地的人民。这正是我们的建国理念。这正是我们的历史使命。这也是克里斯·史蒂文斯恪守不渝、为之奋斗终生的承诺！

我可以向各位保证：在杀人凶手被绳之以法后的岁月里，克里斯·史蒂文斯的精神将长存于每一个被触动的生命体内——那些在班加西市成千上万走上街头抗议暴力的民众，那些把他们的个人主页头像更换成克里斯的照片的利比亚人，还有那面言简意赅的标语牌："克里斯·史蒂文斯是所有利比亚人的朋友！"

这一切应当让我们心存希冀，应当使我们铭记于心，只要我们持之以恒，正义终将得到伸张，历史站在我们一边，自由之潮势不可挡，永无逆转！

谢谢各位。

（杜梦臻/译）

Remarks by Obama
at the 2012 Alfred E. Smith Dinner

Thank you. Thank you. Thank you so much. Thank you. Everyone, please take your seats – otherwise Clint Eastwood will yell at them.

Thank you to Al and Ann. To Your Eminence; Governor, Mrs. Romney; Governor Cuomo; Mayor Bloomberg; Senator Schumer; all the distinguished guests who are here.

In less than three weeks, voters in states like Ohio and Virginia and Florida will decide this incredibly important election – which begs the question, what are we doing here?

Of course, New Yorkers also have a big choice to make – you have to decide which one of us you want holding up traffic for the next four years.

Tonight I am here with a man whose father was a popular governor, and who knows what it's like to run a major Northeastern state, and who could very well be president someday – and I'm hoping it is Andrew Cuomo.

This is the third time that Governor Romney and I have met recently. As some of you may have noticed, I had a lot more energy at our second debate. I felt really well rested after the nice, long nap I had in the first debate.

Although it turns out millions of Americans focused in on the second debate who didn't focus in on the first debate – and I happen to be one of them.

I particularly want to apologize to Chris Matthews. Four years ago, I gave him a thrill up his leg – this time around I gave him a stroke.

And of course, there's a lot of things I learned from that experience. For

奥巴马在2012年
艾尔弗雷德·史密斯慈善晚宴上的讲话 ①

谢谢，谢谢，非常感谢，谢谢。各位请就座，要不然伊斯特伍德又会向椅子吼叫了。

谢谢你们，阿尔和安。主教阁下，罗姆尼州长及夫人，科莫州长，布隆伯格市长，舒默参议员，所有在座的各位嘉宾：

还有不到三周，俄亥俄、弗吉尼亚、佛罗里达等几个州的选民就将决定这场至关重要的大选了，一个问题出现了，我们在这里做什么？

当然了，纽约人也要作出重大抉择——你们要在我们俩中间作出选择，未来四年到底由谁来管制你们的出行，由谁来指挥你们的交通。

今晚到场的一位先生，父亲是一位广受爱戴的州长，懂得如何治理美国东北部的大州，有朝一日有望成为总统，我所希望的人就是你，安德鲁·科莫。

这是我近期第三次与罗姆尼州长会面了，有些人可能已经注意到了，第二场辩论时我精神多了。首场辩论那晚，我在场上睡得特别香，因此，我最近休整的很好。

尽管现在看来，不计其数的美国人更多地关注第二场辩论，对首场辩论没有太在意，我碰巧也是其中之一。

我特别想向克里斯·马修斯说声抱歉，四年前我给他打了鸡血，这一次我差点让他中风。

---

① 美国总统贝拉克·奥巴马和共和党竞选对手米特·罗姆尼于10月18日晚一同出席纽约市一场年度慈善晚宴。与选举电视辩论不同，两名总统候选人一改凌厉语调，大秀幽默，在损人和自嘲中向外界展示另一面。

example, I learned that there are worse things that can happen to you on your anniversary than forgetting to buy a gift. So, take note, gentlemen.

Now, win or lose, this is my last political campaign. So I'm trying to drink it all in. Unfortunately, Mayor Bloomberg will only let me have 16 ounces of it. That's okay, I'm still making the most of my time in the city. Earlier today, I went shopping at some stores in Midtown. I understand Governor Romney went shopping for some stores in Midtown.

And it brought back some great memories because, some of you know, I went to school here in New York, had a wonderful experience here. Used to love walking through Central Park, loved to go to old Yankee Stadium, the house that Ruth built – although he really did not build that. I hope everybody is aware of that.

It's been four years since I was last at the Al Smith Dinner. And I have to admit some things have changed since then. I've heard some people say, "Barack, you're not as young as you used to be. Where's that golden smile? Where's that pep in your step?" And I say, "Settle down, Joe, I'm trying to run a Cabinet meeting." He does smile when he says it, though.

Tomorrow it's back to campaigning. I visit cities and towns across our great country, and I hear the same thing everywhere I go – honestly, we were hoping to see Michelle. And I have to admit it can be a grind. Sometimes it feels like this race has dragged on forever. But Paul Ryan assured me that we've only been running for two hours and 50-something minutes.

Of course, the economy is on everybody's minds. The unemployment rate is at its lowest level since I took office. I don't have a joke here. I just thought it would be useful to remind everybody that the unemployment rate is at the lowest it's been since I took office.

And we're getting to that time when folks are making up their minds. Just the other day, Honey Boo Boo endorsed me. So that's a big relief.

Ultimately, though, tonight is not about the disagreements Governor

当然了，这次经历也让我受益匪浅，比方说，在结婚纪念日上可能会冒出比忘买礼物还要糟糕的情况。所以，男士们，记住我的教训。

不论胜负，这次都是我最后一次政治竞选了，所以我会全力以赴开怀畅饮。不幸的是，布隆伯格市长只允许我喝16盎司的酒，没关系，我还是在城里度过了很美好的时光。今天早些时候，我到市中心的几家商场买了些东西，我知道罗姆尼州长也去了市中心，他买了几家商场。

这唤起了我许多美好的回忆，在座的各位都知道，我在纽约上过学，在这里有着难忘的经历。我曾很喜欢在中央公园散步，喜欢去老洋基体育场，这座被叫做"鲁斯建的房子"，其实并不是鲁斯建的，希望大家都明白这一点。

上一次参加史密斯晚宴已经是四年前了，我不得不承认自那时起许多事情都发生了变化，我听到有人对我说："巴拉克，你不再像过去那样年轻了，你那金子般的笑容哪里去了？你那矫健的步伐哪里去了？"我回答："拜登，你给我老实点，我们正开内阁会议呢。"虽然他说这话的时候面带笑容。

明天我们就要回归竞选活动了，我有幸周游了我们伟大祖国的大小城

Romney and I may have. It's what we have in common – beginning with our unusual names. Actually, Mitt is his middle name. I wish I could use my middle name.

And even though we're enjoying ourselves tonight, we're both thinking ahead to our final debate on Monday. I'm hoping that Governor Romney and I will have a chance to answer the question that is on the minds of millions of Americans watching at home: Is this happening again? Why aren't they putting on The Voice?

Monday's debate is a little bit different because the topic is foreign policy. Spoiler alert: We got bin Laden. Of course, world affairs are a challenge for every candidate. After – some of you guys remember, after my foreign trip in 2008, I was attacked as a celebrity because I was so popular with our allies overseas. And I have to say, I'm impressed with how well Governor Romney has avoided that problem.

Now, just so everyone knows, in our third debate we won't spend a whole lot of time interrupting each other. We will also interrupt the moderator, just to mix things up.

And finally, let me say that I've been doing some thinking, and I've decided that for our final debate I'm going to go back to the strategy I used to prepare for the first debate. I'm just kidding – I'm trying to make Axelrod sweat a little bit. Get him a little nervous.

In all seriousness, I couldn't be more honored to be here this evening. I'm honored to be with leaders of both the private and public sectors, and particularly the extraordinary work that is done by the Catholic Church.

It's written in Scripture that tribulation produces perseverance; and perseverance, character; and character, hope. This country has fought through some very tough years together, and while we still have a lot of work ahead, we've come as far as we have mainly because of the perseverance and character of ordinary Americans. And it says something about who we are as a people that

镇，不管走到哪里，我都听到同样的话："说实话，我们其实想见的是米歇尔。"我得承认这是很折磨人的，有时候我感觉这场赛跑永无止境，但保罗·莱恩让我确信，我们只是才跑了两小时五十多分钟而已。

当然，经济是每个人都关心的问题，失业率现在处于我就职以来的最低水平，我从不在这方面开玩笑，我只是想提醒在座的各位，失业率确实已经降到我就职以来的最低点。

全民决选的时刻很快就要到了，而前几天 Honey Boo Boo 说支持我，真让我松了一口气啊。

当然，今晚不谈我和罗姆尼州长之间的分歧，谈谈我们的共同点吧——首先我们都有奇怪的名字，实际上米特只是他的中间名，我多希望我也能用我的中间名啊。

尽管今晚我们在此度过美好的时光，但脑子里都在纠结着下周一的最终辩论，我希望罗姆尼州长和我能有机会回答电视机前数百万名美国观众心中的疑问：这玩意儿怎么又开始了，干吗不播《美国好声音》呢？

周一的辩论与以往有所不同，因为涉及外交话题。剧透哦，我们干掉了本·拉登。当然，国际事务对于任何候选人都是挑战，你们或许有人记得在我 2008 年的国外访问结束后，我因为在海外盟友中太受欢迎而被攻击为"明星派头儿"，我很惊奇罗姆尼长是如何成功地避免了这样的麻烦的？

当然，告诉大家，在第三场辩论中，我们不会把全部时间用来打断对方的讲话。我们还会打断主持人的讲话，这样才热闹。

最后，我想说，我最近一直在思考，我已经决定最后一场辩论时我要回归首场辩论时的战略，我开玩笑呢——我只是想让阿克塞尔罗德冒冒汗，让他紧张一下。

说正经的，今晚来到这里我无比荣幸，我很荣幸能跟私营和国营企业部门的领袖们共聚一堂，尤其感谢天主教会的出色安排。

圣经中写道："患难造就坚韧，坚韧造就品格，品格造就希望。"我们全国民众上下同心，挺过了艰难的日子，虽然前方还有很多工作亟待完成，但是，平凡的美国同胞的坚韧和品格让我们取得了巨大的成就，这体现了我们民族的特点，在喧嚣的大选中，对立的候选人可以同台逗趣，两

in the middle of a contentious election season, opposing candidates can share the same stage; people from both parties can come together – come together to support a worthy cause.

And I particularly want to thank Governor Romney for joining me, because I admire him very much as a family man and a loving father, and those are two titles that will always matter more than any political ones.

So we may have different political perspectives, but I think – in fact, I'm certain – that we share the hope that the next four years will reflect the same decency and the same willingness to come together for a higher purpose that are on display this evening. May we all, in the words of Al Smith, do our full duty as citizens.

God bless you. God bless your families. And may God bless the United States of America. Thank you very much.

New York, New York, October 18, 2012

党成员可以携手共事，携手支持我们可贵的事业。

我特别要感谢罗姆尼州长跟我一起出席晚宴，因为我十分敬重他，作为爱家的丈夫和慈爱的父亲，这两个头衔比某些政治头衔都更加重要。

我们可能政见不同，但我认为——其实我敢肯定——我们都有共同的希冀：在未来四年内，能以如今晚展现出来的同样的风度和意愿，为一个更高的目标而携手并进。最后，借用阿尔斯密斯的一句话，愿我们都能尽公民的职责。

上帝保佑你们，上帝保佑你们的家人，上帝保佑美利坚合众国，谢谢大家！

（杜梦臻／译）

Obama's Victory Speech in 2012

Thank you. Thank you. Thank you so much.

Tonight, more than 200 years after a former colony won the right to determine its own destiny, the task of perfecting our union moves forward.

It moves forward because of you. It moves forward because you reaffirmed the spirit that has triumphed over war and depression, the spirit that has lifted this country from the depths of despair to the great heights of hope, the belief that while each of us will pursue our own individual dreams, we are an American family, and we rise or fall together as one nation and as one people.

Tonight, in this election, you, the American people, reminded us that while our road has been hard, while our journey has been long, we have picked ourselves up, we have fought our way back, and we know in our hearts that for the United States of America, the best is yet to come.

I want to thank every American who participated in this election. Whether you voted for the very first time or waited in line for a very long time – by the way, we have to fix that whether you pounded the pavement or picked up the phone, whether you held an Obama sign or a Romney sign, you made your voice heard and you made a difference.

I just spoke with Governor Romney and I congratulated him and Paul Ryan on a hard-fought campaign. We may have battled fiercely, but it's only because we love this country deeply and we care so strongly about its future. From George to Lenore to their son Mitt, the Romney family has chosen to give back to America through public service. And that is a legacy that we honour

奥巴马2012年竞选连任获胜演讲 ①

谢谢，非常感谢。

时至今晚已过去200多年，前殖民地赢得权利，主宰了自己的命运，开始了这个国家的前进之旅。

因为你们，美国才得以勇往直前。因为你们不断唤起那种精神，那种曾经帮助我们跨越了战火纷飞和经济萎靡的精神，那种将这个国家拖出绝望的深渊，推向希望彼岸的精神。我们始终坚信：每一个人都可以独立地争取自己的未来，我们将会作为一个国家同起同落。

今夜，在此选举中，你们——美国人民，让我们记得：尽管前路漫漫，充满荆棘，但是我们已重拾信心，重振旗鼓。我们深知，最棒的美国即将来临。

我想感谢每一位参与选举的美国同胞。不管你是从第一天就投票了，还是排队等了很长的时间才投上一票——顺便说一下我会解决这个问题。不管你是亲自去投票站投的票，还是通过电话投的票；不管你投的是奥巴马，还是罗姆尼；你的声音，我们都听到了，你让美国，因你而不同。

我刚刚跟罗姆尼州长通了电话，对他和保罗在这个艰苦卓绝的战役中的出色表现表示祝贺。这场战役本会厮杀得更惨烈，这正是因为我们都深爱着这个国家，都如此在乎它的未来。从乔治到勒诺到他们的儿子米特，罗姆尼的整个家庭，子子孙孙都献给了美国，这种精神我们将永远铭记。未来几周，我将会同罗姆尼坐在一起，讨论我们怎么样推动国家未来的发

---

① 2012年美国大选结果揭晓，民主党候选人奥巴马获得274张选举人票，超过当选总统所需的270张，战胜共和党候选人罗姆尼203张选票，赢得2012年美国总统大选，成功连任，将成为美国第45任总统。11月7日，美国芝加哥麦考米克会展中心，奥巴马在胜选后亮相并发表演说。

and applaud tonight. In the weeks ahead, I also look forward to sitting down with Governor Romney to talk about where we can work together to move this country forward.

I want to thank my friend and partner of the last four years, America's happy warrior, the best vice-president anybody could ever hope for, Joe Biden.

And I wouldn't be the man I am today without the woman who agreed to marry me 20 years ago. Let me say this publicly. Michelle, I have never loved you more. I have never been prouder to watch the rest of America fall in love with you too as our nation's first lady.

Sasha and Malia - before our very eyes, you're growing up to become two strong, smart, beautiful young women, just like your mom. And I am so proud of you guys. But I will say that, for now, one dog's probably enough.

To the best campaign team and volunteers in the history of politics – the best – the best ever – some of you were new this time around, and some of you have been at my side since the very beginning.

But all of you are family. No matter what you do or where you go from here, you will carry the memory of the history we made together. And you will have the lifelong appreciation of a grateful president. Thank you for believing all the way - to every hill, to every valley. You lifted me up the whole day, and I will always be grateful for everything that you've done and all the incredible work that you've put in.

I know that political campaigns can sometimes seem small, even silly. And that provides plenty of fodder for the cynics who tell us that politics is nothing more than a contest of egos or the domain of special interests. But if you ever get the chance to talk to folks who turned out at our rallies and crowded along a rope line in a high school gym or – or saw folks working late at a campaign office in some tiny county far away from home, you'll discover something else.

You'll hear the determination in the voice of a young field organiser who's working his way through college and wants to make sure every child has that

展。

我想对过去四年的朋友和搭档表示感谢——美国的快乐战士、美国历史上最好的副总统：乔·拜登。

当然，如果没有20年前跟我结婚的妻子，我今天也就不会

站在这里。我想公开地表达，米歇尔，我比以前更加爱你，当我看到全国人民也十分热爱你这位第一夫人，这更让我引以为傲。

萨沙，玛利亚，在我们大家的眼里，你们一天天在长大，如今已经出落成了像你们妈妈一样坚强、美丽、富有才华的大姑娘，我也以你们为荣。不过眼下，我觉得家里养一条狗就够了。

我还要感谢我的竞选团队和志愿者，你们是史上最棒的。你们当中有的人是新来的，有的人从一开始就一直伴我左右。

你们都是我的家人。不管你们做了什么，不管你们来自哪里，你们一定会记得今晚我们共同创造的历史。你们将终身铭记，有一个总统，永远对你们心怀感激。谢谢你们一路对我的信任，不论是在顶峰还是低谷，是你们鼓舞我走完全程。我对你们所做的一切都将心怀感激。

我知道政治竞选有时候看起来很琐碎，甚至愚蠢。不少愤世嫉俗者借此攻击政治不过是自负者的争名夺利和利益集团的鹬蚌相争。但要是你们真有机会，去和参加竞选集会的人们聊一聊，去和体育场排队投票的选民聊一聊，或是亲眼看一看那些远离家人彻夜工作的志愿者们，你们的印象定会有所改观。

一名大学生助选活动组织者，话语里充满了决心，他克服困难努力读完大学，而现在希望每一个孩子都能享有和他一样的机会。一名志愿者，言辞中难掩骄傲，她挨家挨户助选拉票，只因哥哥终于找到工作，附近的汽车厂增加了班次给了他这个岗位。

一名军嫂，话语间尽是深深的爱国情怀，她为助选打电话直至深夜，

same opportunity. You'll hear the pride in the voice of a volunteer who's going door to door because her brother was finally hired when the local auto plant added another shift.

You'll hear the deep patriotism in the voice of a military spouse who's working the phones late at night to make sure that no one who fights for this country ever has to fight for a job or a roof over their head when they come home.

That's why we do this. That's what politics can be. That's why elections matter. It's not small, it's big. It's important. Democracy in a nation of 300 million can be noisy and messy and complicated. We have our own opinions. Each of us has deeply held beliefs. And when we go through tough times, when we make big decisions as a country, it necessarily stirs passions, stirs up controversy. That won't change after tonight. And it shouldn't. These arguments we have are a mark of our liberty, and we can never forget that as we speak, people in distant nations are risking their lives right now just for a chance to argue about the issues that matter – the chance to cast their ballots like we did today.

But despite all our differences, most of us share certain hopes for America's future.

We want our kids to grow up in a country where they have access to the best schools and the best teachers – a country that lives up to its legacy as the global leader in technology and discovery and innovation – with all of the good jobs and new businesses that follow.

We want our children to live in an America that isn't burdened by debt, that isn't weakened up by inequality, that isn't threatened by the destructive power of a warming planet.

We want to pass on a country that's safe and respected and admired around the world, a nation that is defended by the strongest military on Earth and the best troops this – this world has ever known – but also a country that moves with confidence beyond this time of war to shape a peace that is built on the

114

只是为了确保那些曾经为国家抛头颅洒热血的军人回家之后，无需再为养家糊口或栖身之所而苦苦相争。

这才是我们选举的本质。这才是政治的真谛。这才是大选如此重要的原因。选举绝非琐碎小事，它至关重要，举足轻重。在一个拥有3亿国民的国家，民主有时候会有些吵闹、混乱和繁复。只因我们每个人都有自己的主张，都有自身的信仰。当我们经历艰难时刻，当我们要作为一个国家作出重大决定，自然会有争论，会有情感的表达。这不会在一夜之间改变，也不应改变。这些争论正是我们自由的体现。我们绝不应忘记，就在此时此刻，在遥远的国度无数人正在为这"争论"的权利舍身赴险，他们想要的正是像我们这样投票的权利。

尽管我们有许多分歧，但我们中的大多数对美国的未来却有着共同的希冀。

我们期望在这个国家，孩子们能上最好的学校，有最好的老师，我们期望这个国家能继承先辈留下的光荣传统，在技术和创新领域培养世界级的领导者。倘若如此，高薪岗位和商业繁荣，定会紧随其后。

promise of freedom and dignity for every human being.

We believe in a generous America, in a compassionate America, in a tolerant America open to the dreams of an immigrant's daughter who studies in our schools and pledges to our flag – to the young boy on the south side of Chicago who sees a life beyond the nearest street corner – to the furniture worker's child in North Carolina who wants to become a doctor or a scientist, an engineer or an entrepreneur, a diplomat or even a president.

That's the – that's the future we hope for. That's the vision we share. That's where we need to go – forward. That's where we need to go.

Now, we will disagree, sometimes fiercely, about how to get there. As it has for more than two centuries, progress will come in fits and starts. It's not always a straight line. It's not always a smooth path. By itself, the recognition that we have common hopes and dreams won't end all the gridlock, resolve all our problems or substitute for the painstaking work of building consensus and making the difficult compromises needed to move this country forward.

But that common bond is where we must begin. Our economy is recovering. A decade of war is ending. A long campaign is now over. And whether I earned your vote or not, I have listened to you. I have learned from you. And you've made me a better president. And with your stories and your struggles, I return to the White House more determined and more inspired than ever about the work there is to do and the future that lies ahead.

Tonight you voted for action, not politics as usual. You elected us to focus on your jobs, not ours.

And in the coming weeks and months, I am looking forward to reaching out and working with leaders of both parties to meet the challenges we can only solve together – reducing our deficit, reforming our tax code, fixing our immigration system, freeing ourselves from foreign oil. We've got more work to do.

But that doesn't mean your work is done. The role of citizens in our democracy does not end with your vote. America's never been about what can

116

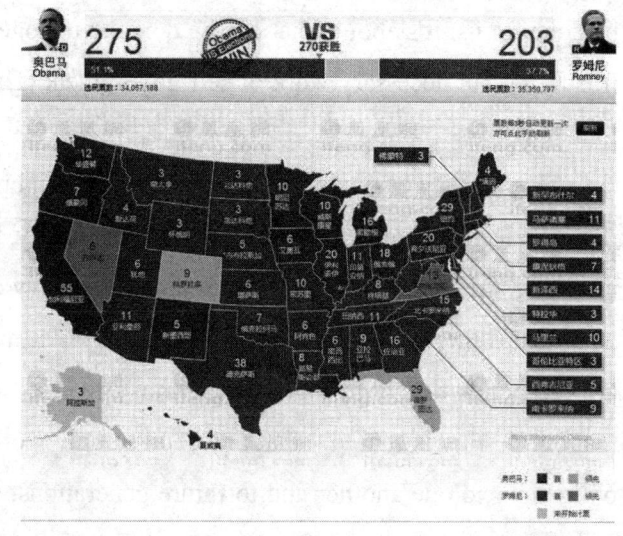

我们绝不希望孩子们未来生活在一个受困于债务、不平等以及气候变暖的美国。

我们希望留给后代的，是一个安全且备受尊重和赞赏的美国。这个国家拥有世界上有史以来最强大的军事实力，但同样也有信心为这个战乱时代带来和平，许诺为每一个人带去自由和尊严。

我们相信美国应该是一个慷慨、富有同情心而包容的国家，欢迎每一个心怀梦想的移民。不管是在我们的学校接受教育、对我们的国旗宣誓效忠的移民儿女，还是梦想改变自己命运的芝加哥南部地区的街头男孩，抑或是希望成为医生、科学家、企业家、外交官或者美国总统的北卡罗来纳州的木匠家的孩子。

这才是我们所希望的未来。这才是我们共同的愿景。这才是我们前进的方向。

然而，关于如何实现目标，我们却时常产生分歧，甚至会发生激烈的冲突。正如美国两个多世纪的历史，这一过程并非一蹴而就，更不是一帆风顺。共同的希望和梦想并不能化解一切僵局，并不能解决所有的问题，也不能代替国家前进所要经历的艰苦工作——作出妥协、建立共识。

但是这些共识是我们的起点。我们的经济正在好转，十年战争也正要告一段落，漫长的竞选也已落下帷幕。不管你是否曾投票给我，我都愿意聆听你们的声音。我从你们身上受益良多，是你们让我成为更好的总统。正是因为你们的奋斗和故事，我才能满怀对未来工作的坚定决心和振奋之情，重返白宫。

今晚不同于往常，你们并不是为政治而投票，而是在为实际行动而投票。你们投票选我们并非为我们自己，而是为了让我们更多地为各位创造

be done for us; it's about what can be done by us together, through the hard and frustrating but necessary work of self-government. That's the principle we were founded on.

This country has more wealth than any nation, but that's not what makes us rich. We have the most powerful military in history, but that's not what makes us strong. Our university, our culture are all the envy of the world, but that's not what keeps the world coming to our shores. What makes America exceptional are the bonds that hold together the most diverse nation on Earth, the belief that our destiny is shared – that this country only works when we accept certain obligations to one another and to future generations, so that the freedom which so many Americans have fought for and died for come with responsibilities as well as rights, and among those are love and charity and duty and patriotism. That's what makes America great.

I am hopeful tonight because I have seen this spirit at work in America. I've seen it in the family business whose owners would rather cut their own pay than lay off their neighbours and in the workers who would rather cut back their hours than see a friend lose a job. I've seen it in the soldiers who re-enlist after losing a limb and in those Seals who charged up the stairs into darkness and danger because they knew there was a buddy behind them watching their back. I've seen it on the shores of New Jersey and New York, where leaders from every party and level of government have swept aside their differences to help a community rebuild from the wreckage of a terrible storm.

And I saw it just the other day in Mentor, Ohio, where a father told the story of his eight-year-old daughter whose long battle with leukaemia nearly cost their family everything had it not been for healthcare reform passing just a few months before the insurance company was about to stop paying for her care. I had an opportunity to not just talk to the father but meet this incredible daughter of his. And when he spoke to the crowd, listening to that father's story, every parent in that room had tears in their eyes because we knew that little girl could be our

118

就业机会。

接下来，在未来的日子里，我期待着与两党的领袖共同应对挑战，这些难题只有同心协力才能攻克——努力减少赤字，改革税收制度，完善移民政策，摆脱对石油进口的依赖，有许多的事情等待着我们努力去做。

但这并不意味着各位的任务就此结束。在美国的民主制度之下，一个公民的职责不会因投下选票而就此终结。美国公民的职责并不在于"国家能为我做什么"，而是在于"我们能为国家做什么"，在于如何通过必要的自我管理和完善去齐心协力战胜困难和挫折。这也是我们的立国之本。

美国是世上最富有的国家，但这种富有不是指如何去发财致富；我们拥有历史上最强大的军队，但让我们充满力量的并非军队；我们拥有最优秀的高等教育和文化成果，但真正吸引世界各国人民涌向美国的魅力不在于此。美国之所以与众不同，是因为能够包容多元化的纽带将我们联系在一起，是因为我们相信彼此拥有共同的命运，是因为我们相信，只有为他人付出，互相帮助才能实现国家的进步，才能为后代创造更美好的未来。前人曾为自由而奋斗甚至是献出生命，而只有权利与义务的结合，只有爱、宽容、责任感及爱国之情才能使我们更好地实现、维护这份来之不易的自由。这才是美国的伟大之处。

在今晚，我满怀希望，因为我见证了这一精神正在美国发扬光大。我看到，一些家族企业宁可给自己减薪也绝不解雇员工，决不让左邻右舍失去工作；我看到，一些工人们宁可减短工时也绝不让同事下岗；我看到，那些在战事中接受截肢的战士们，又再一次选择入伍服役；我看到，那些勇敢的海豹突击队员，在同伴的掩护下，义无反顾冲向黑暗与危险；我还看到了，那些新泽西和纽约的海岸的各界领袖，放下成见与分歧，在桑迪飓风后的废墟上为社区重建而各尽己力——在他们身上，我看到了美国精神。

就在不久前，我还看到了，就在俄亥俄州的门托市，一位为了给八岁女儿治疗白血病的父亲，如果不是因为几个月前通过的医改法案，保险公司就会停止支付医疗费用，他们的家庭将一无所有。我曾经与这位父亲交谈，还有幸去看望了这位八岁的小女孩。当这位父亲向人们叙述着与病魔斗争的故事，已为人父母的在场观众都湿了眼眶——因为我们都知道，他

own. And I know that every American wants her future to be just as bright. That's who we are. That's the country I'm so proud to lead as your president.

And tonight, despite all the hardship we've been through, despite all the frustrations of Washington, I've never been more hopeful about our future. I have never been more hopeful about America. And I ask you to sustain that hope.

I'm not talking about blind optimism, the kind of hope that just ignores the enormity of the tasks ahead or the road blocks that stand in our path. I'm not talking about the wishful idealism that allows us to just sit on the sidelines or shirk from a fight. I have always believed that hope is that stubborn thing inside us that insists, despite all the evidence to the contrary, that something better awaits us so long as we have the courage to keep reaching, to keep working, to keep fighting.

America, I believe we can build on the progress we've made and continue to fight for new jobs and new opportunities and new security for the middle class. I believe we can keep the promise of our founding, the idea that if you're willing to work hard, it doesn't matter who you are or where you come from or what you look like or where you love. It doesn't matter whether you're black or white or Hispanic or Asian or Native American or young or old or rich or poor, abled, disabled, gay or straight. You can make it here in America if you're willing to try.

I believe we can seize this future together because we are not as divided as our politics suggests. We're not as cynical as the pundits believe. We are greater than the sum of our individual ambitions and we remain more than a collection of red states and blue states. We are, and forever will be, the United States of America.

And together, with your help and God's grace, we will continue our journey forward and remind the world just why it is that we live in the greatest nation on earth.

Thank you, America. God bless you. God bless these United States.

Chicago, Illinois, November 7, 2012

的女儿也可能是我们自己的女儿。而我确信，每位父母都真心祝福着这个小女孩也能够拥有光明的未来。这就是美国人，这就是美国，我为自己能领导这样的国家而自豪！

今晚，尽管我们历尽艰辛，尽管我们的政府有诸多不尽如人意之处，但此时此刻，对于未来，对于美国，我的内心却从未如此充满希冀——在此我请求各位坚守住这份希冀。

这一份希冀并不是盲目乐观，并不是无视艰难，并不是逃避责任。我也并不想鼓吹过度的理想主义，并不是鼓励无动于衷或是一味逃避。我一向坚信，不论多少流言飞语，只有守住这份希望，美国才能有勇气向前迈进，全力奋斗。

同胞们，我坚信，美国一定能够再进一步，争取更多的工作岗位、新的机遇和保障措施，让中产阶级的生活状况得到改善。我坚信，我们能够延续开国领袖们的承诺——不论身份、地域、种族和信仰，只要努力奋斗便能够实现自我；无论你是黑人或是白人、西班牙裔、亚裔或是印第安人，无论年少或年长，无论贫穷或富有，无论健全或残疾，无论是同性恋或是非同性恋——只要你愿意去尝试，就能在美国大有作为。

我坚信，未来仍然在美国人自己的手中，因为我们不像政界那样分歧严重，我们并没有在冷嘲热讽中失去希望。美国并不只是个人雄心壮志的简单总和，美国并不只是民主党和共和党两个阵营的简单总和。我们现在是，未来也将永远都是——美利坚合众国！

而在此，在你们的辛勤付出之下，在上帝的仁慈关爱之下，我们将继续前行，并告诉世界为何美利坚合众国是地球上最伟大的国家。感谢你们！

谢谢各位，同胞们，上帝保佑你们，上帝保佑美利坚合众国！

（杜梦臻 / 译）

Romney: Republican Party Presidential Nomination Acceptance

Mr. Chairman and delegates:

I accept your nomination for President of the United States.

I do so with humility, deeply moved by the trust you've placed in me. It's a great honor. It's an even greater responsibility. And tonight I'm asking you to join me to walk together to a better future. And by my side I've chosen a man with a big heart from a small town. He represents the best of America. A man who will always make us very proud: my friend and America's next vice-president, Paul Ryan.

In the days ahead, you're going to get to know Paul and Janna better. But last night America got to see what I saw in Paul Ryan – a strong and caring leader who's down to earth and confident in the challenge this moment demands. And I love the way he lights up around his kids and how he's not embarrassed to show the world how much he loves his mom.

Four years ago, I know that many Americans felt a fresh excitement about the possibilities of a new President. That choice was not the choice of our party but Americans always come together after elections. We're a good and generous people; and we're united by so much more than what divides us. When that election was over, when the yard signs came down and the television commercials finally came off the air, Americans were eager to go back to work, to live our lives the way Americans always have – optimistic and positive and confident in the future.

罗姆尼接受共和党总统候选人提名的演讲

主席先生、各位代表们：

我接受你们的美国总统提名。

我怀着谦卑之心接受提名，你们之信任让我感动不已，你们的决定让我不胜荣幸，但这亦是一种重任。今晚，我将邀请诸位与我一道携手并进，迈向锦绣前程。我选择一位来自于小镇、心胸宽广的人与我一道努力，他是美国的杰出代表——是我们引以自豪的、我的战友、美国的下一任副总统保罗·瑞安。

That very optimism is uniquely American. It's what brought us to America. We're a nation of immigrants. We're the children and grandchildren and great-grandchildren of the ones who wanted a better life, the driven ones, the ones who woke up at night hearing that voice telling them that life in the place called America could be better. They came not just in pursuit of the riches of this world but for the richness of this life. Freedom: freedom of religion; freedom to speak their mind; freedom to build a life; and yes, freedom to build a business with their own hands.

This is the essence of the American experience. We Americans have always felt a special kinship with the future. When every new wave of immigrants looked up and saw the Statue of Liberty, or knelt down and kissed the shores of freedom just 90 miles from Castro's tyranny, these new Americans surely had many questions; but none doubted that here in America they could build a better life, that in America their children would be blessed more than they.

But today, four years from the excitement of that last election, for the first time, the majority of Americans now doubt that our children will have a better future. It's not what we were promised.

Every family in America wanted this to be a time when they could get a little ahead, put aside a little more for college, do more for the elderly mom that's [sic] now living alone, or give a little more to their church or their charity.

Every small business wanted these to be their best years ever, when they could hire more, do more for those who'd stuck with them through the hard times, open a new store or sponsor that Little League team.

Every new college graduate thought they'd have a good job by now, a place of their own; they could start paying back some of their loans and build for the future.

You deserved it because during these years, you worked harder than ever before. You deserved it because when it cost more to fill up your car, you cut out – cut out movie [nights] and put in longer hours. Or when you lost that job that

在接下来的日子里，你们还将会更深入地了解保罗和安娜。但是昨晚，美国已见证了我眼中的保罗·瑞安——一个坚韧不拔、富于同情心的领袖；他具有当世所需要的品质——脚踏实地，临危不惧。我喜欢孩子们身边兴高采烈的他，以及那个毫不羞涩地向世界展示对母亲浓浓爱意的他。

四年前，我知道许多同胞对新总统感到新鲜兴奋，虽然那并不是我们党的选择，但大选过后，美国人总能团结一致。我们是善良慷慨的民族，更多的事情让我们同舟共济而不是四分五裂。选举结束，场地标语落下，电视广告销声匿迹，美国人急切地重返工作岗位，让我们的生活回归常态——乐观、积极、对未来充满信心。

这种乐观是美国人所独有的，正是它把人们汇集在这片土地上，组成了这个移民国度。有一群人想要追寻美好的生活，他们奋发向上，夜深人静的时候，有在一种声音在启迪他们：在一个叫美国的地方可以生活得更加美好。而我们，就是他们的儿辈、孙辈、曾孙辈。我们的前辈来到美国不仅仅是为了追求世俗的财富，而且为了生活的丰富多彩。自由，意味着：信仰自由，表达内心的自由，建设新生活的自由；当然还有用自己的双手开拓一番事业的自由。

这就是美国经验的真谛，我们美国人常常感到与未来有一种特别的血肉之情。每当一批新移民仰头并凝视自由女神的雕像时，或者，每当他们屈膝亲吻这个与卡斯特罗的暴政仅隔九十英里的自由的海岸时，这些新美国人肯定也曾心怀疑惑；但是毋庸置疑，在美国这片土地上，他们能够创造美好的生活，他们的孩子们会拥有更多的庇佑。

时光飞逝，上次选举虽令人激动兴奋，但四载已过，如今许多美国人第一次质疑他们的孩子是否能够享有更好的前程，这并不符合我们曾经得到的许诺。

paid 22.50 an hour with benefits, you took two jobs at nine bucks an hour. You deserve it because your family depended on you. And you did it because you're an American and you don't quit. You did it because it was what you had to do.

This is when our nation was supposed to start paying down the national debt and rolling back those massive deficits.

This was the hope and change America voted for. It's not just what we wanted. It's not just what we expected. It's what Americans deserved.

But driving home late from that second job, or standing there watching the gas pump hit 50 dollars and still going, when the realtor told you that to sell your house you'd have to take a big loss, in those moments you knew that this just wasn't right. But what could you do – except work harder, do with less, try to stay optimistic, hug your kids a little longer, maybe spend a little more time praying that tomorrow would be a better day.

I wish President Obama had succeeded because I want America to succeed. But his promises gave way to disappointments and division. This isn't something we have to accept. Now is the moment when we can do something. And with your help we will do something. Now is the moment when we can stand up and say, "I'm an American. I make my destiny. We deserve better. My children deserve better. My family deserves better. My country deserves better."

So here we stand. Americans have a choice, a decision. To make that choice, you need to know more about me and where I'd lead our country.

I was born in the middle of the century in the middle of the country, a classic baby boomer. It was a time when Americans were returning from war and eager to work. To be an American was to assume that all things were possible. When President Kennedy challenged Americans to go to the moon, the question wasn't whether we'd get there, it was only when we'd get there.

The soles of Neil Armstrong's boots on the moon made permanent impressions on our souls. Ann and I watched those steps together on her parent's sofa. Like all Americans we went to bed that night knowing we lived in the

在美国，每个家庭都希望生活能够蒸蒸日上，多一些积蓄供孩子上大学，对垂老双亲多尽孝道，给教堂或慈善机构多一些捐赠。

每个小企业都希望回到盈利颇丰的年代，雇佣更多的人，同他们一起渡过难关，为那些依靠他们渡过难关的人们做更多的事情，开设新的店面，或者为少年棒球队提供资助。

每位刚走出校园的莘莘学子都希望得到一份属于自己的称心的工作，希望能够偿还贷款，创造自己的未来。

你们理应拥有，是因为这些年，你们比从前工作更加辛苦，是因为你们给汽车加油花费更多，是因为你牺牲夜场电影而延长工作时间。或是因为你失去每小时22.5美元外加津贴的工作，却兼两份每小时9美元的工作；你们理应拥有，因为你的家人都依靠你，你所做的一切都因为你是美国人，你不能放弃，你必须这样做。

这时需要国家开始偿还国债，弥补财政赤字。

就是这份希望和改变，让美国人四年前投下选票。它不仅仅是我们的希冀和期盼，也是同胞们理应拥有的。

然而，当你结束兼职，披星戴月驱车归家时，或当你站在那儿看着加油泵窜上50美元还不断上升时，当你从房产中介得知你的房子变卖会遭受巨大的损失时，那一刻，你才明白，这是多么的不公平。然而除了更辛苦的工作，节约开支，保持乐观，给你孩子一个紧紧的拥抱，也许用更多的时间来为美好的明天祈祷，你还能做些什么。

我真心希望奥巴马总统在过去的四年有所建树，因为我希望美国成功，然而，他的空口承诺到头来只是失望与纷争，我们无法接受。现在，该是我们民主党挺身而出的时候了。在你们的帮助下，我们一定会作出一番事业。现在，是该民主党站起来昭告世人的时候了："我是美国人，我的命运我做主。我们理应更好，我的孩子们理应更好，我的家庭理应更好，我的国家理应更好。"

所以今天，我们站在这里，让同胞们来选择决定，为了这个选择，你们需要更清楚地了解我将带领我们的国家迈向何方。

greatest country in the history of the world.

God bless Neil Armstrong. Tonight that American flag is still there on the moon. And I don't doubt for a second that Neil Armstrong's spirit is still with us: that unique blend of optimism, humility, and the utter confidence that when the world needs someone to do the really big stuff, you need an American.

My dad had been born in Mexico and his family had to leave during the Mexican revolution. I grew up with stories of his family being fed by the U.S. Government as war refugees. My dad never made it through college and he apprenticed as a lath and plaster carpenter. He had big dreams. He convinced my mom, a beautiful young actress, to give up Hollywood to marry him. They moved to Detroit. He led a great – He led a great automobile company and became Governor of the Great State of Michigan.

We were – We were Mormons and growing up in Michigan that might have seemed unusual or out of place, but I really don't remember it that way. My friends cared more about what sports teams we followed than what church we went to. My mom and dad gave their kids the – the greatest gift of all: the gift of unconditional love. They cared deeply about who we would be, and much less about what we would do.

Unconditional love is a gift that Ann and I have tried to pass on to our sons and now to our grandchildren. All the laws and legislation in the world will never heal this world like the loving hearts and arms of mothers and fathers. You know, if every child could drift to sleep feeling wrapped in the love of their family, and God's love, this world would be a far more gentle and better place.

Mom and Dad were married for 64 years. And if you wondered what their secret was, you could have asked the local florist – because every day Dad gave Mom a rose, which he put on her bedside table. That's how she found out what happened on the day my father died: She went looking for him because that morning, there was no rose.

My mom and dad were true partners, a life lesson that shaped me by

上世纪中叶，我出生于美国的中部，是个典型的婴儿潮① 时期出生的人。那个时代，美国人渴望从战场回归正常的工作。作为一个美国人就意味着一切皆有可能，肯尼迪总统激励美国人登月，那么问题就不是我们能否登月，只是我们将何时登月。

尼尔·阿姆斯特朗登月的足迹在我们心中留下了永恒的形象，我和安在她父母家的沙发上一起目睹了那些足迹。和所有的美国人一样，那晚就寝时，我们意识到，自己生活在世界有史以来最伟大的国度。

上帝保佑尼尔·阿姆斯特朗。今晚那面美国国旗仍然在月球上飘扬。不可否认，尼尔·阿姆斯特朗的精神仍然伴随我们左右，美国人将乐观、谦虚与绝对自信融为一身——如果要在世界上找人干一件伟大的事业，你就得找一个美国人。

我的父亲出生于墨西哥，墨西哥革命期间家人被迫离开，因此我成长在一个由美国政府资助的战争难民的家庭里。我父亲半路辍学，当了一名和木板与泥灰打交道的木匠学徒。他抱负远大，说服了我妈妈，一位漂亮年轻的女演员，放弃好莱坞而嫁给他。随后，他们搬家到底特律，成为一家大汽车公司的领导并且担任了密歇根州的州长。

我们作为摩门教徒成长在密歇根州，这似乎看来有些与众不同或者不合时宜，但我的记忆并非完全那样，我的朋友们更关心的是你追随哪支球队而不是你踏进哪个教堂，我的父母给了我们世界上最好的礼物——无条件的爱。他们密切地关注我们未来的人生方向，而对我们未来从事的职业则关心甚少。

这种无条件的爱也是安和我曾经努力传递给我们的儿子们的礼物，也是现在又努力传递给我们的孙子们的礼物。所有世界上的法律法规都无法像父母的爱心与温暖的臂弯一样来拯救世界。你知道，如果每个孩子都能在家庭之爱、上帝之爱的怀抱里恬然入梦，这个世界将会变得更加安宁和美好。

---

① 婴儿潮：美国1946~1964年间出生的人。指二战后生育高峰时出生者。

everyday example. When my mom ran for the Senate, my dad was there for her every step of the way. I could still see her saying in her beautiful voice, "Why should women have any less say than men about the great decisions facing our nation?"

Don't – Don't you wish you could have been here at this convention? And heard leaders like Governor Mary Fallin, Governor Nikki Haley, Governor Susana Martinez, Senator Kelly Ayotte and Secretary of State Condoleezza Rice.

As Governor of Massachusetts, I – I chose a woman Lieutenant Governor, a woman chief of staff; half of my cabinet and senior officials were women. And in business, I mentored and supported great women leaders who went on to run great companies.

I grew up in Detroit in love with cars and wanted to be a car guy, like my dad. But by the time I was out of school, I realized that I had to go out on my own, that if I stayed around Michigan in the same business, I'd never really know if I was getting a break because of my dad. I wanted to go someplace new and – and prove myself.

Those weren't the easiest of days: many long hours and weekends working, five young sons who seemed to have this need to re-enact a different world war every night. But if you ask Ann and I what we'd give to break up just one more fight between the boys, or wake up in the morning and discover a pile of kids asleep in our room – well, every mom and dad knows the answer to that.

Those days were the – These were tough days – on Ann, particularly. She was heroic through it all – five boys, with our families a long way away. I had to travel a lot for my job then and I'd – I'd call and try to offer support. But every mom knows that doesn't help get the homework done or get the kids out the door to school. And I knew that her job as a mom was harder than mine. And I knew without question, that her job as a mom was a lot more important than mine. And as America saw Tuesday night, Ann would have succeeded at

　　我父母的婚姻持续了六十四载，如果你想知道他们白头偕老的秘诀，你可以请教当地的花工——因为每天父亲都送给母亲一枝玫瑰，放在她的床头柜上。这就是为什么父亲去世时母亲立刻感到异常——因为，床头柜上没有了玫瑰。

　　我父母是真正的伴侣，仿佛一本教科书，规范着我每日的行为。当母亲竞选参议员时，父亲始终站在她的身边，陪她走完竞选的每一步。我现在还记得母亲用她那甜美的声音发问："为什么当国家面临重大抉择时妇女不能与男人拥有同样的发言权？"

　　难道你们不希望你们能够在这次大会上，听到像州长玛丽·佛林、州长尼奇·赫利、州长苏珊娜·马提内兹、参议员凯莉·阿约特、国务卿康多莉扎·赖斯这样一些女性领导人的声音吗？

　　我作为马萨诸塞州州长，挑选了一名女性副州长，一名女性的办公室主任；我的半数的内阁成员和高级官员也都是女性。在企业界，我也曾经对一些一直经营着大公司的杰出女领导给予指导和支持。

　　我成长于底特律，热爱汽车并希望成为像我父亲一样的汽车人。但是当我迈出校门时我意识到，我不得不靠自己的力量来取得成功。如果我呆在密歇根一带从事同样的事业，我就无法真实地知道我是否是依靠父亲的力量才出人头地。所以，我要去新的地方，来证明我自己。

　　那些日子十分艰苦：工作时间延长以及周末加班加点，而且似乎每晚五个小男孩之间的世界大战都会再现。我和安试图结束哪怕一次男孩子之间的战争，试图早晨醒来不再看到男孩子们在我们的房里睡成一团的景象，如果你们要问我们是如何做到这些的——我想每个父母都知道答案。

anything she wanted to do.

Like a lot of families in a new place with no family, we – we found kinship with a wide circle of friends through our church. When we were new to the community it was welcoming; and as the years went by it was a joy to help others who'd just moved in to town or just joined our church. We had remarkably vibrant and diverse congregations [sic] from all walks of life, and many who were new to America. We prayed together; our kids played together, and we always stood ready to help each other out in different ways.

That's how it is in America. We look to our communities, our faiths, our families for our joy, our support, in good times and bad. It's both how we live our lives and why we live our lives. The strength and power and goodness of America has always been based on the strength and power and goodness of our communities, our families, and our faiths. That's the bedrock of what makes America, America.

In our best days, we can feel the vibrancy of America's communities, large and small. It's when we see that new business opening up downtown. It's when we go to work in the morning and see everybody else on the block doing the same. It's when our son or daughter calls from college to talk about which job offer they should take, and you try not to choke up when you hear that the one they like is not too far from home. It's that good feeling when you have more time to volunteer to coach your kid's soccer team, or help out on school trips. But for too many Americans, those kind of good days are harder to come by.

How many days have you woken up feeling that something really special was happening in America? Many of you felt that way on Election Day four years ago. "Hope and Change" had a powerful appeal. But tonight I'd ask a simple question: If you felt that excitement when you voted for Barack Obama, shouldn't you feel that way now that he's President Obama?

You know there's something wrong with the kind of job he's done as President when the best feeling you had was the day you voted for him. The

那些日子是艰苦的岁月，对安来说，尤其如此。她英勇地面对了这一切——照顾五个小男孩，住在远离父母的城市。因为工作，我经常出差，那时只能试着通过电话来支持她。但是每个母亲都知道，要让孩子们做家庭作业或让他们出门上学，电话毫无用处。我非常清楚，作为母亲，她要比我辛苦得多；我知道，毫无疑问，作为母亲，她比我重要得多。并且，正如大家在周二晚上看到的那样，只要是安她想做的事，不论什么她都能取得成功。

像许多背井离乡、无依无靠的家庭一样，我们通过教堂与各行各业的朋友建立了亲密的关系。当我们新来到这个社区时，受到了欢迎；随着时间的流逝，帮助那些刚搬进城里或新加入我们教堂的人便成了我们生活中的一种乐趣。我们举办各种各样充满活力的集会，邀请来自各行各业以及刚到美国的人前来参加。我们共同祈祷，我们的孩子一起玩耍，我们时刻准备着用各种方式互相帮助。

这就是美国的行事风格。无论顺境与逆境，我们把我们的欢乐与支持都寄托在我们的社区、我们的信仰、我们的家人。它既是我们的生活方式，又是我们生活的动力。美国的力量、能力和仁慈永远来源于我们的社区、我们的家庭、我们的信仰。这便造就了美国的基石。

在我们最美好的时光里，我们能感受到美国大大小小社区的活力。那时我们看到新的商场在市区开张，那时我们早晨上班看到街区里每个人都同样忙碌，那时我们的子女从大学里打电话谈及他们的工作，当听说他们喜欢的工作离家不远时我们极力掩饰自己的哽咽。那时我们有更多的时间自愿去训练孩子们的足球队，或是帮助安排学校组织的孩子们的远足活动，那时是多么美妙的感觉？但是对太多的美国人来说，那样的好日子是一去不复返了。

President hasn't disappointed you because he wanted to. The President has disappointed America because he hasn't led America in the right direction. He took office with the – without the basic qualification that most Americans have and one that was essential to the task at hand: He had almost no experience working in a business. Jobs to him are about government.

I learned the real lessons about how America works from experience. When I was 37, I helped start a small company. My partners and I had been working for a company that was in the business of helping other businesses. So some of us had this idea that if we really believed our advice was helping companies, we should invest in companies. We should bet on ourselves and our – on our advice.

So we started a new business called Bain Capital. The only problem was, while we believed in ourselves, not many other people did. We were young and had never done this before and we almost didn't get off the ground. In those days, sometimes I wondered if I'd made a really big mistake. By the way, I – I'd thought about asking my church's pension fund to invest, but I didn't. I figured it was bad enough that I might lose my investors' money, but I didn't want to go to hell too. Shows what I know. Another of my partners got the Episcopal Church pension fund to invest. And today there are a lot of happy retired priests who should thank him.

That business we started with 10 people has now grown into a great American success story. Some of the companies we helped start are names you – you know, and you've heard from tonight: an office supply company called Staples, where I'm pleased to see the Obama campaign has been shopping; The Sports Authority, which of course became a favorite of my boys. We helped start an early childhood learning center called Bright Horizons that First Lady Michelle Obama rightly praised. And at a time when nobody thought we'd ever see a new steel mill built in America, we took a chance and built one in a corn field in Indiana. Today – Today Steel Dynamics is one of the largest steel producers in the United States.

有多少日子你们一觉醒来真的发觉美国不同以往了吗？四年前的那个选举日，很多同胞都感同身受。"希望和改变"确实有其强大的吸引力。但是今夜，我想问一个简单的问题：当年你为巴拉克·奥巴马投票时倍感兴奋，这种兴奋不应该在他总统任期内不断延续吗？

各位知道，美妙的感觉只存在于你们为他投下选票的那一刻，而问题出在他身为总统所完成的工作。现任总统并不想让你们失望，但他却使整个美国失望，因为他未能领导国家迈向正确的方向。他就职之时就缺乏很多美国人皆已具备的基本条件，其中重要的一项就是：他几乎没有任何企业工作经验。工作对他而言，就是政府工作。

从自身的经历中，我汲取了许多治理国家的前车之鉴。三十七岁时，我帮忙筹办一家小公司，同合伙人一道就职于一家专门帮助其他企业的公司。因此，我们便萌生了一个念头：若我们的金玉良言果真对这些公司有所帮助，我们何不自己投资公司？我们应该为我们自己和那些"金点子"赌上一把。

所以我们便创办了自己的企业，名字叫做"贝恩资本"。唯一的问题是，虽然我们相信自己，但别人并非如此。那时我年纪尚轻，经验尚浅，公司几乎无法顺利开张。那段日子，有时我怀疑我是否真的铸成大错，顺便说一句，我曾想请求我们教堂的养老会基金来投资，但最终我没那么做。我想，运气再不济也就是把投资人的钱赔个精光，但我可不想下地狱。看吧，我就那么点见识。而我的另一个合伙人得到了圣公会养老基金会的投资，如今，那儿有很多退休牧师都过上了幸福的生活，他们都应该感谢他。

企业创办伊始，只有我们十个人，现在它已经成长为一个美国式伟大的成功传奇。我们帮助创办的一些公司，他们的名字，各位耳熟能详，今晚你们也已经听到了他们的名字：比如办公用品采购公司"Staple"，我高兴地看到奥巴马的竞选团队采购的就是这个品牌；体育用品公司"The Sports Authority"，当然，它是我那几个孩子的最爱；我们帮助创办的早教中心"Bright Horizons"，曾得到第一夫人奥巴马·米歇尔公证的褒扬；在美国无人创建新的钢厂之时，我们抓住时机，在印第安纳州的玉米地里创办了今日的"Steel Dynamics"，如今，它已经是美国最大的钢铁生产商

These – These are American success stories. And yet the centerpiece of the President's entire re-election campaign is attacking success. Is it any wonder that someone who attacks success has led the worst economic recovery since the Great Depression? In America, we celebrate success – we don't apologize for success.

Now – Now we weren't always successful at Bain. But no one ever is in the real world of business. That's what this President doesn't seem to understand. Business and growing jobs is about taking risk, sometimes failing, sometimes succeeding, but always striving. It's about dreams. Usually, it doesn't work out exactly as you might have imagined. Steve Jobs was fired at Apple. And then he came back and changed the world. It's the genius of the American free enterprise system – to harness the extraordinary creativity and talent and industry of the American people with a system that's dedicated to creating tomorrow's prosperity, not trying to redistribute today's.

That's why – That's why every President since the Great Depression who came before the American people asking for a second term could look back at the last four years and say with satisfaction: "You're better off than you were four years ago." Except Jimmy Carter. And except this President.

This President can ask us to be patient. This President can tell us it was someone else's fault. This President can tell us that the next four years he'll get it right. But this President cannot tell us that you're better off today than when he took office. America's been patient. Americans have supported this President in good faith. But today, the time has come to turn the page.

Today the time has come for us to put the disappointments of the last four years behind us; to put aside the divisiveness and the recriminations; to forget about what might have been and to look ahead to what can be. Now is the time to restore the promise of America.

Many Americans have given up on this President but they haven't ever thought about giving up – not on themselves, not on each other, and not on

之一。

这些都是美国人的成功传奇！然而现任总统竞选连任的中心议题竟是对这些成就的抨击。一个诋毁成功的人，居然要带领一个自从大萧条以来最衰败的经济走向复苏，大家认为可能吗？我们美国人向来庆贺成功——我们从不为成功道歉。

当然，现在我们在贝恩公司的发展并非一路天随人意，在真实的企业界也从来没有一帆风顺之事，现任总统似乎并不理解这一点。创办企业，增加就业就是需要承担风险，有时失败，有时成功，但奋斗永不停歇，这就是梦想。通常，结果与我们最初的设想并非完全吻合。史蒂夫·乔布斯曾被苹果公司开除，但后来他凯旋而归，改变了整个世界。这就是美国自由企业制度的天赋特点——调动美国人非凡的创造力、才能与勤奋去创造未来的繁荣，而不是纠结于如何重新分配今天的财富。

这就是为什么，大萧条以来，每位总统来到美国人民面前要求继续连任时，在回顾过去的四年任期时，都会欣慰地说上一句："和四年前相比，大家的日子变好了！"除了吉米·卡特，除了现任总统。

总统可以要求我们忍耐，可以告诉我们那是别人的过错，可以向我们保证，下一个四年他能够打翻身仗。但是他难以启齿的，就是那句："和四年前相比，大家日子变好了！"美国已经足够有耐心了，美国人民满怀

America. What is needed in our country today is not complicated or profound. [It] doesn't take a special government commission to tell us what America needs. What America needs is jobs – lots of jobs.

In the richest country in the history of the world, this Obama economy has crushed the middle class. Family income has fallen by 4,000 dollars, but health insurance premiums are higher, food prices are higher, utility bills are higher, and gasoline prices, they've doubled. Today more Americans wake up in poverty than ever before. Nearly one out of six Americans is living in poverty. Look around you. These aren't strangers. These are our brothers and sisters, our fellow Americans.

His policies have not helped create jobs, they've depressed them. And this I can tell you about where President Obama would take America: His plan to raise taxes on small business won't add jobs – it would eliminate them. His assault on coal and gas and oil will send energy and manufacturing jobs to China. His trillion dollar cuts to our military will eliminate hundreds of thousands of jobs, and also put our security at greater risk. His 716 billion dollar cut to Medicare, to finance Obamacare, will both hurt today's seniors and depress innovation and jobs in medicine. And his trillion-dollar deficits, they slow our economy, restrain employment, and cause wages to stall. To the majority of Americans who now believe that the future will not be better than the past, I can guarantee you this: If Barack Obama is re-elected, you'll be right.

I'm running for President to help create a better future – a future where everyone who wants a job can find a job; where no senior feels for the – fears for the security of their retirement; an America where every parent knows that their child will get an education that leads them to a good job and a bright horizon. And unlike the President, I have a plan to create 12 million new jobs.

Paul Ryan and I have five steps:

First, by 2020 North America will be energy independent by taking full advantage of our oil and our coal, our gas, our nuclear, and renewables.

希冀与信任支持现任总统；但今天，是翻开新的一页的时候了。

今天，该是时候把过去四年来的失望抛在身后，搁置争议，放弃指责，忘记过去该做却未做的事情，想想未来要走的道路。现在就是重新恢复美国希望的时刻。

许多美国人已经放弃了现任总统，但从未想过放弃自己，从未想过放弃彼此，从未想过放弃美国。今天我们的国家需要并不复杂难解也非深奥莫测。不需要一个专门的政府委员会来告诉我们美国需要什么。美国需要的就是就业机会——许许多多的就业机会。

在这个世界历史上最富有的国度，"奥巴马经济"却压垮了中产阶级。家庭收入已缩水了4000美元，而医保费用却水涨船高，食品价格与日俱增，水电费用也连年攀升，连汽油价格也翻了一番。现在一觉醒来一贫如洗的美国人创历史之最。几乎每六个美国人中就有一个生活在贫困之中，看看你们周围，他们不是别人，他们就是我们的兄弟姐妹，我们的美国同胞。

他的政策没有促进就业机会，反而适得其反。这一点我可以告诉你们，奥巴马总统将把美国领向何方：他的小企业增税计划不会增加就业机会，只会减少就业。他对煤、气和石油业的打击，将把能源与制造业的就业机会拱手送给中国。他削减的万亿军费开支将减少几十万个工作岗位，并且让我们在安全方面承受极大的风险。他拨出7160亿美元给医疗保健，来为"奥巴马医改"提供资金支持，既伤害了当今的老人，又抑制了医药领域的创新与就业。至于他的万亿财政赤字，则延缓了我们经济的发展，压抑了就业的增长，导致了工资的停滞。对于大多数对未来持悲观态度的美国人，我敢向你们担保，如果奥巴马再次当选，你们的想法就会成为现实。

我竞选总统为的就是创造一个更加美好的未来：一个职有所求，老无所忧，学有所教的未来，一个理想工作与光明前途并存的美国。不同于现任总统，我计划将创造1200万个新就业机会。

我和保罗·瑞安计划推出五大举措：

第一，通过充分利用本国的石油、煤炭、天然气、核能以及可再生能源，在2020年实现北美洲的能源自给。

Second, we'll give our fellow citizens the skills they need for the jobs of today and the careers of tomorrow. When it comes to the school your child will attend every parent should have a choice and every child should have a chance.

Third, we will make trade work for America by forging new trade agreements. And when nations cheat in trade, there will be unmistakable consequences.

And fourth, to assure every entrepreneur and every job creator that their investments in America will not vanish as have those in Greece; we will cut the deficit and put America on track to a balanced budget.

And fifth, we will champion small businesses, America's engine of job growth. That means reducing taxes on business, not raising them. It means simplifying and modernizing the regulations that hurt small business the most. And it means that we must rein in the skyrocketing cost of healthcare by repealing and replacing Obamacare.

Today, women are more likely than men to start a business. They need a President who respects and understands what they do. And let me make this very clear: Unlike President Obama, I will not raise taxes on the middle class of America. As President, I'll protect the sanctity of life. I'll honor the institution of marriage. And I will guarantee America's first liberty: the freedom of religion.

President Obama promised to begin to slow the rise of the oceans and to heal the planet. My promise is to help you and your family. I will begin my presidency with a jobs tour. President Obama began his presidency with an apology tour. America, he said, had dictated to other nations. No, Mr. President, America has freed other nations from dictators.

Every American – Every American was relieved the day President Obama gave the order, and Seal Team Six took out Osama bin Laden. On another front, every American is less secure today because he has failed to slow Iran's nuclear threat. In his first TV interview as President, he said we should talk to Iran. We're still talking, and Iran's centrifuges are still spinning.

第二，我们将让公民掌握所需的技能，以适应今天的工作，开创明天的事业。至于孩子们入学的学校，每位家长都应有选择权，每个孩子都应拥有就读权。

第三，我们将通过缔结新的贸易协定，让贸易服务于美国，而对于在贸易中使用欺骗手段的国家，将会使他们承担应有后果。

第四，我们向每位企业家及创造工作机会的人保证，他们在美国的投资不会像在希腊那样化为乌有。我们将降低赤字，让美国踏入预算平衡的正轨。

第五，我们将扶持作为美国就业增长引擎的小企业。那就意味着我们将降低而非提高工商税，那就意味着，我们要把那些使小企业蒙受损失最多的规定简化与现代化。那还意味着我们必须取代甚至废止"奥巴马医改"政策，以抑制医疗保健费用的飞涨。

当今，与男人相比，妇女的就业机会更多，她们需要一个尊重和理解她们的总统。明确地说：我不会像奥巴马总统那样对美国的中产阶级增税，作为总统，我将捍卫生命的圣洁，我将尊重婚姻制度，我将保障美国的首要自由——宗教信仰自由。

奥巴马总统承诺过要着手抑制海平面的上升，修缮伤痕累累的星球，我的承诺是帮助你们和你们的家庭。奥巴马总统是从道歉之旅开始他的总统任期的，而我将从创造就业之旅开始我的总统任期。奥巴马曾说过，美国曾对其他国家颐指气使。不，总统先生，是美国把其他国家从独裁者手中解放出来。

在总统奥巴马下令海豹第六突击队铲除奥萨马·本·拉登的那一天，每个美国人都松了一口气。但在另一方面，由于奥巴马总统未能减缓伊朗的核威胁，这又让美国人民心存不安。在作为总统的第一次电视访谈里，他说我们应该同伊朗会谈，我们一直在谈着，而伊朗提炼浓缩铀的离心分离机却仍在不停地运转。

President Obama has thrown allies like Israel under the bus, even as he has relaxed sanctions on Castro's Cuba. He abandoned our friends in Poland by walking away from our missile defense commitments. But he's eager to give Russia's President Putin the flexibility he desires after the election. Under my Administration, our friends will see more loyalty, and Mr. Putin will see a little less flexibility and more backbone. We will honor America's democratic ideals because a free world is a more peaceful world. This is the bipartisan foreign policy legacy of Truman and Reagan. And under my presidency we will return to it once again.

You might have asked yourself if these last years are really the America we want – the America that was won for us by the greatest generation. Does the America we want borrow a trillion dollars from China? Does it fail to find the jobs that are needed for 23 million people and for half the kids graduating from college? Are those schools lagging behind the rest of the developed world? And does the America we want succumb to resentment and division among Americans?

The America we all know has been a story of the many becoming one, uniting to preserve liberty, uniting to build the greatest economy in the world, uniting to save the world from unspeakable darkness. Everywhere I go in America, there are monuments that list those who have given their lives for America. There's no mention of their race, their party affiliation, or what they did for a living. They lived and died under a single flag, fighting for a single purpose. They pledged allegiance to the United States of America.

That America, that united America, can unleash an economy that will put Americans back to work, that will once again lead the world with innovation and productivity, and that will restore every father and mother's confidence that their children's future is brighter even than the past.

That America, that united America, will preserve a military that's so strong, no nation would ever dare to test it.

奥巴马总统居然在放松对古巴卡斯特罗的制裁的同时，对以色列一类的盟友弃如敝屣。他无视我们在导弹防御方面的承诺，对波兰朋友弃好背盟，却在俄罗斯总统普京当选后，迫不及待地给了俄罗斯想要的灵活性。在我的任期里，盟友会看到一个更忠诚的美国，而普京先生会遇到的是一个不再放任其自由，更有骨气的美国。我们将尊重美国的民主理想，因为一个自由的世界才是更加和平的世界。这是杜鲁门和里根两党一致的外交政策留下的宝贵遗产。如果我能当选，我们将重返这一政策。

你们或许已曾扪心自问，难道近几年的美国就是我们真正想要的美国吗？是最伟大的前辈为我们赢来的美国吗？这样的美国需要向中国借债万亿美元吗？这样的美国不能帮助2300万子民和半数大学毕业生找到工作么？这样的美国其大学会被其他发达国家的高等学府抛在身后吗？这样的美国要屈从于内部的怨愤与人民的分裂吗？

众所周知，美国是"合众为一"的传奇，我们团结起来保卫自由，团结起来创造世界上最伟大的经济体，团结起来从无穷的黑暗中拯救世界。无论我走到哪里，美国到处都矗立着英雄纪念碑，上面只镌刻着为国捐躯者的姓名，并不提及他们的种族、他们隶属的党派、他们的职业。他们都在一面旗帜之下出生入死，为一个目的而英勇战斗，誓死效忠于美利坚合众国。

那样的美国，那个团结一致的美国，才能让经济重见天日：让美国人重返岗位，凭借自身的创造力与生产力再次领导世界，让每一位父母重拾信心，相信他们孩子的未来会前程似锦，蒸蒸日上。

那样的美国，那个团结一致的美国，将保持强大的军事力量，没有一个国家敢公然挑衅。

That America – That America, that united America, will uphold the constellation of rights that were endowed by our Creator and codified in our Constitution.

That united America will care for the poor and the sick, will honor and respect the elderly, and will give a helping hand to those in need.

That America is the best within each of us. That America we want for our children.

If I am elected President of these United States, I will work with all my energy and soul to restore that America, to lift our eyes to a better future. That future is our destiny. That future is out there. It is waiting for us.

Our children deserve it.

Our nation depends on it.

The peace and freedom of the world require it.

And with your help we will deliver it. Let us begin that future for America tonight!

Thank you so very much! May God bless you! May God bless the American people!

And may God bless the United States of America.

Tampa, Florida, August 30, 2012

那样的美国，那个团结一致的美国，将保障那些由我们的开国领袖赐予并载入宪法的各种权利。

那个团结一致的美国，将关怀贫弱，将敬老尊贤，将济困扶危！

那样的美国才是我们彼此间最好的美国，那样的美国才是我们希望留给后人的美国。

如果我当选为美国总统，我将全身心地投入到重建那样的美国中，领导美国人民去展望一个更加美好的未来。那个未来是我们的命运，那个未来近在眼前，它正在等待我们的到来。

我们的孩子理应得到它。

我们的国家依赖于它。

世界的和平与自由呼唤着它。

实现这一梦想需要仰仗大家的帮助。让我们从今夜开始走向美国的美好未来。

非常感谢你们！愿意上帝保佑你们！愿意上帝保佑美国人民！

愿上帝保佑美利坚合众国！

（杜梦臻　袁婧／译）

Romney's Concession Speech

Thank you. Thank you. Thank you. Thank you, my friends. Thank you so very much. Thank you. Thank you. Thank you.

I have just called President Obama to congratulate him on his victory. His supporters and his campaign also deserve congratulations. I wish all of them well, but particularly the president, the first lady and their daughters. This is a time of great challenges for America, and I pray that the president will be successful in guiding our nation.

I want to thank Paul Ryan for all that he has done for our campaign. And

罗姆尼告别竞选演讲

谢谢，谢谢，谢谢，朋友们。非常感谢你们。谢谢，谢谢。

我刚刚已致电奥巴马总统，祝贺他连任，同时也祝贺奥巴马的支持者和他的竞选团队，他们如愿以偿赢得胜利。在此祝福的同时，我也要特别祝福总统及总统夫人，及他们的两位千金。对于美国而言，这是一个充满挑战的时代，而我希望总统先生能够引导我们国家走向成功。

在此，我也要感谢保罗·瑞恩[①]为我们的竞选甚至国家所付出的一切。除了我的夫人安，瑞恩是我作过的最明智的选择。而我相信，他的智慧和辛勤工作，以及他对原则的坚守将继续造福美国。

同时，我还要感谢我一生的最爱，我的妻子安，她本可以是一位出色的第一夫人。对于我和我们的家人，以及她用同情心和曾被她的博爱与关怀感染过的所有人来说，她更加的重要。

我还要代表竞选团队感谢我的儿子们所做的辛勤工作，他们离家多时，协助我筹备竞选，对此我要向他们的妻子和孩子们所作的牺牲表示感谢。

我要感谢马特罗迪斯以及他所领导的竞选团队，他们为我和我们所热爱的国家作出了非凡的努力。

今夜，对在座的各位，以及我全国各地的竞选团队——志愿者、资金筹集人、捐赠者、代理人，你们在过去几年所作的一切无与伦比。我向你们表达深深的谢意。

---

① 保罗·瑞恩（Paul D. Ryan, Jr, 1970年1月29日—　）出生于美国威斯康星州，毕业于迈阿密大学。美国众议员、众议院预算委员会首席成员。2012年8月，有消息称其将作为美国共和党总统候选人罗姆尼的副总统候选人而受关注。

for our country. Besides my wife, Ann, Paul is the best choice I've ever made. And I trust that his intellect and his hard work and his commitment to principle will continue to contribute to the good of our nation.

I also want to thank Ann, the love of my life. She would have been a wonderful first lady. She's – she has been that and more to me and to our family and to the many people that she has touched with her compassion and her care.

I thank my sons for their tireless work on behalf of the campaign, and thank their wives and children for taking up the slack as their husbands and dads have spent so many weeks away from home.

I want to thank Matt Rhoades and the dedicated campaign team he led. They have made an extraordinary effort not just for me, but also for the country that we love.

And to you here tonight, and to the team across the country – the volunteers, the fundraisers, the donors, the surrogates – I don't believe that there's ever been an effort in our party that can compare with what you have done over these past years. Thank you so very much.

Thanks for all the hours of work, for the calls, for the speeches and appearances, for the resources and for the prayers. You gave deeply from yourselves and performed magnificently. And you inspired us and you humbled us. You've been the very best we could have imagined.

The nation, as you know, is at a critical point. At a time like this, we can't risk partisan bickering and political posturing. Our leaders have to reach across the aisle to do the people's work.

And we citizens also have to rise to the occasion. We look to our teachers and professors, we count on you not just to teach, but to inspire our children with a passion for learning and discovery.

We look to our pastors and priests and rabbis and counselors of all kinds to testify of the enduring principles upon which our society is built: honesty, charity, integrity and family.

感谢你们的辛勤工作、你们的号召、你们的演讲和挺身而出、你们所贡献的资源和祝福。你们全力以赴并且表现出色，是你们激励了我们，你们使我们谦卑。你们出类拔萃，超出想象。

正如你们所知道的那样，我们的国家正处在关键时期。在这样的时刻，我们不能冒险搞两党纷争和政治攻讦。我们的领导人只有同心协力，才能做好人民的工作。

我们公民也需尽一己之力。我们对教师和教授怀有期望，他们身上肩负的不仅是传道授业的任务，还要激发孩子学习和探索的热情。

我们对牧师及教父怀有期望，期望他们去践行奠基我们社会的经久不衰的原则：诚实、宽容、正直及和睦。

我们对父母怀有期望，因为一切最终都取决于我们家庭的胜利。

我们对各类创业者怀有期望，我们依靠你们来投资、雇佣员工、使整个国家进步。

我们对政府机关的共和党和民主党各级人士怀有期望，希望你们把人民的利益始终放在政治之上。

我相信美国，我也相信美国人民的选择。

We look to our parents, for in the final analysis everything depends on the success of our homes.

We look to job creators of all kinds. We're counting on you to invest, to hire, to step forward.

And we look to Democrats and Republicans in government at all levels to put the people before the politics.

I believe in America. I believe in the people of America.

And I ran for office because I'm concerned about America. This election is over, but our principles endure. I believe that the principles upon which this nation was founded are the only sure guide to a resurgent economy and to renewed greatness.

Like so many of you, Paul and I have left everything on the field. We have given our all to this campaign.

I so wish – I so wish that I had been able to fulfill your hopes to lead the country in a different direction, but the nation chose another leader. And so Ann and I join with you to earnestly pray for him and for this great nation.

Thank you and God bless America. You guys are the best. Thank you so much. Thank you. Thanks, guys.

Boston, Massachusetts, November 7, 2012

我竞选总统，是因为我关心祖国。竞选虽已落下帷幕，但我们的信念将持永存在。我相信我们国家的建国理念将成为我们经济复苏、重振雄风的唯一导向。

和你们大多数人一样，我和保罗都将为了这场角逐竭尽全力，倾其所有。

我期望——我是如此期望我能如你们所愿，领导这个国家迈向截然不同的道路，但是，这个国家选择了另外一位领导者。所以我和安真心地加入你们的行列，一起为他和这个国家祝福。

谢谢。上帝保佑美国。你们是最棒的，谢谢你们。朋友们，谢谢你们！

（杜梦臻　袁婧／译）

Remarks of Michelle
to the Democratic National Convention 2012

Thank you so much! Elaine, we are so grateful for your family's service and sacrifice and we will always have your back.

Over the past few years as First Lady, I have had the extraordinary privilege of traveling all across this country.

And everywhere I've gone, in the people I've met, and the stories I've heard, I have seen the very best of the American spirit.

I have seen it in the incredible kindness and warmth that people have shown me and my family, especially our girls.

I've seen it in teachers in a near-bankrupt school district who vowed to keep teaching without pay.

I've seen it in people who become heroes at a moment's notice, diving into harm's way to save others, flying across the country to put out a fire, driving for hours to bail out a flooded town.

And I've seen it in our men and women in uniform and our proud military families; in wounded warriors who tell me they're not just going to walk again, they're going to run, and they're going to run marathons; in the young man blinded by a bomb in Afghanistan who said, simply, "I'd give my eyes 100 times again to have the chance to do what I have done and what I can still do."

Every day, the people I meet inspire me; every day, they make me proud; every day they remind me how blessed we are to live in the greatest nation on earth.

米歇尔在2012年
民主党全国代表大会上的演讲 ①

（2012年9月4日）

非常感谢，伊莲，我们非常感谢来自你的家人的奉献和牺牲，我们将永远支持你。

在过去的几年，以第一夫人的非凡殊荣，我有幸周游了整个美国。

所到之处，所遇之人，所闻之事，让我见证了美国精神之精髓。

从人们对我和我的家庭，特别是对我的女儿那和蔼与热情当中，我看到了它。

在濒临破产的学区内，教师们无偿执教的誓言中，我看到了它。

在危难时刻，英雄们挺身而出，奋不顾身拯救他人，飞越全国勇战火海，驱车数时去救援被淹没的城镇，在这些英勇壮举中，我看到了它。

在身着戎装的男女军人和光荣自豪的军属身上，在告诉我他们不仅会学着站立行走，学着奔跑，甚至还要参加马拉松的伤残战士身上，在说出"我宁愿为了我所做的事情和我继续做的事情失去眼睛一百次"的阿富汗轰炸中失去光明的年轻人身上，我看到了它。

每一天，所遇之人都在激励着我；每一天，他们都使我引以为傲；每一天，他们都让我意识到，能够生活在这个世界上最伟大的国度中，是多么的幸福。

---

① 9月4日美国第一夫人米歇尔·奥巴马在2012年民主党代表大会上发表了"深情而有力的演讲"。她赞扬奥巴马是勤劳、坚韧和自信的美国精神的分享者，"和你们（所有美国人）一样，即使是四年的总统生涯也没有改变他模范丈夫的本质"。米歇尔短短26分钟的演讲高潮迭起，人们不自觉地多次起立长时间鼓掌。很多听众因米歇尔朴实无华但真切感人的话语激动不已而热泪盈眶。

Serving as your First Lady is an honor and a privilege, but back when we first came together four years ago, I still had some concerns about this journey we'd begun.

While I believed deeply in my husband's vision for this country and I was certain he would make an extraordinary President. Like any mother, I was worried about what it would mean for our girls if he got that chance.

How would we keep them grounded under the glare of the national spotlight? How would they feel being uprooted from their school, their friends, and the only home they'd ever known?

Our life before moving to Washington was filled with simple joys: Saturdays at soccer games, Sundays at grandma's house...and a date night for Barack and me was either dinner or a movie, because as an exhausted mom, I couldn't stay awake for both.

And the truth is, I loved the life we had built for our girls. I deeply loved the man I had built that life with and I didn't want that to change if he became President.

I loved Barack just the way he was.

You see, even though back then Barack was a Senator and a presidential candidate, to me, he was still the guy who'd picked me up for our dates in a car that was so rusted out, I could actually see the pavement going by through a hole in the passenger side door. He was the guy whose proudest possession was a coffee table he'd found in a dumpster, and whose only pair of decent shoes was half a size too small.

But when Barack started telling me about his family – that's when I knew I had found a kindred spirit, someone whose values and upbringing were so much like mine.

You see, Barack and I were both raised by families who didn't have much in the way of money or material possessions but who had given us something far more valuable – their unconditional love, their unflinching sacrifice, and the

能够成为第一夫人，我倍感荣耀和幸运，但回首我们四年前首次相聚，我对已经开始的旅程，我仍然略感忐忑不安。

但是，对我丈夫所绘制的祖国蓝图，我满怀信心；我坚信他可以成为一名杰出卓越的总统！同天下所有的母亲一样，我也曾担心，他若果真当选，将对我们的女儿意味着什么。

身处万众瞩目的聚光灯下，我们要如何让她们保持脚踏实地？当她们被迫离开曾经熟悉的学校、朋友和唯一的家时，会有怎样的感受？

在搬到华盛顿之前，我们的生活简简单单但其乐无穷：周六参加足球赛，周日拜访祖母家，还有我和巴拉克的约会之夜，吃晚饭或者看电影，只能择一而行，因为作为一个筋疲力尽的母亲，我实在没有精力二者兼顾。

说实话，我喜欢我们为女儿们创造的生活环境，我深爱和我一起创造这种生活的男人，我不想一切因为他当了总统而发生丝毫的改变。

我爱的就是巴拉克本来的样子。

即便是巴拉克已经成为一名参议员兼总统候选人的时候，在我眼里，他仍然是那个开着一辆锈迹斑斑的破车来接我去约会的男人，真的，我都

chance to go places they had never imagined for themselves.

My father was a pump operator at the city water plant, and he was diagnosed with Multiple Sclerosis when my brother and I were young.

And even as a kid, I knew there were plenty of days when he was in pain. I knew there were plenty of mornings when it was a struggle for him to simply get out of bed.

But every morning, I watched my father wake up with a smile, grab his walker, prop himself up against the bathroom sink, and slowly shave and button his uniform.

And when he returned home after a long day's work, my brother and I would stand at the top of the stairs to our little apartment, patiently waiting to greet him, watching as he reached down to lift one leg, and then the other, to slowly climb his way into our arms. But despite these challenges, my dad hardly ever missed a day of work. He and my mom were determined to give me and my brother the kind of education they could only dream of.

And when my brother and I finally made it to college, nearly all of our tuition came from student loans and grants.

But my dad still had to pay a tiny portion of that tuition himself. And every semester, he was determined to pay that bill right on time, even taking out loans when he fell short.

He was so proud to be sending his kids to college...and he made sure we never missed a registration deadline because his check was late.

You see, for my dad, that's what it meant to be a man.

Like so many of us, that was the measure of his success in life – being able to earn a decent living that allowed him to support his family.

And as I got to know Barack, I realized that even though he'd grown up all the way across the country, he'd been brought up just like me.

Barack was raised by a single mother who struggled to pay the bills, and by grandparents who stepped in when she needed help.

能透过这侧车门上的破洞看到那飞逝的路面；他仍是那个把从垃圾箱里翻出来的咖啡桌当做自己最了不起的财产的男人，那个仅有一双体面的鞋子，还小了半号的男人。

然而，当巴拉克开始向我讲述他的家庭时——就在那一瞬间，我明白我遇到了一个志同道合的精神伴侣，他的价值观和成长经历与我竟惊人的相似。

大家知道，我和巴拉克的家境都不富裕，但是，家人给予了我们更为珍贵的东西——无条件的爱，无畏的牺牲，以及他们自己未曾想象的机会。

我的父亲是城区水厂的一名水泵操作员，在我和哥哥年幼时，父亲被诊断出患有多发性硬化症。

虽然当时年纪尚小，但我也知道他常常受到病痛的折磨，也知道有很多清晨，仅仅起床对他来说都是一场痛苦的挣扎。

然而每天早晨，我都看到父亲面带微笑地醒来，抓紧他的助步器，用浴室的洗脸池支撑着自己的身体，慢慢地刮好胡须，扣好制服。

在父亲一天漫长的工作之后，我和哥哥会站在自家小公寓的楼梯顶

Barack's grandmother started out as a secretary at a community bank and she moved quickly up the ranks, but like so many women, she hit a glass ceiling.

And for years, men no more qualified than she was – men she had actually trained – were promoted up the ladder ahead of her, earning more and more money while Barack's family continued to scrape by.

But day after day, she kept on waking up at dawn to catch the bus, arriving at work before anyone else, giving her best without complaint or regret.

And she would often tell Barack, "So long as you kids do well, Bar, that's all that really matters."

Like so many American families, our families weren't asking for much.

They didn't begrudge anyone else's success or care that others had much more than they did. In fact, they admired it.

They simply believed in that fundamental American promise that, even if you don't start out with much, if you work hard and do what you're supposed to do, and then you should be able to build a decent life for yourself and an even better life for your kids and grandkids.

That's how they raised us: that's what we learned from their example. We learned about dignity and decency – that how hard you work matters more than how much you make that helping others means more than just getting ahead yourself. We learned about honesty and integrity – that the truth matters; that you don't take shortcuts or play by your own set of rules...and success doesn't count unless you earn it fair and square. We learned about gratitude and humility – that so many people had a hand in our success, from the teachers who inspired us to the janitors who kept our school clean and we were taught to value everyone's contribution and treat everyone with respect.

Those are the values Barack and I – and so many of you – are trying to pass on to our own children.

That's who we are.

And standing before you four years ago, I knew that I didn't want any of

上，耐心地迎接他回家。我们看着他弯下腰，慢慢地抬起腿，蹒跚地爬上楼梯，迎向我们的怀抱。再苦再难，父亲从未请过一天假。他和母亲下定决心，要让我和哥哥接受最好的教育，曾经他们梦寐以求的教育！

我和哥哥最终考上大学，几乎全部的学费都来源于助学贷款和补助金。

但是小部分学费还是压在了父亲的肩头。每个学期，他都坚持按时缴纳学费，在捉襟见肘的时候，他甚至去贷款。

能送子女上大学，他引以为傲；虽然有时学费无法按时到账，但他从未让我们错过任何一次报到。

对我的父亲来说，这是身为一个男人的责任。

和我们大多数人一样，这就是他衡量生命成功与否的标准——能否靠自己的双手让家人过上体面的生活。

当我深入了解巴拉克之后，我发现虽然他成长在美国的另一边，其成长经历却和我极为相似。

巴拉克生于单亲家庭，他的母亲不辞辛劳，支撑家庭，在她实在无能为力的时候，祖父母也会伸出援助的双手。

巴拉克的祖母起初在社区银行当秘书，后来她晋升很快，可惜和很多女性一样，性别让她的升职空间遭遇瓶颈。

数年间，那些资历不如她的男性员工——事实上，还是她亲手培训的男性员工——都升到比她高的职位，挣的钱越来越多，而与此同时，巴拉克一家却只能勉强度日。

但日复一日，她仍然坚持早起去赶公车，比其他任何人都早到公司，对待工作，她总是竭尽全力，无怨无悔。

她常常这样告诉巴拉克：“巴，只要你们过得好，其他什么都不重要。”

像诸多美国家庭一样，我们俩的家庭都知足常乐。

他们既不嫉妒他人的成功，也不在意他人的拥有。事实上，他们为此心存感激。

他们就是心怀着最简单的美国式希望，即，哪怕你出身贫寒，只要你辛勤工作，做好本职，那么你就能过上体面的生活，而你的子孙后代的生活也会蒸蒸日上。

他们就是这样把我们抚养成人，并且成为我们的楷模。从他们身上，

that to change if Barack became President.

Well, today, after so many struggles and triumphs and moments that have tested my husband in ways I never could have imagined, I have seen firsthand that being president doesn't change who you are – it reveals who you are.

You see, I've gotten to see up close and personal what being president really looks like.

And I've seen how the issues that come across a President's desk are always the hard ones – the problems where no amount of data or numbers will get you to the right answer. The judgment calls where the stakes are so high, and there is no margin for error.

And as President, you can get all kinds of advice from all kinds of people.

But at the end of the day, when it comes time to make that decision, as President, all you have to guide you are your values, and your vision, and the life experiences that make you who you are.

So when it comes to rebuilding our economy, Barack is thinking about folks like my dad and like his grandmother.

He's thinking about the pride that comes from a hard day's work.

That's why he signed *the Lilly Ledbetter Fair Pay Act* to help women get equal pay for equal work.

That's why he cut taxes for working families and small businesses and fought to get the auto industry back on its feet.

That's how he brought our economy from the brink of collapse to creating jobs again – jobs you can raise a family on, good jobs right here in the United States of America.

When it comes to the health of our families, Barack refused to listen to all those folks who told him to leave health reform for another day, another president.

He didn't care whether it was the easy thing to do politically – that's not how he was raised – he cared that it was the right thing to do.

我们学会了自尊正派——努力工作远比挣钱重要，帮助他人比超越别人更有意义。我们学会了诚实守信——要追求真理，不能妄图走捷径或耍小伎俩，而且成功要靠公平来争取。我们学会了感激和谦虚——我们的成功依靠许多人的帮助，从启迪我们的老师到保持校园整洁的校工，我们学会珍惜每个人的贡献，并且尊重待人。

这些是巴拉克和我——以及在场的各位——都试图传递给子女的价值观。

我们就是这样的人。

四年前，站在你们面前的我，不想让这一切因为巴拉克当选总统而发生丝毫的改变。

那么，今天，在那么多艰苦奋斗、克敌制胜和难以想象的考验之后，我明白了，当总统并不会改变一个人，却可以证明一个人。

众所周知，我足够幸运，能够近距离地亲眼观察当总统到底是怎么一回事。

我看到，放到总统面前的问题总是难题——困难到无论运用多少资料和数据都无法迎刃而解。作出选择的风险之高，根本容不得一星半点的差错。

作为总统，会有各种各样的人给你提出各种各样的建议。

但到最后需要作出决定的时刻，作为总统，指导你做出选择的其实是你的价值观、判断力，以及那些塑造你人格的成长经历。

因此，当谈到重建经济的时候，巴拉克想到的是像我的父亲和他的祖母一样的人们。

他想到的是一整天兢兢业业之后的自豪感。

这就是他签署《莉莉·列得贝塔同工同酬法》的原因，帮助女性争取到同工同酬的公平权利。

这就是他为工作家庭和小企业主削减了赋税，并努力让汽车工业重振

He did it because he believes that here in America, our grandparents should be able to afford their medicine; our kids should be able to see a doctor when they're sick, and no one in this country should ever go broke because of an accident or illness.

And he believes that women are more than capable of making our own choices about our bodies and our health care. That's what my husband stands for.

When it comes to giving our kids the education they deserve, Barack knows that like me and like so many of you, he never could've attended college without financial aid.

And believe it or not, when we were first married, our combined monthly student loan bills were actually higher than our mortgage.

We were so young, so in love, and so in debt.

That's why Barack has fought so hard to increase student aid and keep interest rates down, because he wants every young person to fulfill their promise and be able to attend college without a mountain of debt.

So in the end, for Barack, these issues aren't political – they're personal.

Because Barack knows what it means when a family struggles.

He knows what it means to want something more for your kids and grandkids.

Barack knows the American Dream because he's lived it, and he wants everyone in this country to have that same opportunity, no matter who we are, or where we're from, or what we look like, or who we love.

And he believes that when you've worked hard, and done well, and walked through that doorway of opportunity. You do not slam it shut behind you. You reach back, and you give other folks the same chances that helped you succeed.

So when people ask me whether being in the White House has changed my husband, I can honestly say that when it comes to his character, and his convictions, and his heart, Barack Obama is still the same man I fell in love with all those years ago.

雄姿的原因。

就是用这种方法，他让我们的经济从崩溃的边缘转危为安，并重新开始创造工作机会——那些可以让人养家糊口的工作机会，那些就在美利坚合众国本土内的理想工作！

至于家庭医保问题，巴拉克拒绝人云亦云，拒绝暂缓医疗改革，把问题留给下一任总统。

这项措施在政治上是否行得通，他毫不在乎，因为这不是他受到的教育，他在乎的是，去做正确的事情。

他这样做，是因为他坚信，在美国，我们的老人必须有能力负担自己的医疗费用，我们的孩子生病时必须能够去看医生，而且坚信，在这个国度里，任何人都不应该因为一场意外或疾病而倾家荡产。

他还坚信，女性完全有能力对自己的身体和健康作出选择。这就是我丈夫的立场。

谈到孩子们应受到的教育问题，巴拉克很清楚，如果没有助学金，像我，像在座的很多人，都永远不可能读完大学。

而且，不管你们相信与否，刚结婚的时候，我们的学生贷款账单合起来比我们的房贷还要高。

我们是那么年轻，那么相恋，又是那样的负债累累。

这就是为什么巴拉克努力增加助学金，并保持低贷款利率的原因，他想让每个年轻人都能如愿以偿，完成学业而不至于债台高筑。

所以归根结底，对巴拉克来说，这些无关政治，而事关个人。

因为巴拉克知道，一个家庭的努力奋斗意味着什么。

他知道想要让子子孙孙过上更好的生活意味着什么。

巴拉克懂得什么是美国梦，因为他正用自己的一生去践行，他想让这个国度里的每一个人，不论身份、地域、肤色、相貌，不管爱的是谁，都能拥有同等的机会。

他相信，当你辛勤工作，卓有成效，跨越了那扇机遇的大门之后，你不应该"砰"的一声将大门关起，你应该伸出援助之手，将成功的机会传递给曾经助你一臂之力的人。

因此，有人问我，入住白宫后，我的丈夫是否发生了改变，我可以诚

He's the same man who started his career by turning down high paying jobs and instead working in struggling neighborhoods where a steel plant had shut down, fighting to rebuild those communities and get folks back to work, because for Barack, success isn't about how much money you make, it's about the difference you make in people's lives.

He's the same man who, when our girls were first born, would anxiously check their cribs every few minutes to ensure they were still breathing, proudly showing them off to everyone we knew.

That's the man who sits down with me and our girls for dinner nearly every night, patiently answering their questions about issues in the news, and strategizing about middle school friendships.

That's the man I see in those quiet moments late at night, hunched over his desk, poring over the letters people have sent him.

The letter from the father struggling to pay his bills, from the woman dying of cancer whose insurance company won't cover her care, from the young person with so much promise but so few opportunities.

I see the concern in his eyes and I hear the determination in his voice as he tells me, "You won't believe what these folks are going through, Michelle, it's not right. We've got to keep working to fix this. We've got so much more to do."

I see how those stories – our collection of struggles and hopes and dreams – I see how that's what drives Barack Obama every single day.

And I didn't think it was possible, but today, I love my husband even more than I did four years ago, even more than I did 23 years ago, when we first met.

I love that he's never forgotten how he started.

I love that we can trust Barack to do what he says he's going to do, even when it's hard – especially when it's hard.

I love that for Barack, there is no such thing as "us" and "them" – he doesn't care whether you're a Democrat, a Republican, or none of the above. He knows that we all love our country, and he's always ready to listen to good

164

实地说，无论是从他的性格、信念和心灵，巴拉克·奥巴马都仍是多年前我爱的那个男人。

他仍是那个会在自己的事业起步之时，拒绝高薪工作，而走入一个因钢铁厂的倒闭而陷入困境的社区，为社区的重建和人们重获工作而奋斗的人。因为在他看来，成功并不能用所赚取的金钱来衡量，而是你在多大程度上，改变了人们的生活。

他仍然是那个当我们的女儿刚出生的时候，每隔几分钟就匆匆赶去查看摇篮，确认她们是否呼吸顺畅，并骄傲地向我们认识的每个人展示自己宝贝女儿的人。

他仍然是那个几乎每晚都会坐下来陪我和女儿们吃晚餐，耐心地回答她们对新闻轶事的疑问，并为孩子们之间的友谊出谋划策的人。

他仍然是那个，在万籁俱寂的深夜里，仍趴在书桌上钻研人们寄来的信件的人。

来信的人有辛苦工作支付账单的父亲，有保险公司拒绝赔付医疗费用而命在旦夕的癌症女病人，还有怀才不遇的年轻人。

那一刻，我能看到他眼里的忧虑，当他对我说："你不会相信这些人们在经历些什么，米歇尔，事情不应该这样的。我们必须不断努力来解决这些问题，还有太多的事情要做。"那一刻，我能听出他声音中的决心。

我看到人生百态，故事里面有挣扎，有希望，有梦想，我终于看到了是什么驱使着巴拉克·奥巴马日复一日地辛勤的工作。

我曾以为我的爱已至极限，然而如今，我比四年前更爱我的丈夫，这份爱，甚至超过了23年前的初次邂逅。

我爱他从未忘记自己是如何开始的。

我爱他哪怕面临困难，尤其是在困难重重之时，也能言行一致，值得信赖。

我爱他从不主观地划分敌我——他才不在意你是民主党人，共和党人，或是别的什么党派。他知道我们都热爱祖国，随时作好静静聆听金玉良言的准备，总是在每个人身上找出闪光点。

我爱他即使在最艰难的时候，在我们都焦灼不安的时候，比如当我们担心法案不能通过，事态看起来已全局皆输的时候——巴拉克也从不受流

ideas. He's always looking for the very best in everyone he meets.

And I love that even in the toughest moments, when we're all sweating it – when we're worried that the bill won't pass, and it seems like all is lost – Barack never lets himself get distracted by the chatter and the noise.

Just like his grandmother, he just keeps getting up and moving forward, with patience and wisdom, and courage and grace.

And he reminds me that we are playing a long game here and that change is hard, and change is slow, and it never happens all at once.

But eventually we get there, we always do.

We get there because of folks like my Dad, folks like Barack's grandmother, men and women who said to themselves, "I may not have a chance to fulfill my dreams, but maybe my children will, maybe my grandchildren will."

So many of us stand here tonight, because of their sacrifice, longing and steadfast love. Because time and again, they swallowed their fears and doubts and did what was hard.

So today, when the challenges we face start to seem overwhelming – or even impossible – let us never forget that doing the impossible is the history of this nation. It's who we are as Americans. It's how this country was built.

And if our parents and grandparents could toil and struggle for us, if they could raise beams of steel to the sky, send a man to the moon, and connect the world with the touch of a button, then surely we can keep on sacrificing and building for our own kids and grandkids.

And if so many brave men and women could wear our country's uniform and sacrifice their lives for our most fundamental rights, then surely we can do our part as citizens of this great democracy to exercise those rights, surely, we can get to the polls and make our voices heard on Election Day.

If farmers and blacksmiths could win independence from an empire, if immigrants could leave behind everything they knew for a better life on our shores, if women could be dragged to jail for seeking the vote, if a generation

言飞语的干扰。

就像他的祖母一样，他只是每天早起，不断前进，心怀耐心、智慧、勇气与风度。

他时常提醒我，我们正在打一场漫长的比赛，改革之路艰难而缓慢，不会一蹴而就。

但我们终会胜利，因为我们一向如此。

我们终会胜利，因为有一群像我父亲这样的人，有一群像巴拉克的祖母这样的人，这一群人会对自己说："也许我没有机会实现梦想，但我的孩子们会的，我的孙子孙女们会的。"

因为他们的牺牲、期盼和坚定的爱，因为他们一次又一次吞噬自己的恐惧和疑虑，去战胜困难，才让我们这么多人，在今夜，站在了这里。

因此，今天，当我们面临的挑战开始势不可挡——甚至无法逾越的时候——让我们永远不要遗忘，"超越一切不可能"正是我们国家的历史写照，正是我们美国人的本性，正是我们的立国之本。

既然我们的前辈能为我们艰苦奋斗，既然他们能建起高耸入云的钢筋大厦，能将人类送上月球，还能轻触按键连接整个世界，那么，我们当然也能为我们的子女和子孙忘我牺牲，建设世界。

既然这么多英勇的男女能换上戎装，为祖国为民权奋不顾身，那么，我们作为这个伟大的民主国家的公民，当然也能承担起自己的责任，去实践权利；当然能够在选举日拿起选票，呐喊出自己的声音。

如果农民和手工业者能从一个帝国手中赢得独立，如果移民能放弃一切，登上我们的海岸，寻求更好的生活，如果妇女们能为争取选举权敢于受牢狱之苦，如果一代人可以战胜经济衰退，让繁荣永垂不朽，如果一位年轻的牧师能用他正义的理想带领我们攀登顶峰①，如果自信的美国人敢于做真正的自己，与自己的所爱之人大胆地站到神的面前，那么，当然，我们当然（重复当然）能够为这个国度中的每一个人都赢得一个公平的机

---

① 《圣经》以色列人出埃及的典故，摩西带领以色列人摆脱埃及法老的奴役，他被上帝带到山顶上，看到了"应许之地"。马丁·路德·金被暗杀之前的最后一场演讲即名为《I've been to the mountaintop》。

could defeat a depression, and define greatness for all time, if a young preacher could lift us to the mountaintop with his righteous dream, and if proud Americans can be who they are and boldly stand at the altar with who they love, then surely, surely we can give everyone in this country a fair chance at that great American Dream.

Because in the end, more than anything else, that is the story of this country – the story of unwavering hope grounded in unyielding struggle.

That is what has made my story, and Barack's story, and so many other American stories possible.

And I say all of this tonight not just as First Lady and not just as a wife.

You see, at the end of the day, my most important title is still "mom-in-chief."

My daughters are still the heart of my heart and the center of my world.

But today, I have none of those worries from four years ago about whether Barack and I were doing what's best for our girls.

Because today, I know from experience that if I truly want to leave a better world for my daughters, and all our sons and daughters, if we want to give all our children a foundation for their dreams and opportunities worthy of their promise, if we want to give them that sense of limitless possibility – that belief that here in America, there is always something better out there if you're willing to work for it, then we must work like never before and we must once again come together and stand together for the man we can trust to keep moving this great country forward—my husband, our President, President Barack Obama.

Thank you, God bless you, and God bless America.

Charlotte, North Carolina, September 4, 2012

会，实现伟大的美国梦。

因为归根结底，我们国家的历史，就是一段顽强斗争、坚忍不拔的奋斗史，它无与伦比，胜过一切。

是它，缔造了我的故事，巴拉克的故事，和其他众多美国人的故事。

今天，我所说的一切，不仅是出于第一夫人的立场，也不仅是出于一个妻子的立场。

最终，各位会发现，我最重要的头衔仍然是那个"老妈总司令"。

我的女儿们仍是我的心头肉，是我的世界的中心。

四年前，我曾怀疑我和巴拉克是否为女儿们做了最正确的事情，但如今我的疑虑早已烟消云散。

因为今天，经历告诉我，如果真要为我的女儿们，以及我们所有人的子女们留下一个更加美好的世界，如果我们想要赋予所有的孩子们实现梦想的根基和与他们能力相称的机遇，如果我们想要让他们感觉到万事皆有可能，让他们拥有一份信念，即相信在美国，只要愿意为之努力，就一定会比现在更好，那么，我们就必须更加卖力地工作，必须再次齐心协力，支持这位值得信任，会将国家推向前进的人。他就是我的丈夫，我们的总统，巴拉克·奥巴马总统！

感谢大家，上帝保佑你们，上帝保佑美国。

（杜梦臻　袁婧 / 译）

Remarks of Clinton to the Democratic National Convention 2012

Now, Mr. Mayor, fellow Democrats, we are here to nominate a president. And I've got one in mind.

I want to nominate a man whose own life has known its fair share of adversity and uncertainty. I want to nominate a man who ran for president to change the course of an already weak economy and then just six weeks before his election, saw it suffer the biggest collapse since the Great Depression; a man who stopped the slide into depression and put us on the long road to recovery, knowing all the while that no matter how many jobs that he saved or created, there'd still be millions more waiting, worried about feeding their own kids, trying to keep their hopes alive.

I want to nominate a man who's cool on the outside – but who burns for America on the inside.

I want – I want a man who believes with no doubt that we can build a new American Dream economy, driven by innovation and creativity, but education and – yes – by cooperation.

And by the way, after last night, I want a man who had the good sense to marry Michelle Obama.

I want – I want Barack Obama to be the next president of the United States. And I proudly nominate him to be the standard-bearer of the Democratic Party.

Now, folks, in Tampa a few days ago, we heard a lot of talk – all about how the president and the Democrats don't really believe in free enterprise

克林顿在2012年民主党
全国代表大会上提名奥巴马的演讲 ①

市长先生，民主党同僚们，此时此刻，我们在这里进行总统提名。而在我心中已经有了一个合适的人选。

我要提名的这个人，他的人生也曾同样经历过艰难困苦和漂泊不定；我要提名的这个人，他竞选总统是为了改变疲软的经济，而就在他当选的六个星期前，却目睹了经济遭受到自大萧条以来史无前例的崩溃，这个人使经济颓势得到遏制，带领我们走向复苏的漫漫长路。他自始至终都很清楚，不管他挽救并创造多少就业机会，仍有不计其数的人一职难求，担心如何养儿育女，他竭尽全力让这些人心怀希望。

我要提名的这个人，他外表冷静，但内心之火却为美国熊熊燃烧。

我要提名的这个人，以创新和创造为桨，以教育与合作为帆，他毫不怀疑我们建立一个崭新的有着美国梦的经济的能力。

顺便说一句，昨晚过后，我发现，我所选的这个人，还拥有睿智的判断力，能娶到米歇尔·奥巴马这样的妻子。

我要推选巴拉克·奥巴马成为美国的下一任总统。并且，能提名他为民主党领导人，我引以为傲。

朋友们，前几天在坦帕，我们听到了许多流言飞语，说总统和民主党并非真的推崇自由企业和个人主动性，说我们如何想让每个人都依赖政府，说在我们的管理下，经济如何糟糕。

---

① 5月晚，美国民主党全国代表大会在北卡罗来纳州的夏洛特市进行第二天的议程，美国第42任总统克林顿为第44任总统奥巴马的连任竞选在会上发表近一个小时的精彩演讲。克林顿的讲话经常被热情的掌声和欢呼声打断，而提词机的出错似乎没有给这位优秀的演讲者造成什么干扰，相反，克林顿很多时候即兴脱稿演讲，并且效果良好。

and individual initiative, how we want everybody to be dependent on the government, how bad we are for the economy.

This Republican narrative – this alternative universe – says that every one of us in this room who amounts to anything, we're all completely self-made. One of the greatest chairmen the Democratic Party ever had, Bob Strauss – used to say that ever politician wants every voter to believe he was born in a log cabin he built himself. But, as Strauss then admitted, it ain't so.

We Democrats – we think the country works better with a strong middle class, with real opportunities for poor folks to work their way into it – with a relentless focus on the future, with business and government actually working together to promote growth and broadly share prosperity. You see, we believe that "we're all in this together" is a far better philosophy than "you're on your own."

So who's right? Well, since 1961, for 52 years now, the Republicans have held the White House 28 years, the Democrats, 24. In those 52 years, our private economy has produced 66 million private sector jobs.

So what's the job score? Republicans, 24 million; Democrats, 42 (million).

Now, there's – there's a reason for this. It turns out that advancing equal opportunity and economic empowerment is both morally right and good economics. Why? Because poverty, discrimination and ignorance restrict growth. When you stifle human potential, when you don't invest in new ideas, it doesn't just cut off the people who are affected; it hurts us all. We know that investments in education and infrastructure and scientific and technological research increase growth. They increase good jobs, and they create new wealth for all the rest of us.

Now, there's something I've noticed lately. You probably have too. And it's this. Maybe just because I grew up in a different time, but though I often disagree with Republicans, I actually never learned to hate them the way the far right that now controls their party seems to hate our president and a lot of other Democrats. I – that would be impossible for me because President Eisenhower

　　共和党跟我们完全是平行宇宙，按照他们的说法，这个房间里的我们，凡是小有成就的人，都是白手起家。民主党最伟大的主席之一，鲍勃·斯特劳先生，曾说过，每个政治家都希望其选民相信，他出生在一个自己建造的小木屋里。但是，施特劳斯也承认，情况并非如此。

　　我们民主党人认为，只有中产阶级变得强大，只有穷人有真正的工作机会加入这个行列，只有坚持不懈地着眼于未来，只有企业和政府强强联合，促进经济增长和共同富裕，我们的国家才能发展壮大。我们相信"共同担当，人人有份"而不是"自顾自，自靠自"。

　　那么，孰对孰错？自 1961 年以来，52 年中，共和党人入主白宫 28 年，民主党人 24 年。在这 52 年里，我们的个体经济已经创造了 6600 万个私人企业的就业岗位。

　　就业量的比分又如何呢？共和党人，2400 万个；民主党人，4200 万个。

　　有果必有因。事实证明，促进机会均等和提升经济能力既符合道义又有利于经济。为什么？因为贫困、歧视和无知会限制发展。如果你扼杀了人的潜能，缺乏创新意识，不仅会与人隔绝，而且害人害己。众所周知，对教育和基础设施以及科学技术研究的投资会促使经济增长，增加好的就业机会并为其他人创造新的财富。

sent federal troops to my home state to integrate Little Rock Central High School. President Eisenhower built the interstate highway system.

When I was a governor, I worked with President Reagan and his White House on the first round of welfare reform and with President George H.W. Bush on national education goals.

I'm actually very grateful to – if you saw from the film what I do today, I have to be grateful, and you should be, too – that President George W. Bush supported PEPFAR. It saved the lives of millions of people in poor countries.

And I have been honored to work with both Presidents Bush on natural disasters in the aftermath of the South Asian tsunami, Hurricane Katrina, the horrible earthquake in Haiti. Through my foundation, both in America and around the world, I'm working all the time with Democrats, Republicans and independents. Sometimes I couldn't tell you for the life who I'm working with because we focus on solving problems and seizing opportunities and not fighting all the time.

And so here's what I want to say to you, and here's what I want the people at home to think about. When times are tough and people are frustrated and angry and hurting and uncertain, the politics of constant conflict may be good. But what is good politics does not necessarily work in the real world. What works in the real world is cooperation. What works in the real world is cooperation, business and government, foundations and universities.

Ask the mayors who are here. Los Angeles is getting green and Chicago is getting an infrastructure bank because Republicans and Democrats are working together to get it. They didn't check their brains at the door. They didn't stop disagreeing, but their purpose was to get something done.

Now, why is this true? Why does cooperation work better than constant conflict?

Because nobody's right all the time, and a broken clock is right twice a day.

And every one of us – every one of us and every one of them, we're

　　我最近注意到一些事情，可能大家也注意到了，是这样，也许只是因为我成长于不同的年代，我虽然常常与共和党人的意见大相径庭，但像操纵该党的极右翼分子对我们的总统和其他民主党人的仇视，其言其行我从未敢效仿一二。

我绝不会如此，毕竟艾森豪威尔总统①曾派出联邦军队来到我的家乡，修缮了小石城中心高中，还修建了州际高速公路。

　　当我担任州长时，我曾和里根总统和他的白宫官员们一起从事第一轮的福利改革，并与乔治·布什总统一起制定国家教育方针。

　　其实我很感激乔治·布什总统，如果你看到了有关我最近制作的电影，你就会知道，我必须感激他，大家也应该感谢他，因为他为美国艾滋病紧急救援计划②提供支持，挽救了贫穷国家数以万计的人的生命。

　　能与两位布什总统一起应对南亚海啸、卡特里娜飓风、令人恐惧的海地地震等自然灾害，我倍感荣幸。通过我在国内外的基金会，我一直与民主党人、共和党人和独立人士合作。有时候，我根本说不清我在和谁并肩协作，因为我们只专注于解决问题，抓住机遇，而不是党派厮杀。

　　所以这就是我想跟各位说的，这也是我希望让坐在家里收看节目的人认真思考的。时局艰难之时，人们心灰意冷，愤怒不堪，伤痕累累却不知所措，不断的政治冲突可能并非坏事。好的政治并不见得非得在现实世界发挥作用。在现实世界需要的是"合作"，企业与政府，基金会和大学的合作。

　　问问在座的市长们。洛杉矶改善了绿化，芝加哥有了基础设施银行，这都是共和党人和民主党人共同合作的成果。他们没有抛开理智，从未停

---

　　①　德怀特·戴维·艾森豪威尔(Dwight David Eisenhower,1890年10月14日至1969年3月28日，79岁)美国第34任总统，陆军五星上将。

　　②　PEPFAR计划是"总统抗击艾滋病紧急救援计划"的简称，这个项目由乔治·布什总统在2003年发起，旨在援助全球15个艾滋病最严重的国家。

compelled to spend our fleeting lives between those two extremes, knowing we're never going to be right all the time and hoping we're right more than twice a day.

Unfortunately, the faction that now dominates the Republican Party doesn't see it that way. They think government is always the enemy, they're always right, and compromise is weakness. Just in the last couple of elections, they defeated two distinguished Republican senators because they dared to cooperate with Democrats on issues important to the future of the country, even national security.

They beat a Republican congressman with almost a hundred percent voting record on every conservative score, because he said he realized he did not have to hate the president to disagree with him. Boy, that was a nonstarter, and they threw him out.

One of the main reasons we ought to re-elect President Obama is that he is still committed to constructive cooperation. Look at his record. Look at his record. Look at his record. He appointed Republican secretaries of defense, the Army and transportation. He appointed a vice president who ran against him in 2008. And he trusted that vice president to oversee the successful end of the war in Iraq and the implementation of the recovery act.

And Joe Biden – Joe Biden did a great job with both.

He – President Obama – President Obama appointed several members of his Cabinet even though they supported Hillary in the primary. Heck, he even appointed Hillary.

Wait a minute. I am – I am very proud of her. I am proud of the job she and the national security team have done for America. I am grateful that they have worked together to make us safer and stronger, to build a world with more partners and fewer enemies. I'm grateful for the relationship of respect and partnership she and the president have enjoyed and the signal that sends to the rest of the world, that democracy does not have a blood – have to be a blood

止争论，但他们的目的是把事情做成。

那么，为什么是这样？为什么团结合作比不断冲突更加有效？

因为没有人永远正确，一个破钟一天也会有两次报对时间。

每位民主党员和每位共和党员，我们都不得不在两种背道而驰的观点之间度过我们稍纵即逝的生命，我们知道我们不会一贯正确，但我们只希望一天能正确两次以上就行了。

不幸的是，目前主导共和党的一小部分人不认同这种观点。他们认为政府永远是敌人，他们永远是对的，妥协就是软弱。就在过去两次选举中，他们让两位杰出的共和党参议员遭遇挫败，因为这两位议员敢于就有关国家未来的重大问题，甚至包括国家安全问题，与民主党合作。

他们在每一项保守的比分上几乎以百分之百的表决记录压制了一位共和党的国会议员，因为这位议员说，他觉得，他虽然和总统持有不同意见，但没有必要怀恨在心。孩子，这是不可能实现的，民主党就不要他了。

我们应当支持奥巴马总统连任，原因之一就是，他仍然致力于建设性的合作。大家来看看他的成就：他曾任命共和党人担任国防部长、陆军部长和运输部长；任命 2008 年大选的竞选对手为副总统，并相信这位副总统有能力让伊拉克战争完美收尾和复苏计划顺利实施。

事实证明，拜登在两件工作上都成绩斐然。

奥巴马总统还任命数名预选时支持希拉里的人为内阁成员，真见鬼！他甚至还将希拉里委以重任。

希拉里让我引以为傲。我为她和国家安全部队为美国所做的工作引以为傲。他们团结一致带来国泰民安、繁荣富强的祖国，他们建立了一个多合作少敌对的世界，为此我心存感激。我很感谢她和总统之间所建立的相互尊重和伙伴关系，以及他们向世界各地所传递的讯息：民主不会流血，不会成为一场流血的游戏，它是一个促进民众利益的崇高事业。

sport, it can be an honorable enterprise that advances the public interest.

Now – besides the national security team, I am very grateful to the men and women who've served our country in uniform through these perilous times. And I am especially grateful to Michelle Obama and to Joe Biden for supporting those military families while their loved ones were overseas – and for supporting our veterans when they came home, when they came home bearing the wounds of war or needing help to find education or jobs or housing.

President Obama's whole record on national security is a tribute to his strength, to his judgment and to his preference for inclusion and partnership over partisanship. We need more if it in Washington, D.C.

Now, we all know that he also tried to work with congressional Republicans on health care, debt reduction and new jobs. And that didn't work out so well. But it could have been because, as the Senate Republican leader said in a remarkable moment of candor two full years before the election, their number one priority was not to put America back to work; it was to put the president out of work. Well, wait a minute. Senator, I hate to break it to you, but we're going to keep President Obama on the job.

Are you ready for that? Are you willing to work for it. Oh, wait a minute.

In Tampa – in Tampa – did y'all watch their convention?

I did. In Tampa, the Republican argument against the president's re-election was actually pretty simple – pretty snappy. It went something like this: We left him a total mess. He hasn't cleaned it up fast enough. So fire him and put us back in.

Now – but they did it well. They looked good; the sounded good. They convinced me that – they all love their families and their children and were grateful they'd been born in America and all that – really, I'm not being – they did.

And this is important, they convinced me they were honorable people who believed what they said and they're going to keep every commitment

除了国家安全部队以外，我还很感激那些在危急时刻武装上阵、报效祖国的青年男女。我还特别要感谢米歇尔·奥巴马和拜登，感谢他们对家人远在海外服役的军属，对返回家园的退伍老兵，对需要教育、工作或住房帮助的负伤军人伸出援助之手。

奥巴马总统在国家安全方面取得的成就都归因于他的坚强力量，他的判断力，他摒弃党派之争的包容性和合作性。我们政府更需要这种作风。

众所周知，他也试图使国会中的共和党人在医疗保健、债务减免和新的就业机会方面进行合作，但障碍重重。这可能是因为，就像参议院共和党领袖在大选前两年直言不讳地说道，他们的首要任务不是使美国重返工作，而是使总统失去工作。好吧，等一下，参议员，我很抱歉把这个信息透露给你，但是我们要让奥巴马总统继续工作。

现在，大家准备好了吗？你愿意为之效劳吗。

在坦帕，你们都观看了大会了吗？

我看了。在坦帕，共和党反对总统连任的理由实际上非常简单、干脆。大意是这样的：我们共和党给总统留下了一个烂摊子，而他没有迅速地收拾好这个烂摊子。所以让他下，我们上！

但他们做得很好，看起来也不错，听起来也很好，由此使我相信，他们都爱自己的家庭和孩子，并为在美国出生而心怀感激，如此等等。说真的，我没有做到，他们做到了。

重要的是：他们让我相信，他们值得尊敬，他们相信自己所言并恪守承诺。我们只想让美国同胞知道，他们的承诺究竟是什么？因为他们为了看上去像一个令人满意、通情达理、沉着稳健的人选来取代奥巴马总统，两年来他们从没有过多地涉及他们许诺过的计划。

they've made. We just got to make sure the American people know what those commitments are – because in order to look like an acceptable, reasonable, moderate alternative to President Obama, they just didn't say very much about the ideas they've offered over the last two years.

They couldn't because they want to the same old policies that got us in trouble in the first place. They want to cut taxes for high- income Americans, even more than President Bush did. They want to get rid of those pesky financial regulations designed to prevent another crash and prohibit future bailouts. They want to actually increase defense spending over a decade $2 trillion more than the Pentagon has requested without saying what they'll spend it on. And they want to make enormous cuts in the rest of the budget, especially programs that help the middle class and poor children.

As another president once said, there they go again.

Now, I like – I like – I like the argument for President Obama's re-election a lot better. Here it is. He inherited a deeply damaged economy. He put a floor under the crash. He began the long, hard road to recovery and laid the foundation for a modern, more well- balanced economy that will produce millions of good new jobs, vibrant new businesses and lots of new wealth for innovators.

Now, are we where we want to be today? No.

Is the president satisfied? Of course not.

But are we better off than we were when he took office?

And listen to this. Listen to this. Everybody – when President Barack Obama took office, the economy was in free fall. It had just shrunk 9 full percent of GDP. We were losing 750,000 jobs a month.

Are we doing better than that today?

The answer is yes.

Now, look. Here's the challenge he faces and the challenge all of you who support him face. I get it. I know it. I've been there. A lot of Americans are

他们没有这样做是因为，他们打算保留那些当初使我们身陷囹圄的老政策。他们要对美国高收入者减税，动作幅度之大甚至超过了布什总统的水平。他们要取消那些麻烦的财政条款，而这些条款旨在预防新的灾难、禁止应急救援。他们把国防开支增加到每 10 年 2 万亿美元，比五角大楼要求的还多，但是却没有说明开支的来龙去脉；而且他们还要减少其他预算内开支，特别是那些帮助中产阶级和贫穷儿童的计划。

另外一位总统曾经说过，他们又老调重谈了。

我更加支持奥巴马连任。他接手了一个伤痕累累的经济，给经济崩溃设定了一个底线，开始了漫长而艰难的复苏之路，并为现代、平衡的经济模式奠定了基础，这一经济将创造数以万计的新的理想的就业机会，生机勃勃的新企业和创业者的丰厚利润。

现在，我们是否处达到了理想的境地？没有。

总统满意了吗？当然不满意。

但我们过得比他就任前要好么？

请注意，各位，当奥巴马总统就任时，经济正在不断下滑。GDP 萎缩了整整 9%。我们每个月都会失去 75 万份的就业机会。

我们现在有所起色吗？

答案是肯定的。

再看看他所面临的挑战，所有支持他的在座同僚所面临的挑战。我深有体会，我知道这种感觉，我曾经处在和他同样的位置上。许多美国人仍然对当前的经济愤怒不已、灰心丧气。但是如果你看一下这些数字，你会发现就业率正在增长，银行正在开始重新放贷。在很多地方，楼市开始回暖，只是很多人没有察觉罢了。

still angry and frustrated about this economy. If you look at the numbers, you know employment is growing, banks are beginning to lend again. And in a lot of places, housing prices are even beginning to pick up. But too many people do not feel it yet.

I had the same thing happen in 1994 and early '95. We could see that the policies were working, that the economy was growing. But most people didn't feel it yet. Thankfully, by 1996 the economy was roaring, everybody felt it, and we were halfway through the longest peacetime expansion in the history of the United States. But – wait, wait. The difference this time is purely in the circumstances. President Obama started with a much weaker economy than I did. Listen to me, now. No president – no president, not me, not any of my predecessors, no one could have fully repaired all the damage that he found in just four years.

Now – but – he has – he has laid the foundation for a new, modern, successful economy of shared prosperity. And if you will renew the president's contract, you will feel it. You will feel it.

Folks, whether the American people believe what I just said or not may be the whole election. I just want you to know that I believe it. With all my heart, I believe it.

Now, why do I believe it?

I'm fixing to tell you why. I believe it because President Obama's approach embodies the values, the ideas and the direction America has to take to build the 21st-century version of the American Dream: a nation of shared opportunities, shared responsibilities, shared prosperity, a shared sense of community.

So let's get back to the story. In 2010, as the president's recovery program kicked in, the job losses stopped and things began to turn around. The recovery act saved or created millions of jobs and cut taxes – let me say this again – cut taxes for 95 percent of the American people. And, in the last 29 m onths, our economy has produced about 4 1/2 million private sector jobs.

1994年和1995年初也出现过类似的情况，那时我们看到政策初见成效、经济开始增长，但大多数民众还没有察觉出来。值得庆幸的是，1996年的经济飞涨所有人都有了明显感觉，当时我们正处在美国历史上最长的平静发展的过程中。但是这次情况有所不同。奥巴马总统就职时，经济状况比我那时候疲软得多，请注意，没有任何一位总统，无论是我，还是我的前任总统们，没有人可以在短短四年中完全修补所有的创伤。

他却为一个崭新的、现代化的、成就显著经济的共同繁荣打下了坚实的基础。如果继续接纳他为总统，你一定会察觉得到这一切。

朋友们，无论美国人民是否相信与否，我只是想让你知道，我相信，我由衷地相信这一点。

为什么相信？

我告诉大家为什么。我相信，这是因为奥巴马总统的举措体现了建设21世纪"美国梦"的价值观、思想内涵和引领方向，即一个民族，能共享机遇，共担责任，共享繁荣，共有社会意识。

让我们回到刚才的话题。2010年，随着总统的复苏计划逐步展开，失业现象得到了遏制，情况日益好转。请允许我再重申一次，"复苏法案"挽救或创造了不计其数的就业机会并减轻了赋税，让95%的美国人民享受到减税福利。而且，在过去的29个月里，我们的经济已经创造了大约450万个私营企业就业岗位。

We could have done better, but last year the Republicans blocked the president's job plan, costing the economy more than a million new jobs.

So here's another job score. Obama: plus 4 1/2 million. Congressional Republicans: zero.

During this period – during this period, more than 500,000 manufacturing jobs have been created under President Obama. That's the first time manufacturing jobs have increased since the 1990s. And I'll tell you something else. The auto industry restructuring worked. It saved – it saved more than a million jobs, and not just at GM, Chrysler and their dealerships but in auto parts manufacturing all over the country.

That's why even the automakers who weren't part of the deal supported it. They needed to save those parts suppliers too. Like I said, we're all in this together. we're all in this together.

So what's happened? There are now 250,000 more people working in the auto industry than on the day the companies were restructured.

So – now, we all know that Governor Romney opposed the plan to save GM and Chrysler. So here's another job score. Are you listening in Michigan and Ohio and across the country? Here – here's another job score: Obama, 250,000; Romney, zero.

Now, the agreement the administration made with the management, labor and environmental groups to double car mileage, that was a good deal too. It will cut your gas prices in half, your gas bill. No matter what the price is, if you double the mileage of your car, your bill will be half what it would have been. It will make us more energy independent. It will cut greenhouse gas emissions. And according to several analyses, over the next 20 years, it'll bring us another half a million good new jobs into the American economy.

The president's energy strategy, which he calls "all of the above," is helping too. The boom in oil and gas production, combined with greater energy efficiency, has driven oil imports to a near-20- year low and natural gas

我们本可以做利益更出色，但是去年共和党阻碍了总统的就业计划，使我们的经济体损失了一百多万个新的就业机会。

所以，另一组就业比分。奥巴马总统：加450万个。国会共和党人：零个。

在奥巴马总统的领导下，增加了超过50万个制造业工作岗位，这是自20世纪90年代以来，制造业就业机会的首次增加。我还要告诉各位一件事，汽车产业重组也效果显著，它挽救了一百多万个就业机会，不仅限于通用、克莱斯勒和他们的经销商，还涉及全国各地的汽车零部件制造业。

这就是为什么整体汽车业之外的汽车制造商也支持这项举措，他们也需要挽救那些零部件供应商。就像我所说的，我们大家"共同担当，人人有份"。

发生了什么变化？现在从事汽车行业的工作人员比汽车行业开始重组时增加了25万人以上。

如今，大家都知道，罗姆尼州长反对拯救通用汽车公司和克莱斯勒汽车公司的计划。这就产生了另一个就业比分。你们是在密歇根州、俄亥俄州或是全国各地听我的讲话吗？那我公布成绩了：奥巴马，25万个，罗姆尼，零个。

近期，政府和管理部门，劳工部门与环保机构达成的有关增加汽车行驶里程的协议是很不错的，这将把你的油价减去一半，也就是把你的汽车油费砍掉一半。无论汽油价格如何，只要你把行驶里程增加一倍，你的油费账单就会享受半价优惠，这将使我们更少地依靠能源并减少温室气体排放。各种分析显示，在未来的20年里，它会给美国经济创造50万个新的就业机会。

总统的能源战略，也就是所谓的"重中之重"的策略，同样效果显著。蓬勃发展的石油和天然气生产，与提高能源效率相结合，使石油进口量达到了近20年来的最低点，也使天然气生产创下新高，再生能源产量增加了一倍。

production to an all-time high. And renewable energy production has doubled.

Of course, we need a lot more new jobs. But there are already more than 3 million jobs open and unfilled in America, mostly because the people who apply for them don't yet have the required skills to do them. So even as we get Americans more jobs, we have to prepare more Americans for the new jobs that are actually going to be created. The old economy is not coming back. We've got to build a new one and educate people to do those jobs.

The president – the president and his education secretary have supported community colleges and employers in working together to train people for jobs that are actually open in their communities – and even more important after a decade in which exploding college costs have increased the dropout rate so much that the percentage of our young people with four-year college degrees has gone down so much that we have dropped to 16th in the world in the percentage of young people with college degrees.

So the president's student loan is more important than ever. Here's what it does – here's what it does. You need to tell every voter where you live about this. It lowers the cost of federal student loans. And even more important, it give students the right to repay those loans as a clear, fixed, low percentage of their income for up to 20 years.

Now what does this mean? What does this mean? Think of it. It means no one will ever have to drop out of college again for fear they can't repay their debt.

And it means – it means that if someone wants to take a job with a modest income, a teacher, a police officer, if they want to be a small-town doctor in a little rural area, they won't have to turn those jobs down because they don't pay enough to repay they debt. Their debt obligation will be determined by their salary. This will change the future for young America.

I don't know about you, but on all these issues, I know we're better off because President Obama made the decisions he did.

当然，我们需要大量新的就业机会。但是美国现在已经有超过3万个空闲就业岗位，无人填补，主要是由于申请者的工作技能不足。因此，即使我们给美国人更多的就业机会，我们也必须为这些新岗位准备更多、更充足的人才储备。旧经济一去不复返，我们必须建立一个新经济，并为这些新岗位培训更多的人才。

社区学院和雇主同心协力，为社区的空缺岗位培训人才，为此总统和教育部长给予有力的支持。十年来大学学费的暴涨使得辍学率猛增，导致具有四年全日制大学学位的年轻人的比例已经大幅度下降，拥有大学学历的年轻人比例已跌至世界第16位。

所以，总统下拨的助学贷款比以往任何时候都更重要。请各位告诉你们地区的每一位选民助学贷款的重要作用。它可以减少联邦学生贷款的成本，更重要的是，它赋予学生一种权利，使他们能在20年里，用他们明确、固定和一少部分的收入来偿还贷款。

这将意味着什么？这将意味着没有人会因担心无力还债而从大学辍学。

这将意味着，如果有人想去从事一份中等收入的工作，例如教师、警察，如果他们想成为一个农村地区小镇的医生，他们不会因为无法偿还债务而推掉这些工作。他们的还债额度将取决于他们的工资，这将改变全美国年轻人的前途。

我不知道各位的想法如何，但就这些问题而言，我认为，奥巴马总统的决定，会让我们过得更好。

Now, that brings me to health care. And the Republicans call it, derisively, "Obamacare." They say it's a government takeover, a disaster, and that if we'll just elect them, they'll repeal it. Well, are they right?

Let's take a look at what's actually happened so far.

First, individuals and businesses have already gotten more than a billion dollars in refunds from insurance companies because the new law requires 80 (percent) to 85 percent of your premium to go to your health care, not profits or promotion. And the gains are even greater than that because a bunch of insurance companies have applied to lower their rates to comply with the requirement.

Second, more than 3 million young people between 19 and 25 are insured for the first time because their parents' policies can cover them.

Millions of seniors are receiving preventive care, all the way from breast cancer screenings to tests for heart problems and scores of other things. And younger people are getting them, too.

Fourth, soon the insurance companies – not the government, the insurance companies – will have millions of new customers, many of them middle-class people with pre-existing conditions who never could get insurance before.

Now, finally, listen to this. For the last two years – after going up at three times the rate of inflation for a decade, for the last two years health care costs have been under 4 percent in both years for the first time in 50 years.

So let me ask you something. Are we better off because President Obama fought for health care reform? You bet we are.

Now, there were two other attacks on the president in Tampa I think deserve an answer. First, both Governor Romney and Congressman Ryan attacked the president for allegedly robbing Medicare of $716 billion. That's the same attack they leveled against the Congress in 2010, and they got a lot of votes on it. But it's not true.

Look, here's what really happened. You be the judge. Here's what really

现在让这我谈谈健康保险问题。共和党人讥讽它为"奥巴马保险"。说这是一种政府接管，一种灾难。如果我们选了他们，他们会废除它。嗯，他们对不对呢？

让我们来看看到目前为止究竟发生了什么事情。

首先，个人和企业都已经从保险公司得到了超过10亿美元的退款，因为新法律要求把80％到85％的保费必须用在医疗保健上，而不能用作利润和促销经费。很多保险公司为此申请降低保费以便符合规定的要求，这使我们受益更多。

第二，由于父母的健康保险政策对自身同样适用，300多万19至25岁的年轻人纷纷投保。

第三，数以百万计的老年人正在接受预防性护理，从乳腺癌筛检到心脏问题测试等等。年轻人也同样适用。

第四，很快保险公司，不是政府，而是保险公司，将会拥有百万计的新客户，他们是众多由于以前存在的情况而从未享受过医保的中产阶级。

最后，请各位注意，以通胀率3倍的速度上涨了10年的健康保险费用，近两年来已经在50年里首次连续两年保持在4％以下。

因此，让我问各位一个问题。奥巴马总统争取医疗改革是不是让我们的日子更好呢？当然是更好。

现在，还有两项在坦帕对总统的攻击应该给予回应。首先，罗姆尼州长和众议员瑞安攻击总统，说他剥夺了医疗保险的7160亿美元。这一次和在2010年对国会的攻击如出一辙，那一次他们为此赢得了了很多选票。但事实并非如此 。

happened. There were no cuts to benefits at all. None. What the president did was to save money by taking the recommendations of a commission of professionals to cut unwarranted subsidies to providers and insurance companies that were not making people healthier and were not necessary to get the providers to provide the service.

And instead of raiding Medicare, he used the savings to close the doughnut hole in the Medicare drug program – and – you all got to listen carefully to this; this is really important – and to add eight years to the life of the Medicare trust fund so it is solvent till 2024.

So – so President Obama and the Democrats didn't weaken Medicare; they strengthened Medicare. Now, when Congressman Ryan looked into that TV camera and attacked President Obama's Medicare savings as, quote, the biggest, coldest power play, I didn't know whether to laugh or cry – because that $716 billion is exactly, to the dollar, the same amount of Medicare savings that he has in his own budget. You got to get one thing – it takes some brass to attack a guy for doing what you did.

So – now, you're having a good time, but this is getting serious, and I want you to listen. It's important, because a lot of people believe this stuff.

Now, at least on this issue, on this one issue, Governor Romney has been consistent. He attacked President Obama too, but he actually wants to repeal those savings and give the money back to the insurance company.

He wants to go back to the old system, which means we'll reopen the doughnut hole and force seniors to pay more for drugs, and we'll reduce the life of the Medicare trust fund by eight full years.

So if he's elected, and if he does what he promised to do, Medicare will now grow (sic/go) broke in 2016. Think about that. That means, after all, we won't have to wait until their voucher program kicks in 2023 – to see the end of Medicare as we know it. They're going to do it to us sooner than we thought.

Now, folks, this is serious, because it gets worse. And you won't be

以下才是事实的真相，请你们来裁决，事实真相是，这项福利根本没有削减。从来没有。总统采纳专业委员会的建议，通过削减对某些医疗服务供应商和保险公司不必要的补贴，因为这些补贴往往适得其反、百无一用，最终达到节约开支的目的。

总统不但没有打击医疗保险，而且还用上述节省下来的钱弥补了医疗保险处方药计划里的差价，请各位听清楚，最重要的是他让医疗保险信托基金延长了8年，从而有能力在2024年之前偿还债务。

所以奥巴马总统和民主党人并没有削减老人医疗保险，相反却巩固了医保的地位。如今，当众议员莱恩在电视上攻击奥巴马总统医疗保险的节省预算为"冷酷无情的权力游戏"时，我真是哭笑不得，因为那7160亿美元正是他自己预算中的节约医疗保险的那部分。你应该清楚，拿你自己做的事情去攻击他人是毫无用处的。

各位现在心情不错，但是接下来的话题会很严肃，请大家注意听，这很重要，因为很多人相信这一套。

至少在这个问题上，罗姆尼州长是始终如一的。他也攻击奥巴马总统，但他希望废除那些节约的开支，把钱归还给保险公司。

他想重蹈覆辙，这意味着我们将重新恢复医疗保险处方药计划的差价漏洞，逼着老年人花更多的钱来支付药物，这样我们将使老人医疗保险信托基金缩短整整8年。

所以，如果他当选，并兑现他的诺言，医疗保险将在2016年破产，大家想想，这意味着，我们等不到他们的"医保优惠券计划"在2023年起步，就将看到我们熟悉的医疗保险寿终正寝了。他们做到这一点的速度要超乎我们的想象。

laughing when I finish telling you this. They also want to block-grant Medicaid, and cut it by a third over the coming 10 years.

Of course, that's going to really hurt a lot of poor kids. But that's not all. Lot of folks don't know it, but nearly two-thirds of Medicaid is spent on nursing home care for Medicare seniors – who are eligible for Medicaid.

It's going to end Medicare as we know it. And a lot of that money is also spent to help people with disabilities, including – a lot of middle-class families whose kids have Down's syndrome or autism or other severe conditions. And honestly, let's think about it, if that happens, I don't know what those families are going to do.

So I know what I'm going to do. I'm going to do everything I can to see that it doesn't happen. We can't let it happen. We can't. Now – wait a minute. Let's look –

Let's look at the other big charge the Republicans made. It's a real doozy. They actually have charged and run ads saying that President Obama wants to weaken the work requirements in the welfare reform bill I signed that moved millions of people from welfare to work. Wait, you need to know, here's what happened. Nobody ever tells you what really happened – here's what happened.

When some Republican governors asked if they could have waivers to try new ways to put people on welfare back to work, the Obama administration listened because we all know it's hard for even people with good work histories to get jobs today. So moving folks from welfare to work is a real challenge.

And the administration agreed to give waivers to those governors and others only if they had a credible plan to increase employment by 20 percent, and they could keep the waivers only if they did increase employment. Now, did I make myself clear? The requirement was for more work, not less.

So this is personal to me. We moved millions of people off welfare. It was one of the reasons that in the eight years I was president, we had a hundred times as many people move out of poverty into the middle class than happened

192

朋友们，事态严重，情况每况愈下。等我把下面的话讲完，大家就笑不出口了。他们，还想阻止医疗补助，在未来十年削减三分之一。

当然，这对贫困儿童无疑是雪上加霜，但这只是一部分。可能很多人还不知道，有将近三分之二的医疗补助是花费在养老院上，为有资格获得医疗补助的老年人提供护理。

众所周知，这些要被他们废除的医疗保险，受益群体很大一部分是伤残人士，包括唐氏综合症患者、自闭症患者或者有其他严重疾病的中产阶级家庭。实话说，如果这种情况真的发生，我不敢设想这些家庭该何去何从。

所以我很清楚我下一步要做什么，我要竭尽全力来阻止它，绝不能让这种事情发生，我们不能。真的不能这样。

让我们再看看共和党人所做的另外一项指控，这真可谓是无稽之谈。但是他们确实指控了，还打出广告说，奥巴马总统要放松由我签署的福利改革法案中的工作要求，这个福利法案曾动员了千百万接受福利的人外出工作。各位同仁，你们需要知道真相，从来没有人告诉你们究竟发生了什么。事情是这样的。

一些共和党州长询问，如果他们尝试一些新的方法动员一些拿福利的人出去工作，是否可以得到一些豁免。奥巴马政府听取了这些意见，因为我们都知道，即使具有良好工作履历的人，如今也很难找到工作。动员拿福利的人出去工作更是一种真正的挑战。

政府同意给予这些州长和其他人一些豁免，只要他们拿得出可信度高的规划来增加20%的就业率，如果他们真的做到了，他们可以保持豁免。现在，各位明白了吧？条件是创造更多的就业，而非更少。

under the previous 12 years, a hundred times as many. It's a big deal. But I am telling you the claim that President Obama weakened welfare reform's work requirement is just not true.

But they keep on running the ads claiming it. You want to know why? Their campaign pollster said, we are not going to let our campaign be dictated by fact-checkers. Now, finally I can say, that is true. I – I couldn't have said it better myself.

And I hope you and every American within the sound of my voice remembers it every time they see one of those ads, and it turns into an ad to re-elect Barack Obama and keep the fundamental principles of personal empowerment and moving everybody who can get a job into work as soon as we can.

Now, let's talk about the debt. Today, interest rates are low, lower than the rate of inflation. People are practically paying us to borrow money, to hold their money for them.

But it will become a big problem when the economy grows and interest rates start to rise. We've got to deal with this big long- term debt problem or it will deal with us. It will gobble up a bigger and bigger percentage of the federal budget we'd rather spend on education and health care and science and technology. It – we've got to deal with it.

Now, what has the president done? He has offered a reasonable plan of $4 trillion in debt reduction over a decade, with 2 1/2 trillion (dollars) coming from – for every $2 1/2 trillion in spending cuts, he raises a dollar in new revenues – 2 1/2-to-1. And he has tight controls on future spending. That's the kind of balanced approach proposed by the Simpson-Bowles Commission, a bipartisan commission.

Now, I think this plan is way better than Governor Romney's plan. First, the Romney plan failed the first test of fiscal responsibility. The numbers just don't add up.

这是我个人的亲身经历，我们使千百万人摆脱了最低福利。这就是为什么，在我担任总统的八年中，摆脱了贫困进入了中产阶级的人数是前十二年的一百倍。这是个壮举，但我告诉你，说奥巴马总统放松了福利改革计划的工作要求不是事实。

但是，他们一直在做广告散布这些言论。想知道为什么吗？他们的竞选民意测验专家说："我们不会让我们的竞选活动接受事实调查员的摆布。"现在，我终于可以说，这是事实真相，这真是恰如其分。

我希望你们和每一个能听到我声音的美国人都记住，每次他们看到这种广告时，就把它换成巴拉克·奥巴马连任的广告，并保持个人权力的基本原则，尽快地动员所有能找到工作的人投入工作。

让我们来谈谈债务问题。如今，利率很低，低于通胀率，人们实际上是付钱给我们借贷，来让我们替他们保管钱财。

但是，当经济增长，利率上升，它就会成为棘手的难题。我们必须处理这个长期债务的难题，否则适得其反，它会吞噬掉越来越多的联邦预算。这部分的钱本来可以花在教育、医疗保健和科技方面，这是我们必须处理的问题。

现在，总统做了什么呢？他提供了一个合理的计划，用10年的工夫削减4万亿美元的债务，每削减2.5万亿美元的开支，他就设法增加1美元的新收入，2.5万亿比1万，并且，他严格控制预算支出。这就是两党联合委员会，辛普森和鲍尔斯委员会，提出的一种平衡的方式。

我觉得这个计划比罗姆尼州长的计划更好。首先，罗姆尼的计划就无法通过财政责任的第一个考验，这些数字就无法合计到一起。

I mean, consider this. What would you do if you had this problem? Somebody says, oh, we've got a big debt problem. We've got to reduce the debt. So what's the first thing you say we're going to do? Well, to reduce the debt, we're going to have another $5 trillion in tax cuts heavily weighted to upper-income people. So we'll make the debt hole bigger before we start to get out of it.

Now, when you say, what are you going to do about this $5 trillion you just added on? They say, oh, we'll make it up by eliminating loopholes in the tax code.

So then you ask, well, which loopholes, and how much?

You know what they say? See me about that after the election.

I'm not making it up. That's their position. See me about that after the election.

Now, people ask me all the time how we got four surplus budgets in a row. What new ideas did we bring to Washington? I always give a one-word answer: Arithmetic.

If – arithmetic! If – if they stay with their $5 trillion tax cut plan – in a debt reduction plan? – the arithmetic tells us, no matter what they say, one of three things is about to happen. One, assuming they try to do what they say they'll do, get rid of – pay – cover it by deductions, cutting those deductions, one, they'll have to eliminate so many deductions, like the ones for home mortgages and charitable giving, that middle-class families will see their tax bills go up an average of $2,000 while anybody who makes $3 million or more will see their tax bill go down $250,000.

Or, two, they'll have to cut so much spending that they'll obliterate the budget for the national parks, for ensuring clean air, clean water, safe food, safe air travel. They'll cut way back on Pell Grants, college loans, early childhood education, child nutrition programs, all the programs that help to empower middle-class families and help poor kids. Oh, they'll cut back on investments in roads and bridges and science and technology and biomedical research. That's what they'll

我的意思是，请大家思考这个问题。如果你面对这个问题，你会怎么做？有人说，哦，我们已经有了一个巨大的债务问题，我们必须减少负债。我们要做的第一件事是什么？好的，为了减少债务，我们对高收入人士再大幅削减5万亿美元的税。所以，在我们摆脱债务以前，我们先扩大这个债务漏洞。

那么，你说你打算如何处理刚加上去的这5万亿美元怎么办呢？他们说："哦，我们会通过消除税务规定中的漏洞来弥补。"

那么你会问，好了，是哪些漏洞，有多少？

你知道他们说什么？选举以后再来找我。

我不是捏造出来的。这就是他们的态度。选举以后再来找我。

现在，人们总是问我，我们怎么会一连得到四个盈余预算。我给政府提了什么新点子？我的答案就两个字：算术。

如果他们在削减债务的计划里，坚持他们的5万亿美元的减税计划，算术告诉我们，不管他们说什么，以下三种情况中的一种就会发生。第一，假设他们竭尽全力实现他们的承诺，通过克扣减免来支付，他们必须克扣许多减免，例如住房抵押贷款和慈善捐助，中产阶级家庭的税款每人将会上涨大概2000美元，而收入300万以上的人们的赋税却下降了25万美元。

第二，他们必须通过减少国家公园建设预算、空气净化预算、水源清洁预算，食品安全预算、航空安全预算等各种方式来削减大额开支。他们会大大削减佩尔助学金、大学贷款、儿童早期教育、儿童营养计划以及所有造福中产阶级家庭和贫穷儿童的计划。哦，他们还会削减对道路桥梁、科学技术和生物医学研究的投资。这是他们要做的。他们要伤害中产阶级和穷人的利益，不顾未来，为的就是削减高收入人群的赋税，这些人其实一直在享受这方面的优惠。

do. They'll hurt the middle class and the poor and put the future on hold to give tax cuts to upper-income people who've been getting it all along. That's what they'll do. They'll hurt the middle class and the poor and put the future on hold to give tax cuts to upper-income people who've been getting it all along.

Or three, in spite of all the rhetoric, they'll just do what they've been doing for more than 30 years. They'll go in and cut the taxes way more than they cut spending, especially with that big defense increase, and they'll just explode the debt and weaken the economy. And they'll destroy the federal government's ability to help you by letting interest gobble up all your tax payments.

Don't you ever forget when you hear them talking about this that Republican economic policies quadrupled the national debt before I took office, in the 12 years before I took office – and doubled the debt in the eight years after I left, because it defied arithmetic. It was a highly inconvenient thing for them in our debates that I was just a country boy from Arkansas, and I came from a place where people still thought two and two was four. It's arithmetic.

We simply cannot afford to give the reins of government to someone who will double down on trickle down. Really. Think about this: President Obama – President Obama's plan cuts the debt, honors our values, brightens the future of our children, our families and our nation. It's a heck of a lot better.

It passes the arithmetic test, and far more important, it passes the values test.

My fellow Americans, all of us in this grand hall and everybody watching at home, when we vote in this election, we'll be deciding what kind of country we want to live in. If you want a winner-take-all, you're-on-your-own society, you should support the Republican ticket. But if you want a country of shared opportunities and shared responsibility, a we're-all-in-this-together society, you should vote for Barack Obama and Joe Biden. If you – if you want –

If you want America – if you want every American to vote and you think it is wrong to change voting procedures – just to reduce the turnout of younger,

第三，不管他们说什么花言巧语，这些都是他们肯定会做的，30多年来始终如一。他们一脚插进来并大力削减税收却不削减开支，尤其是由于国防开支的大幅增加使他们的债务急速膨胀，经济实力由此削弱。他们将让利息一口口吞下大家的全部税款，联邦政府的救助能力因此毁于一旦。

请各位永远不要忘记：在我上任以前的12年里，共和党的经济政策使国家债务翻了四倍，在我卸任以后的8年里，债务增加了一倍，因为他们不会算术。在我们进行辩论时，这对他们来说相当不利，因为我只是一个来自阿肯色州的乡下男孩，在我的家乡，人们仍然认为2加2等于4。这是算术。

让这样的人来掌握政府大权，我们担当不起后果。对于本已岌岌可危的资源，他们用起来却大手大脚。各位想想：奥巴马总统削减债务、尊重我们的劳动所得，给我们的孩子、家庭和国家绘制了一个光明的蓝图。这才是一个更好的计划。

它可以通过算术检测，更为重要的是，它可以通过价值观的检测。

美国同胞们，所有在这个大厅里的与会代表，和每一个在家里收看大会的人们，当我们投下神圣的一票，我们将决定自己要在怎样的国家里生活。如果你想要一个胜者为王、"自靠自，自顾自"的社会，请你支持共和党。但是，如果你想有一个机遇共享和责任共担的国家，一个大家共同担待、人人有份的社会，请你把票投给奥巴马和拜登。

如果你希望每一个美国人都有平等的投票权，如果你认为，为减少年轻、贫穷、少数民族和残疾选民的投票率而改变投票程序的做法是错误的，那么你就应该把票投给巴拉克·奥巴马。

poorer, minority and disabled voters – you should support Barack Obama.

And if you think – if you think the president was right to open the doors of American opportunity to all those young immigrants brought here when they were young so they can serve in the military or go to college, you must vote for Barack Obama. If you want a future of shared prosperity, where the middle class is growing and poverty is declining, where the American dream is really alive and well again and where the United States maintains its leadership as a force for peace and justice and prosperity in this highly competitive world, you have to vote for Barack Obama.

Look, I love our country so much. And I know we're coming back. For more than 200 years, through every crisis, we've always come back. People have predicted our demise ever since George Washington was criticized for being a mediocre surveyor with a bad set of wooden false teeth. And so far, every single person that's bet against America has lost money because we always come back. We come through ever fire a little stronger and a little better.

And we do it because in the end we decide to champion the cause for which our founders pledged their lives, their fortunes, their sacred honor – the cause of forming a more perfect union. My fellow Americans, if that is what you want, if that is what you believe, you must vote and you must re-elect President Barack Obama.

God bless you and God bless America.

Charlotte, North Carolina, September, 5, 2012

如果你认为，总统对所有来到了美国的年轻移民打开了一扇扇机会之门，让他们可以在军队服役，可以去上大学，你就必须投奥巴马的票。如果你想要拥有一个共同繁荣，一个中产阶层的能够发展壮大，贫困人口得以减少的未来，一个"美国梦"能够成为现实的未来，一个能够让美国作为一支维护和平、正义和繁荣的力量，在这个竞争激烈的世界里保持领导地位的未来，那么你就必须投奥巴马的票。

看，我是如此地热爱祖国，坚信我们可以重振雄风。两百多年以来，经过重重的危机，我们总能重归繁荣。乔治·华盛顿是一个戴着一口蹩脚木制假牙的平庸勘探师，受到人们的批评，从那以后，人们一直预言我们会灭亡。到目前为止，每一个打赌美国会失败的人都输了，因为我们总是能够重振旗鼓。我们经过重重烈火的考验，变得更加坚强，更加进步。

我们这样做，是因为我们决心捍卫我们的事业，一个我们的先驱用他们的生命、他们的命运、他们的神圣荣誉来捍卫的事业，一个建立更加完美国度的事业。我的美国同胞们，如果这就是你想要的，如果这就是你所信仰的，那么你就必须拿起选票，再一次把这一票投给奥巴马总统！

愿上帝保佑你们，愿上帝保佑美利坚合众国！

（杜梦臻/译　袁婧/校）

The First Obama–Romney Presidential Debate

Jim Lehrer: Good evening from the Magness Arena at the University of Denver in Denver, Colorado. I'm Jim Lehrer of the PBS NewsHour, and I welcome you to the first of the 2012 presidential debates between President Barack Obama, the Democratic nominee, and former Massachusetts Governor Mitt Romney, the Republican nominee.

This debate and the next three – two presidential, one vice- presidential – are sponsored by the Commission on Presidential Debates.

Tonight's 90 minutes will be about domestic issues, and will follow a format designed by the commission. There will be six roughly 15-minute segments, with two-minute answers for the first question, then open discussion for the remainder of each segment.

Thousands of people offered suggestions on segment subjects of questions via the Internet and other means, but I made the final selections, and for the record, they were not submitted for approval to the commission or the candidates.

The segments, as I announced in advance, will be three on the economy and one each on health care, the role of government, and governing, with an emphasis throughout on differences, specifics and choices. Both candidates will also have two-minute closing statements.

The audience here in the hall has promised to remain silent. No cheers, applause, boos, hisses – among other noisy distracting things – so we may all concentrate on what the candidates have to say. There is a noise exception right

奥巴马—罗姆尼第一场电视辩论 ①

吉姆·莱勒： 我在科罗拉多州丹佛市的丹佛大学马格尼斯竞技场向大家说声晚安。我是美国公共广播公司《新闻时间》节目主持人吉姆·莱勒。欢迎大家参与2012年总统大选首场辩论会，今天辩论双方是民主党候选人、现任总统巴拉克·奥巴马和共和党候选人、前马萨诸塞州州长米特·罗姆尼。

本场以及后面的三场辩论——两场总统辩论和一场副总统辩论——由总统辩论委员会赞助。

今天晚上的90分钟辩论将围绕国内议题并遵守总统辩论委员设计的模式，分为六部分，各约15分钟，在每个部分里，辩论双方各花两分钟回答第一个问题，然后就该部分的其余问题进行自由辩论。

数千人通过因特网和其他方式对每个部分的主题提出了建议，但是，由我做出最终选择。在此我声明，这些议题并未提交辩论委员会或候选人筛选。

提前声明，有三个部分是关于经济的议题，其余三个议题分别是关于医疗服务、政府职能和执政重点的。每个部分都会强调辩论双方的不同意见、具体想法和政策选择。辩论双方还将各有两分钟的总结发言。

现场观众承诺保持鸦雀无声。辩论时不要有喝彩、掌声、嘘声以及其他分散注意力的噪声，确保大家能够把注意力集中在候选人的发言上。不过，现在可以有一个例外，让我们热烈欢迎奥巴马总统和罗姆尼州长。

---

① 美国2012年总统大选首场辩论10月3日在科罗拉多州丹佛大学举行。美国总统奥巴马和共和党总统候选人罗姆尼首次电视辩论以经济和医改为主展开交锋此次辩论未触及外交，主要侧重医改、就业、纳税和联邦政府角色等内政议题。罗姆尼作为"挑战者"暂时赢得首场总统候选人辩论。

now, though, as we welcome President Obama and Governor Romney.

Gentlemen, welcome to you both.

Let's start the economy, segment one. And let's begin with jobs. What are the major differences between the two of you about how you would go about creating new jobs? You have two minutes – each of you have two minutes to start. The coin toss has determined, Mr. President, you go first.

Obama: Well, thank you very much, Jim, for this opportunity. I want to thank Governor Romney and the University of Denver for your hospitality.

There are a lot of points that I want to make tonight, but the most important one is that 20 years ago I became the luckiest man on earth because Michelle Obama agreed to marry me. (Laughter.) And so I just want to wish, Sweetie, you happy anniversary and let you know that a year from now, we will not be celebrating it in front of 40 million people.

You know, four years ago we went through the worst financial crisis since the Great Depression. Millions of jobs were lost. The auto industry was on the brink of collapse. The financial system had frozen up. And because of the resilience and the determination of the American people, we've begun to fight our way back.

Over the last 30 months, we've seen 5 million jobs in the private sector created. The auto industry has come roaring back and housing has begun to rise. But we all know that we've still got a lot of work to do. And so the question here tonight is not where we've been but where we're going. Governor Romney has a perspective that says if we cut taxes, skewed towards the wealthy, and roll back regulations that we'll be better off.

I've got a different view. I think we've got to invest in education and training. I think it's important for us to develop new sources of energy here in America, that we change our tax code to make sure that we're helping small businesses and companies that are investing here in the United States, that we take some of the money that we're saving as we wind down two wars to rebuild

欢迎你们，两位先生！

现在开始第一部分，辩论经济议题，关于如何创造就业机会，两位有什么不同看法？你们都将有两分钟的时间陈述自己观点。根据抽签顺序，您先请，总统先生。

奥巴马：好的。谢谢你给我这个机会，吉姆。我还想感谢罗姆尼州长和丹佛大学的热情。

今晚我想说的很多，但其中最重要的一点，就是20年前米歇尔·奥巴马同意嫁给我，使我成为世界上最幸运的人。因此，亲爱的，我只想祝你结婚纪念日快乐，并想告诉你：一年以后的今天，我们将不会再在4000万众目睽睽之下庆祝我们的纪念日。

大家知道，我们在四年前经历了大萧条以来最严重的金融危机，丧失了数以百万计的工作机会，汽车工业濒临崩溃，整个金融系统已经冻结。但是，由于美国人民乐观向上、坚定不移，我们已经开始起死回生。

在过去的30个月里，我们在私营领域创造了500万份工作，汽车行业恢复迅速，房地产业有所起色，但我们都知道还需要付出许多的努力，因此今晚的问题不是回首过去，而是展望未来。罗姆尼州长认为，如果我们减少税收、倾向于富人、减少规章制度，我们的情况就会好转。

我的看法则有所不同，我认为要投资教育和培训，有必要开拓国内新能源；有必要改变税收政策，为投资美国的小企业提供帮助；有必要把结束两场战争省下来的一部分钱用于重建美国；同时也有必要通过平衡的方式减少赤字，以此来确保我们能够进行重要的投资。

America and that we reduce our deficit in a balanced way that allows us to make these critical investments.

Now, it ultimately is going to be up to the voters, to you, which path we should take. Are we going to double down on the top-down economic policies that helped to get us into this mess, or do we embrace a new economic patriotism that says, America does best when the middle class does best? And I'm looking forward to having that debate.

Lehrer: Governor Romney, two minutes.

Romney: Thank you, Jim. It's an honor to be here with you, and I appreciate the chance to be with the president. I am pleased to be at the University of Denver, appreciate their welcome and also the presidential commission on these debates.

And congratulations to you, Mr. President, on your anniversary. I'm sure this was the most romantic place you could imagine here – here with me, so I – congratulations.

This is obviously a very tender topic. I've had the occasion over the last couple of years of meeting people across the country. I was in Dayton, Ohio, and a woman grabbed my arm, and she said, "I've been out of work since May. Can you help me?"

Ann yesterday was a rally in Denver, and a woman came up to her with a baby in her arms and said, Ann, my husband has had four jobs in three years, part-time jobs. He's lost his most recent job, and we've now just lost our home. Can you help us?

And the answer is yes, we can help, but it's going to take a different path, not the one we've been on, not the one the president describes as a top-down, cut taxes for the rich. That's not what I'm going to do.

My plan has five basic parts. One, get us energy independent, North American energy independent. That creates about four million jobs. Number two, open up more trade, particularly in Latin America; crack down on China if and

现在，我们要走哪条道路，最终要由选举人、在座的你们来决定。我们是要加速跑向那些使我们陷入经济危机的自上而下的经济政策，还是要拥护那种"中产阶级强则美国强"的新的经济爱国主义呢？我十分期待这个辩论。

莱勒：吉姆罗姆尼州长，你有两分钟时间。

罗姆尼：谢谢你，吉姆，很荣幸与你在这里，并有机会和总统进行辩论。我很高兴来到丹佛大学，感谢你们的欢迎，同时也感谢总统委员会举办这次辩论会。

我也对您的结婚纪念日表示祝贺，总统先生。您和我在一起，我相信这是您能想象到的最浪漫的地方了，所以我——祝贺您。

显而易见，这是一个敏感的话题，在过去的几年里，我在全国各地和人们进行交流，在俄亥俄州代顿市的时候，一个妇女抓住我的手臂说："我从5月以来一直失业，你能帮帮我吗？"

昨天我的妻子安在丹佛参加集会，一个抱着孩子的妇女走过来说："我丈夫三年做了四份兼职，他现在失业了，我们刚刚无家可归，你能帮帮我们吗？"

答案是肯定的，我们能帮得上忙，但方式与以往大径相庭，它也不是总统所说的那种自上而下的、为富人减税的方式，这不是我的计划。

我的计划包含五个部分：第一，实现能源独立，北美地区能源独立，这可以创造400万个工作机会；第二，开放更多的贸易，尤其是在拉美地区；如果中国有欺诈行为，我们就予以制裁；第三，确保我们的民众有赖以成功的技能并拥有世界上最好的学校，现在我们相差甚远；第四，实现预算平衡；第五，支持小企业。

when they cheat. Number three, make sure our people have the skills they need to succeed and the best schools in the world. We're far away from that now. Number four, get us to a balanced budget. Number five, champion small business.

It's small business that creates the jobs in America. And over the last four years small-business people have decided that America may not be the place to open a new business, because new business startups are down to a 30-year low. I know what it takes to get small business growing again, to hire people.

Now, I'm concerned that the path that we're on has just been unsuccessful. The president has a view very similar to the view he had when he ran four years ago, that a bigger government, spending more, taxing more, regulating more – if you will, trickle-down government would work. That's not the right answer for America. I'll restore the vitality that gets America working again.

Thank you.

Lehrer: Mr. President, please respond directly to what the governor just said about trickle-down – his trickle-down approach. He's – as he said yours is.

Obama: Well, let me talk specifically about what I think we need to do.

First, we've got to improve our education system. And we've made enormous progress drawing on ideas both from Democrats and Republicans that are already starting to show gains in some of the toughest-to- deal-with schools. We've got a program called Race to the Top that has prompted reforms in 46 states around the country, raising standards, improving how we train teachers. So now I want to hire another hundred thousand new math and science teachers and create 2 million more slots in our community colleges so that people can get trained for the jobs that are out there right now. And I want to make sure that we keep tuition low for our young people.

When it comes to our tax code, Governor Romney and I both agree that our corporate tax rate is too high. So I want to lower it, particularly for manufacturing, taking it down to 25 percent. But I also want to close those loopholes that are giving incentives for companies that are shipping jobs

在美国，创造就业机会的是小企业。在过去四年中，小企业经营者已经认为美国或许不适合开展新业务，因为创业率已经到了30年来的新低水准，而我知道如何让小企业重获发展、雇佣员工。

现在，我们的道路是不成功的，我为此感到担忧。总统的观点与他四年前竞选时的观点大同小异，那就是大政府、多消费、多征税以及多管制——只要你想，这个滴涓式的政府就会奏效，但这些并不能很好地适用于美国。我将会让美国恢复活力，重振雄风。

谢谢大家。

莱勒：总统先生，请您直接回应州长刚才所说的滴涓式政府的言论。他说，你的方式是滴涓式。

奥巴马：好，我来具体谈谈我需要做的事情。

首先，要改善教育体系。通过吸收民主党人和共和党人的意见，我们已取得巨大的进步，已开始在学校教育中最困难的部分取得成果。我们已经有一个名叫"力争上游"的计划，该计划推动全国46个州进行改革，提高标准并改善训练教师的方法，现在，我想另外再聘请10万名新的数学和科技教师，在社区大学再创造200万个入学名额，以便让人们能够接受培训、应对工作，并且我还想确保年轻人的学费保持低位。

关于我们的税收政策，我和罗姆尼州长都认为我们的企业税过高，尤其是在制造业方面，因此我想把它降低到25%。但是我也想解决那些漏洞，为那些把工作岗位转向海外的公司提供激励政策，为在美国投资的公司提供赋税减免。

overseas. I want to provide tax breaks for companies that are investing here in the United States.

On energy, Governor Romney and I, we both agree that we've got to boost American energy production.

And oil and natural gas production are higher than they've been in years. But I also believe that we've got to look at the energy source of the future, like wind and solar and biofuels, and make those investments.

So, all of this is possible. Now, in order for us to do it, we do have to close our deficit, and one of the things I'm sure we'll be discussing tonight is, how do we deal with our tax code, and how do we make sure that we are reducing spending in a responsible way, but also how do we have enough revenue to make those investments? And this is where there's a difference because Governor Romney's central economic plan calls for a $5 trillion tax cut, on top of the extension of the Bush tax cuts, so that's another trillion, and $2 trillion in additional military spending that the military hasn't asked for. That's $8 trillion. How we pay for that, reduce the deficit and make the investments that we need to make without dumping those costs on the middle-class Americans I think is one of the central questions of this campaign.

Lehrer: Both of you have spoken about a lot of different things, and we're going to try to get through them in as specific a way as we possibly can. But first, Governor Romney, do you have a question that you'd like to ask the president directly about something he just said?

Romney: Well, sure. I'd like to clear up the record and go through it piece by piece. First of all, I don't have a $5 trillion tax cut. I don't have a tax cut of a scale that you're talking about. My view is that we ought to provide tax relief to people in the middle class. But I'm not going to reduce the share of taxes paid by high- income people. High-income people are doing just fine in this economy. They'll do fine whether you're president or I am.

The people who are having the hard time right now are middle- income

关于能源问题，我和罗姆尼州长都同意要促进美国能源的生产。

石油和天然气产量这几年有所提高，但我也认为要把目光投向诸如风能、太阳能和生物能等新能源，并作出投资。

所以，一切皆有可能，为此必须减少赤字，所以，今晚无疑还要讨论如何处理税收政策，如何确保负责任地减少支出，如何有足够的收入来投资，这就是分歧所在，因为罗姆尼州长的主要经济方案是要减税5万亿美元，并延续布什政府的减税政策，这又是1万亿元，再加上2万亿美元的额外军费开支，这样总共就是8万亿美元。我们怎样支付这些钱，减少赤字、进行投资而不把这些支出分担到美国中产阶级呢？我想这是本次总统大选的核心问题之一。

莱勒：你们俩都谈到了许多不同之处，我们要设法把它们具体化，但首先，罗姆尼州长，就总统刚才说的一些事情，你有没有想直接问他的问题？

罗姆尼：当然有，我想清理一些记录，一段一段地进行。首先，我没有5万亿美元的减税计划，我没有你谈到的那种规模的减税计划，我的观点是，我们应该为中产阶级提供税额减免，但是我们不会减少高收入人群的纳税份额，高收入群体在这个经济体中表现良好，不管你当总统还是我当总统，他们都会表现良好。

Americans. Under the president's policies, middle-income Americans have been buried. They're – they're just being crushed. Middle-income Americans have seen their income come down by $4,300. This is a – this is a tax in and of itself. I'll call it the economy tax. It's been crushing. The same time, gasoline prices have doubled under the president, electric rates are up, food prices are up, health care costs have gone up by $2,500 a family.

Middle-income families are being crushed. And so the question is how to get them going again, and I've described it. It's energy and trade, the right kind of training programs, balancing our budget and helping small business. Those are the – the cornerstones of my plan.

But the president mentioned a couple of other ideas, and I'll just note: first, education. I agree, education is key, particularly the future of our economy. But our training programs right now, we got 47 of them housed in the federal government, reporting to eight different agencies. Overhead is overwhelming. We got to get those dollars back to the states and go to the workers so they can create their own pathways to getting the training they need for jobs that will really help them.

The second area: taxation. We agree; we ought to bring the tax rates down, and I do, both for corporations and for individuals. But in order for us not to lose revenue, have the government run out of money, I also lower deductions and credits and exemptions so that we keep taking in the same money when you also account for growth.

The third area: energy. Energy is critical, and the president pointed out correctly that production of oil and gas in the U.S. is up. But not due to his policies. In spite of his policies. Mr. President, all of the increase in natural gas and oil has happened on private land, not on government land. On government land, your administration has cut the number of permits and license in half. If I'm president, I'll double them. And also get the – the oil from offshore and Alaska. And I'll bring that pipeline in from Canada.

现在面临困境的是美国的中等收入群体。在总统的政策下，中等收入的美国人已经被埋葬了，他们——他们被压垮了，美国中产阶级的收入下降了4300美元，这本身就是一种税收，我称之为经济税，它压垮了中产阶级，同时在总统就任期间，汽油价格翻番、电费增加、食品价格上涨，每个家庭的医疗保险费用增加了2500美元。

中等收入家庭正被压垮。所以问题是如何让他们再次前行。我已经说过，要通过能源、贸易，还有正确的培训项目、平衡预算、帮助小企业，这些是我的计划的基石。

但是，总统提到其他几个想法，我要评论一下：首先是教育，我同意，教育是关键，特别是对于我们经济的未来发展，但是，我们现在的培训项目，其中47个由联邦政府管辖，向8个不同的机构汇报，日常管理费用大得惊人，我们应该把经费拨到各个州和员工的手里，使他们能够创造自己的道路来获得就业所需，真正对他们有所帮助。

第二个领域：税收，我们同意，我们应该把税率降下来，我认为企业税和个税都应该降，但是为了我们不失去税收，让政府有资金运行，我也赞成降低课税减免、课税抵免和课税豁免，以便我们能够获得相同数额的税收，同时经济也能够保持增长。

第三个领域：能源。能源至关重要，总统正确地指出了美国的石油和天然气产量正在增加，但这并不能归功于他的政策。也跟他的政策关系不大。总统先生，所有天然气和石油产量的增加都发生在私有土地上，而不是在政府土地上，在政府土地上，你的政府将许可和执照砍掉了一半。如果我是总统，我会让他们翻番，也会从近海和阿拉斯加开采石油，我会引进加拿大的石油管线。

And by the way, I like coal. I'm going to make sure we continue to burn clean coal. People in the coal industry feel like it's getting crushed by your policies. I want to get America and North America energy independent, so we can create those jobs.

And finally, with regards to that tax cut, look, I'm not looking to cut massive taxes and to reduce the – the revenues going to the government. My – my number one principle is there'll be no tax cut that adds to the deficit.

I want to underline that – no tax cut that adds to the deficit. But I do want to reduce the burden being paid by middle-income Americans. And I – and to do that that also means that I cannot reduce the burden paid by high-income Americans. So any – any language to the contrary is simply not accurate.

Lehrer: Mr. President.

Obama: Well, I think – let's talk about taxes because I think it's instructive. Now, four years ago when I stood on this stage I said that I would cut taxes for middle-class families. And that's exactly what I did. We cut taxes for middle-class families by about $3,600. And the reason is because I believe we do best when the middle class is doing well.

And by giving them those tax cuts, they had a little more money in their pocket and so maybe they can buy a new car. They are certainly in a better position to weather the extraordinary recession that we went through. They can buy a computer for their kid who's going off to college, which means they're spending more money, businesses have more customers, businesses make more profits and then hire more workers.

Now, Governor Romney's proposal that he has been promoting for 18 months calls for a $5 trillion tax cut on top of $2 trillion of additional spending for our military. And he is saying that he is going to pay for it by closing loopholes and deductions. The problem is that he's been asked a – over a hundred times how you would close those deductions and loopholes and he hasn't been able to identify them.

顺便说一下，我喜欢煤，我要确保我们继续使用洁净煤。煤炭产业的人们感觉这个行业被你的政策压垮了，我想要让美国和北美能源独立，这样我们能够创造一些工作机会。

最后，关于减税问题，看吧，我不指望大幅度减税，也不打算减少政府的税收。

我的首要原则是，减税不能增加赤字，我想要强调这一点——减税不能增加赤字，但是我确实想减轻美国中等收入家庭的负担，那么做也意味着我不能减轻美国高收入家庭的负担，所以任何与其相反的言论都是不准确的。

莱勒：总统先生。

奥巴马：好吧，我认为，我们就应该讨论一下税收问题，因为我认为它的确耐人寻味。四年前，当我站在这个舞台上，我说过我会为中产家庭减税，我确实做到了，我们为中产家庭减税近3600美元，因为我相信，当中产阶级日子好过的时候，我们的经济也表现最佳。

给他们减些税，他们就会有更多一点的钱，他们可能会买一辆新车。他们肯定能在我们经历的经济重大衰退期间过得更好一点。他们能为即将步入大学校门的孩子买一台电脑，这就意味着他们将会花更多的钱，企业将会有更多的客户，有更多的盈利，然后雇佣更多的工人。

现在，罗姆尼州长在过去的18个月里一直宣传的提议就是，在减少5万亿美元税收的基础上，再加上2万亿美元的额外军费开支，说他将通过课税减免和消除漏洞来支付，问题是他已经被问过100多遍了，你将会怎样消除课税减免和弥补漏洞？但他一直没有能够确认。

But I'm going to make an important point here, Jim.

Lehrer: All right.

Obama: When you add up all the loopholes and deductions that upper income individuals can – are currently taking advantage of – if you take those all away – you don't come close to paying for $5 trillion in tax cuts and $2 trillion in additional military spending. And that's why independent studies looking at this said the only way to meet Governor Romney's pledge of not reducing the deficit – or – or – or not adding to the deficit, is by burdening middle-class families.

The average middle-class family with children would pay about $2,000 more. Now, that's not my analysis; that's the analysis of economists who have looked at this. And – and that kind of top – top-down economics, where folks at the top are doing well so the average person making 3 million bucks is getting a $250,000 tax break while middle- class families are burdened further, that's not what I believe is a recipe for economic growth.

Lehrer: All right. What is the difference?

Let's just stay on taxes for –

Romney: But I – but I – right, right.

Lehrer: OK. Yeah, just – let's just stay on taxes for a moment.

Romney: Yeah. Well, but – but –

Lehrer: What is the difference?

Romney: – virtually every – virtually everything he just said about my tax plan is inaccurate.

Lehrer: All right, go –

Romney: So – so if – if the tax plan he described were a tax plan I was asked to support, I'd say absolutely not. I'm not looking for a $5 trillion tax cut. What I've said is I won't put in place a tax cut that adds to the deficit. That's part one. So there's no economist can say Mitt Romney's tax plan adds 5 trillion (dollars) if I say I will not add to the deficit with my tax plan.

Number two, I will not reduce the share paid by high-income individuals.

我在此要指出很重要的一点，吉姆。

莱勒： 好的。

奥巴马： 当你把所有税务漏洞和高收入人群所享受的课税减免加在一起的时候——如果你这些都抛开——也远远不能支付5万亿美元减税和2万亿美元的额外军费开支。这就是为什么独立研究组织在研究了罗姆尼州长的方案后，认为不增加赤字的唯一方法，是扩大中产阶级家庭的税负。

有小孩的中产阶级家庭平均会多支付2000美元，这不是我的分析；这是研究过您方案的经济学家的分析，那种自上而下的经济，使得上层人士顺风顺水，年收入300万美元以上的人士平均获得25万美元的减税，而中产阶级家庭的负担进一步加重，我认为这不是促进经济增长的良药。

莱勒： 好的，区别在哪里？让我们继续讨论税收问题——

罗姆尼： 但是我，但是我——好的，好的。

莱勒： 好的，让我们继续讨论税收问题。

罗姆尼： 恩，好的，但是——但是

莱勒： 区别在那里？

罗姆尼： 实际上——实际上，他刚才讲的关于我的税收计划的事情都

I – I know that you and your running mate keep saying that, and I know it's a popular things to say with a lot of people, but it's just not the case. Look, I got five boys. I'm used to people saying something that's not always true, but just keep on repeating it and ultimately hoping I'll believe it – but that – that is not the case, all right? I will not reduce the taxes paid by high-income Americans.

And number three, I will not, under any circumstances, raise taxes on middle-income families. I will lower taxes on middle-income families. Now, you cite a study. There are six other studies that looked at the study you describe and say it's completely wrong. I saw a study that came out today that said you're going to raise taxes by 3,000 dollars to $4,000 on – on middle-income families. There are all these studies out there.

But let's get to the bottom line. That is, I want to bring down rates. I want to bring down the rates down, at the same time lower deductions and exemptions and credits and so forth so we keep getting the revenue we need.

And you think, well, then why lower the rates? And the reason is because small business pays that individual rate. Fifty-four percent of America's workers work in businesses that are taxed not at the corporate tax rate but at the individual tax rate. And if we lower that rate, they will be able to hire more people. For me, this is about jobs.

Lehrer: All right. That's where we started.

Romney: This is about getting jobs for the American people.

Lehrer: Yeah. Do you challenge what the governor just said about his own plan?

Obama: Well, for 18 months he's been running on this tax plan. And now, five weeks before the election, he's saying that his big, bold idea is "never mind". And the fact is that if you are lowering the rates the way you describe, Governor, then it is not possible to come up with enough deductions and loopholes that only affect high-income individuals to avoid either raising the deficit or burdening the middle class. It's – it's math. It's arithmetic.

是不准确的。

莱勒：好的，继续——

罗姆尼：如果有人要我支持他所形容的税收计划，我会说绝不支持，我没有5万亿美元的减税计划，我说的是，我不会实施增加赤字的减税，这是其一，如果我说我的税收计划不会增加赤字，所以也就没有经济学家会说，罗姆尼的税收计划会增加5万亿美元。

其二，我不会减少高收入群体的纳税份额，我知道你和你的竞争伙伴一直那么说，我知道那么说会受到很多人的欢迎，但情况并非如此。看，我有5个儿子，我对人们说谎已经习以为常，但是如果只是不停地重复，最后让我相信它——但——情况并非如此，对吧？我不会减少美国高收入群体的纳税。

其三，无论什么情况下，我都不会增加中等收入家庭的税额，而是去降低它。现在您援引了一个研究报告，有其他的六个研究机构对你谈到的研究作了调查，称您那个研究报告结果完全错误。我看到的一项今天公布的研究认为，您给中等收入家庭增税3000到4000美元，这些研究遍地都是。

但结论是，我想降低税率，我想减低税率，同时降低课税减免、课税豁免和课税抵免，这样我们可以获得所需的收入。

你会想，为什么要降低税率？原因是，因为小企业在按照个人所得税税率纳税，美国54%的企业工作人员，不是按照企业税率纳税，而是按照个人所得税税率纳税，如果我们降低个人所得税税率，他们将能雇佣更多的人。对我来说，这事关就业。

莱勒：好的，这就是起点。

罗姆尼：这涉及美国人民的就业机会。

莱勒：好的，你是否质疑州长刚才阐述的计划？

奥巴马：好的，18个月来，他一直在宣传他的税收计划，现在在距离大选还有5周的时间，他说那个重大、大胆的计划是"不要在意"。实际上，如果您按照您描述的方法降低税率，州长先生，那么您不可能充足地实现课税减免和弥补漏洞，从而避免增加赤字或者避免加重中产阶级的负担，这是数字，这是算术。

Now, Governor Romney and I do share a deep interest in encouraging small-business growth. So at the same time that my tax plan has already lowered taxes for 98 percent of families, I also lowered taxes for small businesses 18 times. And what I want to do is continue the tax rates – the tax cuts that we put into place for small businesses and families.

But I have said that for incomes over $250,000 a year that we should go back to the rates that we had when Bill Clinton was president, when we created 23 million new jobs, went from deficit to surplus and created a whole lot of millionaires to boot.

And the reason this is important is because by doing that, we can not only reduce the deficit, we can not only encourage job growth through small businesses, but we're also able to make the investments that are necessary in education or in energy.

And we do have a difference, though, when it comes to definitions of small business. Now, under – under my plan, 97 percent of small businesses would not see their income taxes go up. Governor Romney says, well, those top 3 percent, they're the job creators. They'd be burdened.

But under Governor Romney's definition, there are a whole bunch of millionaires and billionaires who are small businesses. Donald Trump is a small business. And I know Donald Trump doesn't like to think of himself as small anything, but – but that's how you define small businesses if you're getting business income. And that kind of approach, I believe, will not grow our economy because the only way to pay for it without either burdening the middle class or blowing up our deficit is to make drastic cuts in things like education, making sure that we are continuing to invest in basic science and research, all the things that are helping America grow. And I think that would be a mistake.

Lehrer: All right.

Romney: Jim, let me just come back on that – on that point.

These small businesses we're talking about –

我和罗姆尼州长在鼓励小企业增长方面都兴趣十足，但同时，我的税收计划已经为98%的家庭减了税，我还为小企业减税18次。我想做的是继续维持这个税率——继续为小企业和家庭减税。

但是我已经说过，对于年收入25万美元以上的家庭，我们应该将税率恢复到克林顿任职时的税率，我们当时创造了2300万新的工作岗位，财政赤字变成了盈余，涌现了很多百万富翁。

那么做重要的原因是，我们不仅能够减少赤字，不仅能够通过小企业创造就业机会，还能够在教育或能源上作必要的投资。

然而，当涉及小企业的定义时，我们确实有分歧，现在根据我的计划，97%的小企业的税收不会增加，而罗姆尼州长认为，出自上层的那3%就是岗位创造者，他们应当承担负担。

但是，根据罗姆尼州长的定义，有很多百万富翁和亿万富翁小企业主，唐纳德·特朗普是小企业主，我知道唐纳德·特朗普并不认为自己渺小，但这就是您的定义，如果你的收入是商业收入，那么你就是小企业主。我相信这种方法不会让我们的经济增长，因为在不加重中产阶级负担或者扩大赤字的情况下，支付这些措施的唯一方法就是大幅度削减在教育等方面的投资，这样就能确保我们继续对基础科学研究领域和有利于美国发展的领域进行投资，我认为那将会是一个错误。

莱勒：好的。

罗姆尼：吉姆，我再回到刚才那一点。

我们谈论的小企——

 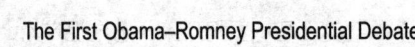

Lehrer: Excuse me. Just so everybody understands –

– we're way over our first 15 minutes.

Romney: It's fun, isn't it?

Lehrer: It's OK. It's great.

Obama: That's OK.

Lehrer: No problem. No, you don't have – you don't have a problem, I don't have a problem, because we're still on the economy, but we're going to come back to taxes and we're going to move on to the deficit and a lot of other things, too.

OK, but go ahead, sir.

Romney: You bet.

Well, President, you're – Mr. President, you're absolutely right, which is that with regards to 97 percent of the businesses are not – not taxed at the 35 percent tax rate, they're taxed at a lower rate. But those businesses that are in the last 3 percent of businesses happen to employ half – half – of all of the people who work in small business. Those are the businesses that employ one quarter of all the workers in America. And your plan is take their tax rate from 35 percent to 40 percent.

Now, I talked to a guy who has a very small business. He's in the electronics business in – in St. Louis. He has four employees.

He said he and his son calculated how much they pay in taxes. Federal income tax, federal payroll tax, state income tax, state sales tax, state property tax, gasoline tax – it added up to well over 50 percent of what they earned.

And your plan is to take the tax rate on successful small businesses from 35 percent to 40 percent. The National Federation of Independent Businesses has said that will cost 700,000 jobs. I don't want to cost jobs. My priority is jobs. And so what I do is I bring down the tax rates, lower deductions and exemptions – the same idea behind Bowles-Simpson, by the way. Get the rates down, lower deductions and exemptions to create more jobs, because there's nothing better

莱勒：对不起，所有人都知道——

我们第一个15分钟已经超时了。

罗姆尼：挺有乐趣的，是不是？

莱勒：好的，好。

奥巴马：好的。

莱勒：没问题。是的，你们没——没有问题，我也没有问题，因为我们仍要继续讨论经济，但先回到税收问题，然后讨论赤字和其他问题。

好的，先生，继续。

罗姆尼：是的。

好的，总统，您是总统先生，您在这方面绝对正确，97%的企业不——不用按35%的税率缴税，而是按更低的税率缴税，但是那些剩余3%的企业却雇佣了半数在小企业工作的员工，雇佣了美国四分之一的员工，您的计划是将他们的税率从35%提高到40%。

最近，我曾和一位小企业主聊过天，他在圣路易斯市的电子行业工作，雇了四个工人。

他说他和他儿子核算过他们缴的税，有联邦所得税、联邦工资税、州所得税、州销售税、州财产税、汽油税——加起来超过盈利的50%。

而您的计划是将成功的小企业的税率从35%提高到40%，全国独立企业联合会表示，这将损失70万个工作岗位，我不愿牺牲就业，就业是重中之重。因此，我所作的就是降低税率，减少扣税和免税——顺便说一句，这与鲍尔斯—辛普森委员会的理念是一致的，那就是，通过降低税率、减少扣税和免税来创造更多的工作岗位，因为让更多的人去工作、赚更多的钱、缴更多的税再平衡不过，这是至今为止最为有效的平衡预算的方法。

for getting us to a balanced budget than having more people working, earning more money, paying – (chuckles) – more taxes. That's by far the most effective and efficient way to get this budget balanced.

Obama: Jim, I – you may want to move on to another topic, but I would just say this to the American people. If you believe that we can cut taxes by $5 trillion and add $2 trillion in additional spending that the military is not asking for – $7 trillion, just to give you a sense, over 10 years that's more than our entire defense budget – and you think that by closing loopholes and deductions for the well-to-do, somehow you will not end up picking up the tab, then Governor Romney's plan may work for you.

But I think math, common sense and our history shows us that's not a recipe for job growth.

Look, we've tried this – we've tried both approaches. The approach that Governor Romney's talking about is the same sales pitch that was made in 2001 and 2003. And we ended up with the slowest job growth in 50 years. We ended up moving from surplus to deficits. And it all culminated in the worst financial crisis since the Great Depression.

Bill Clinton tried the approach that I'm talking about. We created 23 million new jobs. We went from deficit to surplus, and businesses did very well.

So in some ways, we've got some data on which approach is more likely to create jobs and opportunity for Americans, and I believe that the economy works best when middle-class families are getting tax breaks so that they've got some money in their pockets and those of us who have done extraordinarily well because of this magnificent country that we live in, that we can afford to do a little bit more to make sure we're not blowing up the deficit.

Romney: Jim, the president began this segment, so I think I get the last word, so I'm going to take it. All right?

Lehrer: Well, you're going to get the first word in the next segment.

Romney: Well, but – but he gets the first word of that segment. I get the

奥巴马： 吉姆，我——你大概想继续谈下一个议题，但是，我只想对美国人民说：如果你们相信我们可以减税5万亿，再加上2万亿美元的额外军费开支——一共是7万亿，你可以设想一下，10年就比全部国防预算还多——如果你们认为可以靠堵住富人的税法漏洞和减少扣税，最后你们就不用替这个方案买单了，那么罗姆尼州长的计划可能适合你。但是我认为数学、常识以及历史都证明，这不是增加就业的灵丹妙药。

看看吧，我们尝试过这个方法——两种方法都尝试过，罗姆尼州长的方法我们曾在2001及2003年提出过，结果导致了50年来最缓慢的就业增长，财政盈余转为赤字，并且在大萧条以来最严重的经济危机中恶化到极点。

比尔·克林顿尝试过我说的方法，我们曾创造了2300万个新的工作岗位，财政由赤字变为盈余，并且企业发展顺利。

所以，在某种程度上，我们已经获得了为美国人民创造工作岗位和机会的方法，我认为，当中产阶级家庭得到税收优惠，经济发展将处于最佳状态，这样他们口袋中才会有钱，我们中一些人因为生活在这么伟大的国家而取得了卓越的成就，为确保国家赤字不再放大，我们可以多承担一点。

罗姆尼： 吉姆，总统先开始这部分，所以我想我有最后的发言资格，是吧？

莱勒： 好的，下一部分你先开始。

罗姆尼： 嗯，但是他先开始这部分，我希望我能最后发言，让我作一下评论。

last word of that segment, I hope. Let me just make this comment.

Obama: (Chuckles.) He can – you can have it. He can –

Romney: Let me – let me repeat – let me repeat what I said – (inaudible). I'm not in favor of a $5 trillion tax cut. That's not my plan. My plan is not to put in place any tax cut that will add to the deficit. That's point one. So you may keep referring to it as a $5 trillion tax cut, but that's not my plan.

Obama: OK.

Romney: Number two, let's look at history. My plan is not like anything that's been tried before. My plan is to bring down rates but also bring down deductions and exemptions and credits at the same time so the revenue stays in, but that we bring down rates to get more people working. My priority is putting people back to work in America. They're suffering in this country. And we talk about evidence – look at the evidence of the last four years. It's absolutely extraordinary. We've got 23 million people out of work or stop looking for work in this country.

Lehrer: All right.

Rise in Food Stamps

Romney: It's just – it's – we've got – we got – when the president took office, 32 million people on food stamps; 47 million on food stamps today. Economic growth this year slower than last year, and last year slower than the year before. Going forward with the status quo is not going to cut it for the American people who are struggling today.

Lehrer: All right. Let's talk – we're still on the economy. This is, theoretically now, a second segment still on the economy, and specifically on what do about the federal deficit, the federal debt. And the question – you each have two minutes on this – and, Governor Romney you go first because the president went first on segment one. And the question is this: What are the differences between the two of you as to how you would go about tackling the deficit problem in this country?

奥巴马：他可以——你可以这样做，他能——

让我重复——让我重复我刚才说的话，我不赞成减少5万亿美元税收，这不是我的计划，我的计划是不进行任何导致赤字增加的减税，这是其一。您可以继续将其称作5万亿美元的减税计划，但那并不是我的计划。

奥巴马：好。

罗姆尼：其二，让我们翻开历史，我们计划与之前尝试的努力大不相同，我的计划是降低税率并减少课税减免、课税豁免和课税抵免，从而使我们可以获得收入，但降低税率是为了让更多的人工作，我的重点是，让更多的人重返美国本土的工作岗位，他们正在这个国家饱受折磨。我们谈一谈证据——看一下过去四年的证据，这绝对触目惊心，我们已经有2300万人失业或处于待业状态。

莱勒：好的。

食品卷的增加

罗姆尼：——我们知道——总统刚就任时，3200万人领取食品券，现在领取食品券的人达到了4700万。今年经济增长比去年还要缓慢，而去年比前年更加缓慢，如果这种情况继续下去的话，对于当今努力奋斗的美国人来说，领取食物券的人数将不会减少。

莱勒：好吧，我们开始讨论——我们依然讨论经济，理论上说，这是经济话题的第二部分，特别是如何处理联邦赤字，联邦债务的问题——你们各有两分钟的时间回答问题。罗姆尼州长，你先回答，因为在第一部分是总统先回答的。问题是：关于如何处理这个国家的赤字问题，你有什么不同的看法？

Romney: Well, good. I'm glad you raised that. And it's a – it's a critical issue. I think it's not just an economic issue. I think it's a moral issue. I think it's, frankly, not moral for my generation to keep spending massively more than we take in, knowing those burdens are going to be passed on to the next generation. And they're going to be paying the interest and the principle all their lives. And the amount of debt we're adding, at a trillion a year, is simply not moral.

So how do we deal with it? Well, mathematically there are – there are three ways that you can cut a deficit. One, of course, is to raise taxes. Number two is to cut spending. And number three is to grow the economy because if more people work in a growing economy they're paying taxes and you can get the job done that way.

The presidents would – president would prefer raising taxes. I understand. The problem with raising taxes is that it slows down the rate of growth and you could never quite get the job done. I want to lower spending and encourage economic growth at the same time.

What things would I cut from spending? Well, first of all, I will eliminate all programs by this test – if they don't pass it: Is the program so critical it's worth borrowing money from China to pay for it? And if not, I'll get rid of it. "Obamacare" is on my list. I apologize, Mr. President. I use that term with all respect.

Obama: I like it.

Romney: Good. OK, good. So I'll get rid of that. I'm sorry, Jim. I'm going to stop the subsidy to PBS. I'm going to stop other things. I like PBS. I love Big Bird. I actually like you too. But I'm not going to – I'm not going to keep on spending money on things to borrow money from China to pay for it. That's number one.

Number two, I'll take programs that are currently good programs but I think could be run more efficiently at the state level and send them to state.

Number three, I'll make government more efficient, and to cut back the number of employees, combine some agencies and departments. My cutbacks

罗姆尼：好的。好，我很高兴你提出这个问题，这是个至关重要的问题，我认为这不只是一个经济问题，我认为它是一个道德问题。开诚布公地说，我认为，我们这一代人人不敷出、大量花费是不道德的，我知道这将给下一代造成负担，他们将终其一生连本带息偿还这些债务。我们的债务额不断增加，每年一万亿美元，这并不是高尚的行为。

那么我们如何处理这个问题？好的，从数学上有三种方法可以减少赤字：第一，当然是提高税收，第二是减少开支，第三是促进经济增长，因为在经济增长的情况下，有更多的人工作，他们就会缴税，这样问题就迎刃而解。

总统会——总统倾向于提高税率。我理解，提高税率的问题是它减缓了增长率，你就无法完全解决赤字问题。我想要减少开支和经济增长并驾齐驱。

我会削减哪方面的开支？首先，我都会摒弃那些不能通过检验的项目：这个项目真的那么至关重要以至于我们从中国借钱来做么？如果不是，我会取消它。"奥巴马医改"就是需要取消的项目之一，我向你道歉，总统先生，我用这个术语是出于敬意。

奥巴马：我喜欢。

罗姆尼：好，好吧，好，我会取消它，对不起，吉姆，我会停止给公共广播公司补贴，我也会停止其他项目。我喜欢PBS，我喜欢大鸟，实际上我也喜欢你。但我不会——不会继续从中国借钱去做这些事情，这是第一点。

第二点，如果我认为一些当前的好项目在州一级运作会更加高效，我就会把这些项目下放给各个州。

第三，我会让政府更加高效，削减职员数量，合并一些机构和部门。顺便说一下，我的裁员会通过人员的自然耗减来实施。

will be done through attrition, by the way.

This is the approach we have to take to get America to a balanced budget. The president said he'd cut the deficit in half. Unfortunately, he doubled it. Trillion-dollar deficits for the last four years. The president's put it in place as much public debt – almost as much debt held by by the public as all prior presidents combined.

Lehrer: Mr. President. two minutes.

Obama: When I walked in the Oval Office, I had more than a trillion dollar deficit greeting me, and we know where it came from. Two wars that were paid for on a credit card. Two tax cuts that were not paid for, and a whole bunch of programs that were not paid for. And then a massive economic crisis.

And despite that, what we've said is, yes, we had to take some initial emergency measures to make sure we didn't slip into a Great Depression. But what we've also said is, let's make sure that we are cutting out those things that are not helping us grow.

So, 77 government programs – everything from aircrafts that the Air Force had ordered but weren't working very well. Eighteen government – 18 government programs for education that were well- intentioned but weren't helping kids learn. We went after medical fraud in Medicare and Medicaid very aggressively – more aggressively than ever before, and have saved tens of billions of dollars. Fifty billion dollars of waste taken out of the system.

And I worked with Democrats and Republicans to cut a trillion dollars out of our discretionary domestic budget. That's the largest cut in the discretionary domestic budget since Dwight Eisenhower.

Now, we all know that we've got to do more. And so I've put forward a specific $4 trillion deficit-reduction plan.

It's on a website. You can look at all the numbers, what cuts we make and what revenue we raise.

And the way we do it is $2.50 for every cut, we ask for a dollar of additional

这是我们让美国实现平衡预算必须采取的方法，总统说过他会削减一半的赤字，不幸的是，他却适得其反，赤字翻番，过去四年有万亿美元的赤字，总统产生的国债几乎是前几任总统负债量的总和。

莱勒：总统先生，你有两分钟的时间发言。

奥巴马：我就任时就面临一万多亿美元赤字，我们知道它的源头，两场透支的战争，两次未曾清偿的减税，一些没有经费的项目，还有一次大规模的经济危机。

尽管如此，我们说过，好吧，我们必须采取一些初步应急措施来确保我们不会跌入大萧条，但是我们也说过，我们要确保停止那些无益于经济增长的项目。

所以，从77个政府项目——空军订购但运行不佳的飞机到18个政府项目——砍掉18个用意良好、但对孩子们学习帮助不大的教育项目。我们严查老年医疗保险和医疗补助计划中的医疗欺诈事件——比以前任何时候力度都大，挽回了数百亿美元，在系统内避免了500亿美元的浪费。

我同民主党和共和党一起齐心协力，从国内自由支配预算中削减了一万亿美元，这是自埃森豪威尔总统以来对国内自由支配预算最大规模的削减。

现在，我们都知道需要付出更多的努力，因此，我提出4万亿的赤字削减计划。

已经在网上发布，你们可以去看所有的数字，我们削减了哪些内容，增加了哪些收入。

revenue, paid for, as I indicated earlier, by asking those of us who have done very well in this country to contribute a little bit more to reduce the deficit.

And Governor Romney earlier mentioned the Bowles-Simpson commission. Well, that's how the commission – bipartisan commission that talked about how we should move forward suggested we have to do it – in a balanced way with some revenue and some spending cuts. And this is a major difference that Governor Romney and I have.

Let – let me just finish this point because you're looking for contrast. You know, when Governor Romney stood on a stage with other Republican candidates for the nomination, and he was asked, would you take $10 of spending cuts for just $1 of revenue, and he said no. Now, if you take such an unbalanced approach, then that means you are going to be gutting our investments in schools and education. It means that – Governor Romney talked about Medicaid and how we could send it back to the states, but effectively this means a 30 percent cut in the primary program we help for seniors who are in nursing homes, for kids who are with disabilities –

Lehrer: Mr. President, I'm sorry –

Obama: And that is not a right strategy for us to move forward.

Lehrer: Way over the two minutes.

Obama: Sorry.

Lehrer: Governor, what about Simpson-Bowles. Will you support Simpson-Bowles?

Romney: Simpson-Bowles, the president should have grabbed that.

Lehrer: No, I mean do you support Simpson-Bowles?

Romney: I have my own plan. It's not the same as Simpson- Bowles. But in my view, the president should have grabbed it. If you wanted to make some adjustments to it, take it, go to Congress, fight for it.

Obama: That's what we've done, made some adjustments to it; and we're putting it forward before Congress right now, a $4 trillion plan, (a balanced ?) –

我们是这样做的，每减少2.5美元的支出，我们要求增加1美元的财政收入，正如我之前提到过的，通过要求那些发展得比较好的人多贡献一些来减少赤字。

罗姆尼州长之前提到的鲍尔斯·辛普森委员会，好的，这就是委员会——两党组成的委员会所建议的我们如何减少赤字的方法——用平衡的方法，一些措施是增加收入的，一些是减少开支的，这就是罗姆尼州长和我的主要分歧。

让我说完这一点，因为你们要做出对比。你们知道，当罗姆尼州长与其他共和党候选人站在台上竞选提名时，有人问他，你愿意用减少10美元开支来换1美元的收入吗？他说不。现在，如果你采用这种不平衡的方法的话，这意味着你将破坏我们对学校和教育的投资，这意味着——罗姆尼州长提到医疗补助以及我们如何将其下放到各个州，但是实际上，这意味着帮助养老院的老人和残疾儿童的项目经费要减少30%。

莱勒：总统，对不起——

奥巴马：这不是一个引导我们的正确策略。

莱勒：超过两分钟了。

奥巴马：对不起。

莱勒：州长，关于鲍尔斯·辛普森委员会，你是否支持？

罗姆尼：鲍尔斯—辛普森委员会，总统应该抓住这次机会。

莱勒：不，我的意思是你是否支持鲍尔斯—辛普森委员会的议案？

罗姆尼：我有自己的计划，它和鲍尔斯—辛普森委员会不一样。但是我认为，总统应该抓住机会，如果你想作一些调整，那么，就把它带到国会，为它而奋斗。

奥巴马：我们已经这样作了，作了一些调整；我们现在正在把它提交给国会，一个四万亿的计划。

Romney: But you've been – but you've been president four years. You've been president four years. You said you'd cut the deficit in half. It's now four years later. We still have trillion- dollar deficits.

The CBO says we'll have a trillion-dollar deficit each of the next four years. If you're re-elected, we'll get to a trillion-dollar debt. You have said before you'd cut the deficit in half. And this four – I love this idea of 4 trillion (dollars) in cuts. You've found $4 trillion of ways to reduce or to get closer to a balanced budget, except we still show trillion dollar deficits every year. That doesn't get the job done.

Let me come back and say, why is that I don't want to raise taxes? Why don't I want to raise taxes on people? And actually, you said it back in 2010. You said, look, I'm going to extend the tax policies that we have. Now, I'm not going to raise taxes on anyone because when the economy's growing slow like this, when we're in recession you shouldn't raise taxes on anyone.

Well, the economy is still growing slow. As a matter of fact, it's growing much more slowly now than when you made that statement. And so if you believe the same thing, you just don't want to raise taxes on people. And the reality is it's not just wealthy people – you mentioned Donald Trump – it's not just Donald Trump you're taxing; it's all those businesses that employ one-quarter of the workers in America. These small businesses that are taxed as individuals. You raise taxes and you kill jobs. That's why the National Federation of Independent Businesses said your plan will kill 700,000 jobs. I don't want to kill jobs in this environment.

Let me make one more point. And that's – and that –

Lehrer: Let's let him answer the taxes thing for a moment, OK?

Romney: OK.

Lehrer: Mr. President.

Obama: Well, we've had this discussion before.

Lehrer: No, about the idea that in order to reduce the deficit there has to

罗姆尼：但你——你当总统已经四年了，四年了。你说过会减少一半的赤字，但现在四年已经过去了，我们仍然有万亿美元的赤字。

国会预算办公室称我们未来四年每年都会有一万亿美元的赤字。如果你连任，我们会达到万亿美元的债务，你以前说过你会减少一半的赤字，我喜欢这个四万亿美元的减少赤字计划，你找到了平衡四万亿美元赤字的方法，但是我们每年依然显示有万亿美元的赤字，这个任务没有完成。

让我重复一下，为什么我不想提高税收？为什么我不想提高人们的税收？实际上，你在2010年说过这话，你说，看吧，我要继续我们已有的税收政策。现在，我不会提高任何人的税收，因为当经济增长如此缓慢时，当我们处于经济衰退之时，你不应该增加任何人的税收。

经济增长依然十分缓慢，事实上，现在的增长速度比你发表那个声明时还要慢得多，所以如果你相信同样的事情，你就不会增加人们的税收，现实是不只富人——你提到的唐纳德·特朗普——你不只是对唐纳德·特朗普征税；它涉及所有雇用了1/4美国劳动力的企业，这些小企业按照个人所得税税率纳税，你提高了税率，就是扼杀了就业。这就是为什么全国独立企业联合会说，你的计划将会扼杀70万个工作岗位，我不想在这个环境下扼杀就业，我再说一点，那就是——那——

莱勒：请回答税收议题，可以么？

罗姆尼：好的。

莱勒：总统先生。

奥巴马：好，我们之前讨论过这个问题。

莱勒：不，就减少赤字的想法，除了削减开支之外，还有收入。

be revenue in addition to cuts.

Obama: There has to be revenue in addition to cuts. Now, Governor Romney has ruled out revenue. He's – he's ruled out revenue.

Lehrer: That's true, right?

Romney: Absolutely.

Obama: OK, so –

Lehrer: Completely?

Romney: I – look, the revenue I get is by more people working, getting higher pay, paying more taxes. That's how we get growth and how we balance the budget. But the idea of taxing people more, putting more people out of work – you'll never get there. You never balance the budget by raising taxes.

Spain – Spain spends 42 percent of their total economy on government. We're now spending 42 percent of our economy on government.

I don't want to go down the path to Spain. I want to go down the path of growth that puts Americans to work, with more money coming in because they're working.

Lehrer: Yeah.

But Mr. President, you're saying in order to get it – the job done, it's got to be balanced. You've got to have –

Obama: If we're serious, we've got to take a balanced, responsible approach. And by the way, this is not just when it comes to individual taxes.

Let's talk about corporate taxes. Now, I've identified areas where we can, right away, make a change that I believe would actually help the economy. The – the oil industry gets $4 billion a year in corporate welfare. Basically, they get deductions that those small businesses that Governor Romney refers to, they don't get. Now, does anybody think that ExxonMobil needs some extra money when they're making money every time you go to the pump? Why wouldn't we want to eliminate that?

Why wouldn't we eliminate tax breaks for corporate jets? My attitude is

奥巴马：除了削减开支，必须要有收入。现在，罗姆尼州长已经排除了收入，他已经排除了收入。

莱勒：是这样么？

罗姆尼：完全正确。

奥巴马：好的，所以——

莱勒：完全排除么？

罗姆尼：我——看吧，收入的增加是让更多的人工作，得到更高的薪水，缴纳更多的税款，那就是我们实现增长和平衡预算的方式，但是，如果向人们征收更多的税款，让更多的人失业——那么，你就永远不能实现它，你无法通过增税来平衡预算。

西班牙——西班牙把经济总量的42%用于政府开支，我们现在也把我们经济总量的42%用在了政府上。

我不想延续西班牙的做法，我想迈向让美国人工作的发展道路，因为他们工作，所以就会有更多的收入。

莱勒：是的。

但是总统先生，你说为了实现目标，需要保持平衡，你已经——

奥巴马：如果我们是认真的，我们应采取平衡、负责任的方法，顺便说一下，这不仅仅是涉及个人所得税时才这样做。

我们来谈谈公司税，现在，我已经确认了一些领域，能够马上作出改变，我相信那实际上会促进经济的发展，石油行业每年得到40亿美元的公司福利，基本上，他们获得了罗姆尼所指的这些小企业所没有得到的课税减免。是否有人认为埃克森美孚石油公司还需要额外的钱？每次你去加油，他们都有利可图。为什么我们不想取消那种补贴？

if you got a corporate jet, you can probably afford to pay full freight, not get a special break for it.

When it comes to corporate taxes, Governor Romney has said he wants to, in a revenue-neutral way, close loopholes, deductions – he hasn't identified which ones they are – but thereby bring down the corporate rate. Well, I want to do the same thing, but I've actually identified how we can do that.

And part of the way to do it is to not give tax breaks to companies that are shipping jobs overseas. Right now you can actually take a deduction for moving a plant overseas. I think most Americans would say that doesn't make sense. And all that raises revenue.

And so if we take a balanced approach, what that then allows us to do is also to help young people, the way we already have during my administration, make sure that they can afford to go to college. It means that the teacher that I met in Las Vegas, wonderful young lady, who describes to me – she's got 42 kids in her class.

The first two weeks, she's got them – some of them sitting on the floor until finally they get reassigned. They're using textbooks that are 10 years old. That is not a recipe for growth; that's not how America was built.

And so budgets reflect choices. Ultimately we're going to have to make some decisions. And if we're asking for no revenue, then that means that we've got to get rid of a whole bunch of stuff, and the magnitude of the tax cuts that you're talking about, Governor, would end up resulting in severe hardship for people, but more importantly, would not help us grow.

As I indicated before, when you talk about shifting Medicaid to states, we're talking about potentially a – a 30 – a 30 percent cut in Medicaid over time. Now, you know, that may not seem like a big deal when it just is – you know, numbers on a sheet of paper, but if we're talking about a family who's got an autistic kid and is depending on that Medicaid, that's a big problem. And governors are creative. There's no doubt about it. But they're not creative

为什么我们不取消对公司专机的税收优惠？我的态度是，如果你有公务机，你很有可能支付得起全部费用，而不需要得到特殊的减税优惠。

当涉及公司税时，罗姆尼州长说过，他想要通过中立的原则来弥补漏洞和课税减免——他还没有确认——就想把公司税率降下来，我想做同样的事情，但是，我实际上已经确认了我们能够做到这一点。

措施之一是不给工作转移到海外的公司提供减税优惠。现在你把工厂转移到海外实际上就能够获得课税减免。我想大部分美国人会说这没道理。所有这些能够增加税收。

所以，如果我们采取平衡的方法，就能帮助年轻人，在我的政府我们已经采用了这种方法，确保他们能够上得起大学，这就意味着我在拉斯韦加斯遇到的那个老师，一个出色的年轻女士，她对我说——她班里有42个孩子。

前两个星期，她发现在她们重新分班之前，一些孩子是坐在地上的，他们使用的教材是十年前的，那不是成长的良药，不是美国的发展方式。

预算反映出抉择，最终我们必须要作出一些决定，如果我们不要求收入，那就意味着我们要取消很多东西。您谈论的减税规模，州长，最后会导致人民陷入艰难的困境，更重要的是，它并不能有助于我们的发展。

就像我曾指出的，当你谈论把医疗补助计划转移到各州时，我们谈论的是医疗补助的经费可能会被削减30%。现在，你知道，它只是纸上的一些数字，好像没什么大不了的，但是，如果我们谈到有自闭症孩子的家庭，他们依靠医疗补助计划时，那就是大问题了。州长们很有创意，这点毫无疑问，但是他们的创造力，不足以弥补像医疗补助计划所缺少的30%的经费短缺，最后的情况是一些人最终得不到帮助。

enough to make up for 30 percent of revenue on something like Medicaid. What ends up happening is some people end up not getting help.

Romney: Jim, let's – we – we've gone on a lot of topics there, and – so I've got to take – it's going to take a minute to go from Medicaid to schools to –

Lehrer: Come back to Medicaid, here, yeah, yeah, right.

Romney: – oil to tax breaks and companies overseas. So let's go through them one by one. First of all, the Department of Energy has said the tax break for oil companies is $2.8 billion a year. And it's actually an accounting treatment, as you know, that's been in place for a hundred years. Now –

Obama: It's time to end it.

Romney: And – and in one year, you provided $90 billion in breaks to the green energy world. Now, I like green energy as well, but that's about 50 years' worth of what oil and gas receives, and you say Exxon and Mobil – actually, this $2.8 billion goes largely to small companies, to drilling operators and so forth.

But you know, if we get that tax rate from 35 percent down to 25 percent, why, that $2.8 billion is on the table. Of course it's on the table. That's probably not going to survive, you get that rate down to 25 percent.

But – but don't forget, you put $90 billion – like 50 years worth of breaks – into solar and wind, to – to Solyndra and Fisker and Tesla and Enerl. I mean, I – I had a friend who said, you don't just pick the winners and losers; you pick the losers. All right? So – so this is not – this is not the kind of policy you want to have if you want to get America energy-secure.

The second topic, which is you said you get a deduction for getting a plant overseas. Look, I've been in business for 25 years. I have no idea what you're talking about. I maybe need to get a new accountant.

But the – the idea that you get a break for shipping jobs overseas is simply not the case.

Lehrer: Let's have –

Romney: What we do have right now is a setting –

罗姆尼： 吉姆，我们已经谈过许多这方面的议题了，所以我想——我想从医疗补助话题转到学校——

莱勒： 回到医疗补助话题，是的。

罗姆尼： ——从石油谈到税收优惠和公司转移到海外，我们一个一个地讨论，首先，能源部说，对石油公司的税收优惠每年是28亿美元，这实际上是一种会计核算，我们知道，这种方法已经使用100年了。现在——

奥巴马： 现在该结束了。

罗姆尼： 你一年就给绿色能源行业提供了900亿美元的税收优惠，现在，我也喜欢绿色能源，但那相当于石油和天然气行业50年的税收优惠，你说到埃克森和美孚公司——实际上，这28亿美元大部分都流向了小公司，流向了钻探公司等等。

但你们知道，如果我们把税率从35%降到25%，为什么还公开讨论那28亿美元呢？当然还要讨论，如果你把税率降到25%，它可能就不会存在了。

但是——不要忘了，你把900亿美元——差不多石油公司50年的税收优惠，给了太阳能和风能公司，给了索林德拉、菲斯科、特斯拉和恩尔1公司。我有一个朋友说过，你不只是在挑选赢家和输家；你在选择输家，对吧？所以这不是——如果你想实现美国能源安全，这不是你想要的政策。

第二个话题，你说人们把工厂转移到海外就获得了课税减免，看吧，我做企业已经25年了，我根本不知道你在说什么，我可能需要找一个新会计了。

但是这个把工作转移到海外从而获得课税减免的概念，根本不是那么回事儿。

莱勒： 让我们——

罗姆尼： 我们现在的情况是——

Lehrer: Excuse me.

Romney: – where I'd like to bring money from overseas back to this country.

And finally, Medicaid to states, I'm not quite sure where that came in, except this, which is, I would like to take the Medicaid dollars that go to states and say to a state, you're going to get what you got last year plus inflation – inflation – plus 1 percent. And then you're going to manage your care for your poor in the way you think best.

And I remember as a governor, when this idea was floated by Tommy Thompson, the governors, Republican and Democrats, said, please let us do that. We can care for our own poor in so much better and more effective a way than having the federal government tell us how to care for our poor.

So let states – one, of the magnificent things about this country is the whole idea that states are the laboratories of democracy. Don't have the federal government tell everybody what kind of training programs they have to have and what kind of Medicaid they have to have. Let states do this.

And by the way, if a states get – gets in trouble, why, we could step in and see if we could find a way to help them. But –

Lehrer: Let's go.

Romney: But – but the right – the right approach is one which relies on the brilliance –

Lehrer: Two seconds.

Romney: – of our people and states, not the federal government.

Lehrer: Two seconds and we're going on, still on the economy on another – but another part of it.

Obama: OK.

Lehrer: All right? All right, this is this is segment three, the economy, entitlements.

First answer goes to you. It's two minutes. Mr. President, do you see a

莱勒：打扰一下。

罗姆尼：我想让资金流回美国。

最后，把医疗补助计划交给各个州，我不清楚这种说法是从哪儿来的，除了我想把医疗补助计划的资金交给州政府，然后对州政府说，你们会得到你们去年的收入并加上通货膨胀——通货膨胀——加上1%，你们要想出最佳的策略来关照穷人们。

我记得我当州长时，当汤米·汤普森把这个想法付诸实践时，共和党和民主党的州长都说，请让我们也这么做吧，与联邦政府告诉我们的方法相比，我们能够行之有效地照顾我们的穷人。

所以让各个州——这个国家的一个卓越特性是，各个州是民主的试验田地，不要让联邦政府告诉每个人他们要有什么样的培训计划，他们要有什么样的医疗补助计划，让州政府去做这事。

顺便说一下，如果某个州陷入了困境——为什么，我们能够介入，找到方法帮助他们。

莱勒：继续。

罗姆尼：但——但正确的方法是依赖智慧——

莱勒：2秒钟时间。

罗姆尼：依赖我们人民和各州的智慧，而不是联邦政府。

莱勒：两秒钟后我们继续经济议题——但是是另外一个部分。

奥巴马：好的。

莱勒：好吗？好的，这是这是第三部分，关于经济，关于福利。

首先请您来回答，两分钟时间。总统先生，您认为你们在社保方面有什么重大区别？

243

major difference between the two of you on Social Security?

Obama: You know, I suspect that on Social Security, we've got a somewhat similar position. Social Security is structurally sound. It's going to have to be tweaked the way it was by Ronald Reagan and Speaker – Democratic Speaker Tip O'Neill. But it is – the basic structure is sound. But – but I want to talk about the values behind Social Security and Medicare and then talk about Medicare, because that's the big driver –

Lehrer: Sure – it – you bet.

Obama: of our deficits right now.

You know, my grandmother, some of you know, helped to raise me. My grandparents did. My grandfather died awhile back. My grandmother died three days before I was elected president. And she was fiercely independent. She worked her way up, only had a high school education, started as a secretary, ended up being the vice president of a local bank. And she ended up living alone by choice. And the reason she could be independent was because of Social Security and Medicare. She had worked all her life, put in this money and understood that there was a basic guarantee, a floor under which she could not go.

And that's the perspective I bring when I think about what's called entitlements. You know, the name itself implies some sense of dependency on the part of these folks. These are folks who've worked hard, like my grandmother. And there are millions of people out there who are counting on this.

So my approach is to say, how do we strengthen the system over the long term? And in Medicare, what we did was we said, we are going to have to bring down the costs if we're going to deal with our long- term deficits, but to do that, let's look where some of the money is going. Seven hundred and sixteen billion dollars we were able to save from the Medicare program by no longer overpaying insurance companies, by making sure that we weren't overpaying providers.

And using that money, we were actually able to lower prescription drug costs for seniors by an average of $600, and we were also able to make a –

奥巴马： 你们知道，我怀疑我们在社保方面可能有些类似的观点，社保在结构是健全的。不过它需要用罗纳德·里根和民主党发言人蒂普·奥尼尔的方式稍作调整一下。但是——基本结构是健全的，但是——但是我想要谈论的是社保和医保背后的价值观，然后谈谈医保，因为这才是主要原因——

莱勒： 当然——这个——是的。

奥巴马： ——我们现在存在赤字的主要原因。

你们知道，有些人知道，我的祖母把我养大，我的祖父母都抚养了我，祖父不久前去世了，祖母也在我当选总统的前三天去世。她非常独立，她靠自己的努力前进，她只有高中文凭，开始做秘书，后来当上当地银行的副行长，最后她选择独自生活，她之所以能这样做是因为有社保和医保，她一辈子都在工作，攒钱，她知道只要她有个基本保障就不会过得很差。

当我想到福利的时候，我是从这个角度来看的。你们知道，这个词本身对于某些人来说包含了某种意义上的依赖关系，有些人像我祖母那样努力工作，但也有数以百万计的人依靠社保。

因此，我的方法是，如何长期加强这个系统？关于医保，我们言行一致，要应对长期赤字，必须降低费用。为此，来看看一些资金的去向。如果我们不再支付保险公司和供应商过高的费用，就可以从医保项目里节约7160亿美元。

实际上，我们可以利用这些钱来减少老人的医药费，平均每人600美元，也可以在提供的预防保健方面取得重大进展，从而最终达到节省经费的目标。

make a significant dent in providing them the kind of preventive care that will ultimately save money through the – throughout the system.

So the way for us to deal with Medicare in particular is to lower health care costs. But when it comes to Social Security, as I said, you don't need a major structural change in order to make sure that Social Security is there for the future.

Lehrer: We'll follow up on this. First, Governor Romney, you have two minutes on Social Security and entitlements.

Romney: Well, Jim, our seniors depend on these programs. And I know any time we talk about entitlements, people become concerned that something's going to happen that's going to change their life for the worst, and the answer is, neither the president nor I are proposing any changes for any current retirees or near retirees, either to Social Security or Medicare. So if you're 60 or around 60 or older, you don't need to listen any further.

But for younger people, we need to talk about what changes are going to be occurring.

Oh, I just thought about one, and that is in fact I was wrong when I said the president isn't proposing any changes for current retirees. In fact, he is on Medicare. On Social Security, he's not.

But on Medicare, for current retirees he's cutting $716 billion from the program. Now, he says by not overpaying hospitals and providers, actually just going to them and saying we're going to reduce the rates you get paid across the board, everybody's going to get a lower rate. That's not just going after places where there's abuse, that's saying we're cutting the rates. Some 15 percent of hospitals and nursing homes say they won't take anymore Medicare patients under that scenario.

We also have 50 percent of doctors who say they won't take more Medicare patients. This – we have 4 million people on Medicare Advantage that will lose Medicare Advantage because of those $716 billion in cuts. I can't understand how you can cut Medicare $716 billion for current recipients of Medicare.

所以，我们应对医疗保险的特别之处就是降低健康保险费用。但是说到社保，正如我之前所说的，并不需要为了确保社保将来存在而做重大结构上的改变。

莱勒： 我们继续这个话题，首先，罗姆尼州长，你有两分钟的时间来谈一谈社保和福利。

罗姆尼： 好的，吉姆，老年人依赖这些保障计划，我知道每次谈到社保福利问题，大家都关心生活会变差。说到这个，总统先生和我都没有想要更改社保计划或是医保计划中有关已经退休或者接近退休人士的那部分，所以如果你60岁了，或者大概在60岁左右，可以不必再关注这个话题了。

但是对于年轻人来说，我们得谈谈将会发生哪些改变。

哦，我刚刚想到一个变化，那就是我刚刚说，总统先生没有改变针对当前退休人群的保障政策，我说错了。事实上，他对医保计划作出了变动，而社保没有。

但是在医保问题上，对于当前的退休人群来说，总统要削减7160亿开支。现在，他说不再支付医院和供应商过高的费用，事实上，就是去跟他们说，要全面降低支付给你们的费用，所有人都将得到更低的比率。这不仅是减少了医疗费用被滥用的部分，而是减少了比率，因此现在有大约15%的医院和养老院都称他们不愿意在这种情况下接受来自医保的病人。

还有50%的医生也称他们不愿意再接受医保病人了，因为要削减7160亿美元，这就使得我们现在的400万的医保补助对象不能再享受医保优惠计划，我无法理解您如何从目前的医疗保险用户那里减少这7160亿美元？

Now, you point out, well, we're putting some back; we're going to give a better prescription program. That's one – that's $1 for every 15 (dollars) you've cut. They're smart enough to know that's not a good trade.

I want to take that $716 billion you've cut and put it back into Medicare. By the way, we can include a prescription program if we need to improve it, but the idea of cutting $716 billion from Medicare to be able to balance the additional cost of "Obamacare" is, in my opinion, a mistake. And with regards to young people coming along, I've got proposals to make sure Medicare and Social Security are there for them without any question.

Lehrer: Mr. President.

Obama: First of all, I think it's important for Governor Romney to present this plan that he says will only affect folks in the future. And the essence of the plan is that he would turn Medicare into a voucher program. It's called premium support, but it's understood to be a voucher program. His running mate –

Lehrer: And you – and you don't support that?

Obama: I don't. And – and let me explain why.

Romney: Again, that's for future people –

Obama: I understand.

Romney: – right, not for current retirees.

Obama: For – for – so if you're – if you – you're 54 or 55, you might want to listen, because this – this will affect you. The idea, which was originally presented by Congressman Ryan, your running mate, is that we would give a voucher to seniors, and they could go out in the private marketplace and buy their own health insurance. The problem is that because the voucher wouldn't necessarily keep up with health care inflation, it was estimated that this would cost the average senior about $6,000 a year.

Now, in fairness, what Governor Romney has now said is he'll maintain traditional Medicare alongside it. But there's still a problem, because what happens is those insurance companies are pretty clever at figuring out who are

现在，您指出，对，是要给一些补偿措施；要给大家一个更好的处方计划。这确实是一种补偿，就是您每削减15美元，就补偿1美元。大家都很精明，知道这并非一笔好交易。

而我想要把您要削减的7160亿放回到医保计划里面去。顺便提一句，如果我们想改善处方计划可以把它列入其中，但我认为，要从现有医保计划里面削减7160亿来填补"奥巴马医改"计划的开销，这绝对是个错误，而考虑到年轻一代的需求，我已经作出计划以确保医保和社保都能够为他们准备就位，万无一失。

莱勒：总统先生，该您了。

奥巴马：首先，我想让罗姆尼州长来谈谈他的那个只会影响未来人群的医改计划，这很重要。那个计划的核心是要把医保计划变成优惠券计划，它名为"保费支持计划"，其实大家知道这是一个优惠券计划。他的竞选搭档——

莱勒：那您——不支持那个计划么？

奥巴马：我不支持，而且——让我来阐释一下原因。

罗姆尼：再说一次，那是针对未来人群的——

奥巴马：我知道。

罗姆尼：好，不是针对当前退休人群的。

奥巴马：所以如果你——如果你现在54岁或者55岁，你可能想要听罗姆尼州长的计划，因为这确实会影响你的生活。这个想法，最早是由你的竞选搭档议员瑞恩提出的，说我们把优惠券给老年人，然后他们可以用这些优惠券去私人市场购买医疗保险。问题是优惠券并不会跟着医疗费用一起水涨船高，据估计这会使老年人每年平均费用增加6000美元。

现在，公平地讲，罗姆尼州长刚刚说他会保留医保计划，并同时推行优惠券计划，但是这仍有问题，因为那些保险公司很精明，他们知道如何分辨出哪些老年人更年轻、更健康。

the younger and healthier seniors.

They recruit them leaving the older, sicker seniors in Medicare. And every health care economist who looks at it says over time what'll happen is the traditional Medicare system will collapse. And then what you've got is folks like my grandmother at the mercy of the private insurance system, precisely at the time when they are most in need of decent health care.

So I don't think vouchers are the right way to go. And this is not my own – only my opinion. AARP thinks that the – the savings that we obtained from Medicare bolster the system, lengthen the Medicare trust fund by 8 years. Benefits were not affected at all and ironically if you repeal "Obamacare" – and I have become fond of this term, "Obamacare" – if you repeal it, what happens is those seniors right away are going to be paying $600 more in prescription care. They're now going to have to be paying copays for basic check-ups that can keep them healthier.

And the primary beneficiary of that repeal are insurance companies that are estimated to gain billions of dollars back when they aren't making seniors any healthier. And I – I don't think that's right approach when it comes to making sure that Medicare is stronger over the long term.

Lehrer: We'll talk about – specifically about health care in a moment, but what is – do you support the voucher system, Governor?

Romney: What I support is no change for current retirees and near-retirees to Medicare and the president supports taking $716 billion out of that program.

Lehrer: What about the vouchers?

Romney: So that's – that's number one.

Lehrer: OK. All right.

Romney: Number two is for people coming along that are young. What I'd do to make sure that we can keep Medicare in place for them is to allow them either to choose the current Medicare program or a private plan – their choice.

他们会把年岁已久、受病患折磨的老年人丢给传统医保体系，因此每个研究过这个计划的经济学家都说，随着时间的推移，传统的医保体系会因此崩溃。然后你们面临的情况就是很多像我的祖母一样的人，在他们最迫切需要良好健康保险的时候，不得不任由私营保险制度发落。

所以我不认为实行优惠券政策是好主意，而这不仅仅是我自己一个人的观点。美国退休人员协会认为——我们从医保项目节省的经费加强了制度，并使医保信托基金期限延长了8年时间，福利不受影响，具有讽刺性的是，如果您废除"奥巴马医改"——现在我也开始喜欢这个术语，"奥巴马医改"——如果您废除它的话，就意味着那些老年人将为处方保险多付600美元，现在他们就开始自费作常规检查来保持健康。

废除奥巴马医改的主要的受益者就是那些保险公司，估计他们会得到几十亿美元，但却未使老年人健康，而我认为，如果我们要确保我们的医保体系能够保持长期稳定，这不是正确的方法。

莱勒：我们将讨论——特别讨论医疗保健问题，但是——州长先生，您支持这个优惠券计划吗？

罗姆尼：我的立场是不更改针对当前和即将退休者的医保计划，而总统先生支持从这个计划里削减7160亿美元。

莱勒：那优惠券呢？

罗姆尼：那是——那是第一点。

莱勒：好的，行。

罗姆尼：第二，针对年轻人，我要做的是确保他们能够享受医保计划，然后让他们能够从现有的医保计划或者是一个私人保险计划中作出选择。他们——他们至少会有两个毫无开销的计划，不必付额外的钱，不用多付那6000美元，这不会发生。

251

They get to – and they'll have at least two plans that will be entirely at no cost to them. So they don't have to pay additional money, no additional $6,000. That's not going to happen.

They'll have at least two plans.

And by the way, if the government can be as efficient as the private sector and offer premiums that are as low as the private sector, people will be happy to get traditional Medicare, or they'll be able to get a private plan. I know my own view is I'd rather have a private plan. I – I'd just as soon not have the government telling me what kind of health care I get. I'd rather be able to have an insurance company. If I don't like them, I can get rid of them and find a different insurance company. But people will make their own choice.

The other thing we have to do to save Medicare, we have to have the benefits high for those that are low-income, but for higher-income people, we're going to have to lower some of the benefits. We have to make sure this program is there for the long term. That's the plan that I've put forward.

And by the way, the idea came not even from Paul Ryan or – or Senator Wyden, who's a co-author of the bill with – with Paul Ryan in the Senate, but also it came from Bill Clinton's – Bill Clinton's chief of staff. This is an idea that's been around a long time, which is saying, hey, let's see if we can't get competition into the Medicare world so that people can get the choice of different plans at lower cost, better quality. I believe in competition.

Obama: Jim, if I – if I can just respond very quickly, first of all, every study has shown that Medicare has lower administrative cost than private insurance does, which is why seniors are generally pretty happy with it. And private insurers have to make a profit. Nothing wrong with that; that's what they do. And so you've got higher administrative costs, plus profit on top of that, and if you are going to save any money through what Governor Romney's proposing, what has to happen is is that the money has to come from somewhere.

他们至少可以有两个计划可供选择。

顺便说一下，如果政府机关能够像私营企业那样高效并提供私营企业一样价格低廉的保险费，人们就愿意参与传统医保，或者也可以选择参与私有保险计划。我认为我宁愿参与私有保险计划。我——我不愿意政府来告诉我我需要怎样的医保计划，我宁愿选择保险公司。如果我不喜欢这家保险公司，我可以换一家保险公司，但人们将作出自己的选择。

对于挽救医保计划，我们要做的另一件事情是，需要提高低收入者的医保补助，而对于高收入者，要降低一些补助，我们需要确保这个计划能够长期运作，这就是我提出的医保计划。

顺便说一下，这个想法不只是来自于保罗·瑞安，或是——和保罗一起起草法案的参议员维登，而是来自比尔·克林顿——比尔·克林顿的白宫办公室主任。这个想法存在已久，就是说要大家来看是否为医保体系引入一些竞争，这样大家就能够去选择一些性价比高的保险计划，我相信竞争。

奥巴马：吉姆，请允许我立刻作出回应。首先，所有研究都表明，医保体系的管理成本低于私营保险公司，这是老年人对于医保比较满意的原因。而私营保险公司是要盈利的，这没有什么不对；他们就是要赚钱，所以说，你要支付更高的管理成本，再加上利润，如果你想要从罗姆尼州长提议的计划中节省开支，那么这笔钱总得从什么地方挤出来才行。

And when you move to a voucher system, you are putting seniors at the mercy of those insurance companies. And over time, if traditional Medicare has decayed or fallen apart, then they're stuck. And this is the reason why AARP has said that your plan would weaken Medicare substantially, and that's why they were supportive of the approach that we took.

One last point I want to make. We do have to lower the cost of health care. Not just in Medicare and –

Lehrer: We'll talk about that in a minute.

Obama: – but – but overall.

Lehrer: Go. OK.

Obama: And so –

Romney: That's – that's a big topic. Could we – could we stay on Medicare?

Obama: Is that a – is that a separate topic? I'm sorry.

Lehrer: Yeah, we're going to – yeah. I want to get to it, but all I want to do is very quickly –

Romney: Let's get back to Medicare.

Lehrer: – before we leave the economy –

Romney: Let's get back to Medicare.

Lehrer: No, no, no, no –

Romney: The president said that the government can provide the service at lower —cost and without a profit.

If that's the case, then it will always be the best product that people can purchase. But my experience –

Lehrer: Wait a minute, Governor.

Romney: My experience is the private sector typically is able to provide a better product at a lower cost.

Lehrer: Can we – can the two of you agree that the voters have a choice, a clear choice between the two of you –

　　而如果你要采用优惠券系统，你就会使老人们任由那些商业保险公司摆布，随着时间的推移，如果传统医保体系衰落，或者彻底崩溃，老年人就会陷入困境。这就是为什么美国退休人员协会说您的医改计划会大幅削弱传统医保系统，这也是为什么他们愿意支持我们采取的方法。

　　我想说最后一点，我们需要降低国家的医疗费用，不只是在医保和——

　　莱勒：我们马上会谈到这个。

　　奥巴马：但——但是总体上

　　莱勒：继续，好的。

　　奥巴马：所以——

　　罗姆尼：这是个大议题。我们可以——我们可以继续讨论医保话题吗？

　　奥巴马：这是——这是不同的议题么？对不起。

　　莱勒：嗯，我们将——嗯，我想再谈一下——但我想要的是快速地讨论一下。

　　罗姆尼：让我们回到医保话题。

　　莱勒：——在我们结束经济话题之前——

　　罗姆尼：让我们回到医保话题。

　　莱勒：不，不——

　　罗姆尼：总统称政府可以以更低——成本，不盈利的情况下，提供服务。

　　如果是这样的话，它将成为人们可以购买的最好的产品。但我的经验是——

　　莱勒：等一下，州长。

　　罗姆尼：我的经验是私营企业能够以更低的成本提供更好的产品。

　　莱勒：我们能——你们两位是否认同你们立场分明？这样选民好作出选择。

　　罗姆尼：当然。

Romney: Absolutely.

Obama: Yes.

Lehrer: – on Medicare?

Romney: Absolutely.

Lehrer: All right. So, to finish quickly, briefly, on the economy, what is your view about the level of federal regulation of the economy right now? Is there too much, and in your case, Mr. President, is there – should there be more? Beginning with you – this is not a new two-minute segment – to start, and we'll go for a few minutes and then we're going to go to health care. OK?

Romney: Regulation is essential. You can't have a free market work if you don't have regulation. As a business person, I had to have – I needed to know the regulations. I needed them there. You couldn't have people opening up banks in their – in their garage and making loans. I mean, you have to have regulations so that you can have an economy work. Every free economy has good regulation.

At the same time, regulation can become excessive.

Lehrer: Is it excessive now, do you think?

Romney: In some places, yes, in other places, no.

Lehrer: Like where?

Romney: It can become out of date. And what's happened in – with some of the legislation that's been passed during the president's term, you've seen regulation become excessive and it's hurt the – it's hurt the economy. Let me give you an example. Dodd- Frank was passed, and it includes within it a number of provisions that I think have some unintended consequences that are harmful to the economy. One is it designates a number of banks as too big to fail, and they're effectively guaranteed by the federal government.

This is the biggest kiss that's been given to – to New York banks I've ever seen. This is an enormous boon for them. There's been – 122 community and small banks have closed since Dodd-Frank. So there's one example.

奥巴马：是的。

莱勒：医保问题上也是这样？

罗姆尼：没错。

莱勒：好的。所以，我们快点结束这个话题。简单来说，你们对于当前政府对于经济的监管政策怎么看？对您来说，总统先生，是否应该加大监管力度？从您（罗姆尼）先开始——这不是一个新的两分钟的议题——我们先就这个话题谈几分钟，然后我们回头再谈医保问题，怎么样？

罗姆尼：监管是必不可少的，如果没有监管，自由市场就无法发挥作用。作为生意人，我必须得——我必须知道那些规章制度，我需要监管。你不能随随便便就让人可以在——在车库里开银行提供贷款服务。我认为必须要有监管，经济才能良好地运转，每一个自由经济都有良好的监管。

与此同时，监管也可能会过度。

莱勒：现在你认为是过度的吗？

罗姆尼：在有些地方过度了，有些地方则不是。

莱勒：比如说呢？

罗姆尼：监管不会与时俱进，你们可以看到有一些总统在任期内通过的法案监管过度，破坏了经济运行。我来举个例子，《多德—弗兰克法》颁布了，它的大量条款引发了无法想象的严重后果，破坏了经济，其中有一条认为一些大银行应该大而不倒，他们得到了联邦政府的有力担保。

这是我所见过的给予纽约银行家们的最大的示好，对他们来说这是个巨大的恩惠，而在《多德—弗兰克法》通过之后，却有122家社区和小型银行倒闭，这就是一例。

还有一个例子。《多德—弗兰克法》认为——

Here's another. In Dodd-Frank, it says that –

Lehrer: You want to repeal Dodd-Frank?

Romney: Well, I would repeal it and replace it. You – we're not going to get rid of all regulation. You have to have regulation. And there's some parts of Dodd-Frank that make all the sense in the world. You need transparency, you need to have leverage limits for institutes –

Lehrer: Well, here's a specific – let's – excuse me –

Romney: Let me mention the other one. Let's talk the –

Lehrer: No, no, let's do – right now, let's not. Let's let him respond.

Lehrer: Let's let him respond to this specific on Dodd-Frank and what the governor just said.

Obama: Well, I think this is a great example. The reason we have been in such a enormous economic crisis was prompted by reckless behavior across the board. Now, it wasn't just on Wall Street. You had – loan officers were – they were giving loans and mortgages that really shouldn't have been given, because they're – the folks didn't qualify. You had people who were borrowing money to buy a house that they couldn't afford. You had credit agencies that were stamping these as A-1 (ph) great investments when they weren't. But you also had banks making money hand-over-fist, churning out products that the bankers themselves didn't even understand in order to make big profits, but knowing that it made the entire system vulnerable.

So what did we do? We stepped in and had the toughest reforms on Wall Street since the 1930s. We said you've got – banks, you've got to raise your capital requirements. You can't engage in some of this risky behavior that is putting Main Street at risk. We're going to make sure that you've got to have a living will, so – so we can know how you're going to wind things down if you make a bad bet so we don't have other taxpayer bailouts.

In the meantime, by the way, we also made sure that all the help that we

莱勒： 您想要废除《多德—弗兰克法》？

罗姆尼： 对，废而换之，我们不应该废除所有的监管政策，我们需要有监管才行。在《多德—弗兰克法》当中，有一些条款是全球适用的，比如说需要更多的透明度、对于金融机构需要有杠杆限制——

莱勒： 好，这是一个具体的例子——让我们—打扰一下——

罗姆尼： 让我再举一个例子。我们来谈——

莱勒： 别，别，让我们—现在，别着急。我们来听听总统的回应。

罗姆尼： 好的。

莱勒： 让他回应一下这项有关《多德—弗兰克法》的具体细节，回应一下州长先生刚刚讲的话。

奥巴马： 对，我觉得这确实是一个很好的例子。我们遭遇这么严重的金融危机就是金融界的鲁莽行为所致，并不只是华尔街，还有很多——信贷官员——他们发放很多贷款和按揭贷款，这是不应该的，因为他们——这些借款人并不具备资质。有人借钱买房子，但是无法偿还。我们有信用机构将这些投资评为 A-1 级，但是事实上并非这么好。还有很多银行日进斗金，为了盈利，明明知道会给整个金融系统带来危险，但还是大量推出不明不白的金融产品。

那么，我们是怎么解决这些问题的呢？我们着手干预，在华尔街进行了自从1930年代以来最严厉的改革。我们说你得——银行，你们得提高资本准备金，你们不能到处投机，而让普通人处于风险之中，我们要确保你们有生存下去的意志，所以——所以如果投机失败的话，我们就能知道你们怎么进行事后处理，这样我们就不用再拿纳税人的钱来为你们买单了。

与此同时，顺便说一句，我们也确保所有我们提供给银行的帮助连本带息，一分不少地还回来。

provided those banks was paid back, every single dime, with interest.

Now, Governor Romney has said he wants to repeal Dodd-Frank, and, you know, I appreciate, and it appears we've got some agreement that a marketplace to work has to have some regulation, but in the past, Governor Romney has said he just wants to repeal Dodd-Frank, roll it back. And so the question is does anybody out there think that the big problem we had is that there was too much oversight and regulation of Wall Street? Because if you do, then Governor Romney is your candidate. But that's not what I believe.

Romney: – sorry, Jim. That – that's just not – that's just not the facts. Look, we have to have regulation of Wall Street.

Obama: Yeah.

Romney: That – that's why I'd have regulation. But I wouldn't designate five banks as too big to fail and give them a blank check. That's one of the unintended consequences of Dodd-Frank. It wasn't thought through properly. We need to get rid of that provision, because it's killing regional and small banks. They're getting hurt.

Let me mention another regulation of Dodd-Frank. You say we were giving mortgages to people who weren't qualified. That's exactly right. It's one of the reasons for the great financial calamity we had. And so Dodd-Frank correctly says we need to –

Lehrer: All right.

Romney: – have qualified mortgages, and if you give a mortgage that's not qualified, there are big penalties. Except they didn't ever go on to define what a qualified mortgage was.

Lehrer: All right.

Romney: It's been two years. We don't know what a qualified mortgage is yet. So banks are reluctant to make loans, mortgages. Try and get a mortgage these days. It's hurt the housing market –

Lehrer: All right –

现在，罗姆尼州长曾说他希望废除《多德—弗兰克法》，大家知道，似乎我们两个都认为市场需要监管，我很欣赏我们的共同之处，但是罗姆尼州长曾说他就是想要彻底推翻《多德—弗兰克法》，所以现在的问题就是，是不是大家都认为我们对于华尔街监督监管的太多了呢？因为如果你是这么想的话，那么你应该投票给罗姆尼州长，而这不是我的想法。

罗姆尼：——不好意思，吉姆，那并非事实。看吧，我们需要对于华尔街进行监管。

奥巴马：好的。

罗姆尼：这是为什么我希望有监管的原因。但我并不会指定5家银行大而不倒，然后开空头支票，这就是《多德—弗兰克法》未曾预想的后果之一，法案并没有经过仔细考证。我们需要取消这些特别援助的条款，因为这伤害了区域银行和小型银行的利益。

让我来谈谈《多德—弗兰克法》的另一项监管措施，您说我们给予很多不够资质的人以分期贷款，说得很对，这就是我们金融危机的原因之一，所以《多德—弗兰克法》在这方面讲得很有道理，我们需要——

莱勒：好的。

罗姆尼：——我们需要有足够资质才能给予分期贷款，如果你给那些不够资质的人分期贷款，将会有大麻烦，但是他们却没有对足够资质的贷款进行界定。

莱勒：好的。

罗姆尼：这种情况已经持续两年了，我们到现在还不知道分期贷款需要什么资格。因此银行并不愿意给出贷款或是分期贷款。最近你可以试着去银行贷一笔款看看情况，这种定义不明确的状况伤害了房产市场——

莱勒：好的——

261

Romney: – because Dodd-Frank didn't anticipate putting in place the kinds of regulations you have to have. It's not that Dodd- Frank always was wrong with too much regulation. Sometimes they didn't come out with a clear regulation.

Lehrer: OK.

Romney: I will make sure we don't hurt the functioning of our – of our marketplace and our businesses, because I want to bring back housing and get good jobs.

Lehrer: All right, I think we have another clear difference between the two of you. Now let's move to health care, where I know there is a clear difference – and that has to do with the Affordable Care Act, "Obamacare."

And it's a two-minute new segment, and it's – that means two minutes each. And you go first, Governor Romney. You wanted repeal. You want the Affordable Care Act repealed. Why?

Deficit and Health Care

Romney: I sure do. Well, in part, it comes, again, from my experience. I was in New Hampshire. A woman came to me, and she said, look, I can't afford insurance for myself or my son. I met a couple in Appleton, Wisconsin, and they said, we're thinking of dropping our insurance; we can't afford it. And the number of small businesses I've gone to that are saying they're dropping insurance because they can't afford it – the cost of health care is just prohibitive. And – and we've got to deal with cost.

And unfortunately, when – when you look at "Obamacare," the Congressional Budget Office has said it will cost $2,500 a year more than traditional insurance. So it's adding to cost. And as a matter of fact, when the president ran for office, he said that by this year he would have brought down the cost of insurance for each family by $2,500 a family. Instead, it's gone up by that amount. So it's expensive. Expensive things hurt families. So that's one reason I don't want it.

罗姆尼：——因为《多德—弗兰克法》并没提前把所需的监管部署到位。并非是《多德—弗兰克法》因为监管太多而错误，而是有时监管并不明晰。

莱勒：好的。

罗姆尼：我想要确保我们不会损伤我们的市场和企业功效，因为我想要重振房产市场，为大家创造好的工作机会。

莱勒：好的，我认为这是二位另一个明确的不同点。现在我们来继续谈论医疗保健问题，我知道在这个问题上有迥异的观点，这个问题和《合理医疗费用法》——"奥巴马医改"有关。

这是一个新的两分钟的议题——每人各两分钟。现在您先开始，罗姆尼州长，您想要废除《合理医疗费用法》，原因是什么？

赤字和医疗保健

罗姆尼：我确实想这样，嗯，部分是因为自己的经历。在新罕布什尔州，一个女人走过来对我说，看，我负担不起我和儿子的医疗保险。我在威斯康星州的阿普尔顿遇到一对夫妇，他们说，我们正在考虑放弃我们的保险，因为我们付不起保险金。我还遇到很多的小型企业，他们说想要取消员工的医疗保险计划，因为他们付不起——医疗开销让人望而却步——我们得解决这些费用才行。

但是很不幸，当你考虑"奥巴马医改"时，国会预算办公室已经说了这会比传统的保险计划每年多开销2500美元，所以，这项计划增加了开销。事实上，在总统先生竞选的时候，他曾说过，今年为止他会为每个家庭减少2500美元的保险开支，但是却适得其反，所以这项计划是很昂贵的，伤害了千家万户，所以这是我想废除这项计划的原因之一。

Second reason, it cuts $716 billion from Medicare to pay for it. I want to put that money back in Medicare for our seniors.

Number three, it puts in place an unelected board that's going to tell people, ultimately, what kind of treatments they can have. I don't like that idea.

Fourth, there was a survey done of small businesses across the country. It said, what's been the effect of "Obamacare" on your hiring plans? And three-quarters of them said, it makes us less likely to hire people. I just don't know how the president could have come into office, facing 23 million people out of work, rising unemployment, an economic crisis at the – at the kitchen table and spent his energy and passion for two years fighting for "Obamacare" instead of fighting for jobs for the American people.

It has killed jobs. And the best course for health care is to do what we did in my state, craft a plan at the state level that fits the needs of the state. And then let's focus on getting the costs down for people rather than raising it with the $2,500 additional premium.

Lehrer: Mr. President, the argument against repeal.

Obama: Well, four years ago when I was running for office I was traveling around and having those same conversations that Governor Romney talks about. And it wasn't just that small businesses were seeing costs skyrocket and they couldn't get affordable coverage even if they wanted to provide it to their employees; it wasn't just that this was the biggest driver of our federal deficit, our overall health care costs. But it was families who were worried about going bankrupt if they got sick – millions of families, all across the country.

If they had a pre-existing condition they might not be able to get coverage at all. If they did have coverage, insurance companies might impose an arbitrary limit. And so as a consequence, they're paying their premiums, somebody gets really sick, and behold they don't have enough money to pay the bills because the insurance companies say that they've hit the limit. So we did work on this alongside working on jobs, because this is part of making sure that middle-class

原因之二是这项计划从医保计划中削减7160亿美元，我想把这些钱放回去，还给老年人。

第三条，该计划设置了一个未经选举就成立的委员会，这个委员会将告诉大家，我们究竟可以获得怎样的健康保险，我不喜欢这种方式。

第四条，有一项针对全国小企业的调查，其中有一个问题，"奥巴马医改"对你的招聘规划有什么样的影响？有四分之三的小企业回答，这让我们不愿多雇员工。我非常不明白，总统上任时面临2300万人失业，失业率攀升，在经济危机威胁人们生活的情况下，竟然可以为了他自己的医改计划耗费两年的时间和精力，而不去提升美国人民的就业。

这项计划事实上抹杀了工作岗位，而最好的医保方法其实是我们州实行的政策——根据每个州的具体需求拟订方案，关键是要将大家的医疗费用降下来，而不是要让大家多付2500美元的额外保险费。

莱勒：总统先生，您对于取消医改计划的提议，有什么论点？

奥巴马：好的，四年前我竞选总统，在全国各地也听到过罗姆尼州长刚刚提到的对话，这其实并不仅仅是小型企业费用猛增、想给员工们提供医疗保障却无能为力的问题，这也不仅仅是医疗费用导致联邦政府赤字增加的最大因素的问题，这其实是关系到我们国家千家万户担心生病就可能破产的问题。

如果他们过去有病史可能就无法保险。如果他们投保了，那些保险公司可能会任意地给他们规定一个报销限额。结果是，他们付了保险金，生病了，却发现他们付不起医药费，因为保险公司说已经超过限额了。所以，我们从过去到现在一直都在解决这个问题，这些都是为了让中产阶级家庭可以有一个稳定的生活。

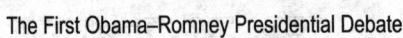

families are secure in this country.

And let me tell you exactly what "Obamacare" did. Number one, if you've got health insurance it doesn't mean a government take over. You keep your own insurance. You keep your own doctor. But it does say insurance companies can't jerk you around. They can't impose arbitrary lifetime limits. They have to let you keep your kid on their insurance – your insurance plan till you're 26 years old. And it also says that they're – you're going to have to get rebates if insurance companies are spending more on administrative costs and profits than they are on actual care.

Number two, if you don't have health insurance, we're essentially setting up a group plan that allows you to benefit from group rates that are typically 18 percent lower than if you're out there trying to get insurance on the individual market.

Now, the last point I'd make before –

Lehrer: Two minutes –

Obama: – before –

Lehrer: Two minutes is up, sir.

Obama: No, I – I think I've – I had five seconds before you interrupted me – was – that the irony is that we've seen this model work really well in Massachusetts, because Governor Romney did a good thing, working with Democrats in the state to set up what is essentially the identical model. And as a consequence, people are covered there. It hasn't destroyed jobs. And as a consequence, we now have a system in which we have the opportunity to start bringing down cost, as opposed to just –

Lehrer: Your five –

Obama: – leaving millions of people out in the cold.

Lehrer: Your five seconds went away a long time ago.

Obama: That –

Lehrer: All right, Governor. Governor, tell the – tell the president directly

我来给大家讲讲"奥巴马医改计划"到底做了什么。第一，如果你有医疗保险，并不是说政府要把你的保险拿掉，你可以保留自己的保险，自己的医生。医改计划是说，那些保险公司不能随便对你指手画脚，他们不能随便指定保险期限限制，他们必须得保证你的小孩在他们的保险范围之内——直到26岁为止。医改计划还要求他们——如果那些保险公司在管理成本和利润上的花费大于它们实际用于医疗保险的费用，你的部分款项将被退回。

　　第二条，如果你现在没有医疗保险，我们其实是设立了一个集体保险计划，让你可以享受到比个人投保低18%的保险费率。

　　现在，最后我要再讲一点——

　　莱勒：到两分钟了——

　　奥巴马：最后再——

　　莱勒：两分钟到了，先生。

　　奥巴马：没有，我——我认为我有——在您打断我之前我还有5秒钟——很讽刺的是这项医改计划在马萨诸塞州运作得很好，因为罗姆尼做得很好，和州里面的民主党同仁们一起树立了这项医改的典范。因此，州里面的居民们获得了医疗保障，这并没有让就业减少。结果，我们现在有了一项可以让我们有机会削减开支的医疗体系，而不是只是说——

　　莱勒：您的5秒钟——

　　奥巴马：让千百万人没有保障，无依无靠。

　　莱勒：您5秒钟已经超时很久了。

　　奥巴马：那个——

　　莱勒：好的，州长先生，州长，直接告诉总统先生为什么您认为他刚刚讲的"奥巴马医改"并不符合事实？

why you think what he just said is wrong about "Obamacare."

Romney: Well, I did with my first statement.

Obama: You did.

Romney: But I'll go on.

Obama: Please elaborate.

Romney: I'll elaborate. Exactly right.

First of all, I like the way we did it in Massachusetts. I like the fact that in my state, we had Republicans and Democrats come together and work together. What you did instead was to push through a plan without a single Republican vote. As a matter of fact, when Massachusetts did something quite extraordinary, elected a Republican senator to stop "Obamacare", you pushed it through anyway. So entirely on a partisan basis, instead of bringing America together and having a discussion on this important topic, you pushed through something that you and Nancy Pelosi and Harry Reid thought was the best answer and drove it through.

What we did, in a legislature 87 percent Democrat, we worked together. Two hundred legislators in my legislature – only two voted against the plan by the time we were finished.

What were some differences?

We didn't raise taxes. You've raised them by a trillion dollars under "Obamacare." We didn't cut Medicare. Of course, we don't have Medicare, but we didn't cut Medicare by $716 billion. We didn't put in place a board that can tell people ultimately what treatments they're going to receive.

We didn't – we didn't also do something that I think a number of people across this country recognize, which is put – put people in a position where they're going to lose the insurance they had and they wanted. Right now, the CBO says up to 20 million people will lose their insurance as "Obamacare" goes into effect next year. And likewise, a study by McKinsey & Company of American businesses said 30 percent of them are anticipating dropping people

罗姆尼： 好，我已经在第一部分的陈述里面讲过了。

奥巴马： 您确实讲过了。

罗姆尼： 但我会继续。

奥巴马： 请详述您的观点。

罗姆尼： 我会详述的。完全正确。

首先，我喜欢我们在马萨诸塞州推行医改的方式。我觉得在我的州里面，共和党和民主党同仁们能够携手努力、共同奋斗是一件非常好的事情。而您所做的，则是在没有一个共和党人投您票的情况下，要强行推进这项医改计划。事实上，当马萨诸塞州做了件不同寻常的事情，选出一名共和党参议员来制止"奥巴马医改"的时候，您还是强行推进该计划。所以在两党合作的这个问题上，您没有联合美国各界来讨论这个重要的议题，而是强行推行了您的医改计划，因为您，还有南希·佩洛西以及哈里·瑞德认为这就是最好的答案，可以推行。

而我们所做的则是，在一个由87%的民主党构成的立法机关携手合作，我们的立法机关有200个立法工作者——最后投票时，只有两个人投票反对这个计划。

所以，我和总统先生的区别在哪里呢？

区别在于，我们没有提税。您因为要推动"奥巴马医疗"增加了1万亿美元的税收。我们没有削减医保计划。当然，我们也没有医保计划，但是我们没有从中削减7160亿美元。我们没有设立一个委员会，来告诉人们究竟他们可以获得怎样的健康保险。

而我们也没有做许多国人已经认识到的事情，那就是——让人们失去已经拥有的和想要拥有的医疗保险。就在现在，国会预算办公室称，如果"奥巴马医改计划"在下一年度继续实行的话，将会有2000万人失去医疗保险。与此相似的是，一份研究美国企业的麦肯锡公司的报告指出，30%的企业正在提前让员工脱离医保体系。所以因为这些，因为税收，因为医保体系，因为这个委员会，因为失去医保的人们，美国人民并不想要——不想要"奥巴马医改"，这就是为什么共和党人说不做这件事的原因。

from coverage. So for those reasons, for the tax, for Medicare, for this board and for people losing their insurance, this is why the American people don't want – don't want "Obamacare." It's why Republicans said, do not do this.

And the Republicans had a – had a plan. They put a plan out. They put out a plan, a bipartisan plan. It was swept aside. I think something this big, this important has to be done in a bipartisan basis. And we have to have a president who can reach across the aisle and fashion important legislation with the input from both parties.

Obama: Governor Romney said this has to be done on a bipartisan basis. This was a bipartisan idea. In fact, it was a Republican idea.

And Governor Romney, at the beginning of this debate, wrote and said, what we did in Massachusetts could be a model for the nation. And I agree that the Democratic legislators in Massachusetts might have given some advice to Republicans in Congress about how to cooperate, but the fact of the matter is, we used the same advisers, and they say it's the same plan.

It – when Governor Romney talks about this board, for example – unelected board that we've created – what this is, is a group of health care experts, doctors, et cetera, to figure out how can we reduce the cost of care in the system overall, because the – there are two ways of dealing with our health care crisis.

One is to simply leave a whole bunch of people uninsured and let them fend for themselves, to let businesses figure out how long they can continue to pay premiums until finally they just give up and their workers are no longer getting insured, and that's been the trend line. Or, alternatively, we can figure out how do we make the cost of care more effective. And there are ways of doing it.

So at – at Cleveland Clinic, one of the best health care systems in the world, they actually provide great care cheaper than average. And the reason they do is because they do some smart things. They – they say, if a patient's coming in, let's get all the doctors together at once, do one test instead of having the patient

共和党人曾经，有——有一个医改计划，他们推出这项计划，这项两党合作的计划。但该计划被搁置，我觉得这么重大的事情，还是需要在两党合作的基础上去做的。因此，我们需要有一个能够领导两党合作的总统，来从两党的立场上推动立法。

奥巴马：罗姆尼州长说这事儿必须由两党合作。其实这项医改是两党共同的主意。事实上，这是共和党提出来的想法。

而罗姆尼州长在这场辩论开始的时候写道并说道，我们在马萨诸塞州所做的事情可以成为全国的表率。马萨诸塞州的民主党立法者们可能给了国会的共和党议员们一些关于如何与总统的医改方案配合的建议，我同意这点，但是，实际情况是，我们两党聘请了相同的顾问团队，而他们说这是同一个计划。

当罗姆尼州长说到这个委员会的时候，举个例子来说——我们成立的未经选举的委员会——这是一个什么委员会呢？这是一个由医保专家、医生等组成的团体，来研究如何能够减少医疗体系总体开销，因为——有两种方法来处理我们的医疗问题。

方法之一是让大部分人没有医疗保险，自生自灭，让企业们去考虑他们还要支付多久的医保费用，直到最后他们放弃医保，让员工不再拥有保障，而这已经成为了一个趋势。或者，我们有另外一个办法，就是去考虑我们怎样才能让医疗体系更具效率，当然我们可以想出具体的办法。

所以，在世界上最好的医疗系统之一的克利夫兰医学中心，事实上它们的保险价格比起全国平均水平要低，因为他们的确很精明。他们认为，如果病人来看病，我们就让所有的医生都为他看病，做一次测试，而不是要让病人跑来跑去做10次测试。我们要确保提供预防性的保健，这样就能发现像糖尿病这样的疾病的苗头。我们要根据保险供应商的服务表现来付钱，而不是根据他们参与的程序数量来付钱。现在，我们这个委员会所做的事情就是要识别医疗业界的最佳做法，然后说，让我们使用医保和医疗救助的购买力来将所有这些好的做法固化下来，让它们成为医疗体系的一部分。

run around with 10 tests. Let's make sure that we're providing preventive care so we're catching the onset of something like diabetes. Let's – let's pay providers on the basis of performance as opposed to on the basis of how many procedures they've – they've engaged in. Now, so what this board does is basically identifies best practices and says, let's use the purchasing power of Medicare and Medicaid to help to institutionalize all these good things that we do.

And the fact of the matter is that when "Obamacare" is fully implemented, we're going to be in a position to show that costs are going down. And over the last two years, health care premiums have gone up, it's true, but they've gone up slower than any time in the last 50 years. So we're already beginning to see progress. In the meantime, folks out there with insurance, you're already getting a rebate.

Let me make one last point. Governor Romney says we should replace it. I'm just going to repeal it, but we can replace it with something. But the problem is he hasn't described what exactly we'd replace it with other than saying we're going to leave it to the states.

But the fact of the matter is that some of the prescriptions that he's offered, like letting you buy insurance across state lines, there's no indication that that somehow is going to help somebody who's got a pre-existing condition be able to finally buy insurance. In fact, it's estimated that by repealing "Obamacare," you're looking at 50 million people losing health insurance at a time when it's vitally important.

Lehrer: Let's let the governor explain what you would do if "Obamacare" is repealed. How would you replace it? What do you have in mind?

Romney: Let – well, actually – actually it's – it's – it's a lengthy description, but number one, pre-existing conditions are covered under my plan. Number two, young people are able to stay on their family plan. That's already offered in the private marketplace; you don't have – have the government mandate that for that to occur.

事实是，当"奥巴马医改"最终得到完全实施时，我们会看到成本会有所降低，在过去两年之中，医保费的确上升了，但是这些开销比过去50年上升的都慢，因此初见成效。同时，那些拥有医保的人们已经享受到部分退款。

让我强调最后一点，罗姆尼州长说我们应该替换医改计划，说他就是要废除该计划，然后用其他的计划替代，但问题是，他并没有讲清楚我们到底用什么方案来替代这个计划，他只是说，要把这些计划丢给各个州来做。

而事实是，他提出的一些方案，比如让你能够跨州购买医保服务，但并没有指出如何让那些已经患病的人最终得以买到保险。事实上，据估计，如果废除"奥巴马医改"，你将会看到有5000万人丢掉医保，而这对他们来说是至关重要的。

莱勒：我们来让州长先生讲讲如果废除"奥巴马医改计划"，您会怎么做？您要怎么替换它？您有什么计划呢？

罗姆尼：嗯——事实上——事实上这会是一个很庞大的计划，但是第一条就是，已经患病的人们会在我的医保计划中得到保障。第二条，年轻人可以享有他们家庭的医保计划，私人医保市场其实已经有这样的服务了；你并不需要政府的命令。

But let's come back to something the president – I agree on, which is the – the key task we have in health care is to get the costs down so it's more affordable for families, and – and then he has as a model for doing that a board of people at the government, an unelected board, appointed board, who are going to decide what kind of treatment you ought to have.

Obama: No, it isn't.

Romney: In my opinion, the government is not effective in – in bringing down the cost of almost anything. As a matter of fact, free people and free enterprises trying to find ways to do things better are able to be more effective in bringing down the costs than the government will ever be. Your example of the Cleveland clinic is my case in point, along with several others I could describe. This is the private market. These are small – these are enterprises competing with each other, learning how to do better and better jobs.

I used to consult to businesses – excuse me, to hospitals and to health care providers. I was astonished at the creativity and innovation that exists in the American people. In order to bring the cost of health care down, we don't need to have a – an – a board of 15 people telling us what kinds of treatments we should have. We instead need to put insurance plans, providers, hospitals, doctors on targets such that they have an incentive, as you say, performance pay, for doing an excellent job, for keeping costs down, and that's happening. Intermountain Health Care does it superbly well.

Obama: They do.

Romney: Mayo Clinic is doing it superbly well, Cleveland Clinic, others. But the right answer is not to have the federal government take over health care and start mandating to the providers across America, telling a patient and a doctor what kind of treatment they can have. That's the wrong way to go. The private market and individual responsibility always work best.

Obama: Let me just point out, first of all, this board that we're talking about can't make decisions about what treatments are given. That's explicitly

但是让我们回到总统的观点——我赞同——说医保的关键任务，就是要降低医疗花销，让我们的家庭能够负担得起这些费用，然后——然后他让一个政府的委员会，一个未经选举的委员会，一个指定的委员会来决定你会得到怎样的健康保险。

奥巴马： 不是这样的。

罗姆尼： 依我所见，政府向来不擅长——降低花销。事实上，自由的人，自由的企业想找到好方法降低花销的话，总是能够比政府更有效率。您说的克利夫兰医学中心就是一个好的例子，还有我说过的其他例子，这就是私有市场的好处。这些是小型企业，互相竞争的企业，它们一直在努力做得越来越好。

我曾经咨询过一些公司——抱歉，是医院和健康保险供应商，我对美国人民所拥有的创造力和创新能力惊讶不已。如果我们要降低医疗开销，并不需要一个——由15人组成的委员会来告诉我们需要怎样的健康保险，相反的，我们要给保险方案、供应商、医院和医生制定目标，给他们提供动力来做这件事情，就像您说的那样，用绩效报酬的形式，来让他们做好自己的工作，降低费用，而这就是现在正在发生的事情。山间医疗保健公司就做的十分出色。

奥巴马： 他们是这样。

罗姆尼： 梅约诊所也做得非常好，还有克利夫兰医学中心，等等。正确的解决方案是不要让联邦政府接管医疗系统，然后开始对全美国的健康保险供应商发号施令，来告诉病人和医生他们可以有什么样的健康保险，这是不对的，而私有市场和个人责任心才是最有效果的。

奥巴马： 我想指出的是，首先，我们所说的这个委员会并不能决定给予人们哪些健康保险，这是法律明文禁止的。

prohibited in the law.

But let's go back to what Governor Romney indicated, that under his plan he would be able to cover people with pre-existing conditions. Well, actually, Governor, that isn't what your plan does. What your plan does is to duplicate what's already the law, which says if you are out of health insurance for three months then you can end up getting continuous coverage and an insurance company can't deny you if you've – if it's been under 90 days.

But that's already the law. And that doesn't help the millions of people out there with pre-existing conditions. There's a reason why Governor Romney set up the plan that he did in Massachusetts. It wasn't a government takeover of health care. It was the largest expansion of private insurance. But what it does say is that insurers, you've got to take everybody. Now, that also means that you've got more customers.

But when Governor Romney says that he'll replace it with something but can't detail how it will be in fact replaced, and the reason he set up the system he did in Massachusetts is because there isn't a better way of dealing with the pre-existing conditions problem, it – it just reminds me of – you know, he says that he's going to close deductions and loopholes for his tax plan.

That's how it's going to be paid for. But we don't know the details. He says that he's going to replace Dodd-Frank, Wall Street reform. But we don't know exactly which ones. He won't tell us. He now says he's going to replace "Obamacare" and assure that all the good things that are in it are going to be in there and you don't have to worry.

And at some point, I think the American people have to ask themselves, is the reason that Governor Romney is keeping all these plans to replace secret because they're too good? Is – is it because that somehow middle-class families are going to benefit too much from them? No, the – the reason is because when we reform Wall Street, when we tackle the problem of pre-existing conditions, then, you know, these are tough problems, and we've got to make choices. And

还是让我们回到罗姆尼州长所指出的，说他的医改计划能够使已经患病的人士投保。好吧，事实上，州长先生，您的计划并不会这么做。您的计划其实是重复法律中存在的东西，说如果你有3个月时间没有医保保障，你最后可以继续得到保险，如果不超过90天的话，保险公司并不能拒绝你。

但法律中已经有这些内容了，而这也不能帮助那些已经患病的人士。罗姆尼州长要采用在马萨诸塞州使用的医改计划，是有原因的，那个计划并不是政府接管医疗系统，这是私人医疗保险公司的最大范围的扩张，该计划认为，保险公司应将所有的人都纳入保障范围。现在意味着你有了更多的顾客。

罗姆尼州长说要用别的计划来替代医改计划，但却说不出具体替代细节，而他在马萨诸塞州设立那个医改计划并非是因为有更好的方法解决已经患病者的医保问题，而是——让我想起了，大家知道，他在他的税收计划中提及的，他要降低课税减免，弥补漏洞。

而这就是他的医改计划的资金来源，但我们并不知道具体细节。他说他要替换华尔街的改革计划——《多德—弗兰克法》，但我们并不知道他究竟要替换哪些条款，他也不会告诉我们，他现在说他要替换"奥巴马医改计划"，然后又保证该计划的优势会保留，而你不必担心。

有时候，我想美国人民不得不问问自己，是因为罗姆尼的这些替代计划太好了，以至于需要被保密吗？是——是因为中产阶级将从这些替代计划中获得太多的好处所以才要保密呢？不是的——原因是因为当我们要改革华尔街的时候，当我们解决已有患病者的医保问题的时候，你知道，这些都是非同寻常的难题，我们必须得做出抉择的。而我们这边做出的抉择会保证使全国的中产阶级受益。

the choices we've made have been ones that ultimately are benefiting middle-class families all across the country.

Lehrer: All right, we're going to move to a –

Romney: No, I – I have to respond to that –

Lehrer: No, but –

Romney: – which is – which is my experience as a governor is if I come in and – and lay down a piece of legislation and say it's my way or the highway, I don't get a lot done. What I do is the same way that Tip O'Neill and Ronald Reagan worked together some years ago. When Ronald Reagan ran for office, he laid out the principles that he was going to foster. He said he was going to lower tax rates. He said he was going to broaden the base. You've said the same thing: You're going to simplify the tax code, broaden the base. Those are my principles.

I want to bring down the tax burden on middle-income families. And I'm going to work together with Congress to say, OK, what are the various ways we could bring down deductions, for instance? One way, for instance, would be to have a single number. Make up a number – 25,000 (dollars), $50,000. Anybody can have deductions up to that amount. And then that number disappears for high-income people. That's one way one could do it. One could follow Bowles-Simpson as a model and take deduction by deduction and make differences that way.

There are alternatives to accomplish the objective I have, which is to bring down rates, broaden the base, simplify the code and create incentives for growth.

And with regards to health care, you had remarkable details with regards to my pre-existing condition plan. You obviously studied up on – on my plan. In fact, I do have a plan that deals with people with pre-existing conditions. That's part of my health care plan. And what we did in Massachusetts is a model for the nation, state by state. And I said that at that time. The federal government taking over health care for the entire nation and whisking aside the 10th Amendment,

莱勒：好的，继续下一个话题——

罗姆尼：别，我还要回应这个话题——

莱勒：不，但——

罗姆尼：——我要回应的是，以我做州长时候的经验，如果我走过来，并——制定一个立法方案，然后对大家说，没得商量，你们必须照做的话，我是不会做成很多事情的。我做事采用的方式，与蒂普奥尼尔和罗纳德·里根多年前合作的时候一样。当罗纳德·里根竞选总统的时候，他制定了一些治理原则，他说要降低税率，扩大税基。您也说了相同的事情：您要简化税法，扩大税基，那些也是我的原则。

我想降低中等收入家庭的税收负担。我要与国会合作，来考虑一下——例如，有哪些方法可以降低课税减免。有一个办法，就是要提出一个简单的数字，提出一个数字——25000美元，或者50000美元，说每个人都可以减掉这么多的税收，然后让这笔数字从高收入群体的收入中消失，这是方法之一。我们可以采用鲍尔斯·辛普森委员会减赤委员会的方式，来逐步削减税收，改变现状。

要达到我的目标，也有别的方案，就是降低税率，扩大税基，简化税法，以提供经济增长的动力。

说到医疗体系改革，您对我解决已经患病人士的医保问题的方案其实非常了解。很明显您对我的计划做了一番研究。事实上，我对于已患病人士确实有一个计划，这是我的医改计划的一部分，而我们在马萨诸塞州所做的改革为全国各州各自的改革树立了榜样，我当时就这么说过。联邦政府现在的做法是要接管全国的医保，把宪法第十修正案扔在一边，不顾各州医改的权力，这无法让美国拥有生机勃勃的经济。

which gives states the rights for these kinds of things, is not the course for America to have a stronger, more vibrant economy.

Lehrer: That is a terrific segue to our next segment, and is the role of government. And let's see, role of government and it is – you are first on this, Mr. President. The question is this. Do you believe – both of you – but you have the first two minutes on this, Mr. President – do you believe there's a fundamental difference between the two of you as to how you view the mission of the federal government?

Obama: Well, I definitely think there are differences.

Lehrer: And – yeah.

Obama: The first role of the federal government is to keep the American people safe. That's its most basic function. And as commander in chief, that is something that I've worked on and thought about every single day that I've been in the Oval Office.

But I also believe that government has the capacity – the federal government has the capacity to help open up opportunity and create ladders of opportunity and to create frameworks where the American people can succeed. Look, the genius of America is the free enterprise system, and freedom, and the fact that people can go out there and start a business, work on an idea, make their own decisions.

But as Abraham Lincoln understood, there are also some things we do better together.

So in the middle of the Civil War, Abraham Lincoln said, let's help to finance the Transcontinental Railroad. Let's start the National Academy of Sciences. Let's start land grant colleges, because we want to give these gateways of opportunity for all Americans, because if all Americans are getting opportunity, we're all going to be better off. That doesn't restrict people's freedom; that enhances it.

And so what I've tried to do as president is to apply those same principles.

莱勒：现在是继续我们下一个议题的绝好时间，下一个议题是谈论政府的职责问题。好，我们来看一下，政府的职责——总统先生，您先谈谈这个话题——您认为——你们两个各有两分钟时间，总统先生——你们两位对于联邦政府的职责的看法有没有本质性的区别？

奥巴马：好的，我认为肯定是有差别的。

莱勒：好的——对。

奥巴马：联邦政府的首要职责是保护美国人民的安全，这是它的最基本的职能。而作为三军总司令，这也是我努力工作的目的，也是我就任了每天都在思考的事情。

但是我也认为联邦政府有能力——来帮助创造机会，提供渠道，拟定框架，使美国人民获得成功。大家知道，美国的非凡之处就在于它的自由企业体系，以及自由本身。这些让人民能够创立企业，实现创意和想法，作出自己的抉择。

按照亚伯拉罕·林肯的理解，有一些事情是我们最好一起携手努力来做。

所以，就在内战正酣之际，林肯总统说过，让我们资助州际铁路，让我们设立美国国家科学院，让我们开始政府赠地建立学院，因为我们想要给所有的美国人民提供这些机遇，因为如果所有的美国人都能得到机会，我们所有的人就会生活得更好，这些做法并没有限制人们的自由，反而增进了人们的自由。

所以作为总统，我所做的就是要采用相同的原则，当提到教育的时候，我说过我们要改革那些运作不善的学校，我们使用了一项叫做"力争上游"的计划，这不是一个自上向下的计划，州长先生。我们对各州说，如果你们要开始教育改革的话，我们会给你们更多的资助。结果，现在全国有46个州的改革初见成效。

And when it comes to education, what I've said is we've got to reform schools that are not working. We use something called Race to the Top. Wasn't a top-down approach, Governor. What we've said is to states, we'll give you more money if you initiate reforms. And as a consequence, you had 46 states around the country who have made a real difference.

But what I've also said is let's hire another hundred thousand math and science teachers to make sure we maintain our technological lead and our people are skilled and able to succeed. And hard-pressed states right now can't all do that. In fact, we've seen layoffs of hundreds of thousands of teachers over the last several years, and Governor Romney doesn't think we need more teachers. I do, because I think that that is the kind of investment where the federal government can help. It can't do it all, but it can make a difference, and as a consequence, we'll have a better-trained workforce, and that will create jobs, because companies want to locate in places where we've got a skilled workforce.

Lehrer: Two minutes, Governor, on the role of government, your view.

Romney: Well, first, I love great schools. Massachusetts, our schools are ranked number one of all 50 states. And the key to great schools: great teachers. So I reject the idea that I don't believe in great teachers or more teachers. Every school district, every state should make that decision on their own.

The role of government – look behind us: the Constitution and the Declaration of Independence.

The role of government is to promote and protect the principles of those documents. First, life and liberty. We have a responsibility to protect the lives and liberties of our people, and that means the military, second to none. I do not believe in cutting our military. I believe in maintaining the strength of America's military.

Second, in that line that says, we are endowed by our Creator with our rights – I believe we must maintain our commitment to religious tolerance and

而我也说过，如果我们聘用更多的数学和科技教师，以确保我国的科技领先地位，确保人民受到良好培训，能够成功。而经济拮据的州可能目前还做不到这些。事实上，过去几年，我们已经发现有成百上千的教师下岗，而罗姆尼州长却不认为我们需要更多的教师。我认为我们需要这些教师，因为我认为这是一种投资，联邦政府也可以提供帮助，虽然它不能万事包办，但是确实可以做一些事情来改变现状。最后，我们会有一个训练有素的劳动力供给，而这会带来更多的工作岗位，因为公司们都希望选址在有训练有素的劳动力的地方。

莱勒：两分钟，州长先生，谈谈政府的职责问题，您的观点是什么？

罗姆尼：好的，首先，我喜欢一流的学校。在马萨诸塞州，我们的学校是所有50个州里面排名第一的，而一流学校的关键是优秀的师资力量。所以那种说我不喜欢好教师或者我不愿意雇佣更多教师的说法是不对的。每一个学区，每一个州都应该自行决定聘请教师的问题。

谈到政府的职责问题——请大家看看我们身后：《宪法》以及《独立宣言》。

政府的职责就是要促进和保护这些文件所述及的原则，其首要原则就是，生命和自由。我们有责任保卫我们人民的生命和自由，而这意味着军事力量责无旁贷。我不想要削减我们的军费开支，我要保持美国军力强大。

第二条原则是，有句话说创造者赐予了我们权利——我相信我们必须在这个国家保持宗教宽容和宗教自由，这一声明也提到，造物者赐予了我们追求自己选择幸福的权利。我对此的理解是，要确保每一个不幸，不能够照顾自己的人——受到他人的照顾。

freedom in this country. That statement also says that we are endowed by our Creator with the right to pursue happiness as we choose. I interpret that as, one, making sure that those people who are less fortunate and can't care for themselves are cared by – by one another.

We're a nation that believes we're all children of the same God. And we care for those that have difficulties – those that are elderly and have problems and challenges, those that disabled, we care for them. And we look for discovery and innovation, all these thing desired out of the American heart to provide the pursuit of happiness for our citizens.

But we also believe in maintaining for individuals the right to pursue their dreams, and not to have the government substitute itself for the rights of free individuals. And what we're seeing right now is, in my view, a – a trickle-down government approach which has government thinking it can do a better job than free people pursuing their dreams. And it's not working.

And the proof of that is 23 million people out of work. The proof of that is one out of six people in poverty. The proof of that is we've gone from 32 million on food stamps to 47 million on food stamps. The proof of that is that 50 percent of college graduates this year can't find work.

We know that the path we're taking is not working. It's time for a new path.

Lehrer: All right, let's go through some specifics in terms of what – how each of you views the role of government. How do – education. Does the federal government have a responsibility to improve the quality of public education in America?

Romney: Well, the primary responsibility for education is – is of course at the state and local level. But the federal government also can play a very important role. And I – and I agree with Secretary Arne Duncan. He's – there's some ideas he's put forward on Race to the Top – not all of them but some of them I agree with, and congratulate him for pursuing that. The federal government can get local and – and state schools to do a better job.

我们作为一个国家相信，我们同是一个上帝的子民的国家。我们关心那些遇到困难的人们——那些年岁已老、遇到难处、面临挑战、身体残疾的人们，我们关心他们。我们也追寻

探索和发现，追寻创新，所有这些都是为了我们的公民们能够追寻幸福，这些都是美国人民的热切期待。

而我们也认为每个人都有权利去追寻梦想，而不是让政府代替个人来行使这些权利。而我们现在看到的是，在我看来——这是一种涓滴式政府方法，认为能够比自由追寻梦想人们做得更好，而这是无济于事的。

证据就是现在有2300万人失业，证据就是我们有六分之一的人穷困潦倒，证据就是，我们的国家领取食品券的人数已经从3200万增加到4700万，证据就是今年有50%的大学生找不到工作。

罗姆尼： 我们知道我们现在选择的路径是不对的，应该选择一条新的路径的时刻到了。

莱勒： 好的，让我们从一些具体的方面——来看看你们两位各自怎么看待政府的职责。怎样看待——教育。联邦政府有没有责任来提升美国的公共教育质量？

罗姆尼： 好的，对于教育的主要责任理所当然是落到州级政府和地方政府的头上。但是联邦政府在这里也扮演了一个非常重要的角色。而我赞同教育部长阿恩·邓肯的想法，他在"力争上游"计划中提出的一些想法——不是所有的想法，而是有一部分，我是赞同的，我很赞赏他追求这些想法。联邦政府确实是可以让地方——以及州一级的学校变得更好。

My own view, by the way, is I've added to that. I happen to believe – I want the kids that are getting federal dollars from IDEA or – or Title I – these are disabled kids or – or poor kids or – or lower-income kids, rather. I want them to be able to go to the school of their choice. So all federal funds, instead of going to the – to the state or to the school district, I'd have go – if you will, follow the child and let the parent and the child decide where to send their – their – their student.

Lehrer: How do you see the federal government's responsibility to – as I say, to improve the quality of public education in this country?

Obama: Well, as I've indicated, I think that it has a significant role to play. Through our Race to the Top program, we've worked with Republican and Democratic governors to initiate major reforms, and they're having an impact right now.

Lehrer: Do you think you have a difference with your views and those of Governor Romney on – about education and the federal government?

Obama: You know, this is where budgets matter because budgets reflect choices. So when Governor Romney indicates that he wants to cut taxes and potentially benefit folks like me and him, and to pay for it, we're having to initiate significant cuts in federal support for education, that makes a difference.

You know, his running mate, Congressman Ryan, put forward a budget that reflects many of the principles that Governor Romney's talked about. And it wasn't very detailed. This seems to be a trend. But – but what it did do is to – if you extrapolated how much money we're talking about, you'd look at cutting the education budget by up to 20 percent.

When it comes to community colleges, we are seeing great work done out there all over the country because we have the opportunity to train people for jobs that exist right now. And one of the things I suspect Governor Romney and I probably agree on is getting businesses to work with community colleges so that they're setting up their training programs –

顺便提一下，我的观点是在支持联邦政府参与发展教育的基础上发展出来的。我恰好认为——我想让那些从联邦政府的"IDEA"计划或者"TitleI"计划获得资助的学生——这些是残疾的孩子——或者是贫穷的孩子——或者是低收入家庭的孩子，能够选择他们的学校。所有这些联邦政府的钱，与其说是分配给各个州，或者是分配给各个学区，不如直接给——如果你赞同的话——给这些小孩自己，然后让他们的家长和学生自己来决定去就读哪所学校。

莱勒：总统先生，您如何看待联邦政府的职责——就像我说的那样，来提升这个国家的公共教育的质量？

奥巴马：好的，如我所言，联邦政府在这当中扮演了非常重要的角色，通过我们的"力争上游"计划，我们已经与共和党州长以及民主党州长们一起来开展了很多重大改革，并取得了重大成效。

莱勒：关于教育和联邦政府，您和罗姆尼州长的观点有什么区别吗？

奥巴马：说到区别，大家知道，预算很重要，因为预算反映了抉择，所以当罗姆尼州长说，他要减税以使得像我和他这样的人能够受益的时候，我们就不得不大幅削减联邦政府对于教育的资助，这就是我们俩的区别所在。

大家知道，他的竞选搭档，瑞恩议员提出的预算计划反映了罗姆尼州长所谈论的不少原则，这份预算并不是很详细，似乎这是一种趋势。但是——这份预算是要——如果你推测一下我们是在谈论多少钱的话，你就知道他们削减了20%的教育预算。

说到社区大学，我们发现它在全国范围内做的十分出色，因为我们有机会为现有的工作岗位提供人们所需要的培训。我自己是赞同这一点的，但我怀疑罗姆尼州长是否希望企业和社区学院能够联合起来启动培训计划——

莱勒：你同意么，州长先生？

Lehrer: Do you agree, Governor?

Obama: Let – let – let me just finish the point.

Romney: Oh, yeah. Oh, yeah.

Obama: I suspect it'll be a small agreement.

Romney: It's going over well in my state, by the way, yeah.

Obama: The – where their partnering so that – they're designing training programs, and people who are going through them know that there's a job waiting for them if they complete them. That makes a big difference. But that requires some federal support.

Let me just say one final example. When it comes to making college affordable – whether it's two-year or four-year – one of the things that I did as president was we were sending $60 billion to banks and lenders as middle men for the student loan program, even though the loans were guaranteed. So there was no risk for the banks or the lenders but they were taking billions out of the system.

And we said, why not cut out the middle man? And as a consequence, what we've been able to do is to provide millions more students assistance, lower or keep low interest rates on student loans. And this is an example of where our priorities make a difference. Governor Romney, I genuinely believe, cares about education. But when he tells a student that, you know, you should borrow money from your parents to go to college, you know, that indicates the degree to which, you know, there may not be as much of a focus on the fact that folks like myself, folks like Michelle, kids probably who attend University of Denver just don't have that option.

And for us to be able to make sure that they've got that opportunity and they can walk through that door, that is vitally important – not just to those kids. It's how we're going to grow this economy over the long term.

Lehrer: We're running out of time.

Romney: Jim, Jim –

Lehrer: I'm certainly going give you a chance to respond to that. Yes, sir,

奥巴马：让我把这点说完。

罗姆尼：对的，我同意，我是同意这么做的。

奥巴马：我怀疑您并不是完全同意。

罗姆尼：顺便提一下，在我的州里面都是这么做的，是的。

奥巴马：——如果他们联合起来就会一起设计培训项目，然后那些参加培训的人们就知道培训结束后，他们会找到工作。这就大大改变了就业问题的现状，但这种合作需要联邦政府的支持。

我来说说最后一个例子。当我们说到让人们可以负担学费时——不管是两年还是四年的大学——我作为总统做的其中一件事情就是，给银行和贷款方600亿美元，让他们作为中间人，来向学生提供助学贷款。因为贷款是被担保的，所以银行或者贷款方在这当中是没有风险的，但是他们需要从系统中抽出几十亿美元。

我们说为什么不取消这些中间人呢？这样，我们的钱就可以多给几百万的学生提供援助，降低助学贷款的利息或者保持低利息，这就是我们两个重点不同的地方。我真诚地相信罗姆尼州长关心教育。但他对学生说，你应该向家长借钱来上大学，这在某种程度上反映了，州长并没有太关心那些像我或米歇尔一样的学生，或者是很有可能就是在丹佛大学上学的学生，没有办法从家里借到钱的这种情况。

而我们所要做的，就是要确保这些学生能够获得机会，跨过上大学的门槛，这是尤其重要的——不只是对这些学生而言。这是我们经济长远发展的必经之路。

莱勒：我们没有时间了。

罗姆尼：吉姆，吉姆——

莱勒：当然，我会给您一个机会来回应。请吧，州长先生。

Governor.

Romney: Mr. – Mr. President, you're entitled, as the president, to your own airplane and to your own house, but not to your own facts – (laughter) – all right? I'm – I'm not going to cut education funding. I don't have any plan to cut education funding and grants that go to people going to college. I'm planning on continuing to grow, so I'm not planning on making changes there.

But you make a very good point, which is that the – the place you put your money makes a pretty clear indication of where your heart is. You put $90 billion into – into green jobs. And – and I – look, I'm all in favor of green energy. Ninety billion (dollars) – that – that would have – that would have hired 2 million teachers. Ninety billion dollars. And these businesses – many of them have gone out of business. I think about half of them, of the ones have been invested in, they've gone out of business. A number of them happened to be owned by – by people who were contributors to your campaigns.

Look, the right course for – for America's government – we were talking about the role of government – is not to become the economic player picking winners and losers, telling people what kind of health treatment they can receive, taking over the health care system that – that has existed in this country for – for a long, long time and has produced the best health records in the world. The right answer for government is to say, how do we make the private sector become more efficient and more effective?

How do we get schools to be more competitive? Let's grade them. I propose we grade our schools so parents know which schools are succeeding and failing, so they can take their child to a – to a school that's being more successful. I don't – I don't want to cut our commitment to education; I wanted to make it more effective and efficient.

And by the way, I've had that experience. I don't just talk about it. I've been there. Massachusetts schools are ranked number one in the nation. This is not because I didn't have commitment to education. It's because I care about

罗姆尼：——总统先生，您作为总统，拥有自己的飞机，拥有自己的房子，但是似乎却搞不清楚自己的状况——对不对？我并不是要削减教育经费。我没有任何计划要削减教育经费，或是要让人们上不了大学。我想要持续地发展经济，所以我不会更改教育方案。

但是您说得非常好，您的资金投入清晰地反映出您的内心想法。您把900亿美元投入了清洁能源行业。我——大家看，我非常支持清洁能源。但是，900亿美元——那是——那是可以用来聘请200万个教师的数目。900亿呀，现在这些清洁能源企业当中很多都倒闭了。我相信您投资的那些企业半数都已停业，而其中大部分企业碰巧是——是您竞选活动的赞助商。

大家看，对于美国政府的正确思路是——我们在谈论政府的职责——而不是要成为经济的参与者来挑选赢家和输家，不是来告诉人们可以获得怎样的健康保险，不是来接管在这个国家已经存在已久，拥有世界最高卫生水准的医疗系统。正确的思路应该是说，我们要怎样才能提高私有领域的效率？

怎样才能让学校变得更具竞争力？让我们给他们评级。我提议，我们给学校评级，这样家长们就知道哪些学校成功，哪些失败，这样他们就可以把小孩送到那些更好的学校去。我不想要降低对于教育的投入；我想要让教育变得更加廉洁和高效。

顺便提一下，我有亲身经验，而不是纸上谈兵。我确实做到了这一点。马萨诸塞州的学校在全国排名是第一的。这并不是因为我对于教育没有投入，而是因为我对教育是非常关心的，因为这关系到我们所有的孩子。

education for all of our kids.

Lehrer: All right, gentlemen, look –

Obama: Jim, I –

Lehrer: Excuse me, one sec – excuse, me sir. (Laughter.) We've got – we've got – barely have three minutes left. I'm not going to grade the two of you and say you've – your answers have been too long or I've done a poor job –

Obama: You've done a great job, Jim.

Lehrer: Oh, well, no. But the fact is, government – the role of government and governing, we've lost a pod in other words, so we only have three minutes left in the – in the debate before we go to your closing statements. And so I want to ask finally here – and remember, we've got three minutes total time here.

And the question is this: Many of the legislative functions of the federal government right now are in a state of paralysis as a result of partisan gridlock. If elected in your case, if re-elected in your case, what would you do about that?

Governor?

Romney: Jim, I had the great experience – it didn't seem like it at the time – of being elected in a state where my legislature was 87 percent Democrat, and that meant I figured out from day one I had to get along and I had to work across the aisle to get anything done. We drove our schools to be number one in the nation. We cut taxes 19 times.

Lehrer: Well, what would you do as president?

Romney: We – as president, I will sit down on day one – actually the day after I get elected, I'll sit down with leaders – the Democratic leaders as well as Republican leaders and – as we did in my state. We met every Monday for a couple hours, talked about the issues and the challenges in the – in the – in our state, in that case. We have to work on a collaborative basis – not because we're going to compromise our principle(s), but because there's common ground.

And the challenges America faces right now – look, the reason I'm in this race is there are people that are really hurting today in this country, and we face –

莱勒：好的，先生们，听着——

奥巴马：吉姆，我——

莱勒：不好意思，等会儿——等会儿，先生——我们已经只剩下不到三分钟的时间。我不会为你们两个打分了，我得说——你们的回答都太长了，或者说是我做得很不到位——

奥巴马：你做得很不错，吉姆。

莱勒：哦，好吧，我没有。事实上，有关政府和执政的问题，我们略去一个，也就是说在最后的陈词之前，我们只剩下三分钟了。现在我想最后一次请求两位记住，我们总共只剩三分钟了。

接下来的问题：现在因为两党之间的僵局，联邦政府的很多立法职能其实陷于瘫痪状态。所以州长先生，如果您当选，或者总统先生，如果您连任，你们会怎么解决这个问题？

州长您先请？

罗姆尼：吉姆，我有一段美好的经历——一开始并没有发觉——那就是，在我的州的立法机关有87%的民主党人，而我当选为州长。这就意味着，我从上任第一天起就必须和大家共同协作，才能把事情做好。我们把我们州的学校打造成全国第一，并进行了19次减税。

莱勒：那么，如果您当选总统了会怎么做呢？

罗姆尼：我们——作为总统，我会第一天就坐下来——其实是我当选的第一天，我会和民主党的领袖以及共和党的领袖们一起坐下来——就像我当州长时那样。我们每个星期一都会面几个小时，来谈论一下我们州的议题和挑战。我们必须携手努力——这不是因为我们要在原则问题上进行妥协，而是因为我们有共同的立场。

this deficit could crush the future generations. What's happening in the Middle East? There are developments around the world that are of real concern. And Republicans and Democrats both love America, but we need to have leadership – leadership in Washington that will actually bring people together and get the job done and could not care less if it's a Republican or a Democrat. I've done it before. I'll do it again.

Lehrer: Mr. President.

Obama: Well, first of all, I think Governor Romney's going to have a busy first day, because he's also going to repeal "Obamacare," which will not be very popular among Democrats as you're sitting down with them.

But look, my philosophy has been I will take ideas from anybody, Democrat or Republican, as long as they're advancing the cause of making middle-class families stronger and giving ladders of opportunity into the middle class. That's how we cut taxes for middle-class families and small businesses. That's how we cut a trillion dollars of spending that wasn't advancing that cause. That's how we signed three trade deals into law that are helping us to double our exports and sell more American products around the world. That's how we repealed "don't ask, don't tell." That's how we ended the war in Iraq, as I promised, and that's how we're going to wind down the war in Afghanistan. That's how we went after al-Qaida and bin Laden.

So we've – we've seen progress even under Republican control of the House of Representatives. But ultimately, part of being principled, part of being a leader is, A, being able to describe exactly what it is that you intend to do, not just saying, I'll sit down, but you have to have a plan.

Number two, what's important is occasionally you've got to say no to – to – to folks both in your own party and in the other party. And you know, yes, have we had some fights between me and the Republicans when they fought back against us, reining in the excesses of Wall Street? Absolutely, because that was a fight that needed to be had. When – when we were fighting about whether

而现在美国所面临的挑战十分严峻——大家看，我在这里参加总统竞选的原因是因为这个国家现在很多人受到了巨大的伤害，我们面临的赤字问题很可能毁掉未来美国人的生活。现在中东那边的情况如何？世界范围内正在发生的一些事情值得人们去关注。其实共和党人和民主党人都很爱美国，但是，我们需要有一个领袖出现——需要一个领袖到华盛顿，让人民团结一致共同奋斗，而不是关心他是共和党人还是民主党人。而我之前正是这么做的，今后我也会一如既往地这样做。

莱勒：总统先生您请。

奥巴马：好的，首先，我认为罗姆尼州长的第一天会很忙碌，因为他要废除"奥巴马医改划"，与您坐在一起交谈的那些民主党人可能对此并不赞同。

但大家看，我的观点是广泛吸收各方意见，无论是民主党还是共和党，只要这些意见是要促进中产阶级家庭强大，只要是推进机会平等的就可以，这就是我们为中产家庭和小企业减税的方式，这就是我们能够削减不利于我们发展的1万亿美元开支的方式，这就是我们把三项贸易协定纳入法规，以帮助我们提高一倍出口量并在全球销售美国制造的产品的方式，这就是我们做到废止"不问不说"的规定的方式，这就是我们按照我的承诺结束在伊拉克的战争的方式，这也就是我们做到逐步从阿富汗撤军的计划的方式，这也是我们找到基地组织和本·拉登的方式。

即使是在共和党控制众议院的情况下，我们——我们仍然已经取得了很多进展。但是说到底，要成为一个有原则的人，要成为一个领袖，最重要的是，要能够清楚地描述你的想法，而不是只是说我会坐下来谈，必须有自己的计划才行。

第二条，关键的是，有时候您需要能够对您自己党派的人以及对方党派的人说不。大家知道，是的，我们不是曾经和共和党们就有关加强华尔街监管的问题打得火热吗？这场争斗绝对是必要的，是必须要进行的争斗。当——当我们在决定美国人民是否需要更多的医疗保障的问题上进行争论，而共和党人说不需要的时候，是的，我们必须要争斗。所以，要成为一个领袖，一个能够驾驭局势的人，您需要能够对一些事情说不，并且有意愿来这么做。

or not we were going to make sure that Americans had more security with their health insurance and they said no, yes, that was a fight that we needed to have. And so part of leadership and governing is both saying what it is that you are for, but also being willing to say no to some things.

And I've got to tell you, Governor Romney, when it comes to his own party during the course of this campaign, has not displayed that willingness to say no to some of the more extreme parts of his party.

Lehrer: That brings us to closing statements. There was a coin toss. Governor Romney, you won the toss, and you elected to go last.

So you have a closing two minutes, Mr. President.

Obama: Well, Jim, I want to thank you and I want to thank Governor Romney, because I think this was a terrific debate and I very much appreciate it.

And I want to thank the University of Denver.

You know, four years ago we were going through a major crisis, and yet my faith and confidence in the American future is undiminished. And the reason is because of its people. Because of the woman I met in North Carolina who decided at 55 to go back to school because she wanted to inspire her daughter, and now has a new job from that new training that she's gotten. Because of the company in Minnesota who was willing to give up salaries and perks for their executives to make sure that they didn't lay off workers during a recession. The auto workers that you meet in Toledo or Detroit take such pride in building the best cars in the world – not just because of a paycheck, but because it gives them that sense of pride, that they're helping to build America.

And so the question now is, how do we build on those strengths? And everything that I've tried to do and everything that I'm now proposing for the next four years in terms of improving our education system, or developing American energy, or making sure that we're closing loopholes for companies that are shipping jobs overseas and focusing on small businesses and companies that are creating jobs here in the United States, or – or closing our deficit in a responsible,

而现在我要告诉你们，当说到罗姆尼州长的竞选路线时，他并没有展示出敢于跟自己极端分子说不的决心。

莱勒：好的，我们将进行总结陈词。随机选择的结果是，罗姆尼州长，您赢了，可以最后发言。

现在，总统先生，您有两分钟的总结陈词时间。

奥巴马：好的，吉姆，我想感谢你，也感谢罗姆尼州长，因为我认为这是一次极好的辩论，我非常感激。

我也想要感谢丹佛大学。

大家知道，四年前，我们经历了重大危机，而我对美国未来的信念和信心却没有因此消失。因为美国人民给了我信心。这是因为，我在北卡罗来纳州遇到的一位妇女，在55岁的时候重返校园，来给她的女儿加油鼓劲。她现在已经通过了培训计划，获得了一份新的工作。这是因为，在明尼苏达的一个公司，宁愿放弃自己管理层的薪水和津贴，来确保自己不会在经济衰退的时候辞掉员工。这是因为，我在托莱多或者底特律遇到的汽车工人，他们对于制造世界上最好的汽车感到无比自豪——不是因为丰厚的薪水，而是因为这份工作给予他们的那份建设祖国的自豪感。

所以，现在的问题是，我们如何将这样的力量发扬光大？过去我所做的一切，以及在未来的四年里面我将要做的事情，就是要提升我们的教育体系，要发展美国的本土能源，要填补那些把工作机会迁移到国外的公司的税务漏洞，要着重发展本国的小型企业，为本土提供更多的工作机会，要以一种负责任的、平衡的方式减少赤字，使得我们能够投资于未来——所有这些事情都是为了确保美国人民，确保他们的天赋，他们的勇气，他们的决心得到发挥和利用——并最终有机会获得成功。

balanced way that allows us to invest in our future – all those things are designed to make sure that the American people, their genius, their grit, their determination is – is channeled, and – and – and they have an opportunity to succeed.

And everybody's getting a fair shot and everybody's getting a fair share. Everybody's doing a fair share and everybody's playing by the same rules.

You know, four years ago I said that I'm not a perfect man and I wouldn't be a perfect president. And that's probably a promise that Governor Romney thinks I've kept. But I also promised that I'd fight every single day on behalf of the American people and the middle class and all those who are striving to get in the middle class.

I've kept that promise and if you'll vote for me, then I promise I'll fight just as hard in a second term.

Lehrer: Governor Romney, your two-minute closing.

Romney: Thank you, Jim and Mr. President. And thank you for tuning in this evening. This is a – this is an important election. And I'm concerned about America. I'm concerned about the direction America has been taking over the last four years. I know this is bigger than election about the two of us as individuals. It's bigger than our respective parties. It's an election about the course of America – what kind of America do you want to have for yourself and for your children.

And there really are two very different paths that we began speaking about this evening. And over the course of this month we're going to have two more presidential debates and vice presidential debate. We'll talk about those two paths. But they lead in very different directions. And it's not just looking to our words that you have to take in evidence of where they go; you can look at the record.

There's no question in my mind that if the president were to be re-elected you'll continue to see a middle-class squeeze with incomes going down and prices going up. I'll get incomes up again. You'll see chronic unemployment. We've had 43 straight months with unemployment above 8 percent. If I'm

这也是要确保每个人都能够享有公平的机会，确保每个人都能够公平地分享成果，确保每个人都能够在相同的规则下公平竞争。

大家知道，四年前我说过我并不是一个完美的人，我也不会成为一个完美的总统。这可能是罗姆尼州长认为我遵守的承诺之一。但我也承诺，我会为了美国人民，为了中产阶级，为了所有那些努力成为中产阶级的人们而奋斗每一天。

我一直坚守着这些承诺，如果你们投票选择我，我会承诺连任期间会一如既往地努力。

莱勒：罗姆尼州长，现在是该您做两分钟总结陈词。

罗姆尼：谢谢您，吉姆，还有总统先生，也谢谢大家今晚收看这个节目。这是非常重要的选举。我对美国非常关切，我对美国过去四年中所选择的道路非常关切。我知道这次选举举足轻重，它比起我们两个竞选人来说要重要得多，比起我们两人的党派也要重要得多。这次涉及美国的道路——你想为你和你的孩子选择一个怎样的美国。

而从今天晚上的讨论开始，确实有两条截然不同道路在等待我们。在接下来的这个月里，我们还会有两场总统辩论和一场副总统辩论。我们会谈一谈两条不同的道路，它们代表着不同方向的未来。这不是说要大家只是听着我们的辩论来判断这两条道路的方向，大家也可以看看我们过去的业绩来做出判断。

在我心中毫无疑问的是，如果总统获得连任，大家会看到中产阶级被继续挤压，收入不断降低，而物价不断攀升，而我会让收入重新回升。大家看到长期的失业现象，我们的失业率已连续43个月超过8%。如果我当选，我会帮助这个国家创造1200万新的就业岗位，提高大家的收入。

president, I will create – help create 12 million new jobs in this country with rising incomes.

If the president's re-elected, "Obamacare" will be fully installed. In my view, that's going to mean a whole different way of life for people who counted on the insurance plan they had in the past. Many will lose it. You're going to see health premiums go up by some $2,500 per – per family. If I'm elected, we won't have "Obamacare". We'll put in place the kind of principles that I put in place in my own state and allow each state to craft their own programs to get people insured. And we'll focus on getting the cost of health care down.

If the president were to be re-elected, you're going to see a $716 billion cut to Medicare. You'll have 4 million people who will lose Medicare advantage. You'll have hospitals and providers that'll no longer accept Medicare patients. I'll restore that $716 billion to Medicare.

And finally, military. If the president's re-elected, you'll see dramatic cuts to our military. The secretary of defense has said these would be even devastating. I will not cut our commitment to our military. I will keep America strong and get America's middle class working again.

Thank you, Jim.

Lehrer: Thank you, Governor.

Thank you, Mr. President.

The next debate will be the vice presidential event on Thursday, October 11th at Center College in Danville, Kentucky. For now, from the University of Denver, I'm Jim Lehrer. Thank you, and good night.

the University of Denver, Denver, Colorado, October, 3, 2012

如果总统获得连任，"奥巴马医改"就会得到全面落实。我认为，这对于那些依赖过去的医保计划的人来说，生活会大有不同，许多人都会失去保险，每个家庭会多支出大约2500美元的医保费用。如果我当选，我们就不会有"奥巴马医改计划"了，我们会让我们州的医改原则在全国生效，那就是让每个州来因地制宜地制定医疗保险计划，为居民提供保障。我们会着重关注于如何减少医疗开销。

如果总统获得了连任，医保体系将被削减7160亿美元。400万人不再享受医保体系的优惠，很多医院和健康保险供应商不再愿意接纳医保的病人了。而我会把这7160亿还给医保体系。

最后，谈到军事问题。如果总统连任，你会看到军费开支将大幅缩减，国防部长说这会造成灾难。我不会削减军事开支，我会让美国保持强力，让美国中产阶级重振雄风。

谢谢你，吉姆。

莱勒：谢谢您，州长先生。

也谢谢您，总统先生。

下一场辩论会是副总统辩论会，在肯塔基州的丹维尔市的中央学院举行，时间是10月11日，星期四。现在，在丹佛大学为您播报，我是吉姆·莱勒，今晚的辩论会到此结束，谢谢大家，晚安。

（袁　婧／译　杜梦臻／校）

The Second Obama – Romney
Presidential Debate

President Barack Obama and Republican presidential nominee Mitt Romney met in Hempstead, New York Tuesday evening for the second of three presidential debates, moderated by CNN Chief Political Correspondent Candy Crowley.

Crowley: Good evening from Hofstra University in Hempstead, New York. I'm Candy Crowley from CNN's "State of the Union". We are here for the second presidential debate, a town hall, sponsored by the Commission on Presidential Debates.

The Gallup organization chose 82 uncommitted voters from the New York area. Their questions will drive the night. My goal is to give the conversation direction and to ensure questions get answered.

The questions are known to me and my team only. Neither the commission, nor the candidates have seen them. I hope to get to as many questions as possible. And because I am the optimistic sort, I'm sure the candidates will oblige by keeping their answers concise and on point. Each candidate has as much as two minutes to respond to a common question, and there will be a two-minute follow-up.

The audience here in the hall has agreed to be polite and attentive – no cheering or booing or outbursts of any sort.

We will set aside that agreement just this once to welcome President Barack Obama and Governor Mitt Romney.

Gentlemen, thank you both for joining us here tonight. We have a lot

奥巴马—罗姆尼第二场电视辩论 ①

克劳利：晚上好，这里是位于纽约州亨普斯特德市的霍夫斯特拉大学。我是美国有线电视新闻网"国情咨文"主持人坎迪·克劳利。我们在此举行第二场总统候选人辩论，这是一场由总统候选人辩论委员会组织的市政厅模式辩论。

民调机构盖洛普公司从纽约地区选出了82名未确定投票立场的选民，他们的提问将是今晚的主要内容。我的目标是引导辩论的方向，并确保所有问题都能够得到回答。

目前只有我和我的团队知晓今晚的问题，无论是委员会还是总统候选人都未被提前告知。我希望各位能够尽可能多地提问题。作为一个乐观主义者，我希望两位候选人都能确保他们的回答简洁到位。对同一个问题，两位候选人均有两分钟的作答时间，之后还有两分钟的后续问答。

请在座的听众务必保持礼貌与专心，不喝彩，不喝倒彩，冷静淡定。

不过此时此刻我们可以破个例，欢迎巴拉克·奥巴马总统和米特·罗姆尼州长。

感谢今晚两位先生的到来。现场有很多观众已经等了一整天，想与你们交流，那我们就进入正题吧。罗姆尼州长，你知道，掷硬币您赢了，所以第一个问题先由你来回答。有请第一次投票的杰瑞米·艾普斯坦提问。

---

① 距离美国总统大选投票日仅剩三周，现任总统奥巴马作为民主党候选人于当地时间10月16日（星期二）同共和党总统候选人罗姆尼进行了第二场电视辩论。对于在首轮辩论中表现不佳的奥巴马来说，这场辩论容不得再有闪失。奥巴马和罗姆尼在90分钟的时间内回答了现场观众提出的11个问题。辩论地点在纽约州的亨普斯特德市。辩论是由美国有线电视新闻网"国情咨文"主持人坎迪·克劳利主持的。

of folks who've been waiting all day to talk to you, so I want to get right to it.Governor Romney, as you know, you won the coin toss, so the first question will go to you. And I want to turn to a first-time voter, Jeremy Epstein, who has a question for you.

Question: Mr. President, Governor Romney, as a 20-year-old college student, all I hear from professors, neighbors and others is that when I graduate, I will have little chance to get employment. What can you say to reassure me, but more importantly my parents, that I will be able to sufficiently support myself after I graduate?

Romney: Thank you, Jeremy. I appreciate your – your question, and thank you for being here this evening and to all of those from Nassau County that have come, thank you for your time. Thank you to Hofstra University and to Candy Crowley for organizing and leading this – this event. Thank you, Mr. President, also for being part of this – this debate.

College kids all over this country. I was in Pennsylvania with someone who had just graduated – this was in Philadelphia – and she said, "I've got my degree. I can't find a job. I've got three part-time jobs. They're just barely enough to pay for my food and pay for an apartment. I can't begin to pay back my student loans".

So what we have to do is two things. We have to make sure that we make it easier for kids to afford college. And also make sure that when they get out of college, there's a job. When I was governor of Massachusetts, to get a high school degree, you had to pass an exam. If you graduated in the top quarter of your airlines, we gave you a John and Abigail Adams scholarship, four years tuition free in the college of your choice in Massachusetts, it's a public institution.I want to make sure we keep our Pell grant program growing. We're also going to have our loan program, so that people are able to afford school.

But the key thing is to make sure you can get a job when you get out of school. And what's happened over the last four years has been very, very hard

创造就业谁更能干？

选民提问：总统先生，罗姆尼州长，我是一名在校大学生，今年20岁，无论是教授、邻居，还是其他人，他们都告诉我，当我毕业时，我可能很难找到工作。您如何打消我这个疑虑呢？尤其是更要让我的父母相信，我能够在毕业后自食其力？

罗姆尼：谢谢你，杰瑞米。谢谢你的提问，感谢你今晚到来，也感谢现场各位观众的到来，感谢霍夫斯特拉大学，坎迪·克劳利，谢谢你们组织并主持这场辩论，也感谢总统先生参与此次辩论。

你的问题也是全国的大学生都关心的问题。我在宾夕法尼亚州的费城时遇到过一位大学毕业生，她说，"我拿到了学位，却找不到工作。我打了三份零工，勉强够我吃饭、付房租。我无力偿还助学贷款"。

所以我们必须做两件事：一是要确保孩子们能上得起大学，二是要确保他们毕业后能找到工作。当我是马萨诸塞州州长时，你只有通过了考试，才能获得高中学位。如果你的毕业成绩排在班级前25%，那么你能够得到John& Abigail Adams 奖学金，州里任何一所公立大学，四年学费全免，这个奖学金是公立机构提供的。我将确保联邦政府佩尔助学金项目继续发展，我们将同时通过发放助学贷款，保证大家上得起大学。

for America's young people. I want you to be able to get a job.I know what it takes to get this economy going. With half of college kids graduating this year without a college – excuse me, without a job. And without a college level job, that's just unacceptable. And likewise you've got more and more debt on your back. So more debt and less jobs.

I'm going to change that. I know what it takes to create good jobs again. I know what it takes to make sure that you have the kind of opportunity you deserve. And kids across this country are going to recognize, we're bringing back an economy. It's not going to be like the last four years. The middle-class has been crushed over the last four years, and jobs have been too scarce. I know what it takes to bring them back, and I'm going to do that, and make sure that when you graduate – when do you graduate?

Question: 2014.

Romney: 2014. When you come out in 2014, I presume I'm going to be president. I'm going to make sure you get a job. Thanks Jeremy. Yeah, you bet.

Crowley: Mr. President?

Obama: Jeremy, first of all, your future is bright. And the fact that you're making an investment in higher education is critical. Not just to you, but to the entire nation. Now, the most important thing we can do is to make sure that we are creating jobs in this country. But not just jobs, good paying jobs, ones that can support a family.

And what I want to do, is build on the five million jobs that we've created over the last 30 months in the private sector alone. And there are a bunch of things we can do to make sure your future is bright.

Number one, I want to build manufacturing jobs in this country again. Now when Governor Romney said we should let Detroit go bankrupt. I said we're going to bet on American workers and the American auto industry and it's come surging back. I want to do that in industries, not just in Detroit, but all across the country and that means we change our tax code so we're giving incentives

　　但最关键是要确保各位毕业之后有份工作。过去四年的情况，对美国年轻人而言，是非常非常艰难的。我要让你们能够找到一份工作。我知道如何搞活经济。今年有一半的本科生找不到工作，或者找不到一份能与其大学毕业生身份相符的工作，这种情况简直无法接受。而且，你们会背上越来越多的债务。结果就是，负债更多，工作机会反而更少。

　　我要改变这种现状。我知道如何重新创造优良的就业机会，我知道如何确保你学有所用，人尽其才。全国的孩子们都将发现，经济形势有所好转，而不会再像过去四年那样。在过去的四年，中产阶级遭受到极大的打击，工作机会少之又少。我知道如何重新创造大量的就业机会，我会做到，待到你毕业那年……你什么时候毕业？

　　选民：2014年。

　　罗姆尼：2014年，等你2014年毕业的时候，假设那时候我是总统，我会保证你有一份工作。谢谢，杰瑞米。相信我，没错的！呵呵。

　　克劳利：总统先生。

　　奥巴马：杰瑞米，首先，你的未来一片光明。你接受高等教育，为自己投资，这一点至关重要。不仅是对于你，更是对于整个国家。当前我们能做的最重要的事情，就是创造国内就业机会，不仅仅是工作，而且是薪酬优厚的工作，能糊口，能养家的工作。

　　我想要做的是，在过去30个月里，仅私营部门就创造了500万份工作，我们想要再接再厉，创造出更多的就业。我们还能做很多事情，确保你拥有一个光明的未来。

　　第一，我要在这个国家重新创造制造业的工作机会。你知道，当罗姆尼州长说我们应该让底特律破产的时候，我说，我们必须依靠美国的劳动人民和美国汽车业，我们也看到了汽车业的确起死回生。不止底特律，我

to companies that are investing here in the United States and creating jobs here. It also means we're helping them and small businesses to export all around the world to new markets.

Number two, we've got to make sure that we have the best education system in the world. And the fact that you're going to college is great, but I want everybody to get a great education and we've worked hard to make sure that student loans are available for folks like you, but I also want to make sure that community colleges are offering slots for workers to get retrained for the jobs that are out there right now and the jobs of the future.

Number three, we've got to control our own energy. Now, not only oil and natural gas, which we've been investing in; but also, we've got to make sure we're building the energy source of the future, not just thinking about next year, but ten years from now, 20 years from now. That's why we've invested in solar and wind and biofuels, energy efficient cars.

We've got to reduce our deficit, but we've got to do it in a balanced way. Asking the wealthy to pay a little bit more along with cuts so that we can invest in education like yours. And let's take the money that we've been spending on war over the last decade to rebuild America, roads, bridges schools. We do those things, not only is your future going to be bright but America's future is going to bright as well.

Crowley: Let me ask you for more immediate answer and begin with Mr. Romney just quickly what – what can you do? We're looking at a situation where 40 percent of the unemployed have been unemployed have been unemployed for six months or more. They don't have the two years that Jeremy has. What about those long term unemployed who need a job right now?

Romney: Well what you're seeing in this country is 23 million people struggling to find a job. And a lot of them, as you say, Candy, have been out of work for a long, long, long time.

The president's policies have been exercised over the last four years and

想让全国工业都有这样的机会。这意味着我们要改变我们的税收政策，激励在美投资的企业，创造国内就业。同时，我们还要帮助这些企业与小企业向全球出口，开拓新市场。

第二，我们将确保我们拥有全世界最好的教育体系。你现在上大学，这真的很好。而我更希望每一个人都能得到良好的教育。我们努力确保，和你一样的大学生都能获得助学贷款。同时我也要确保，社区大学能够针对现有工作和未来工作的需求，为广大劳动者提供就业再培训。

第三，我们将掌控我们自己的能源，我们一直在投资石油和天然气，但这还不够。我们还应该确保未来的能源的开发，不能只考虑明年，还要考虑10年、20年以后的情况。这就是我们为什么要投资太阳能、风能和生物燃料以及节能汽车的原因。

我们已经减少了我们的赤字，但方法则要讲究平衡，让富人多交一点点税，政府再减少一些开支，这样我们才能投资教育，比如，资助你的学业。同时，让我们把过去10年花在战争上的钱，都用于重建美国——修路、建桥、兴办学校。上面几点，如果我们都做到了，不仅你的未来一片光明，美国的未来也会一片光明的。

克劳利：我想听听你们更直接的回答。从罗姆尼先生开始吧。现在的情况是，四成失业者失业半年以上。杰瑞米还有两年时间，但他们没有，远水解不了近渴，对于长期失业、亟需就业的人们，您能做点什么？

罗姆尼：好，如今这个国家有2300万人正在艰难地寻找工作，其中许多人，如您所言，坎迪，已经失业很久很久了。

they haven't put Americans back to work. We have fewer people working today than we had when the president took office. If the – the unemployment rate was 7.8 percent when he took office, it's 7.8 percent now. But if you calculated that unemployment rate, taking back the people who dropped out of the workforce, it would be 10.7 percent. We have not made the progress we need to make to put people back to work.

That's why I put out a five-point plan that gets America 12 million new jobs in four years and rising take-home pay. It's going to help Jeremy get a job when he comes out of school. It's going to help people across the country that are unemployed right now.

And one thing that the president said, which I want to make sure that we understand, he said that I said we should take Detroit bankrupt. And that's right. My plan was to have the company go through bankruptcy like 7-Eleven did and Macy's and Condell (ph) Airlines and come out stronger. And I know he keeps saying, you want to take Detroit bankrupt. Well, the president took Detroit bankrupt. You took General Motors bankrupt. You took Chrysler bankrupt. So when you say that I wanted to take the auto industry bankrupt, you actually did. And I think it's important to know that that was a process that was necessary to get those companies back on their feet, so they could start hiring more people. That was precisely what I recommended and ultimately what happened.

Crowley: Let me give the president a chance. Go ahead.

Obama: Candy, what Governor Romney said just isn't true. He wanted to take them into bankruptcy without providing them any way to stay open. And we would have lost a million jobs.

And that — Don't take my word for it, take the executives at GM and Chrysler, some of whom are Republicans, may even support Governor Romney. But they'll tell you his prescription wasn't going to work.

And Governor Romney's says he's got a five-point plan? Governor Romney doesn't have a five-point plan. He has a one-point plan. And that plan is

奥巴马总统的政策已经实施了四年之久，但并未能让美国人重新返回工作岗位。现在有工作的人，人数还没有总统上任的时候多。当时的失业率是7.8%，现在还是7.8%。可是算上彻底退出劳动市场的人，现在的失业率高达10.7%。我们没有取得我们需要取得的成绩，没有让人们重新返回工作岗位。

因此，我提出五点计划，它能让美国在未来的四年增加1200万个新岗位，同时提升工作者税后的实际收入。这将有助于杰瑞米在毕业后找到工作，也将有助于目前国内失业者现在就找到工作。

我要澄清一点，刚才总统说，我说应该让底特律破产，这个没错。我的计划就是让公司经历破产，类似7—11连锁店、梅西百货和大陆航空公司一样，历经破产后，脱胎换骨，然后变得更加强大。我知道，他不断地说：你想要底特律破产。可最后呢，是总统让底特律破了产。你让通用汽车破了产，你让克莱斯勒公司破了产。因此，当你说我想要汽车工业破产的时候，实际上你做到了。我要强调的是，认识到破产是让这些公司重新站起来的一个过程是非常重要的，这样他们才能开始雇佣更多的人。这恰恰正是我的建议，事实最终也的确如此。

克劳利：让我给总统先生一个机会。开始吧。

奥巴马：坎迪，罗姆尼州长说的并不属实。他所说的破产是不以任何形式帮助他们经营，如果那样的话，我们将损失上百万个就业岗位。

大家也别光听信我的，听听通用和克莱斯勒的董事们怎么说，他们中的一些还是共和党人，甚至是罗姆尼州长的支持者。但是他们会告诉你，罗姆尼开的药方不顶用。

to make sure that folks at the top play by a different set of rules. That's been his philosophy in the private sector, that's been his philosophy as governor, that's been his philosophy as a presidential candidate. You can make a lot of money and pay lower tax rates than somebody who makes a lot less. You can ship jobs overseas and get tax breaks for it. You can invest in a company, bankrupt it, lay off the workers, strip away their pensions, and you still make money.

That's exactly the philosophy that we've seen in place for the last decade. That's what's been squeezing middle class families. And we have fought back for four years to get out of that mess. The last thing we need to do is to go back to the very same policies that got us there.

Crowley: Mr. President, the next question is going to be for you here. And, Mr. Romney – Governor Romney – there'll be plenty of chances here to go on, but I want to... We have all these folks.

Romney: That – that Detroit – that Detroit answer... and the rest of the answer, way off the mark.

Crowley: OK. Will – will – you certainly will have lots of time here coming up.

Because I want to move you on to something that's sort of connected to cars here, and – and go over. And we want to get a question from Phillip Tricolla.

Question: Your energy secretary, Steven Chu, has now been on record three times stating it's not policy of his department to help lower gas prices. Do you agree with Secretary Chu that this is not the job of the Energy Department?

Obama: The most important thing we can do is to make sure we control our own energy. So here's what I've done since I've been president. We have increased oil production to the highest levels in16 years. Natural gas production is the highest it's been in decades. We have seen increases in coal production and coal employment.

But what I've also said is we can't just produce traditional source of energy. We've also got to look to the future. That's why we doubled fuel

罗姆尼州长说到了他的五点计划。罗姆尼州长并没有什么五点计划，他只有一点计划，而这个计划就是让富人享受特殊的优待。这就是他在私营部门的原则，也是他作为州长的原则，当然也是他作为总统候选人的原则。在这一原则下，你可以挣大钱，交小税，挣钱比你少的人，居然税费比你还高。你可以把工作机会运送到海外，并因此获得减税。你可以投资一家公司，搞得它破产，解雇工人，剥夺他们的养老金，然后你居然还挣着钱！

这正是我们在过去10年所看到的周而复始的原则，正是它压榨了中产家庭。而我们奋战了四年就是想摆脱这一团糟，我们最不想的就是回到当初这一团糟的局面。

"新老"能源如何权衡？

克劳利： 总统先生，下一个问题请您先回答。罗姆尼州长，您还有很多发言机会。我们必须继续了，大家都……

罗姆尼： 底特律……底特律还有其他回答，简直离题万里。

克劳利： 您待会儿还有很多时间继续。我希望两位开始回答下一个问题，算是和汽车扯上点儿关系。有请菲利普·崔克拉提问。

选民提问： 您的能源部长朱棣文，曾公开讲过三次，他们部门不负责降低油价。你同意朱部长说的吗？这不是能源部长的职责吗？

奥巴马： 现在要做的最重要的事，是掌控自己的能源。这也是我一就任总统就着手做的。我们的石油产量达到16年来的最高。天然气产量为数十年来最高。煤炭和煤炭相关产业的就业人数也有所上升。

efficiency standards on cars. That means that in the middle of the next decade, any car you buy, you're going to end up going twice as far on a gallon of gas. That's why we doubled clean – clean energy production like wind and solar and biofuels. And all these things have contributed to us lowering our oil imports to the lowest levels in 16 years.

Now, I want to build on that. And that means, yes, we still continue to open up new areas for drilling. We continue to make it a priority for us to go after natural gas. We've got potentially 600,000 jobs and 100 years worth of energy right beneath our feet with natural gas. And we can do it in an environmentally sound way. But we've also got to continue to figure out how we have efficiency energy, because ultimately that's how we're going to reduce demand and that's what's going to keep gas prices lower.

Now, Governor Romney will say he's got an all-of-the-above plan, but basically his plan is to let the oil companies write the energy policies. So he's got the oil and gas part, but he doesn't have theclean energy part. And if we are only thinking about tomorrow or the next day and not thinking about 10 years from now, we're not going to control our own economic future. Because China, Germany, they're making these investments. And I'm not going to cede those jobs of the future to those countries. I expect those new energy sources to be built right here in the United States. That's going to help Jeremy get a job. It's also going to make sure that you're not paying as much for gas.

Crowley: Governor, on the subject of gas prices?

Romney: Well, let's look at the president's policies, all right, as opposed to the rhetoric, because we've had four years of policies being played out. And the president's right in terms of the additional oil production, but none of it came on federal land. As a matter of fact, oil production is down 14 percent this year on federal land, and gas production was down 9 percent. Why? Because the president cut in half the number of licenses and permits for drilling on federal lands, and in federal waters. So where'd the increase come from? Well a lot of

但是我也说过，我们不能只生产传统能源，也要着眼于未来的发展。这是为什么我们将汽车燃料效率标准提高一倍的原因所在。这样，到了2020年中期，你随便买辆车，一加仑的油能当现在两加仑使。这也是为什么我们将风能、太阳能和生物燃料等清洁能源的产量提高一倍的原因。所有这些努力让我们的石油进口量降至16年来的最低。

现在，我想在这个基础上更进一步。这意味着，我们仍将继续开辟新的区域用于开采，继续优先开发天然气。我们脚下的天然气资源可以带来60万份工作，可供使用100年。而且我们可以以环保的方式开发。但是我们还要继续探索，如何拥有高效的能源，因为最终，我们要以此降低能源需求，借此保持低油价。

现在，罗姆尼州长会说，他也有以上计划，但是归根结底，他的计划就是让石油公司主导能源政策。他考虑了石油和天然气，但他不重视清洁能源。如果我们只想到明天，而不为十年之后多做打算，我们就无法控制我们的经济前景，因为中国、德国，正在进行投资。我不会把那些未来的工作机会，拱手相让给这些国家。我希望看到，美国的能源美国造。这有助于杰瑞米找到工作，同时也有助于油价降低。

克劳利：州长，关于汽油价格的看法。

罗姆尼：好，让我们来看一下总统的政策，不要只听他的豪言壮语。他的政策已经实施了四年，玩完了。关于石油产量增加这一点，没错，但是没有一滴石油的增产是来自联邦的土地。事实上，今年联邦土地上的石油产量下降了14%，天然气产量则下降了9%。为什么？因为总统把联邦土地及水域开采许可证的数量砍掉了一半。那么，增长来自哪里？很多是北达科他州的巴肯油田产的。那么总统在那里干了什么？有人在那儿勘探石油，当局却对其提起刑事诉讼。可惜了多么庞大的资源啊。这些石油开采的代价是什么？死了二十几只鸟儿，然后他们就根据《候鸟保护法》，对那些人提起刑事诉讼。

it came from the Bakken Range in North Dakota. What was his participation there? The administration brought a criminal action against the people drilling up there for oil, this massive new resource we have. And what was the cost? 20 or 25 birds were killed and brought out a migratory bird act to go after them on a criminal basis.

Look, I want to make sure we use our oil, our coal, our gas, our nuclear, our renewables. I believe very much in our renewable capabilities; ethanol, wind, solar will be an important part of our energy mix.But what we don't need is to have the president keeping us from taking advantage of oil, coal and gas. This has not been Mr. Oil, or Mr. Gas, or Mr. Coal. Talk to the people that are working in those industries. I was in coal country. People grabbed my arms and said, "Please save my job". The head of the EPA said, "You can't build a coal plant. You'll virtually – it's virtually impossible given our regulations". When the president ran for office, he said if you build a coal plant, you can go ahead, but you'll go bankrupt. That's not the right course for America. Let's take advantage of the energy resources we have, as well as the energy sources for the future. And if we do that, if we do what I'm planning on doing, which is getting us energy independent, North America energy independence within eight years, you're going to see manufacturing jobs come back.

Because our energy is low cost, that are already beginning to come back because of our abundant energy. I'll get America and North America energy independent. I'll do it by more drilling, more permits and licenses. We're going to bring that pipeline in from Canada. How in the world the president said no to that pipeline? I will never know. This is about bringing good jobs back for the middle class of America, and that's what I'm going to do.

Crowley: Mr. President, let me just see if I can move you to the gist of this question, which is, are we looking at the new normal? I can tell you that tomorrow morning, a lot of people in Hempstead will wake up and fill up and they will find that the price of gas is over $4 a gallon. Is it within the purview of

　　我将确保我们能够使用我们的石油、煤炭、天然气、核能和可再生能源，我深信我们在可再生能源方面的潜力——乙醇、风能、太阳能会成为我们能源组合中的重要组成部分。但是我们不需要总统阻止我们开发石油、煤炭和天然气。这并不是石油大王或者煤炭大王的事情。跟在这些行业里工作的人们谈谈心吧。我曾到过一些产煤大区，人们抓住我的手说：求求你，保住我们的饭碗吧。国家环保局局长说："你不能建煤厂。根据我们的规定，建厂根本是不可能的。"总统当年竞选时说过："如果你要建一个煤炭工厂，那就建吧，但是你会因此破产。"这不应该是美国选择的道路。我们要利用好手头的能源资源，也要利用好未来的能源资源。如果让我们按着我的计划行动，我们将实现能源独立，在八年内实现北美洲能源独立，你们就能看到制造业工作回归。

　　因为我们的能源成本低，而且我们能源充足，现在制造业已经开始回归。我会为美国和北美争取能源独立，通过更多的钻探，颁发更多的执照和许可证。我们将从加拿大建输油管道，引进来。总统怎么能、怎么会拒绝输油管道计划呢？我这辈子都想不通。这可是事关中产阶级的就业大计，我将为此而努力。

　　克劳利：总统先生，我想试试我能否帮您回到问题的关键点上，就是，这个问题会不会成为一种新常态？我可以告诉您，明天早上，很多本地市民起床出门开车加油，发现汽油价格超过了每加仑4美元。降低油价是否在政府的政策范围内？还是说高油价将成为新常态？

the government to bring those prices down, or are we looking at the new normal?

Obama: Candy, there's no doubt that world demand's gone up, but our production is going up, and we're using oil more efficiently. And very little of what Governor Romney just said is true. We've opened up public lands. We're actually drilling more on public lands than in the previous administration and my – the previous president was an oil man. And natural gas isn't just appearing magically. We're encouraging it and working with the industry.

And when I hear Governor Romney say he's a big coal guy, I mean, keep in mind, when – Governor, when you were governor of Massachusetts, you stood in front of a coal plant and pointed at it and said, "This plant kills", and took great pride in shutting it down. And now suddenly you're a big champion of coal. So what I've tried to do is be consistent.

With respect to something like coal, we made the largest investment in clean coal technology, to make sure that even as we're producing more coal, we're producing it cleaner and smarter. Same thing with oil, same thing with natural gas. And the proof is our oil imports are down to the lowest levels in 20 years. Oil production is up, natural gas production is up, and, most importantly, we're also starting to build cars that are more efficient.

And that's creating jobs. That means those cars can be exported, 'cause that's the demand around the world, and it also means that it'll save money in your pocketbook. That's the strategy you need, an all-of-the-above strategy, and that's what we're going to do in the next four years.

Romney: But that's not what you've done in the last four years. That's the problem. In the last four years, you cut permits and licenses on federal land and federal waters in half.

Obama: Not true, Governor Romney.

Romney: So how much did you cut?

Obama: Not true.

Romney: How much did you cut them by, then?

奥巴马：坎迪，毫无疑问，世界的需求在上升。但是我们的产量也在上升，而且我们的石油利用更加有效率。罗姆尼州长刚才所言几乎全都不属实。我们已经开放公共用地。目前，公共用地的开采比前任政府要多。而且，我的前任总统还是一位"石油派"的。因此，天然气不会如魔法般的出现，我们鼓励这个行业，并一起想办法。

当我听罗姆尼州长说他是个"煤炭派"，大家别忘了，州长，你当马萨诸塞州州长时，你站在一家煤厂前，指着它说，这家厂子可真要命，然后关停了这家厂子，并引以为傲。而你现在又突然化身为"煤斗士"，而我一直希望始终如一。

就煤炭能源而言，我们对清洁煤技术做了大规模的投资，以确保在煤炭产量提高的情况下，生产过程更优更洁。石油如此，天然气亦如此。有证据表明，我们的石油进口降到20年最低，石油、天然气产量上升，更重要的，我们同样开始制造能效更高的汽车。

这就意味着，有更多的就业机会。意味着那些车可以出口，因为全球的需求增加。也意味着我们可以因此节省开支。这才是你们需要的、全面的、一揽子计划，这就是我们接下来四年的工作。

罗姆尼：但过去四年，你们没有做到。这才是问题的关键。过去四年，你把联邦土地和水域开采许可砍掉了一半。

奥巴马：并非如此，罗姆尼州长。

罗姆尼：那你砍了多少？

奥巴马：你说的不对。

罗姆尼：那你到底砍了多少？

Obama: Governor, we have actually produced more oil –

Romney: No, no. How much did you cut licenses and permits on federal land and federal waters?

Obama: Governor Romney, here's what we did. There were a whole bunch of oil companies.

Romney: No, no, I had a question and the question was how much did you cut them by?

Obama: You want me to answer a question –

Romney: How much did you cut them by?

Obama: I'm happy to answer the question.

Romney: All right. And it is –

Obama: Here's what happened. You had a whole bunch of oil companies who had leases on public lands that they weren't using. So what we said was you can't just sit on this for 10, 20, 30 years, decide when you want to drill, when you want to produce, when it's most profitable for you. These are public lands. So if you want to drill on public lands, you use it or you lose it.

Romney: OK, –

Obama: And so what we did was take away those leases. And we are now reletting them so that we can actually make a profit.

Romney: And production on private – on government land –

Obama: Production is up.

Romney: – is down.

Obama: No, it isn't.

Romney: Production on government land of oil is down 14 percent.

Obama: Governor –

Romney: And production on gas –

Obama: It's just not true.

Romney: It's absolutely true. Look, there's no question but the people recognize that we have not produced more (inaudible) on federal lands and in

320

奥巴马：州长，事实上，我们开采了更多的石油。

罗姆尼：不不，你就告诉我，你到底砍了多少联邦土地和水域的开采许可？

奥巴马：罗姆尼州长，我们所做的是，有一大批石油企业……

罗姆尼：不不，回答我的问题，我问你砍了多少？

奥巴马：你是想叫我回答问题……

罗姆尼：你砍了多少？

奥巴马：我很乐意回答这个问题。

罗姆尼：好啊，那是多少？

奥巴马：情况是这样的，罗姆尼州长。有大量的石油公司拥有公地的租约，却不去用。那么我们就说，你不能就这样白白地占着这块地10年、20年、30年，来决定什么时候钻井，什么时候生产，什么时候对你来说利润最大。这是公地。所以，如果你想要在公地钻井，你要么动手就干，要么走人。

罗姆尼：那么——

奥巴马：我们所做的是收回那些租约，然后现在重新发放租约，以实现真正盈利。

罗姆尼：但私有土地……政府土地——

奥巴马：增产了。

罗姆尼：不，减产了。

奥巴马：不，是增产了。

罗姆尼：政府油田产量下降了14%。

奥巴马：州长——

罗姆尼：天然气产量——

奥巴马：你所言完全失实。

federal waters. And coal, coal production is not up; coal jobs are not up. I was just at a coal facility, where some 1,200 people lost their jobs. The right course for America is to have a true all-of-the-above policy. I don't think anyone really believes that you're a person who's going to be pushing for oil and gas and coal. You'll get your chance in a moment. I'm still speaking.

Obama: Well –

Romney: And the answer is I don't believe people think that's the case –

Obama: OK.

Romney: That was a statement. I don't think the American people believe that. I will fight for oil, coal and natural gas. And the proof, the proof of whether a strategy is working or not is what the price is that you're paying at the pump. If you're paying less than you paid a year or two ago, why, then, the strategy is working. But you're paying more. When the president took office, the price of gasoline here in Nassau County was about $1.86 a gallon. Now, it's $4.00 a gallon. The price of electricity is up.

If the president's energy policies are working, you're going to see the cost of energy come down. I will fight to create more energy in this country, to get America energy secure. And part of that is bringing in a pipeline of oil from Canada, taking advantage of the oil and coal we have here, drilling offshore in Alaska, drilling offshore in Virginia where the people want it. Those things will get us the energy we need.

Crowley: Mr. President, could you address, because we did finally get to gas prices here, could you address what the governor said, which is if your energy policy was working, the price of gasoline would not be $4 a gallon here. Is that true?

Obama: Well, think about what the governor – think about what the governor just said. He said when I took office, the price of gasoline was $1.80, $1.86. Why is that? Because the economy was on the verge of collapse, because we were about to go through the worst recession since the Great Depression,

罗姆尼：我所言绝对是属实的。你看，毫无疑问人们意识到我们在联邦的土地和水域上，没有生产出更多的石油和天然气。还有煤炭产量和就业也没有上升。我曾去过一个煤厂，那里就有1200名员工失业。对美国来说，正确的道路应该是真正的一揽子能源计划。我认为没有人真正地相信你是一个会推动石油、天然气和煤炭行业的人。你稍等，我还在说呢。

奥巴马：好吧……

罗姆尼：我不相信人们会这么认为。

奥巴马：好吧。

我没有问你问题，那只是一个陈述句。我不认为美国人民会相信你这一套。而我，会为石油、煤炭和天然气而奋斗。至于证据，证明我的战略是否有效，就是你们的加油钱。如果你比一年或两年前付的少了，那么这个策略就奏效了。但是你们如今付的更多，当总统上任时，本地油价是一加仑1.86美元，现在一加仑4美元了。电价也节节高了。

如果总统的能源政策是有效的，你应该看到能源价格下调才对。我将为在这个国家创造更多的能源，为美国在能源上更安全而奋斗。而其中的一个方法，就是通过从加拿大引入输油管，利用好我们所拥有的石油和煤炭，在阿拉斯加州近海、在维吉尼亚州近海钻井，这是民意所向，这些都会带给我们所需要的能源。

克劳利：总统先生，您能否谈谈——我们终于说到油价问题了——刚才州长说，如果你的能源政策是有效的，那么这里的汽油价格不应该是4美元每加仑。这种说法对吗？

奥巴马：好，让我们回顾一下州长刚才说的话。他说，在我就任时，汽油的价格是1.8美元、1.86美元。为什么？因为当时的经济正处于崩溃的边缘，因为当时我们正在遭遇自大萧条以来最大的经济衰退，而衰退的原因，恰恰就和罗姆尼州长现在支持的一些政策有关。所以，可以想象，罗姆尼州长也许能把油价压下来，但也因为通过他的政策，我们的经济可能会回到当初的一团糟。

as a consequence of some of the same policies that Governor Romney's now promoting. So, it's conceivable that Governor Romney could bring down gas prices because with his policies, we might be back in that same mess.

What I want to do is to create an economy that is strong, and at the same time produce energy. And with respect to this pipeline that Governor Romney keeps on talking about, we've – we've built enough pipeline to wrap around the entire earth once. So, I'm all for pipelines. I'm all for oil production.

What I'm not for is us ignoring the other half of the equation. So, for example, on wind energy, when Governor Romney says "these are imaginary jobs." When you've got thousands of people right now in Iowa, right now in Colorado, who are working, creating wind power with good-paying manufacturing jobs, and the Republican senator in that – in Iowa is all for it, providing tax breaks (ph) to help this work and Governor Romney says I'm opposed. I'd get rid of it. That's not an energy strategy for the future. And we need to win that future. And I intend to win it as President of the United States.

Crowley: I got to – I got to move you on –

Romney: He gets the first –

Crowley: – and the next question –

Romney: He actually got the first question. So I get the last question – last answer –

Crowley: in the follow up, it doesn't quite work like that. But I'm going to give you a chance here. I promise you, I'm going to. And the next question is for you. So if you want to, you know, continue on – but I don't want to leave all – sitting here –

Romney: Candy, Candy, I don't have a policy of stopping wind jobs in Iowa and that – they're not phantom jobs. They're real jobs.

Crowley: OK.

Romney: I appreciate wind jobs in Iowa and across our country. I appreciate the jobs in coal and oil and gas. I'm going to make sure –we're taking

我要做的是建立一个强大的经济，同时生产能源。至于罗姆尼州长再三提及的石油管道问题，我们修建好的石油管道已足够绕地球一圈。所以，我是支持修建石油管道的，我也是支持石油生产的。

而我不支持的是我们忽略了另一部分能源。比如，风能，当罗姆尼州长说，这些是"想象中的工作机会"，你可以看到成千的人就在衣阿华州、就在科罗拉多州从事风能行业，拥有薪酬优厚的制造业工作，衣阿华州的共和党参议员也全力支持，并为其提供税收减免，但罗姆尼州长却说："我反对，我要清除掉它"，这绝不是我们未来的能源战略。而我们亟需在未来赢得这些，我希望我以美国总统的身份，赢得这个未来。

克劳利：我必须——我必须——让你们继续下一个话题。

罗姆尼：他回答了第一个问题——

克劳利：下一个问题——

罗姆尼：他回答了第一个问题，所以我应该回答最后一个。

克劳利：后续回答流程不是这样的。但我会给你一个机会的，我保证给你机会。下一个问题是给你的。如果你想继续上一个问题——但我不想让这么人干坐在这里。

罗姆尼：坎迪，坎迪——我没有打算叫停衣阿华州与风能相关的工作，而且这些工作不是幻影，他们是实实在在的职位。

克劳利：好的。

罗姆尼：我很喜欢衣阿华州以及全国的与风能相关的工作，我也看好煤炭、石油和天然气方面的工作。我将确保我们能很好地利用我们的能源资源。我们会为美国找回更多的制造业岗位。我们将实行激进的能源政策，在国内创造350万个岗位。这对我们的未来至关重要。

advantage of our energy resources. We'll bring back manufacturing to America. We're going to get through a very aggressive energy policy, 3.5 million more jobs in this country. It's critical to our future.

Obama: Candy, it's not going to –

Crowley: We're going to move you along –

Obama: Used to being interrupted.

Crowley: We're going to move you both along to taxes over here and all these folks that have been waiting. Governor, this question is for you. It comes from Mary Follano – Follano, sorry.

Romney: Hi, Mary.

Question: Governor Romney, you have stated that if you're elected president, you would plan to reduce the tax rates for all the tax brackets and that you would work with the Congress to eliminate some deductions in order to make up for the loss in revenue. Concerning the – these various deductions, the mortgage deductions, the charitable deductions, the child tax credit and also the – oh, what's that other credit? I forgot.

Obama: You're doing great.

Question: Oh, I remember. The education credits, which are important to me, because I have children in college. What would be your position on those things, which are important to the middle class?

Romney: Thank you very much. And let me tell you, you're absolutely right about part of that, which is I want to bring the rates down, I want to simplify the tax code, and I want to get middle- income taxpayers to have lower taxes.

And the reason I want middle-income taxpayers to have lower taxes is because middle-income taxpayers have been buried over the past four years. You've seen, as middle-income people in this country, incomes go down $4,300 a family, even as gasoline prices have gone up $2,000. Health insurance premiums, up $2,500. Food prices up. Utility prices up. The middle-income families in America have been crushed over the last four years. So I want to get

326

奥巴马：坎迪，继续下一个话题吧——

克劳利：我们要谈谈——

奥巴马：我已经习惯被打断了。

谁的减税政策更实在？

克劳利：我们要谈谈税收的话题了。大家伙儿都在等着呢，州长，这个问题是问您的。有请玛丽·弗拉诺。

罗姆尼：你好，玛丽。

选民提问：罗姆尼州长，你说过，如果你当选总统，你计划将为所有税收层次的人减税，你还将与国会合作，取消一些税收减免项目以补偿国家税收的减少，其中包括很多减免项目，如，住房抵押贷款减免、慈善事业减免、儿童税收抵免以及——我忘了。

奥巴马：你做得很棒了！

选民提问：我想起来了，教育税收抵免。这对我来说很重要，因为我的孩子在上大学。您对此态度如何？对中产阶级来说这可是相当重要的。

罗姆尼：非常感谢你。你说的一部分毫无疑问是对的，我想要调低税率，简化税收制度，还有我想要让中等收入的纳税人缴纳更少的税。

而我想让中产少纳税的原因是，中产阶级在过去的四年里，简直快被税务给埋葬了。如你所见，我国的中等收入家庭，收入减少了4300美元，而汽油支出却升高了2000美元，医疗保险费用提高了2500美元。食品价格上升了，水电价格上升了。美国中等收入家庭在过去的四年被压垮了。所以我想要减轻中等收入家庭的负担。这是一个方面。

some relief to middle-income families. That's part – that's part one.

Now, how about deductions? 'Cause I'm going to bring rates down across the board for everybody, but I'm going to limit deductions and exemptions and credits, particularly for people at the high end, because I am not going to have people at the high end pay less than they're paying now. The top 5 percent of taxpayers will continue to pay 60 percent of the income tax the nation collects. So that'll stay the same. Middle-income people are going to get a tax break.

And so, in terms of bringing down deductions, one way of doing that would be say everybody gets – I'll pick a number – $25,000 of deductions and credits, and you can decide which ones to use. Your home mortgage interest deduction, charity, child tax credit, and so forth, you can use those as part of filling that bucket, if you will, of deductions. But your rate comes down and the burden also comes down on you for one more reason, and that is every middle-income taxpayer no longer will pay any tax on interest, dividends or capital gains. No tax on your savings. That makes life a lot easier.

If you're getting interest from a bank, if you're getting a statement from a mutual fund or any other kind of investment you have, you don't have to worry about filing taxes on that, because there'll be no taxes for anybody making $200,000.00 per year and less, on your interest, dividends and capital gains. Why am I lowering taxes on the middle-class? Because under the last four years, they've been buried. And I want to help people in the middle-class.

And I will not – I will not under any circumstances, reduce the share that's being paid by the highest income taxpayers. And I will not, under any circumstances increase taxes on the middle-class. The president's spending, the president's borrowing will cost this nation to have to raise taxes on the American people. Not just at the high end. A recent study has shown the people in the middle-class will see $4,000.00 per year in higher taxes as a result of the spending and borrowing of this administration.

I will not let that happen. I want to get us on track to a balanced budget,

那么，减免额度呢？因为我想降低税率，这适用于所有的纳税人，但我同时会限制减免额度，免税额度，以及退税额度，特别是针对那些高收入群体，因为我不会让高收入者比现在交更少的税。收入前5%的纳税人仍将继续上缴这个国家所得税的60%，因此这方面保持不变，而中等收入群体则将获得税收减免。

至于降低减税额度，一个方法是，我将选择一个数字——比如25000美元的减税额。这个钱由你来决定你想用在哪儿，按揭贷款利息减免、慈善减免、儿童税收抵免等等。你可以用它来填写税收减免表。但由于另一个原因，你的税率和税收负担将下降。那就是中等收入的纳税人不再需要缴纳利息税、红利税或者资本所得税，你将不用为你的储蓄交税。这将让生活变得容易。

当你从银行获得利息，或者当你从共同基金或者其他投资那里拿到一份对账单，你将不用担心为这些报税，因为对于收入在20万美元及以下的任何人，你将不用为你的利息、红利和资本所得交税。为什么我要降低中产阶级的税收呢？因为在过去的四年里，他们被税单掩埋了。而我想帮助中产阶级的人们。

任何情况下，我都不会减少最高收入纳税人的税收份额，同时不论在什么情况下，我也不会向中产阶级增税。总统的支出与借债会让全体美国人民都缴纳更多的税收，而不仅仅针对高收入群体。最近一份调查显示，中产阶级的美国人，每年多交4000美元的税款，以覆盖这届政府的支出和借贷。

and I'm going to reduce the tax burden on middle income families. And what's that going to do? It's going to help those families, and it's going to create incentives to start growing jobs again in this country.

Crowley: Thanks, Governor.

Obama: My philosophy on taxes has been simple. And that is, I want to give middle-class families and folks who are striving to get into the middle-class some relief. Because they have been hit hard over the last decade, over the last 15, over the last 20 years. So four years ago I stood on a stage just like this one. Actually it was a town hall, and I said I would cut taxes for middle-class families, and that's what I've done, by $3,600.00. I said I would cut taxes for small businesses, who are the drivers and engines of growth. And we've cut them 18 times. And I want to continue those tax cuts for middle-class families, and for small business.

But what I've also said is, if we're serious about reducing the deficit, if this is genuinely a moral obligation to the next generation, then in addition to some tough spending cuts, we've also got to make sure that the wealthy do a little bit more.

So what I've said is, your first $250,000.00 worth of income, no change. And that means 98 percent of American families, 97 percent of small businesses, they will not see a tax increase. I'm ready to sign that bill right now. The only reason it's not happening is because Governor Romney's allies in Congress have held the 98 percent hostage because they want tax breaks for the top 2 percent.

But what I've also says is for above $250,000, we can go back to the tax rates we had when Bill Clinton was president. We created 23 million new jobs. That's part of what took us from deficits to surplus. It will be good for our economy and it will be good for job creation.

Now, Governor Romney has a different philosophy. He was on 60 like you, making $20 million a year, to pay a lower tax rate than a nurse or a bus driver, somebody making $50,000 year? And he said, "Yes, I think that's fair." Not only that, he said, "I think that's what grows the economy."

我决不允许这种事情发生。我要把大家带回到平衡的预算中去，我要减轻中等收入家庭的负担。效果是什么呢？这会帮助这些家庭，而且会刺激就业，创造更多的国内工作岗位。

克劳利：谢谢州长的发言。

奥巴马：我在税收上的观点很简单，那就是，我将为中产阶级家庭以及那些正在努力进入中产阶级的人们提供一些帮助，因为不管是过去的10年、15年、20年，他们已经遭受了重创。所以，四年前，我站在一个像今晚这样的舞台上，我要为中产阶级家庭减税，我做到了，我为中产阶级家庭减税3600美元。我说我要为中小企业减税，它们是经济增长的推动者和发动机，我们为它们减税18次。我还将继续为中产阶层家庭和中小企业减税。

但是我同样指出，如果我们真心想要降低赤字，如果这真是我们对下一代的道德职责，那么，除了一些艰难的支出消减，我们同样需要确保那些富人多交一些税。

所以正如我所说，你的收入起步25万美元，不会有变化。这意味着98%的美国家庭、97%的中小企业不会增税。我已准备好签署这项法案。但是这项法案没签成，唯一的原因是罗姆尼州长在国会的盟友们，他们为了给那些最富有的2%的人减税，把98%的人劫为了人质。

但是我也同样指出，对于超过25万美元的人群，我们可以回到克林顿总统时期的税率，那时我们创造了2300万个新的就业岗位。那是当时让我们从赤字走向盈余的部分原因。这样做无论对经济还是对创造就业岗位都是有益的。

现在，罗姆尼州长有另外一套不同的观点。在两周前"60分钟"节目上，当他被问及，"像你这样每年挣2000万美元的人，所交的税率比每年挣5万美元的护士或者公车司机还要低，你认为公平吗？"他答："是的，我认为这是公平的。"不仅如此，他还说："这有助于经济增长。"

Well, I fundamentally disagree with that. I think what grows the economy is when you get that tax credit that we put in place for your kids going to college. I think that grows the economy. I think what grows the economy is when we make sure small businesses are getting a tax credit for hiring veterans who fought for our country. That grows our economy. So we just have a different theory. And when Governor Romney stands here, after a year of campaigning, when during a Republican primary he stood on stage and said "I'm going to give tax cuts" – he didn't say tax rate cuts, he said "tax cuts to everybody", including the top 1 percent, you should believe him because that's been his history. And that's exactly the kind of top-down economics that is not going to work if we want a strong middle class and an economy that's striving for everybody.

Crowley: Governor Romney, I'm sure you've got a reply there.

Romney: You're absolutely right. You heard what I said about my tax plan. The top 5 percent will continue to pay 60 percent, as they do today. I'm not looking to cut taxes for wealthy people. I am looking to cut taxes for middle-income people.

And why do I want to bring rates down, and at the same time lower exemptions and deductions, particularly for people at the high end? Because if you bring rates down, it makes it easier for small business to keep more of their capital and hire people. And for me, this is about jobs. I want to get America's economy going again. Fifty-four percent of America's workers work in businesses that are taxed as individuals. So when you bring those rates down, those small businesses are able to keep more money and hire more people.

For me, I look at what's happened in the last four years and say this has been a disappointment. We can do better than this. We don't have to settle for, how many months, 43 months with unemployment above 8 percent, 23 million Americans struggling to find a good job right now. There are 3.5 million more women living in poverty today than when the president took office. We don't have to live like this. We can get this economy going again.

我从根本上反对这种说法。我认为，推动我们经济增长的是，你能用这部分钱支付孩子的大学学费，这才是真正推动经济增长。我认为推动经济增长的是，当我们确保，小企业因雇佣为国而战的老兵而得到减税，这才是真正推动经济增长。因此，我们的理论根本就不一样。罗姆尼州长站在这儿，竞选活动都持续一年了，想想共和党初选时，他曾在台上说，"我要减税"，他没有说降低税率，他说的是减税。每个人都减，包括最富有的那1%的人。你应该相信他，因为那就是他的历史。而这却恰恰就是那种没用的、自上而下的经济。不适用于我们想要的强健的中产阶级，不是有益于每个美国人的经济。

克劳利：罗姆尼州长，我相信你一定有话要回应。

罗姆尼：完全正确。你们刚才听了我的税收计划，最富有的5%将继续缴纳和现在一样的60%的所得税。我并没有追求给富人减税。我希望给中等收入的群体减税。

那么为什么我要在降低税率的同时减少税收豁免和税收减免，特别是针对高收入群体？因为降低了税率，中小企业就能保有更多的资本并且雇佣更多的人。对我来说，这事关就业岗位。我要让美国经济重新启动。54%的美国工人工作的企业是按个人课税的。因此当你调低税率，这些中小企业就能保有更多的资金同时雇佣更多的人。

看到过去四年所发生的事情，我说，这是一个失望的结果。我们原本能做得比这更好。我们不应该落得43个月失业率超过8%，如今2300万美国人为找到一个好工作而挣扎着，这位总统就任后，如今生活窘迫的女性增加了350万。我们没有必要活的这么惨，我们能让经济复苏起来。

My five-point plan does it. Energy independence for North America in five years. Opening up more trade, particularly in Latin America. Cracking down on China when they cheat. Getting us to a balanced budget. Fixing our training programs for our workers. And finally, championing small business. I want to make small businesses grow and thrive. I know how to make that happen. I spent my life in the private sector. I know why jobs come and why they go. And they're going now because of the policies of this administration.

Crowley: Governor, let me ask the president something about what you just said. The governor says that he is not going to allow the top 5 percent, believe is what he said, to have a tax cut, that it will all even out, that what he wants to do is give that tax cut to the middle class. Settled?

Obama: No, it's not settled. Look, the cost of lowering rates for everybody across the board, 20 percent. Along with what he also wants to do in terms of eliminating the estate tax, along what he wants to do in terms of corporates, changes in the tax code, it costs about $5 trillion. Governor Romney then also wants to spend $2 trillion on additional military programs even though the military's not asking for them. That's $7 trillion. He also wants to continue the Bush tax cuts for the wealthiest Americans. That's another trillion dollars – that's $8 trillion.

Now, what he says is he's going to make sure that this doesn't add to the deficit and he's going to cut middleclass taxes deductions, which loopholes are you going to close? He can't tell you. The – the fact that he only has to pay 14 percent on his taxes when a lot of you are paying much higher. He's already taken that off the board, capital gains are going to continue to be at a low rate so we – we're not going to get money that way. We haven't heard from the governor any specifics beyond Big Bird and eliminating funding for Planned Parenthood in terms of how he pays for that.

Now, Governor Romney was a very successful investor. If somebody came to you, Governor, with a plan that said, here, I want to spend $7 or $8 trillion,

我的五点计划能够做到这点：用五年的时间实现北美能源独立；开辟更多的贸易，特别是与拉丁美洲之间，当中国欺诈时就给予其制裁；平衡预算；重整我们的工人培训项目；最后，支持中小企业。我要帮助中小企业成长与勃兴。我知道如何实现这些。我的一生都在私人部门工作，我知道就业岗位是怎样产生与失去的。而现在，由于本届政府的政策，就业岗位正在失去。

克劳利：州长，让我根据你刚才说的向总统提个问题。州长说，他将不会给最富有的5%人群，我相信他说的是享受减税，他要给中产阶级减税。同意吗？

奥巴马：不，我不同意啊。你看，为所有人减税20%，同时他还要取消房产税，给公司更改税收制度，所有这些的成本是5万亿美元。罗姆尼州长还要增加2万亿美元的额外军事项目开支，尽管军方并没有做此要求。这加起来就是7万亿美元。他还要继续布什时期的税收减免政策，为最富有的美国人减税。这是另外的1万亿美元。所有这些加起来就是8万亿美元。

现在，他说他将确保所有这些不会增加赤字，他还要给中产阶级减税。但是当被问及，你要怎么做，有哪些减税项目？哪些漏洞你能补上？他无言以对。事实是，他只需要交14%的税，而你们当中的许多人却比他交的还要高——你们知道，他已将此扣除。资本所得将继续保持在低税率。所以我们无法从中获益。我们还没有从州长那里听到任何细节，除了"巨鸟项目"和撤销"计划生育"资金，他就没有说出任何支付细节。

and then we're going to pay for it, but we can't tell you until maybe after the election how we're going to do it, you wouldn't take such a sketchy deal and neither should you, the American people, because the math doesn't add up.

And – and what's at stake here is one of two things, either Candy – this blows up the deficit because keep in mind, this is just to pay for the additional spending that he's talking about, $7 trillion ~ $8 trillion before we even get to the deficit we already have. Or, alternatively, it's got to be paid for, not only by closing deductions for wealthy individuals, that – that will pay for about 4 percent reduction in tax rates. You're going to be paying for it. You're going to lose some deductions, and you can't buy the sales pitch. Nobody who's looked at it that's serious, actually believes it adds up.

Crowley: Mr. President, let me get – let me get the governor in on this. And Governor, let's – before we get into a... vast array of who says – what study says what, if it shouldn't add up. If somehow when you get in there, there isn't enough tax revenue coming in. If somehow the numbers don't add up, would you be willing to look again at a 20 percent...

Romney: Well of course they add up. I – I was – I was someone who ran businesses for 25 years, and balanced the budget. I ran the Olympics and balanced the budget. I ran the – the state of Massachusetts as a governor, to the extent any governor does, and balanced the budget all four years.

When we're talking about math that doesn't add up, how about $4 trillion of deficits over the last four years, $5 trillion? That's math that doesn't add up. We have – we have a president talking about someone's plan in a way that's completely foreign to what my real plan is. And then we have his own record, which is we have four consecutive years where he said when he was running for office, he would cut the deficit in half. Instead he's doubled it.

We've gone from $10 trillion of national debt, to $16 trillion of national debt. If the president were reelected, we'd go to almost $20 trillion of national debt. This puts us on a road to Greece. I know what it takes to balance budgets.

罗姆尼州长是一个非常成功的投资者。州长，如果有一个人拿着一个计划来找你，说，我打算花7—8万亿美元，我们会付钱，只是在大选没结束前我不能告诉你我打算怎么付，你不会接受这档子含糊不清的买卖吧。美国同胞们——你们也不应该接受吧，因为这个算数是有问题的。

可能会出现两种危险。要么，坎迪，这会让赤字膨胀——因为，大家要记得，这些钱只是拿来支付他所说的那些额外开支，7万亿、8万亿，这些都还没有涉及我们目前的赤字。要么，他不仅减少富人的税收减免，同时还要减少你们的税收减免，还要因此承担4%的财产损失。这些损失是要各位来承担的。你们会失去几项免税项目的，你们不能陷入这笔交易的。真正有研究的人，都知道这算数是有问题的。

克劳利：总统先生，让我叫州长来谈几句。州长，如果你到了那里，但是没有足够的税收来源，如果这些数字不能算平，你还会考虑20%这个数字吗？

罗姆尼：它们当然能够算平。我是一个在商界摸爬滚打长达25年并且平衡了预算的人，我办了奥运会，预算也是平衡的。我作为州长主政马萨诸塞州四年，我平衡了预算。

当我们讨论数字不能算平的时候，怎么看过去四年来产生的4万亿美元、5万亿美元的赤字？这些数字才不能算平。我们这位总统讨论别人的计划时使用的是一种与我的真实计划完全不相关的方式，那么我们看看他连续四年的记录。在他刚就任时，他说他能砍掉一半赤字，结果相反，他翻了一倍。

我们国家的债务已经从10万亿美元攀升到了16万亿美元。如果这位总统先生赢得连任，我们的国债将达到近20万亿美元。这将把我们带向希腊的境地。我知道如何平衡预算，我一辈子就是干这个的。所以，比如当他说，你的计划砍掉了5万亿收入，不对，这是不对的，因为我通过减少税收减免对此做了抵消。而且……

I've done it my entire life. So for instance when he says, "Yours is a $5 trillion cut." Well, no it's not. Because I'm offsetting some of the reductions with holding down some of the deductions. And...

Crowley: Governor, I've gotta – gotta – actually, I need to have you both. I understand the stakes here. I understand both of you. But I – I will get run out of town if I don't...

Romney: And I just described – I just described to you, Mr. President – I just described to you precisely how I'd do it which is with a single number that people can put – and they can put they're – they're deductions and credits...

Crowley: Mr. President, we're keeping track, I promise you. And Mr. President, the next question is for you, so stay standing.

Obama: Great. Looking forward to it.

And it's Katherine Fenton, who has a question for you.

Question: In what new ways to you intend to rectify the inequalities in the workplace, specifically regarding females making only 72 percent of what their male counterparts earn?

Obama: Well, Katherine, that's a great question. And, you know, I was raised by a single mom who had to put herself through school while looking after two kids. And she worked hard every day and made a lot of sacrifices to make sure we got everything we needed. My grandmother, she started off as a secretary in a bank. She never got a college education, even though she was smart as a whip. And she worked her way up to become a vice president of a local bank, but she hit the glass ceiling. She trained people who would end up becoming her bosses during the course of her career. She didn't complain. That's not what you did in that generation.

And this is one of the reasons why one of the first – the first bill I signed was something called The Lily Ledbetter bill. And it's named after this amazing woman who had been doing the same job as a man for years, found out that she was getting paid less, and the Supreme Court said that she couldn't bring

职场平等谁有高招？

克劳利：州长，我必须让你俩都暂停一下，我知道这个议题很重要。两边我都能理解。但我得请下一位观众提问了，不然他们……

罗姆尼：总统先生，我刚才也跟您详细描述了我的措施。其实就很简单，一个数字。他们是税收减免和税收抵免……

克劳利：总统先生，我记着这个话题，我保证。总统先生，下一个问题是提给您的，您先别坐。

奥巴马：好。我期待。

有请，凯瑟琳·芬顿。

选民提问：针对就业方面的不平等，尤其针对女性员工工资只有男性员工工资的72%这一事实，您有哪些新的改进措施？

奥巴马：好，凯瑟琳，这个问题提的非常好。你知道，我是由一位单亲母亲抚养长大的，她不得不边照顾两个孩子边完成学业。她每天刻苦工作，为了确保我们能够得到我们日常所需付出了很大的牺牲。我的外祖母，她最初是银行的书记员。她从来没有上过大学，但她非常聪明，她朝着自己的方向工作，最终做到了当地银行的副总裁。但她遭遇了职场瓶颈，无法再晋升，她培训出来的那些男性员工，最终却成为了她的上司。她没有抱怨，这不是她们那代人会做的事。

这就是为什么我最早签署的法案之一就是《莉莉·列得贝塔同工同酬法》。它以一位了不起的女性命名，她多年来，都和男人们做着一样的工作，后来却发现，她的薪水比他们少。最高法院认为，她不能就此提起诉讼，因为她早先时候就应该发现这种情况，可是她根本没有办法了解这些情况。

suit because she should have found about it earlier, whereas she had no way of finding out about it.

So we fixed that. And that's an example of the kind of advocacy that we need, because women are increasingly the breadwinners in the family. This is not just a women's issue, this is a family issue, this is a middle-class issue, and that's why we've got to fight for it.

It also means that we've got to make sure that young people like yourself are able to afford a college education. Earlier, Governor Romney talked about he wants to make Pell Grants and other education accessible for young people. Well, the truth of the matter is, is that that's exactly what we've done. We've expanded Pell Grants for millions of people, including millions of young women, all across the country. We did it by taking $60 billion that was going to banks and lenders as middlemen for the student loan program, and we said, let's just cut out the middleman. Let's give the money directly to students. And as a consequence, we've seen millions of young people be able to afford college, and that's going to make sure that young women are going to be able to compete in that market place.

But we've got to enforce the laws, which is what we are doing, and we've also got to make sure that in every walk of life we do not tolerate discrimination.

That's been one of the hallmarks of my administration. I'm going to continue to push on this issue for the next four years.

Crowley: Governor Romney, pay equity for women?

Romney: Thank you. And important topic, and one which I learned a great deal about, particularly as I was serving as governor of my state, because I had the chance to pull together a cabinet and all the applicants seemed to be men. And I – and I went to my staff, and I said, "How come all the people for these jobs are – are all men." They said, "Well, these are the people that have the qualifications." And I said, "Well, gosh, can't we – can't we find some – some women that are also qualified?"

所以我们对此做了修正。这个例子就说明了我们应当倡导的理念，由于越来越多的女性成了家里的顶梁柱。这不仅仅是女性的问题，也是一个家庭问题，一个中产阶级的问题。所以我们必须努力争取。

同时也说明，我们得保证，像你们这样的年轻人，能付得起大学学费。早些时候，罗姆尼州长谈到，他要让年轻人得到佩尔助学金和其他教育支持。事实上，我们已经做到了。我们扩展了佩尔助学金令数百万学子受惠，包括全国范围的数百万的年轻女性。在操作过程中，我们的600亿美元学生贷款项目原本通过银行和其他借贷机构作为中间人发放，但我们说，我们要取消中间人，让我们直接把钱交给学生。结果我们看到，几百万年轻人能够支付得起大学学费，这将确保这些年轻女性能够在职场上展现她们的竞争力。

但法令一定要严格执行，这也是我们正在做的。并且要确保在所有行业，我们都绝不能容忍歧视。

这是我们这届政府的特色之一。在接下来的四年里，我将继续推进这方面的工作。

克劳利：罗姆尼州长，给女人同工同酬的问题。

罗姆尼：谢谢，这是一个重要话题，我对此深有体会，特别是当我作为州长的时候，因为我有机会组建州内阁，结果我发现申请者几乎都是男性。我就问我的职员们，怎么来应聘这些工作的都是男性？他们说，这些人都符合申请资格啊。然后我说，我的天，难道我们就找不到同样符合条件的女性吗？

And – and so we – we took a concerted effort to go out and find women who had backgrounds that could be qualified to become members of our cabinet. I went to a number of women's groups and said, "Can you help us find folks," and they brought us whole binders full of women.

I was proud of the fact that after I staffed my Cabinet and my senior staff, that the University of New York in Albany did a survey of all 50 states, and concluded that mine had more women in senior leadership positions than any other state in America.

Now one of the reasons I was able to get so many good women to be part of that team was because of our recruiting effort. But number two, because I recognized that if you're going to have women in the workforce that sometimes you need to be more flexible. My chief of staff, for instance, had two kids that were still in school. She said, I can't be here until 7 or 8 o'clock at night. I need to be able to get home at 5 o'clock so I can be there for making dinner for my kids and being with them when they get home from school. So we said fine. Let's have a flexible schedule so you can have hours that work for you.

We're going to have to have employers in the new economy, in the economy I'm going to bring to play, that are going to be so anxious to get good workers they're going to be anxious to hire women. In the – in the last women have lost 580,000 jobs. That's the net of what's happened in the last four years. We're still down 580,000 jobs. I mentioned 31/2 million women, more now in poverty than four years ago.

What we can do to help young women and women of all ages is to have a strong economy, so strong that employers that are looking to find good employees and bringing them into their workforce and adapting to a flexible work schedule that gives women opportunities that they would otherwise not be able to afford.

This is what I have done. It's what I look forward to doing and I know what it takes to make an economy work, and I know what a working economy looks like.

　　然后大家就一起开始找符合我们州内阁要求的女性人选。我去了不少女性团体，问能否帮我们找到人选？然后我带回来成沓的女性候选人资料。

　　我很自豪地告诉大家，我的员工和高级官员的女性比例，根据纽约州立大学阿尔巴尼分校对全美50个州的调查，我的领导班子里，女性和女性高级官员的比例是全美最高的。现在看来，我的州内阁有这么多优秀的女性，一是因为，我们在招募时所花费的努力。二是因为我意识到，要女性来为你工作，有时候得学会变通。比如，我的办公厅主任，她有两个上学的孩子。她说："我不能在晚上7点或者8点还不下班。我得5点到家，好给孩子做晚饭，免得他们放学后独自在家。"我说，可以啊，那时间上我们就变通一下，这样你就可以有时间照顾孩子。

　　我会给经济带来新的气象，会有更多像我这样的雇主，他们非常想聘用好的员工，非常想聘用女员工。在过去的四年，我们的女性丧失了58万个就业岗位。仅仅是过去四年啊，就有58万。我也提到了，现在相比四年前，贫困线以下的女性又多了350万。

　　想要帮助年轻女性以及其他年龄段的女性，就要有个极好的经济环境，好到让雇主主动去寻找好员工，给她们工作，还能采取一个灵活的工作时间，让女性享受到各种机会，否则她们无力承担。

And an economy with 7.8 percent unemployment is not a real strong economy. An economy that has 23 million people looking for work is not a strong economy. An economy with 50 percent of kids graduating from college that can't finds a job, or a college level job, that's not what we have to have. I'm going to help women in America get good work by getting a stronger economy and by supporting women in the workforce.

Crowley: Mr. President why don't you get in on this quickly, please?

Obama: Katherine, I just want to point out that when Governor supported it? He said, "I'll get back to you." And that's not the kind of advocacy that women need in any economy.

Now, there are some other issues that have a bearing on how women succeed in the workplace. For example, their healthcare. You know a major difference in this campaign is that Governor Romney feels comfortable having politicians in Washington decide the health care choices that women are making. I think that's a mistake. In my health care bill, I said insurance companies need to provide contraceptive coverage to everybody who is insured. Because this is not just a – a health issue, it's an economic issue for women. It makes a difference. This is money out of that family's pocket.

Governor Romney not only opposed it, he suggested that in fact employers should be able to make the decision as to whether or not a woman gets contraception through her insurance coverage. That's not the kind of advocacy that women need. When Governor Romney says that we should eliminate funding for Planned Parenthood, there are millions of women all across the country, who rely on Planned Parenthood for, not just contraceptive care, they rely on it for mammograms, for cervical cancer screenings. That's a pocketbook issue for women and families all across the country.

And it makes a difference in terms of how well and effectively women are able to work. When we talk about child care, and the credits that we're providing. That makes a difference in whether they can go out there and – and

这是我已经实践了的，并且希望推广的。我知道如何搞活经济，我知道有生命力的经济是什么样子。有7.8%失业率的经济环境，真算不上好环境。有2300万人求职无门，这样的环境真算不上好。50%的本科毕业生找不到工作，或者找不到与所受教育相符的工作，这真算不上好。我会用一个更好的经济，来帮助美国女性找到好的工作。

克劳利：总统先生，您简短回应一下吧。

奥巴马：凯瑟琳，我只想说明一下。我刚想指出的是，当州长在竞选中被问及是否支持《莉莉·列得贝塔同工同酬法》时，他说，以后再说吧。在任何的经济环境下，这都是女性不想看到的态度。

现在，有一些其他问题也与女性如何在职场上获得成功有关：比如，她们的医疗护理。在这场选举中，我们两方重大的分歧就是，罗姆尼州长丝毫不介意让华府政客代替女性作医保方面的决定。但我认为那是错误的。在我的医疗法案中，我指出，保险公司需要为每一个被保险人提供避孕服务，因为这不仅是一个健康问题，对女性来说，这还是一个经济问题。钱虽小，但问题的性质不同，这钱是要从家庭开支里掏的。

罗姆尼州长不仅反对它，而且他还暗示，雇主实际上应该能够决定女性员工的保险范围是否包括避孕服务。这不是女性想看到的主张。当罗姆尼州长说，我们应该取消计划生育项目的拨款时，全国有几百万的女性需要计划生育联合会，不仅是避孕，她们还需要依靠这个项目做乳腺癌检查，做宫颈癌检查。这对全国的女性和家庭来说是一项关于钱袋子的问题。

earn a living for their family. These are not just women's issues. These are family issues. These are economic issues. And one of the things that makes us grow as an economy is when everybody participates and women are getting the same fair deal as men are. And I've got two daughters and I want to make sure that they have the same opportunities that anybody's sons have. That's part of what I'm fighting for as president of the United States.

Crowley: I want to move us along here to Susan Katz, who has a question. And, Governor, it's for you.

Question: Governor Romney, I am an undecided voter, because I'm disappointed with the lack of progress I've seen in the last four years. However, I do attribute much of America's economic and international problems to the failings and missteps of the Bush administration. Since both you and President Bush are Republicans, I fear a return to the policies of those years should you win this election. What is the biggest difference between you and George W. Bush, and how do you differentiate yourself from George W. Bush?

Romney: Thank you. And I appreciate that question. I just want to make sure that, I think I was supposed to get that last answer, but I want to point out that that I don't believe...

Obama: I don't think so, Candy. I want to make sure our timekeepers are working here.

Crowley: OK. The timekeepers are all working. And let me tell you that the last part, it's for the two of you to talk to one another, and it isn't quite as you think. But go ahead and use these two minutes any way you'd like to, the question is on the floor.

Romney: I'd just note that I don't believe that bureaucrats in Washington should tell someone whether they can use contraceptives or not. And I don't believe employers should tell someone whether they could have contraceptive care of not. Every woman in America should have access to contraceptives. And – and the – and the president's statement of my policy is completely and totally wrong.

这是事关女性工作的质量和效率的问题。还有，儿童保育以及我们提供的补助金，这是事关女性能否走出家门、工作养家的问题。这些是家庭问题，也是经济问题。经济的发展，一定需要每个人的参与。让女性能够享受与男性一样的职场待遇。我有两个女儿，我要确保她们能够和任何人的儿子一样拥有同样的机会。这是我作为美国总统，要去努力争取的一件事。

罗姆尼是小布什吗？

克劳利：接下来把话筒递给苏珊·卡茨，州长，这个问题是提给您的。

选民提问：罗姆尼州长，我至今还未作出投票决定，因为过去的四年缺乏进展，让我感到失望。尽管如此，我认为，美国经济以及全球面临的困境与布什政府所走的歧途有关。您和布什总统都是共和党人，我担心若你当选总统，又会重复从前的那些措施。您和小布什总统之间最大的差别是什么？为使自己有别于小布什，您将如何去做？

罗姆尼：谢谢。谢谢您的提问。只是确认一下，我应该可以回应上一个问题吧。我只想说明我并不相信……

奥巴马：我看这可不行，坎迪，计时员得认真计时吧？

克劳利：计时员在计时。但最后那个部分，本应该是你俩有互动的，不过这两分钟，要说什么，全看您自己。问题已经提出来了。

罗姆尼：我只是想说，我并不觉得华府的官员，有资格或者有义务告诉别人她们能不能使用避孕药物。我也不认为雇主有权利左右任何人能否投保避孕医保，应该让每一位美国的女性，都能获取避孕药物。总统先生对我的陈述，是完全彻底的曲解。

Let me come back and – and answer your question. President Bush and I are – are different people and these are different times and that's why my five point plan is so different than what he would have done. I mean for instance, we can now, by virtue of new technology actually get all the energy we need in North America without having to go to the – the Arabs or the Venezuelans or anyone else. That wasn't true in his time, that's why my policy starts with a very robust policy to get all that energy in North America – become energy secure.

Number two, trade – I'll crack down on China, President Bush didn't. I'm also going to dramatically expand trade in Latin America. It's been growing about 12 percent per year over a long period of time. I want to add more free trade agreements so we'll have more trade.

Number three, I'm going to get us to a balanced budget. President Bush didn't. President Obama was right, he said that that was outrageous to have deficits as high as half a trillion dollars under the Bush years. He was right, but then he put in place deficits twice that size for every one of his four years. And his forecast for the next four years is more deficits, almost that large. So that's the next area I'm different than President Bush.

And then let's take the last one, championing small business. Our party has been focused too long. I came through small business. I understand how hard it is to start a small business. That's why everything I'll do is designed to help small businesses grow and add jobs. I want to keep their taxes down on small business. I want regulators to see their job as encouraging small enterprise, not crushing it.

And the thing I find the most troubling about Obama Care, well it's a long list, but one of the things I find most troubling is that when you go out and talk to small businesses and ask them what they think about it, they tell you it keeps them from hiring more people.

My priority is jobs. I know how to make that happen. And President Bush has a very different path for a very different time. My path is designed in getting

我回到你的问题，布什总统和我是不同的人，时代也不同了。这就是为什么我的五点计划与他执政时的措施是很不一样的，比如说，我们现在能够通过技术在北美获取我们所需的所有能源，而不需要从阿拉伯国家或者委内瑞拉或者其他国家进口。而在布什时期，并非如此。这就是为什么我的政策起点是在北美获取所有能源的强力能源政策，以保证我们的能源安全。

其二，贸易。我将制裁中国。布什总统没有这么做。我将显著地推进与拉丁美洲的贸易，在相当长的一段时间里，两地之间的贸易平均每年增长12%。我将增加更多的贸易协定以促进更多的贸易。

其三，我将实现预算平衡。布什总统没有这么做。奥巴马总统当年说的没错，他说，布什政府的5000亿美元真让人忍无可忍。他说得对，可是他把这数字翻了一番，四年来每年翻一番。而他对未来四年赤字的预期，只增不减，几乎又要翻番。所以，这是我和布什总统第二个不同点。

还有最后一点，我将鼓励中小企业发展。我们共和党长久以来，都把重点放在大企业上。我出身于小企业，我体会得到创建一家小企业有多么不容易。这也是为什么我要在帮助促进中小企业发展的同时增加就业。我将保持中小企业的低税收。我要让监管者明白，他们的工作是鼓励中小企业，而不是压垮它们。

而"奥巴马医保"中最让我担忧的一点是——这要是说起来可就多了——但其中的一项是，如果你去问问那些小企业主对医保有何看法，他们会告诉你，这会给他们招人带来困难。

对我来说，就业是第一位的，而我也知道如何去实现。布什总统在一个非常不同的时期走了一条非常不一样的路。我所设计的路径是让小企业成长并创造更多的就业。

small businesses to grow and hire people.

Crowley: Thanks, Governor. Mr. President?

Obama: Well, first of all, I think it's important to tell you that we did come in during some tough times. We were losing 800,000 jobs a month when I started.

But we had been digging our way out of policies that were misplaced and focused on the top doing very well and middle class folks not doing well.

Now, we've seen 30 consecutive – 31 consecutive months of job growth; 5.2 million new jobs created. And the plans that I talked about will create even more. But when Governor Romney says that he has a very different economic plan, the centerpiece of his economic plan are tax cuts. That's what took us from surplus to deficit. When he talks about getting tough on China, keep in mind that Governor Romney invested in companies that were pioneers of outsourcing to China, and is currently investing in countries – in companies that are building surveillance equipment for China to spy on its own folks. That's – Governor, you're the last person who's going to get tough on China.

And what we've done when it comes to trade is not only sign three trade deals to open up new markets, but we've also set up a task force for trade that goes after anybody who is taking advantage of American workers or businesses and not creating a level playing field. We've brought twice as many cases against unfair trading practices than the previous administration and we've won every single one that's been decided.

When I said that we had to make sure that China was not flooding our domestic market with cheap tires, Governor Romney said I was being protectionist; that it wouldn't be helpful to American workers. Well, in fact we saved 1,000 jobs. And that's the kind of tough trade actions that are required.

But the last point I want to make is this. You know, there are some things where Governor Romney is different from George Bush. George Bush didn't propose turning Medicare into a voucher. George Bush embraced comprehensive immigration reform. He didn't call for self-deportation. George Bush never

克劳利：谢谢州长。请总统先生发言。

奥巴马：好的。首先，我觉得我有必要告诉大家，我们确实经历了非常困难的时期。在我就任的时候，我们每月丧失80万个工作岗位。

但是我们一直在深究政策方面的问题，那些政策的重点，放在了生活滋润的巨富以及艰难度日的中产阶级上。

我们已经看到了连续30到31个月的就业增长，我们创造了520万个新的就业岗位，我一直在说的这个计划，还有更多的突破。但是，当罗姆尼州长说他有一个非常不一样的经济计划时，其核心部分就是减税。那正是让我们从盈余走向赤字的原因。当他说要对中国强硬时，记住，罗姆尼州长曾投资的公司是把业务外包给中国的急先锋。而他还在投资一些国家，一些公司。他们向中国提供监控设备，好让中国监视自己的国民。州长，你是最不可能对中国强硬的人。

在贸易问题上，我们所做的事情不仅是签订三份贸易协议以开拓新的市场，而且我们也设立了贸易专门工作组，追踪调查任何占美国工人或企业便宜、不公平竞争的人和机构。我们针对不公平贸易提起的案件比前任政府多一倍，而且我们还赢得了每一个已经裁决了的案件。

当我说我们得保证中国便宜的轮胎不会大量涌入国内市场，罗姆尼州长说这是贸易保护主义，不会对美国工人有益。但实际上，我们拯救了1000个就业岗位。这正是我国贸易需要的强硬措施。

suggested that we eliminate funding for Planned Parenthood, so there are differences between Governor Romney and George Bush, but they're not on economic policy. In some ways, he's gone to a more extreme place when it comes to social policy. And I think that's a mistake. That's not how we're going to move our economy forward.

Crowley: I want to move you both along to the next question, because it's in the same wheelhouse, so you will be able to respond. But the president does get this question. I want to call on Michael Jones.

Question: Mr. President, I voted for you in 2008. What have you done or accomplished to earn my vote in 2012? I'm not that optimistic as I was in 2012. Most things I need for everyday living are very expensive.

Obama: Well, we've gone through a tough four years. There's no doubt about it. But four years ago, I told the American people and I told you I would cut taxes for middle class families. And I did. I told you I'd cut taxes for small businesses, and I have. I said that I'd end the war in Iraq, and I did. I said we'd refocus attention on those who actually attacked us on 9/11, and we have gone after Al Qaeda's leadership like never before and Osama bin Laden is dead.

I said that we would put in place health care reform to make sure that insurance companies can't jerk you around and if you don't have health insurance, that you'd have a chance to get affordable insurance, and I have. I committed that I would rein in the excesses of Wall Street, and we passed the toughest Wall Street reforms since the 1930s. We've created five million jobs, and gone from 800 jobs a month being lost, and we are making progress. We saved an auto industry that was on the brink of collapse.

Now, does that mean you're not struggling? Absolutely not. A lot of us are. And that's why the plan that I've put forward for manufacturing and education, and reducing our deficit in a sensible way, using the savings from ending wars, to rebuild America and putting people back to work. Making sure that we are controlling our own energy, but not only the energy of today, but also the energy

最后我想说的是，罗姆尼州长和小布什确实有不同之处。乔治·布什没有什么提议，要把医保做成代金券，乔治·布什启动了全面的移民政策改革，他也没有呼吁非法移民"自我驱逐出境"。乔治·布什从未呼吁减少对计划生育组织的资助，所以罗姆尼州长和乔治布什确有不同。但不在经济方面，在某种程度上，罗姆尼在社会议题上要更加极端。这样无法推动经济向前发展。

奥巴马四年政绩几何？

克劳利： 我想进入到下一个问题了，因为都是同一领域的，所以你会有机会作出回应。但是，下面这个问题是给总统的。有请迈克尔·琼斯。

选民提问： 总统先生，我在2008年时把选票投给了你。你做了些什么或者取得了什么成绩值得我在2012年再次投票给你？此时此刻，我没有上次那么乐观了。大多数日常必需品都变得太贵了。

奥巴马： 我们经历了严峻的四年，这是毋庸置疑的。但四年前，我告诉美国人民，包括你，我将为中产阶级家庭减税，我做到了。我说我要给中小企业减税，我做到了。我说我将结束伊拉克战争，我做到了。我说我将把我们的注意力重新集中到那些在"9·11"幕后真正的元凶，我们对塔利班基地组织高层的打击程度，前所未有，奥萨马·本·拉登也死了。

我说我会实施医保改革，这样你们不会再被保险公司玩得团团转，如果你没有医保，你会有机会买到便宜的保险，我也做到了。我保证我将控制华尔街的过分行为，我们通过了自20世纪30年代以来最严厉的金融改革。我们创造了500万个工作岗位，摆脱了每月失掉80万工作岗位的困境。我们收获了很多，我们还拯救了濒临破产的汽车工业。

of the future. All of those things will make a difference, so the point is the commitments I've made, I've kept. And those that I haven't been able to keep, it's not for lack of trying and we're going to get it done in a second term.

But, you should pay attention to this campaign, because Governor Romney has made some commitments as well. And I suspect he'll keep those too. You know when members of the Republican Congress say, "We're going to sign a no tax pledge, so that we don't ask a dime for millionaires and billionaires to reduce our deficit so we can still invest in education, and helping kids go to college." He said, "Me too." When they said, "We're going to cut Planned Parenthood funding." He said, "Me too." When he said, "We're going to repeal Obamacare. First thing I'm going to do", despite the fact that it's the same health care plan that he passed in Massachusetts and is working well. He said, "Me too." That is not the kind of leadership that you need, but you should expect that those are promises he's going to keep.

Crowley: Mr. President, let me let...

Obama: ...the choice in this election is going to be whose promises are going to be more likely to help you in your life? Make sure your kids can go to college. Make sure that you are getting a good paying job, making sure that Medicare and Social Security... will be there for you.

Crowley: Mr. President. Thank you. Governor?

Romney: I think you know better. I think you know that these last four years haven't been so good as the president just described and that you don't feel like your confident that the next four years are going to be much better either. I can tell you that if you were to elect President Obama, you know what you're going to get. You're going to get a repeat of the last four years. We just can't afford four more years like the last four years.

He said that by now we'd have unemployment at 5.4 percent. The difference between where it is and 5.4 percent is 9 million Americans without work. I wasn't the one that said 5.4 percent. This was the president's plan.

这是否意味着你们日子好过了呢？当然不是。我们中的许多人还在勉强度日。所以我才推出了计划振兴制造业、发展教育、用合理的方法减少赤字，用结束战争节省下来的资金来重建美国，让人们重新拥有工作，确保我们能够掌控自己的能源，而且不仅仅是眼前的能源，还有未来的能源——所有这些做法都会收到卓越的成效。所以重点是，我作出的承诺，我都兑现了。对于那些目前为止我没能兑现的承诺，不是因为我们不够努力，而是因为我们将在第二个任期去完成。

但是你们应该注意这次竞选，罗姆尼州长也作了一些承诺，而我很怀疑他能否将其变为现实。有共和党国会议员说，我们将要签署一项无增税承诺，这样我们就不用向百万富翁、亿万富翁要一个子儿来削减赤字，同时我们依旧可以投资教育帮助孩子们上大学，罗姆尼说他赞成。当他们说，我们将削减计划生育组织的资助，他也说他赞成。他们说上任第一件事就是要废除我的医改，尽管这一方案和马萨诸塞州通过并实施顺利的方案一样，他也说他赞成。这不是你们需要的领导力，但你们应该注意，这些承诺，他必须兑现。

克劳利：总统先生，请让我……

奥巴马：你们需要选择的是，谁的承诺更有可能有助于你的人生，确保你孩子能够上大学，保证你能找得到薪酬不错的工作，保证你能够享受到医保和社会保障……

克劳利：谢谢，总统先生。州长你怎么看？

罗姆尼：我觉得你可能知道得更清楚，过去四年没有像总统刚才描绘的那样美好，而且你也不会觉得今后的四年会比现在好多少。我可以告诉你，如果你投票给了奥巴马总统，你知道会是什么结果，你将重复过去四年的生活。你已经无法再经历一次四年悲惨生活了。

Didn't get there. He said he would have by now put forward a plan to reform Medicare and Social Security, because he pointed out they're on the road to bankruptcy. He would reform them. He'd get that done. He hasn't even made a proposal on either one. He said in his first year he'd put out an immigration plan that would deal with our immigration challenges. Didn't even file it. This is a president who has not been able to do what he said he'd do. He said that he'd cut in half the deficit. He hasn't done that either. In fact, he doubled it. He said that by now middle-income families would have a reduction in their health insurance premiums by $2,500 a year. It's gone up by $2,500 a year. And if Obamacare is passed, or implemented – it's already been passed – if it's implemented fully, it'll be another $2,500 on top.

The middle class is getting crushed under the policies of a president who has not understood what it takes to get the economy working again. He keeps saying, "Look, I've created 5 million jobs." That's after losing 5 million jobs. The entire record is such that the unemployment has not been reduced in this country. The unemployment, the number of people who are still looking for work, is still 23 million Americans. There are more people in poverty, one out of six people in poverty.

How about food stamps? When he took office, 32 million people were on food stamps. Today, 47 million people are on food stamps. How about the growth of the economy? It's growing more slowly this year than last year, and more slowly last year than the year before.

The president wants to do well. I understand. But the policies he's put in place from Obamacare to Dodd-Frank to his tax policies to his regulatory policies, these policies combined have not let this economy take off and grow like it could have. You might say, "Well, you got an example of one that worked better?" Yeah, in the Reagan recession where unemployment hit 10.8 percent, between that period – the end of that recession and the equivalent of time to today, Ronald Reagan's recovery created twice as many jobs as this president's

他曾说，我们现在的失业率应该是5.4%，而如今我们现在还有900万美国人没有工作。承诺5.4%的人不是我罗姆尼，而是总统先生，他没能说到做到。他曾说，他会制定改革医保和社会保障，因为现有计划正在面临破产，他要改革，他说他会做到。可是他现在连方案都还没提，两项都只字未提。他曾说上任的首年将提出移民计划，以应对移民形式的新变化，他甚至连档都还没建。事实证明，这是个无法信守承诺的总统，他说他会削减一半赤字，他也没能做到，他做了，他让赤字翻了一倍。他曾说，到现在，中等收入家庭每年能够减少2500美元的医保支出，结果每年却上升了2500美元。如果"奥巴马医疗"完全得到执行，那么每年又会新增2500美元的支出。

面对这样的总统，中产阶级很煎熬，他根本不懂如何怎么重振经济。他总说，你看，我创造了500万个工作岗位，可是前提是，我们当初失去了500万份工作。数据显示，全国的失业率并没有下降。失业人口，那些仍旧在寻找工作的人口，仍有2300万。还有1/6的人身陷贫困。

那食品救济呢？在他刚就任时，有3200万人依靠食品券过活；而现在则有4700万人依靠食品券度日。经济增长呢？今年的增长速度比去年要慢，去年的增长速度比前年更慢。

这位总统想把这些工作做好，这个我理解。但是他提出的举措，从"奥巴马医改"到《多得—弗兰卡法》，从他的税收政策到他的监管政策——这些政策结合在一起没有让经济取得应有的复苏，没有像它原本应该的那样增长。你可能会问，你有经济复苏的正面例子吗？是的，在里根执政时期，经济衰退造成10.8%的失业率，在那期间，衰退结束之后，和如今差不多的时间段，里根总统的复苏计划创造了现任总统计划两倍的新工作。500万的就业甚至无法跟上我们的人口增长。而如今失业率稍低的唯一原因，是总劳动的基数有很大的下降。

recovery. Five million jobs doesn't even keep up with our population growth. And the only reason the unemployment rate seems a little lower today is because of all the people that have dropped out of the workforce.

The president has tried, but his policies haven't worked. He's great as a – as a – as a speaker and describing his plans and his vision. That's wonderful, except we have a record to look at. And that record shows he just hasn't been able to cut the deficit, to put in place reforms for Medicare and Social Security to preserve them, to get us the rising incomes we need. Median income is down $4,300 a family and 23 million Americans out of work. That's what this election is about. It's about who can get the middle class in this country a bright and prosperous future and assure our kids the kind of hope and optimism they deserve.

Crowley: Governor, I want to move you along. Don't – don't go away, and we'll have plenty of time to respond. We are quite aware of the clock for both of you. But I want to bring in a different subject here. Mr. President, I'll be right back with you. Lorraine Osorio has a question for you about a topic we have not...

Obama: This is for Governor Romney?

Crowley: It's for Governor Romney, and we'll be right with you, Mr. President. Thanks.

Romney: Is it Loraina?

Question: Lorraine.

Romney: Lorraine?

Question: Yes, Lorraine.

Romney: Lorraine.

Question: How you doing?

Romney: Good, thanks.

Question: Mr. Romney, what do you plan on doing with immigrants without their green cards that are currently living here as productive members of society?

Romney: Thank you. Lorraine? Did I get that right? Good. Thank you for

总统先生已经很努力了，但是他的政策却没有奏效。他是一个伟大的演说家，能够绘声绘色地描述他的计划与愿景。但我们得看数据，数据显示他没有能力削减赤字，没有能力改革医保和社保，使其免于破产，没有能力让我们的收入增长，家庭收入中位数下降了4300美元，2300万美国人失业，这才是这次竞选的核心，谁能给中产阶级一个美好的未来，谁能保证我们的孩子拥有一个他们应当拥有的希望和乐观。

对非法移民持何立场？

克劳利：州长先生，我想进行下一个问题。您先别回座位，我们还有很多时间作回答。我们在严格为两位计时，但我想抛出一个新的话题，总统先生，我稍后会给您时间。罗琳娜·萨瑞尔，问到了一个新话题——

奥巴马：问罗姆尼州长？

克劳利：是的，问罗姆尼州长，我稍后会给你时间，总统先生。谢谢。

罗姆尼：罗琳娜？

选民：罗琳。

罗姆尼：罗琳？

选民：是的，罗琳。

罗姆尼：罗琳，好的。

选民：感觉如何？

罗姆尼：不错。谢谢。

选民提问：罗姆尼先生，对于那些没有绿卡但却对社会有贡献的移民，你们将如何对待他们？

罗姆尼：谢谢罗琳，名字没念错吧？谢谢你的提问。让我先回顾一下，告诉你我的移民政策的大的方面，其中就包含了对你这个问题的回答。

your question. And let me step back and tell you what I would like to do with our immigration policy broadly and include an answer to your question.

But first of all, this is a nation of immigrants. We welcome people coming to this country as immigrants. My dad was born in Mexico of American parents; Ann's dad was born in Wales and is a first-generation American. We welcome legal immigrants into this country.

I want our legal system to work better. I want it to be streamlined. I want it to be clearer. I don't think you have to – shouldn't have to hire a lawyer to figure out how to get into this country legally. I also think that we should give visas to people – green cards, rather, to people who graduate with skills that we need. People around the world with accredited degrees in science and math get a green card stapled to their diploma, come to the U.S. of A. We should make sure our legal system works.

Number two, we're going to have to stop illegal immigration. There are 4 million people who are waiting in line to get here legally. Those who've come here illegally take their place. So I will not grant amnesty to those who have come here illegally.

What I will do is I'll put in place an employment verification system and make sure that employers that hire people who have come here illegally are sanctioned for doing so. I won't put in place magnets for people coming here illegally. So for instance, I would not give driver's licenses to those that have come here illegally as the president would.

The kids of those that came here illegally, those kids, I think, should have a pathway to become a permanent resident of the United States and military service, for instance, is one way they would have that kind of pathway to become a permanent resident.

Now when the president ran for office, he said that he'd put in place, in his first year, a piece of legislation – he'd file a bill in his first year that would reform our – our immigration system, protect legal immigration, stop illegal immigration.

首先，这是一个移民国家。我们欢迎移民到这里的人们。我的父亲作为一对美国夫妇的孩子，出生在墨西哥。安（编注：罗姆尼夫人）的父亲出生在威尔士，是他们家第一代美国移民。我们欢迎合法的移民。

我要让我们的法律体系更好地运作。更加简洁高效，更加清晰。我不希望你得请个律师才能搞清楚如何才能合法移民到这个国家。对于有能力的毕业生，我们也应该提供签证甚至绿卡，全世界拥有认可学位的毕业生，学科学的，学数学的，给他们的学位证盖上章让他们来到美国。我们应该确保法律程序运作良好。

其次，我们得阻止非法移民。我们有400万人等着通过合法的途径移民到美国，而他们的位置却被那些通过非法途径过来的人们挤占了。因此我不会给那些非法的移民提供特赦。

我推行雇员身份核实系统，让雇佣非法移民的雇主受到处罚。我不会放一个磁铁来吸引非法移民，比如，我不会给那些非法移民发放驾照，而总统先生会。

对于那些通过非法的方式来到美国的孩子，我认为应该有一条通道可以让他们成为一个永久的美国居民。比如参军，就是一条途径。

在这位总统竞选时，他说他在就任第一年就会提出一项法案来改革我们的移民系统，保护合法移民，阻止非法移民。但他没有这样做。他同时兼有由民主党控制的众议院和参议院，但他甚至没有能够推动立法，给那些想通过合法途径移民到美国的人和那些现在已经非法移入美国的人一个答案。我认为，总统先生现在正好来回答一下这个问题。

He didn't do it. He had a Democrat House, a Democrat Senate, super majority in both Houses. Why did he fail to even promote legislation that would have provided an answer for those that want to come legally and for those that are here illegally today? What's a question I think the – the president will have a chance to answer right now.

Obama: Good, I look forward to it. Was – Lorranna? - Lorraine – we are a nation of immigrants. I mean we're just a few miles away from Ellis Island. We all understand what this country has become because talent from all around the world wants to come here. People are willing to take risks. People who want to build on their dreams and make sure their kids have even bigger dreams than they have.

But we're also a nation of laws. So what I've said is we need to fix a broken immigration system and I've done everything that I can on my own and sought cooperation from Congress to make sure that we fix the system.

The first thing we did was to streamline the legal immigration system, to reduce the backlog, make it easier, simpler and cheaper for people who are waiting in line, obeying the law to make sure that they can come here and contribute to our country and that's good for our economic growth. They'll start new businesses. They'll make things happen to create jobs here in the United States.

Number two, we do have to deal with our border so we put more border patrol on the – any time in history and the flow of undocumented works across the border is actually lower than it's been in 40 years.

What I've also said is if we're going to go after folks who are here illegally, we should do it smartly and go after folks who are criminals, gang bangers, people who are hurting the community, not after students, not after folks who are here just because they're trying to figure out how to feed their families. And that's what we've done.

And what I've also said is for young people who come here, brought here often times by their parents. Had gone to school here, pledged allegiance to

奥巴马： 好，很期待，罗琳娜？罗琳。我们是一个移民国家。我们处在离埃利斯岛几英里的地方。我们都知道，全世界的优秀人才都期望来到这里会给这个国家带来什么变化，包括那些有冒险精神的人，那些希望实现梦想的人，以及那些为了让他们的孩子拥有更大的梦想的人。

但是我们同样也是一个法治国家。所以我指出，我们需要修补我们的移民系统的漏洞。我做了我所能做的所有事情，并寻求与众议院合作以确保重新修正这个系统。

我们所做的第一件事是优化合法移民系统，减少积压，让那些等待合法入境的人们来得更容易、更简单、更便宜，能到这里为国家作出贡献。同时这也有助于我们经济的增长。他们将开创新的企业，会在美国创造就业岗位。

其次，我们也需要应对边境问题。我们投入了世界上最多的边境巡逻，如今非法入境量，已经达到了40年来的最低水平。

我也说过，对于那些非法移民的追踪，我们应该更巧妙一些，我们应该调查那些罪犯与黑帮分子，他们伤害到了社区生活。我们并不针对学生，不针对那些入境只为赚钱养家的人。这是我们做的事情。

我还说过，对于来到美国的年轻人，他们常常是被父母带过来的，他们在这里上学，面对国旗发誓效忠这个国家，他们认为这里是他们的国家，除了没有一张纸面文件以外，他们在所有方面与美国人完全一样。因此，我们应当确保为他们提供成为公民的途径，这是我的内阁所做的事情。

the flag. Think of this as their country. Understand themselves as Americans in every way except having papers. And we should make sure that we give them a pathway to citizenship. And that's what I've done administratively.

Now, Governor Romney just said, you know he wants to help those young people too, but during the Republican primary, he said, "I will veto the DREAM Act", that would allow these young people to have access. His main strategy during the Republican primary was to say, "We're going to encourage self-deportation." Making life so miserable on folks that they'll leave. He called the Arizona law a model for the nation. Part of the Arizona law said that law enforcement officers could stop folks because they suspected maybe they looked like they might be undocumented workers and check their papers. You know what? If my daughter or yours looks to somebody like they're not a citizen, I don't want – I don't want to empower somebody like that.

So, we can fix this system in a comprehensive way. And when Governor Romney says, the challenge is, "Well Obama didn't try." That's not true. I have sat down with Democrats and Republicans at the beginning of my term. And I said, let's fix this system. Including Senators previously who had supported it on the Republican side. But it's very hard for Republican's in Congress to support comprehensive immigration reform, if their standard bearer has said that, this is not something I'm interested in supporting.

Crowley: Let me get the governor in here, Mr. President. Let's speak to, if you could... the idea of self-deportation?

Romney: Yes.

No, let – let – let me go back and speak to the points that the president made and – and – and let's get them correct. I did not say that the Arizona law was a model for the nation in that aspect. I said that the E-Verify portion of the Arizona law, which is – which is the portion of the law which says that employers could be able to determine whether someone is here illegally or not illegally, that that was a model for the nation. That's number one.

刚才，罗姆尼州长说，他也想要帮助那些年轻人。但是在共和党初选时，他却说他会否决能够帮助年轻人得到永久居住权的"梦想法案"，他在初选中的主要策略是，鼓励"自我驱逐"，让这些人的生活更加悲惨好让他们自动离开。他把亚利桑那州的移民法案当成全国部分的楷模。该州的部分法律规定，执法人员可以拦下任何看似非法移民的路人，验证他们的证件。如果我的女儿或者你们的女儿看起来不像本国公民，我可不想给某些人以这种权利。

因此我们可以更全面地改善这个体系。当罗姆尼州长说，他认为奥巴马从未尝试挑战，这是不对的。我在任职初期就与民主党人、共和党人促膝长谈，商讨改善移民体系，其中包括曾支持改革的共和党人。但要国会的共和党人支持全面的移民改革，很难。他们的倡导者说，这不是我们有兴趣支持的东西。

克劳利：总统先生，让我们听听罗姆尼州长对自我驱逐的想法吧。

罗姆尼：好的。

我们回头来看看总统的观点，来做一些纠正。我并没有说亚利桑那州的法律全国都应该效仿。而是说，该法律中的"电子身份验证"即允许雇主审核雇员的身份合法性的那部分，这一部分是可以普及到全国的。这是第一点。

Number two, I asked the president the question, I think Hispanics and immigrants all of the nation have asked. He was asked on "Univision" the other day. Why, when you said you'd filed legislation in your first year didn't you do it? And he didn't answer. He – he doesn't answer that question. He said the standard bearer wasn't for it. I'm glad you thought I was a standard bearer four years ago, but I wasn't. Four years ago you said in your first year you would file legislation. In his first year, I was just getting – licking my wounds from having been beaten by John McCain, all right. I was not the standard bearer. My – my view is that this president should have honored his promise to do as he said.

Now, let me mention one other thing, and that is self-deportation says let people make their own choice. What I was saying is, we're not going to round up 12 million people, undocumented illegals, and take them out of the nation. Instead let people make their own choice. And if they – if they find that – that they can't get the benefits here that they want and they can't – and they can't find the job they want, then they'll make a decision to go a place where – where they have better opportunities. But I'm not in favor of rounding up people and – and – and taking them out of this country. I am in favor, as the president has said, and I agree with him, which is that if people have committed crimes we got to get them out of this country.

Let me mention something else the president said. It was a moment ago and I didn't get a chance to, when he was describing Chinese investments and so forth.

Obama: Candy? Hold on a second. The...

Romney: Mr. President, I'm still speaking. Mr. President, let me finish. I've gotta continue.

Crowley: Governor Romney, you can make it short. See all these people? They've been waiting for you. make it short.

Romney: Just going to make a point. Any investments I have over the last eight years have been managed by a blind trust. And I understand they do include investments outside the United States, including in – in Chinese

第二点，我问总统一个问题，我想这个问题是全国所有拉美裔和移民都问过的。之前他在西语电视台"Univision"做客时就被问及，为什么当你说你会在就任的第一年提出立法，但没有履行？但他没有作答。他说共和党的领袖对此不感兴趣。我很高兴你四年前就把我当领袖了，但我当时不是。四年前，你说你会在任期的第一年就提出立法。在他任职的第一年，我正在舔舐被麦凯恩击败的伤口。我并不是什么领袖，总统先生。我的观点是你应该接受并履行自己的承诺。

说到"自我驱逐入境"的问题，即给予那些人以自主选择权。我的观点是，我们不应该把1200万未登记的非法移民集中赶走。相反，我让他们自己作出选择。如果他们发现自己得不到想要的好处，找不到想要的工作，那么他们可以作出决定，去一个能给他们带来更多机会的地方。但我并不支持把大家伙儿集体赶走。我支持总统刚才说的，对于那些犯罪分子，我们应该把他们驱逐出境。

之前总统先生谈到，就在刚才，我一直没有机会回应。关于中国投资等等问题。

奥巴马： 坎迪？稍等。

罗姆尼： 总统先生，请让我说完，能让我说完吗？

克劳利： 罗姆尼州长，请继续，但请简短一些。看到了吗？大家都在等着你。

罗姆尼： 我只说一点。过去的八年，我的所有投资，都是由保密信托基金管理，我也知道，这其中确实包括美国以外的投资，比如向中国企业的投资。总统先生，您关注过您的养老金吗？

companies. Mr. President, have you looked at your pension? Have you looked at your pension?

Obama: I've got to say...

Romney: Mr. President, have you looked at your pension?

Obama: You know, I – I don't look at my pension. It's not as big as yours so it doesn't take as long.

Romney: Well, let me give you some advice.

Obama: I don't check it that often.

Romney: Let me give you some advice. Look at your pension. You also have investments in Chinese companies. You also have investments outside the United States. You also have investments through a Cayman's trust.

Crowley: We're way off topic here, Governor Romney.

Obama: I thought we were talking about immigration. I do want to make sure that...

Crowley: If I could have you sit down, Governor Romney. Thank you.

Obama: I do want to make sure that – I do want to make sure that we just understand something. Governor Romney says he wasn't referring to Arizona as a model for the nation. His top adviser on immigration is the guy who designed the Arizona law, the entirety of it; not E-Verify, the whole thing. That's his policy. And it's a bad policy. And it won't help us grow. Look, when we think about immigration, we have to understand there are folks all around the world who still see America as the land of promise. And they provide us energy and they provide us innovation and they start companies like Intel and Google. And we want to encourage that.

Now, we've got to make sure that we do it in a smart way and a comprehensive way, and we make the legal system better. But when we make this into a divisive political issue, and when we don't have bipartisan support – I can deliver, Governor, a whole bunch of Democrats to get comprehensive immigration reform done, and we can't...

奥巴马：坎迪，我得说几句——

罗姆尼：总统先生，你关注过您的养老金吗？

奥巴马：不怎么关注，我的养老金可没您的丰厚，花不了多长时间。

罗姆尼：我给您一些建议吧。

奥巴马：我没你那么常看。

罗姆尼：我建议，您关注一下自己的养老金，您在中国企业也有投资，在国外也有投资，也有开曼的基金投资。

克劳利：我们跑题了，罗姆尼州长。

奥巴马：我们是在讨论移民问题吧，我不确定——

克劳利：罗姆尼州长，请您先坐下，谢谢。

奥巴马：我只想确保我们明白一些事情。罗姆尼州长说，他将亚利桑那州的那部法律视作全国的典范。他在移民问题上的首席顾问参与起草了那部法律，大家注意，是设计了整套法案，而不只是"电子身份验证系统"。这是他的政策，而且这是一个糟糕的政策。它不会帮助我们增长。说到移民问题时，我们必须清楚，全世界仍有许多人将美国视为一个梦想之地。他们为我们带来了活力、创新，创造出英特尔、谷歌这样的公司，因此我们要鼓励他们。

现在，我们将确保，以一种明智和全面的举措，让我们的法律体系更完善。但当我们将此事政治化后，如果两党不能保持一致——州长，我还是可以让一批民主党人进行全面的移民改革的。

罗姆尼：我也会解决，上任第一年就解决。

Romney: I'll get it done. I'll get it done. First year...

Obama: ... we can't – we have not seen Republicans serious about this issue at all. And it's time for them to get serious on it. This used to be a bipartisan issue.

Crowley: Mr. President, let me move you on here please. Mr. President, Don't go away, though – right. Don't go away because I – I want you to talk to Kerry Ladka who wants to switch the topic for us.

Obama: OK.

Question: Good evening, Mr. President.

Obama: I'm sorry. What's your name?

Question: It's Kerry, Kerry Ladka.

Obama: Great to see you.

Question: This question actually comes from a brain trust of my friends at Global Telecom Supply (ph) in Minneola yesterday. We were sitting around, talking about Libya, and we were reading and became aware of reports that the State Department refused extra security for our embassy in Benghazi, Libya, prior to the attacks that killed four Americans. Who was it that denied enhanced security and why?

Obama: Well, let me first of all talk about our diplomats, because they serve all around the world and do an incredible job in a very dangerous situation. And these aren't just representatives of the United States, they are my representatives. I send them there, oftentimes into harm's way. I know these folks and I know their families. So nobody is more concerned about their safety and security than I am.

So as soon as we found out that the Benghazi consulate was being overrun, I was on the phone with my national security team and I gave them three instructions. Number one, beef up our security and procedures, not just in Libya, but at every embassy and consulate in the region. Number two, investigate exactly what happened, regardless of where the facts lead us, to make sure folks

奥巴马：但我们没有看到共和党人会严肃地看待此问题。该是时候让他们认真对待此事了。这是一个需要两党共同支持的问题。

大使之死谁该负责？

克劳利：总统先生，我们要进行下一个问题了。请您留步，下面有请凯瑞·拉德加。

奥巴马：好的。

选民提问：晚上好，总统先生。

奥巴马：抱歉，您的名字是？

选民：我是凯瑞。凯瑞·拉德加。

奥巴马：见到你很高兴。

选民提问：晚上好，总统先生。这个问题实际上是我的智囊团里的一个朋友提出来的，我们来自米尼奥拉的 GTS 公司，我们坐在一起谈论利比亚问题，看到一些报告说，在袭击发生前，国务院曾拒绝为在利比亚班加西的大使馆增加安全措施，结果四位美国人被杀死。是谁拒绝加强安保措施的，为什么？

奥巴马：好，首先，让我谈一下我们的外交官们，在危险的地方，做着相当出色的工作。他们不仅代表了美国，也代表了我。是我多次委以重任，将他们派往危险之地。我认识他们，也认识他们的家人。因此没有人比我更关心他们的安全和安保。

因此我们一得知驻班加西领事馆遭到袭击，就马上打电话给我的国家安全小组，作出了三条指示。第一，对我们在利比亚以及该地区的所有大使馆都增加安全措施。第二，彻查真相，不管线索指向哪里，务必追究到责任人，并不让类似事件再次发生。第三，找出祸凶，同时将他们捉拿归案，自从我上任起，我就强调，谁要是伤害美国人，我们绝不会放过他们。

are held accountable and it doesn't happen again. And number three, we are going to find out who did this and we're going to hunt them down, because one of the things that I've said throughout my presidency is when folks mess with Americans, we go after them.

Now Governor Romney had a very different response. While we were still dealing with our diplomats being threatened, Governor Romney put out a press release, trying to make political points, and that's not how a commander in chief operates. You don't turn national security into a political issue. Certainly not right when it's happening.

And people – not everybody agrees with some of the decisions I've made. But when it comes to our national security, I mean what I say. I said I'd end the war in Libya – in – in Iraq, and I did. I said that we'd go after al-Qaeda and bin Laden, we have. I said we'd transition out of Afghanistan, and start making sure that Afghans are responsible for their own security, that's what I'm doing.

And when it comes to this issue, when I say that we are going to find out exactly what happened, everybody will be held accountable. And I am ultimately responsible for what's taking place there because these are my folks, and I'm the one who has to greet those coffins when they come home. You know that I mean what I say.

Crowley: Mr. President, I'm going to move us along. Governor?

Romney: Thank you Kerry for your question, it's an important one. And – and I – I think the president just said correctly that the buck does stop at his desk and – and he takes responsibility for – for that – for the failure in providing those security resources, and – and those terrible things may well happen from time to time.

I – I'm – I feel very deeply sympathetic for the families of those who lost loved ones. And today there's a memorial service for one of those that was lost in this tragedy. We – we think of their families and care for them deeply. There were other issues associated with this – with this tragedy.

而罗姆尼州长却作出了截然不同的反应。当我们还在为外交官的安全担忧时，罗姆尼州长却召开了新闻发布会，大作政治文章。这不是一个最高执行长官应该表现出的所作所为。你不能将一个国家问题变成一个政治问题，特别是在这件事的当口。

并非每个人都同意我的决定。但是，当它事关我们国家的安全时，我言出必行。我说我将结束在伊拉克的战争，我做到了。我说要追踪基地组织和本·拉登，我们做到了。我说我们要淡出阿富汗并且开始确保阿富汗人能够为自己国家的安全负责，这是我正在做的。

而在这件事情上，当我说我们将彻查真相、相关人员都将被追查责任时，而我，应对此事负有最终的责任，因为这些人是我的属下，我得迎接他们的灵柩返乡，你们明白的，我言出必行。

克劳利：总统先生，我们得继续了。州长先生？

罗姆尼：谢谢你的问题，凯瑞。这是一个重要问题。我认为总统刚才说得没错，他确实备受压力，未能提供安保措施，这类恐怖袭击可能随时再次发生。他应对此事负责。

我对遇难者家属深表同情。今天早些时候，还举行了一位遇难者的悼念仪式，我们的心，和他们的家人在一起。此次惨剧，也牵扯到其他的一些问题。

There were many days that passed before we knew whether this was a spontaneous demonstration or actually whether it was a terrorist attack. And there was no demonstration involved. It was a terrorist attack and it took a long time for that to be told to the American people. Whether there was some misleading, or instead whether we just didn't know what happened, you have to ask yourself why didn't we know five days later when the ambassador to the United Nations went on TV to say that this was a demonstration. How could we have not known?

But I find more troubling than this, that on – on the day following the assassination of the United States ambassador, the first time that's happened since 1979, when – when we have four Americans killed there, when apparently we didn't know what happened, that the president, the day after that happened, flies to Las Vegas for a political fund-raiser, then the next day to Colorado for another event, other political event. I think these – these actions taken by a president and a leader have symbolic significance and perhaps even material significance in that you'd hope that during that time we could call in the people who were actually eyewitnesses. We've read their accounts now about what happened. It was very clear this was not a demonstration. This was an attack by terrorists.

And this calls into question the president's whole policy in the Middle East. Look what's happening in Syria, in Egypt, now in Libya. Consider the distance between ourselves and – and Israel, the president said that – that he was going to put daylight between us and Israel. We have Iran four years closer to a nuclear bomb. Syria – Syria's not just a tragedy of 30,000 civilians being killed by a military, but also a strategic – strategically significant player for America.

The president's policies throughout the Middle East began with an apology tour and – and – and pursue a strategy of leading from behind, and this strategy is unraveling before our very eyes.

Crowley: Because we're – we're closing in, I want to still get a lot of people in. I want to ask you something, Mr. President, and then have the governor

在这件事情过去很多天之后，我们才弄清楚这到底是一场自发的游行示威还是一次恐怖袭击。这并非示威游行，它确实是一次恐怖袭击，但美国人民很晚才被告知真相。不管是我们被误导了，还是事实的确不明确，我想大家都该自问，袭击发生五天后，驻联合国代表在电视上露面，称此次事件是示威行动，可是我们怎么就不知道呢？

但我觉得更为忧心的是，美国大使刚刚遇袭身亡，这可是1979年以来的头一次，共有四名美国人身亡，国人也显然对此事一无所知。袭击发生后的第二天，总统就飞往拉斯维加斯，进行政治筹款活动，紧接着又飞往科罗拉多州参加另外一项政治活动——我认为一个总统和领导人的这些行动有着标志性的意义，甚至是实质性意义，我认为我们原本可以在那段时间传唤目击者，我们现在都看过目击者的陈述了，很显然这不是一次游行示威，这是一次恐怖袭击事件。

而且此事足以让我们质疑总统的整个中东政策。看看在叙利亚、埃及以及现在的利比亚发生了一些什么事情。看看我们和以色列的关系，总统先生曾说，他要改善美以关系。伊朗呢？距离核导弹又更近一步。在叙利亚，三万平民被军队屠杀，但叙利亚也是美国的重要战略成员。

纵观总统先生的整个中东政策，以道歉之旅开始，接着采取"幕后领导"的战略，而这种战略已经在我们的眼前慢慢展开。

克劳利：时间已经不多了，我希望更多的人能有机会参与进来。我想问总统先生一些问题，州长先生稍后。国务卿女士称，她对班加西外交使团被袭事件负全责。是不是责任追究到国务卿就为止了？

just quickly. Your secretary of state, as I'm sure you know, has said that she takes full responsibility for the attack on the diplomatic mission in Benghazi. Does the buck stop with your secretary of state as far as what went on here?

Obama: Secretary Clinton has done an extraordinary job. But she works for me. I'm the president and I'm always responsible, and that's why nobody's more interested in finding out exactly what happened than I do. The day after the attack, governor, I stood in the Rose Garden and I told the American people in the world that we are going to find out exactly what happened. That this was an act of terror and I also said that we're going to hunt down those who committed this crime. And then a few days later, I was there greeting the caskets coming into Andrews Air Force Base and grieving with the families.

And the suggestion that anybody in my team, whether the Secretary of State, our U.N. Ambassador, anybody on my team would play politics or mislead when we've lost four of our own, governor, is offensive. That's not what we do. That's not what I do as president, that's not what I do as Commander in Chief.

Crowley: Governor, if you want to quickly to this please.

Romney: Yes, I – I... I – I think interesting the president just said something which – which is that on the day after the attack he went into the Rose Garden and said that this was an act of terror.

Obama: That's what I said.

Romney: You said in the Rose Garden the day after the attack, it was an act of terror. It was not a spontaneous demonstration, is that what you're saying?

Obama: Please proceed governor.

Romney: I want to make sure we get that for the record because it took the president 14 days before he called the attack in Benghazi an act of terror.

Obama: Get the transcript.

Crowley: It – it – it – he did in fact, sir. So let me – let me call it an act of terror...

Obama: Can you say that a little louder, Candy?

奥巴马：克林顿国务卿做了非常出色的工作，但是她是为我工作的，我是总统，我总是要负责任的。所以我最有动力去调查整个事件的来龙去脉。在事件发生次日，州长，我站在白宫玫瑰园，向全世界和美国人民宣布，这是一次恐怖袭击，必须彻底查明真相。同时我也指出，我们会将那些罪犯捉拿归案。几天后，我在安德鲁斯空军基地迎接遇难者返乡的灵柩，与他们的家人一起吊唁。

州长先生，我们失去了四位至亲，如果说我们团队中的任何人，国务卿也好，驻联合国代表也好，在这个时候大打政治牌，或者发表误导性言论，州长先生，这对我们来说，是一种侮辱。我们并没有这么做。作为总统，作为三军总司令，我也不会这么做。

是否支持攻击性武器禁令？

克劳利：州长先生，请简短回应。

罗姆尼：总统刚才说，袭击发生后的第二天，他便在玫瑰园宣布，这是恐怖袭击，我倒是觉得很有意思。

奥巴马：是的，我是这么说的。

罗姆尼：你说袭击发生后的第二天，就在玫瑰园宣布，这是恐怖袭击。不是示威行动，是这么说的吗？

奥巴马：州长先生，请继续。

罗姆尼：好吧，我想让大家都记下，事实上，总统先生在14天之后，才称这次事件为恐怖袭击。

奥巴马：去查讲话记录。

克劳利：州长先生，他确实宣布了。

Crowley: He – he did call it an act of terror. It did as well take – it did as well take two weeks or so for the whole idea there being a riot out there about this tape to come out. You are correct about that.

Romney: This – the administration – the administration indicated this was a reaction to a video and was a spontaneous reaction. It took them a long time to say this was a terrorist act by a terrorist group. And to suggest – am I incorrect in that regard, on Sunday, the – your secretary –

Excuse me. The ambassador of the United Nations went on the Sunday television shows and spoke about how this was a spontaneous.

Obama: Candy, I'm – I'm happy to have a longer conversation – about foreign policy.

Crowley: Mr. President, let me – Absolutely. But I want to – I want to move you on and also-

Obama: OK. I'm happy to do that, too.

Crowley: – the transcripts and –

Obama: I just want to make sure that all of these wonderful folks are going to have a chance to get some of their questions answered.

Crowley: Because what I – what I want to do, Mr. President, stand there a second, because I want to introduce you to Nina Gonzalez, who brought up a question that we hear a lot, both over the Internet and from this crowd.

Question: President Obama, during the Democratic National Convention in 2008, you stated you wanted to keep AK-47s out of the hands of criminals. What has your administration done or planned to do to limit the availability of assault weapons?

Obama: We're a nation that believes in the Second Amendment, and I believe in the Second Amendment. We've got a long tradition of hunting and sportsmen and people who want to make sure they can protect themselves.

But there have been too many instances during the course of my presidency, where I've had to comfort families who have lost somebody. Most

奥巴马：能大声点说吗，坎迪？

克劳利：他当时确实宣布了，这是恐怖袭击，但也确实是两周之后，才确认当地发生骚乱，这一点您没搞错。

罗姆尼：政府曾暗示，这是针对某段录像的自发示威行动。过了很久，他们才宣布，这是恐怖组织发起的恐怖袭击，并且声称……我说错了？周日，国务卿女士……

对不起，是驻联合国代表，周日在电视节目中，称此次事件为示威行动。

奥巴马：坎迪，我很愿意就此事谈下去，关于外交事务——

克劳利：当然，但我们继续下一个话题好吗？

奥巴马：我也希望下一个话题。

克劳利：大家可以去看一下讲话记录。

奥巴马：我只是想确保大家的问题都有机会得到解答。

克劳利：总统先生，请留步，下面有请妮娜·冈萨雷斯，她的问题，我们也听说过许多次了。不管是在网上，还是在这里。

选民提问：奥巴马总统，在2008年的民主党全国代表大会上，您说将保证AK-47等不会落入罪犯的手中。在限制攻击性武器方面，您的政府都做了些什么，或者有何打算？

奥巴马：你知道，我们的国家是相信《宪法第二修正案》的。我也相信《宪法第二修正案》。长久以来，我们有悠久的打猎、运动传统，人们要确保他们能够保护自己。

但我上任以来，经历了太多安抚死难者家属的场景，就是由于枪支的滥用，最近的一次发生在奥罗拉市。就在几周前，可能是一个月之前，我

recently out in Aurora. You know, just a couple of weeks ago, actually, probably about a month, I saw a mother, who I had met at the bedside of her son, who had been shot in that theater. And her son had been shot through the head. And we spent some time, and we said a prayer and, remarkably, about two months later, this young man and his mom showed up, and he looked unbelievable, good as new. But there were a lot of families who didn't have that good fortune and whose sons or daughters or husbands didn't survive.

So my belief is that, (A), we have to enforce the laws we've already got, make sure that we're keeping guns out of the hands of criminals, those who are mentally ill. We've done a much better job in terms of background checks, but we've got more to do when it comes to enforcement.

But I also share your belief that weapons that were designed for soldiers in war theaters don't belong on our streets. And so what I'm trying to do is to get a broader conversation about how do we reduce the violence generally. Part of it is seeing if we can get an assault weapons ban reintroduced. But part of it is also looking at other sources of the violence. Because frankly, in my home town of Chicago, there's an awful lot of violence and they're not using AK-47s. They're using cheap hand guns.

And so what can we do to intervene, to make sure that young people have opportunity; that our schools are working; that if there's violence on the streets, that working with faith groups and law enforcement, we can catch it before it gets out of control.

And so what I want is a – is a comprehensive strategy. Part of it is seeing if we can get automatic weapons that kill folks in amazing numbers out of the hands of criminals and the mentally ill. But part of it is also going deeper and seeing if we can get into these communities and making sure we catch violent impulses before they occur.

Crowley: Governor Romney, the question is about assault weapons, AK-47s.

Romney: Yeah, I'm not in favor of new pieces of legislation on – on guns

在一位伤者的病榻前，见到了他的母亲，她的儿子在影院的枪击事件中头部中了弹。我陪她呆了一会儿，我们一起祷告。令人惊奇的是，大约两个月之后，这位年轻小伙子和他的母亲出现了，而且看起来不可置信地完好如初。但是有许多家庭没有这样好的运气，他们的儿子或者女儿或者丈夫没有活下来。

所以我相信，第一，要执行现有法律，不让罪犯和精神疾病患者接触枪支。我们在背景审查方面的工作已经有了改善，但是在强制执行方面还有待加强。

但是我和大家同样相信，那些为战区士兵设计的武器不应该被带到我们的大街上去。因此我努力在做的事情是，就如何从总体上降低暴力展开更广泛的对话。对话的内容之一就是，我们能否重新推出攻击性武器禁令，因为坦率地讲，在我的家乡芝加哥，那里有许多可怕的暴力活动，他们没有使用 AK–47，他们使用便宜的手枪。

所以我们该采用哪些干预措施，能让年轻人拥有机会，能让学校的系统行之有效，如果街头发生暴力事件，能在宗教团体和执法部门的协作下，我们可以在事态失控前抓住祸首？

因此我想要的是一个综合性的战略。其中之一就是，我们是否能够让那些具有超强杀伤能力的自动武器远离罪犯与精神疾病患者之手。但是其中的另一些内容将更加深入，看我们能否深入社区，确保我们能够在暴力事件发生之前找到暴力爆发点。

克劳利： 罗姆尼州长，请您谈一下这个关于攻击武器的话题，关于 AK–47。

罗姆尼： 好，我不支持关于没收枪支或者规定特定枪支为非法的新立法。我们当然不想要自动武器，而且持有自动武器在这个国家已经是非法活动。

and taking guns away or making certain guns illegal. We, of course, don't want to have automatic weapons, and that's already illegal in this country to have automatic weapons.

What I believe is we have to do, as the president mentioned towards the end of his remarks there, which is to make enormous efforts to enforce the gun laws that we have, and to change the culture of violence that we have. And you ask how – how are we going to do that? And there are a number of things.

He mentioned good schools. I totally agree. We were able to drive our schools to be number one in the nation in my state. And I believe if we do a better job in education, we'll – we'll give people the – the hope and opportunity they deserve and perhaps less violence from that.

But let me mention another thing. And that is parents. We need moms and dads, helping to raise kids. Wherever possible the – the benefit of having two parents in the home, and that's not always possible. A lot of great single moms, single dads. But gosh to tell our kids that before they have babies, they ought to think about getting married to someone, that's a great idea. Because if there's a two parent family, the prospect of living in poverty goes down dramatically. The opportunities that the child will – will be able to achieve increase dramatically.

So we can make changes in the way our culture works to help bring people away from violence and give them opportunity, and bring them in the American system.

The – the greatest failure we've had with regards to – to gun violence in some respects is what – what is known as Fast and Furious. Which was a program under this administration, and how it worked exactly I think we don't know precisely, where thousands of automatic, and AK-47 type weapons were – were given to people that ultimately gave them to – to drug lords.

They used those weapons against – against their own citizens and killed Americans with them. And this was a – this was a program of the government. For what purpose it was put in place, I can't imagine. But it's one of the great tragedies related to violence in our society which has occurred during this

　　我相信我们不得不像总统刚才在最后指出的那样做，努力强化执行我们已有的枪支法律，并且改变我们的暴力文化。你问我们将会怎么做？有很多事情可以做。

　　他提到良好的学校教育，我完全同意。我们曾推动我们州的学校发展，并成为全国最好的学校。我相信，如果我们的教育工作做得更好，我们就会给人们带来他们值得拥有的希望与机会，这样暴力或许就会少一些。

　　但是让我提及另外一件事情，那就是父母。我们需要更多的母亲和父亲帮助抚养孩子。如果有可能，尽量让每一个孩子的家里都有父亲和母亲——但这常常不是每个孩子都有的。虽然有许多伟大的单亲母亲、单亲父亲，但是要在他们有自己的孩子之前告诉我们的孩子，他们应该考虑结婚，这是一个很好的想法，因为在一个双亲家庭，生活贫困的可能性就会大幅减少，而孩子将能够取得成就的可能性也会大幅度提升。

　　所以，我们可以在我们的文化工作上作一些调整，把人们带离暴力，给他们机会，将他们纳入美国的制度之下。

　　我们在枪支暴力问题上的最大失败就是所谓的"速度与激情"项目，这是这届政府的一个项目，我认为我们确实不清楚这个项目的细节，但是数千支自动的、AK-47类型的武器被人们持有，这些武器最终落入了毒贩之手。

　　他们利用这些武器攻击自己的公民，杀害美国人。而这是一个政府项目。这个项目缘何而生？我实在想不出。但是，与我们社会中的暴力有关的一个大悲剧在于，这些都发生在这届政府的任期之内，我认为美国人民想知道全部。调查某种程度上在展开，但是，政府却通过执行的便利阻碍所有这些信息透露给公众。我想要明白是谁做了这些，以及隐藏其后的想法，为什么它导致了暴力——数千枪支流入到墨西哥毒枭之手。

administration. Which I think the American people would like to understand fully, it's been investigated to a degree, but – but the administration has carried out executive privilege to prevent all of the information from coming out. I'd like to understand who it was that did this, what the idea was behind it, why it led to the violence, thousands of guns going to Mexican drug lords.

Obama: Candy?

Crowley: Governor, Governor, if I could, the question was about these assault weapons that once were once banned and are no longer banned. I know that you signed an assault weapons ban when you were in Massachusetts, obviously, with this question, you no longer do support that. Why is that, given the kind of violence that we see sometimes with these mass killings? Why is it that you have changed your mind?

Romney: Well, Candy, actually, in my state, the pro-gun folks and the anti-gun folks came together and put together a piece of legislation. And it's referred to as an assault weapon ban, but it had, at the signing of the bill, both the pro-gun and the anti-gun people came together, because it provided opportunities for both that both wanted. There were hunting opportunities, for instance, that haven't previously been available and so forth, so it was a mutually agreed – upon piece of legislation.

That's what we need more of, Candy. What we have right now in Washington is a place that's gridlocked.

Crowley: So I could – if you could get people to agree to it, you would be for it?

Romney: – we haven't had the leadership in Washington to work on a bipartisan basis. I was able to do that in my state and bring these two together.

Crowley: Quickly, Mr. President.

Obama: The – first of all, I think Governor Romney was for an assault weapons ban before he was against it. And he said that the reason he changed his mind was, in part, because he was seeking the endorsement of the National

奥巴马：坎迪？

克劳利：州长，州长，如果可以的话，我想说，这个问题是关于这些攻击性武器曾被禁止而现在不再禁止的问题。我知道您在马萨诸塞州任州长时签署了一项攻击性武器禁令。很明显，在这个问题上，你现在不再支持禁令。为什么？鉴于我们间或看到的各种各样造成大规模杀伤的暴力事件，为什么您改变了您的想法？

罗姆尼：好，坎迪，实际上，在我所任职的州，就攻击性武器禁令，支持枪支的人与抵制枪支的人他们走到了一起，共同完成了一项立法。在这项法令的签署过程中，支持枪支与反对枪支的人能够走到一起，是因为它给双方都提供了他们所需要的机会。比如，这包括打猎的机会，这在之前是不可以的。因此这是一项体现双方共识的立法。

这就是我们更需要的东西，坎迪。现在的华府，是一个僵死的状态。我们没有在华盛顿形成一种基于两党合作的领导能力。

克劳利：所以，如果你能争取到别人的同意，你就会去做了？

罗姆尼：在华盛顿没有一个人站出来，领导一个真正的两党合作，在我的州，我做到了，我们让两党走到了一起。

克劳利：总统先生，请作简短回答。

奥巴马：首先，我认为罗姆尼州长在反对攻击性武器禁令之前曾是持支持态度的。他改变其想法的部分原因在于，他在寻求国家手枪协会的支持。这是有记录可查的。

Rifle Association. So that's on the record.

But I think that one area we agree on is the important of parents and the importance of schools, because I do believe that if our young people have opportunity, then they are less likely to engage in these kinds of violent acts. We're not going to eliminate everybody who is mentally disturbed and we have got to make sure they don't get weapons. Because I do believe that if our young people have opportunity, then they're less likely to engage in these kinds of violent acts. We're not going to eliminate everybody who is mentally disturbed, and we've got to make sure they don't get weapons. But we can make a difference in terms ensuring that every young person in America, regardless of where they come from, what they look like, have a chance to succeed.

And, Candy, we haven't had a chance to talk about education much, but I think it is very important to understand that the reforms we've put in place, working with 46 governors around the country, are seeing schools that are some of the ones that are the toughest for kids starting to succeed. We're starting to see gains in math and science.

When it comes to community colleges, we are setting up programs, including with Nassau Community College, to retrain workers, including young people who may have dropped out of school but now are getting another chance, training them for the jobs that exist right now.

And in fact, employers are looking for skilled workers. And so we're matching them up. Giving them access to higher education. As I said, we have made sure that millions of young people are able to get an education that they weren't able to get before.

Crowley: Mr. President, I have to – I have to move you along here. You said you wanted to... We need to do it here.

Obama: ... just one second. Because – because this is important. This is part of the choice in this election. Teachers were important to growing our economy, Governor Romney said that doesn't grow our economy.

但是我认为我们有一点是一致的，就是强调父母与学校的重要性，因为我相信，如果我们的年轻人拥有机会，那么他们参与暴力活动的可能性就会降低一些。我们不是要消除任何一位受精神病困扰的人，我们要确保的是他们没有持有枪支。但是，我们与罗姆尼他们的区别在于，我们将确保那些在美国国土上的年纪非常小的人，不管他们来自哪里，相貌如何，都有机会成功。

坎迪，我们还没有机会好好谈教育，很重要的一点是，要看到，我们与全国46位州长合作所进行的改革，让最差的学校也有了起色，我们在数学和理科方面看到了进步。

提到社区大学，我们正在设立项目，包括拿索社区大学，开展再培训，面向劳动者和得到第二次机会的辍学的年轻人，培训他们胜任现在亟需的工作岗位。

实际上，雇主们正在寻找熟练工，我们就为他们牵线搭桥，让他们能有机会接受高等教育，我说过，我们已确保数以万计的年轻人能够得到原本不能得到的教育。

克劳利：但是，总统先生，我不得不进入下一个问题了，您说过您想听听这些问题。我们得继续了。

奥巴马：就一秒钟，这很重要。这是本次选举中的重要选题之一，当罗姆尼州长被问到，要发展经济，多聘请教师是否重要时，罗姆尼州长回答："那不会促进经济增长。"

Crowley: The question, Mr. President, was guns here, so I need to move us along.

Obama: I understand.

Crowley: You know, the question was guns. So let me – let me bring in another...

Obama: But this will make a difference in terms of whether or not we can move this economy forward for these young people...

Crowley: I understand.

Obama: ... and reduce our violence.

Crowley: OK. Thank you so much. I want to ask Carol Goldberg to stand up, because she gets to a question that both these men have been passionate about. It's for Governor Romney.

Question: The outsourcing of American jobs overseas has taken a toll on our economy. What plans do you have to put back and keep jobs here in the United States?

Romney: Boy, great question and important question, because you're absolutely right. The place where we've seen manufacturing go has been China. China is now the largest manufacturer in the world. It used to be the United States of America. A lot of good people have lost jobs. A half a million manufacturing jobs have been lost in the last four years. That's total over the last four years.

One of the reasons for that is that people think it's more attractive in some cases to go offshore than to stay here. We have made it less attractive for enterprises to stay here than to go offshore from time to time.

What I will do as president is make sure it's more attractive to come to America again. This is the way we're going to create jobs in this country. It's not by trickle-down government, saying we're going to take more money from people and hire more government workers, raise more taxes, put in place more regulations. Trickle-down government has never worked here, has never worked

克劳利：总统先生，我们在谈论有关枪支的话题。我必须让我们紧扣话题。

奥巴马：明白。

克劳利：咱们的话题是枪支管制，我将有请——

奥巴马：但这事关乎我们能否为年轻人发展经济。

克劳利：我明白。

奥巴马：……并减少暴力事件。

谁能把就业岗位留在美国？

克劳利：谢谢。我想有请卡罗·古德伯格，她有两个两位都关注的问题。请罗姆尼州长先回答。

选民提问：外包对工作岗位乃至美国经济产生了负面影响。你们有什么计划可以令这些工作岗位重返美国并保持在美国境内？

罗姆尼：很好，这是一个非常好也非常重要的问题，因为你说的确实是对的。我们看到制造业已经流向了中国。中国现在是头号制造大国，而这曾是美国的头衔。过去四年我们丧失了50万个制造业工作岗位，许多善良的美国人失去了工作。

造成这种情况的一个原因是，人们认为，在某些情况下，海外更加具有吸引力，把企业吸引了过去。我们国内的商业环境发生了变化，对企业来说，国外比国内更具有吸引力。

我上台后要做的，是让美国重新找回吸引力。这是我们在这个国家重新创造就业的途径。不是要先富带动后富，也就是说，从人民那儿拿钱，聘用更多的公务员，增税，制定更多规则。先富带动后富从来就没有成功过，在哪儿都没有。我想让美国变成一个全球最具吸引力的地方，无论是对企业家、对中小企业还是对大企业，他们将来美国投资，促进美国的经济增长。

anywhere. I want to make America the most attractive place in the world for entrepreneurs, for small business, for big business, to invest and grow in America.

Now, we're going to have to make sure that as we trade with other nations that they play by the rules. And China hasn't. One of the reasons – or one of the ways they don't play by the rules is artificially holding down the value of their currency. Because if they put their currency down low, that means their prices on their goods are low. And that makes them advantageous in the marketplace. We lose sales. And manufacturers here in the U.S. making the same products can't compete.

China has been a currency manipulator for years and years and years. And the president has a regular opportunity to label them as a currency manipulator, but refuses to do so. On day one, I will label China a currency manipulator, which will allow me as president to be able to put in place, if necessary, tariffs where I believe that they are taking unfair advantage of our manufacturers.

So we're going to make sure that people we trade with around the world play by the rules. But let me – let me not just stop there. Don't forget, what's key to bringing back jobs here is not just finding someone else to punish, and I'm going to be strict with people who we trade with to make sure they – they follow the law and play by the rules, but it's also to make America the most attractive place in the world for businesses of all kinds. That's why I want to down the tax rates on small employers, big employers, so they want to be here. Canada's tax rate on companies is now 15 percent. Ours is 35 percent. So if you're starting a business, where would you rather start it?

We have to be competitive if we're going to create more jobs here. Regulations have quadrupled. The rate of regulations quadrupled under this president. I talk to small businesses across the country. They say, "We feel like we're under attack from our own government." I want to make sure that regulators see their job as encouraging small business, not crushing it. And there's no question but that Obamacare has been an extraordinary deterrent to

　　我们要保证和别的国家有贸易往来，要和遵守规则的国家，而中国就没有遵守规则。原因之一，他们一直在人为地压低他们的币值，因为他们的汇率越低，他们的产品价格看起来就越便宜。这使得他们在市场上占尽优势。我们在美国失去了市场份额，在美国生产产品的制造商根本无法与其竞争。

　　多年以来，中国一直在操纵汇率。总统先生也有许多机会挑明他们是汇率操纵国，但他一直不肯。如果我当选总统，我将在就任的第一天就把中国列为汇率操纵国，如果需要的话，我将对他们的不公平竞争行为征收关税。

　　所以我们将确保与全球那些遵守规则的国家进行贸易往来。但我的论点并不只停留于此。不要忘记：把就业岗位重新夺回的关键不仅仅是去寻找惩罚对象——我将对我们的贸易伙伴严格要求，确保它们遵守法律和规则——还有，就是要把美国建成一个对各种生意人都有吸引力的地方。这就是为什么我要对中小企业、大企业减税的原因，这样他们就会留在美国。加拿大的公司税率是15%，而美国是35%。如果是你想创业，你会选择哪里？

　　想要创造更多的就业岗位，我们就要有竞争力。在总统的治理之下，监管数量翻了四倍。我在全国各地与中小企业交谈，他们说，他们似乎遭受了来自本国政府的打压。我将确保监管者将自己的工作视为鼓励中小企业，而不是去压垮企业。毫无疑问，"奥巴马医改"已经让企业在雇佣更多人员的时候心怀恐惧。

enterprises of all kinds hiring people.

My priority is making sure that we get more people hired. If we have more people hired, if we get back manufacturing jobs, if we get back all kinds of jobs into this country, then you're going to see rising incomes again. The reason incomes are down is because unemployment is so high. I know what it takes to get this to happen, and my plan will do that, and one part of it is to make sure that we keep China playing by the rules.

Crowley: Mr. President, two minutes here, because we are then going to go to our last question.

Obama: OK. We need to create jobs here. And both Governor Romney and I agree actually that we should lower our corporate tax rate. It's too high.

But there's a difference in terms of how we would do it. I want to close loopholes that allow companies to deduct expenses when they move to China; that allow them to profit offshore and not have to get taxed, so they have tax advantages offshore. All those changes in our tax code would make a difference.

Now, Governor Romney actually wants to expand those tax breaks. One of his big ideas when it comes to corporate tax reform would be to say, if you invest overseas, you make profits overseas, you don't have to pay U.S. taxes. But, of course, if you're a small business or a mom-and-pop business or a big business starting up here, you've got to pay even the reduced rate that Governor Romney's talking about. And it's estimated that that will create 800,000 new jobs. The problem is they'll be in china. Or India or Germany.

That's not the way we're going to create jobs here. The way we're going to create jobs here is not just to change our tax code, but also to double our exports. And we are on pace to double our exports, one of the commitments I made when I was president. That's creating tens of thousands of jobs all across the country. That's why we've kept on pushing trade deals, but trade deals that make sure that American workers and American businesses are getting a good deal.

Now, Governor Romney talked about China, as I already indicated. In

我将给予优先考虑的是，确保我们能够雇佣更多的人。如果我们重新夺回了制造业的工作岗位，如果我们能把各类工作引回到国内，那时你们将看到我们的工资又将增长。收入下降的原因是因为失业率太高。我知道要实现这一切需要做哪些事情，我的计划将解决这些问题。而计划的一部分则是保证让中国遵守游戏规则。谢谢。

克劳利：总统先生，两分钟时间，之后将是我们的最后一个问题。

奥巴马：好。我们需要创造更多的就业机会。罗姆尼州长和我都同意，实际上我们应该降低我们的公司所得税。它实在是太高了。

但我们的做法不同。我想堵塞漏洞，这些漏洞允许公司搬到中国后减少成本，比如它们投资中国，在海外盈利，但却不用在美国交税，这就造成了它们在海外投资的税收优势。我的税收政策中的所有这些变化都会让我们有所不同。

现在罗姆尼州长实际上想要扩大这些税收优惠。在公司税的改革问题上，他的一个重点就是，如果你在海外投资，你就在海外盈利，你不需要给美国政府交税。当然了，如果是中小企业、私营企业或者在美国起步的大企业，你还是得交税，即使是罗姆尼州长所说的减免后的税率，这种政策预计能创造80万个就业岗位。问题是这些机会在中国，在印度，或在德国。

我们创造就业岗位的途径不仅仅是改变我们的税收政策，还要成倍地增加我们的出口。我们正在按部就班地推进出口倍增计划，这是我刚就任总统时所作的承诺。这会在全国范围内创造成千上万的工作岗位。这就是为什么我们不断推动贸易协定的原因，贸易协定将确保美国工人和美国企业做成好生意。

the private sector, Governor Romney's company invested in what were called pioneers of outsourcing. That's not my phrase. That's what reporters called it.

And as far as currency manipulation, the currency has actually gone up 11 percent since I've been president because we have pushed them hard. And we've put unprecedented trade pressure on China. That's why exports have significantly increased under my presidency. That's going to help to create jobs here.

Crowley: Mr. President, we have a really short time for a quick discussion here. iPad, the Macs, the iPhones, they are all manufactured in China. One of the major reasons is labor is so much cheaper here. How do you convince a great American company to bring that manufacturing back here?

Romney: The answer is very straightforward. We can compete with anyone in the world as long as the playing field is level. China's been cheating over the years. One by holding down the value of their currency. Number two, by stealing our intellectual property; our designs, our patents, our technology. There's even an Apple store in China that's a counterfeit Apple store, selling counterfeit goods. They hack into our computers. We will have to have people play on a fair basis, that's number one.

Number two, we have to make America the most attractive place for entrepreneurs, for people who want to expand their business. That's what brings jobs in. The president's characterization of my tax plan...is completely...is completely... false. Let me tell you....

Crowley: Let me to go the president here because we really are running out of time. And the question is can we ever get – we can't get wages like that. It can't be sustained.

Obama: Candy, there are some jobs that are not going to come back. Because they are low wage, low skill jobs. I want high wage, high skill jobs. That's why we have to emphasize manufacturing. That's why we have to invest in advanced manufacturing. That's why we've got to make sure that we've got the best science and research in the world.

现在，罗姆尼州长谈到中国。正如我之前所指出的，在私营部门，罗姆尼州长投资的公司正是外包行业的先驱者。这不是我的说法，这是记者们的原话。

就汇率操纵而言，在我就任以来，通过我们坚持不懈的压力，人民币汇率实际上上升了11%。我们对中国形成了空前的贸易压力。这样，我们的出口才能在我的任期内实现如此显著的增长。这将帮助美国创造就业。

克劳利：总统先生，我们时间有限，请简短地辩论一下，像苹果公司的产品，它们都在中国生产，其中一个主要的原因是，他们的劳动力成本比我们便宜许多。你如何才能说服一家美国大公司将这些制造业挪回国内呢？

罗姆尼：这个答案是直截了当的。只要竞争发生在公平的领域，我们就能够与世界上任何国家的人竞争。中国的欺诈行为持续多年了，一个是压低汇率，另一个是窃取我们的知识产权、设计、专利、技术。在中国甚至有山寨的苹果专卖店，出售山寨的苹果产品。他们的黑客进入我们的电脑。我将不得不让所有人在公平的基础上竞争。这是第一点。

第二点，我们不得不让美国成为对企业家最具吸引力的国家，让那些想开拓商业梦想的人视美国为天堂，这样就业就会源源不断地被创造出来。总统先生对我的税收计划的描述，是完全错误的。

克劳利：轮到总统先生了，因为我们真的没时间了。问题是我们能不能……我们不可能开出那种工资，至少不可能持续那种工资水平。

奥巴马：坎迪，有一些工作是不会重返美国的，因为那是一些低工资、低技术含量的工作。我要的是高工资、高技术含量的工作。这就是为什么我们不得不重视制造业、投资高端制造业，为什么我们必须确保我们的科研水平是全世界最高的。

And when we talk about deficits, if we're adding to our deficit for tax cuts for folks who don't need them, and we're cutting investments in research and science that will create the next Apple, create the next new innovation that will sell products around the world, we will lose that race.

If we're not training engineers to make sure that they are equipped here in this country. Then companies won't come here. Those investments are what's going to help to make sure that we continue to lead this world economy, not just next year, but 10 years from now, 50 years from now, 100 years from now.

Crowley: Thanks Mr. President. Governor Romney?

Romney: Government does not create jobs.

Crowley: Governor Romney, I want to introduce you to Barry Green, because he's going to have the last question to you first?

Romney: Barry? Where is Barry?

Question: Hi, Governor. I think this is a tough question. To each of you. What do you believe is the biggest misperception that the American people have about you as a man and a candidate? Using specific examples, can you take this opportunity to debunk that misperception and set us straight?

Romney: Thank you, and that's an opportunity for me, and I appreciate it. In the nature of a campaign, it seems that some campaigns are focused on attacking a person rather than prescribing their own future and the things they'd like to do. In the course of that, I think the president's campaign has tried to characterize me as – as someone who's very different than who I am.

I care about 100 percent of the American people. I want 100 percent of the American people to have a bright and prosperous future. I care about our kids. I understand what it takes to make a bright and prosperous future for America again. I spent my life in the private sector, not in government. I'm a guy who wants to help with the experience I have, the American people.

My – my passion probably flows from the fact that I believe in God. And I believe we're all children of the same God. I believe we have a responsibility

而说到赤字，如果我们为不需要减税的人提供减税从而导致赤字增加，同时却削减对科研经费的投入，那么我们将无法创造出下一个苹果公司，也无法创造出下一个能够行销全世界的创新产品，这样，我们将在全球竞争中落败。

如果我们不去培养工程师，让他们在本国获得充分的装备。那么就不会有公司来到这里。那些投资将有助于确保我们继续领导世界经济。不只是明年，而是10年，50年，100年以后。

克劳利：谢谢总统先生。罗姆尼州长怎么看？

罗姆尼：政府不会创造就业。

克劳利：罗姆尼州长，我想向你介绍，巴里·格林，他会先向您提出本场最后一个问题。

罗姆尼：巴里？巴里在哪儿？

说说真实的自己

选民提问：州长先生，您好，我觉得这个问题挺难的。你们都说说，您认为美国人民对你们作为您本人和您作为候选人，最大的误解是什么？通过具体的例子，您能利用这个机会纠正我们、消除误解吗？

罗姆尼：谢谢。我很感激有这么一个机会来澄清自己。由于竞选的性质使然，许多竞选看起来都把重点放在了攻击人而不是阐述自己的未来和想要做的事情上面。在这些过程中，我认为总统先生的竞选团队努力把我塑造成完全另外的一个人。

我关心百分之百的美国人民。我想要百分之百的美国人拥有一个光明和繁荣的未来。我关心我们的下一代。我懂得如何让美国重返光明与繁荣之路途。我的大半生都在私营领域里摸爬滚打，而不是在政府部门里。我希望我能凭着平生的积累来帮助美国人民。

to care for one another. I – I served as a missionary for my church. I served as a pastor in my congregation for about 10 years. I've sat across the table from people who were out of work and worked with them to try and find new work or to help them through tough times. I went to the Olympics when they were in trouble to try and get them on track. And as governor of my state, I was able to get 100 percent of my people insured, all my kids, about 98 percent of the adults. I was able also to get our schools ranked number one in the nation, so 100 percent of our kids would have a bright opportunity for a future.

I understand that I can get this country on track again. We don't have to settle for what we're going through. We don't have to settle for gasoline at four bucks. We don't have to settle for unemployment at a chronically high level. We don't have to settle for 47 million people on food stamps. We don't have to settle for 50 percent of kids coming out of college not able to get work. We don't have to settle for 23 million people struggling to find a good job.

If I become president, I'll get America working again. I will get us on track to a balanced budget. The president hasn't. I will. I'll make sure we can reform Medicare and Social Security to preserve them for coming – coming generations. The president said he would. He didn't.

Crowley: Governor...

Romney: I'll get our incomes up. And by the way, I've done these things. I served as governor and showed I could get them done.

Crowley: Mr. President, last two minutes belong to you.

Obama: Barry, I think a lot of this campaign, maybe over the last four years, has been devoted to this nation that I think government creates jobs, that that somehow is the answer. That's not what I believe. I believe that the free enterprise system is the greatest engine of prosperity the world's ever known.

I believe in self-reliance and individual initiative and risk takers being rewarded. But I also believe that everybody should have a fair shot and everybody should do their fair share and everybody should play by the same

我之所以能够激情迸发，或许缘于我相信上帝，我相信我们都是同一个上帝的子民。我相信我们有责任互相依偎，照顾对方。我曾是我们教堂的传教士，我曾作过十年的牧师。我曾与失业者同坐一桌，与他们一起努力寻找新的工作或者帮助他们渡过难关。当奥运会运行遇到问题时，我加入他们，通过努力，终于将其扶上正轨。作州长期间，我让我们本州百分之百的人都上了保险——所有的孩子和大约98%的成人。我同样让我们的学校在全美排名第一，这样我们百分之一百的孩子的未来将会有一个光明的前途。

我知道我也能将这个国家重新扶上正轨。我们不需要遭受我们正在遭受的东西，我们不需要遭受4美元的油价，我们不需要遭受长期的高失业率。我们不需要让4700万人靠食品券度日。我们不需要让50%的毕业生找不到工作。我们不需要让2300万的人民去苦苦地寻求一个好的工作。

如果我成为总统，我会让美国重新运转起来。我将让我们回到平衡预算的轨道。总统先生未能做到的，我能做到。为了我们的下一代，我将确保能够改革医疗与社会保障体系。这是总统先生说他会做的，但是他没能做得到。

克劳利：州长先生……

我会让我们的收入增长。顺便提一下，我曾经做成了这些事情。我曾经作为一个州长并且把这些事情都搞定了。

克劳利：总统先生，最后两分钟，交给你。

奥巴马：巴里，我认为在这次竞选过程中，或者在过去的四年，人们都专注于一个观念，那就是我认为政府会创造就业，这某种程度上就是人们误解我最深的地方。实际上我不是这样认为的。

我相信自由企业制度是我们推动经济向前发展的最大引擎。我相信自力更生与个人主动性。我相信冒险者应该获得奖赏，每一个人应该有一个公平的机会，每一个人应该承当公平的负担，每一个人应该按同一规则行事，因为这是我们经济增长的根源。我们也正是这样，建立了世界上最伟大的中产阶级。

rules, because that's how our economy's grown. That's how we built the world's greatest middle class.

And – and that is part of what's at stake in this election. There's a fundamentally different vision about how we move our country forward.

I believe Governor Romney is a good man. Loves his family, cares about his faith. But I also believe that when he said behind closed doors that 47 percent of the country considered themselves victims who refuse personal responsibility, think about who he was talking about. Folks on Social Security who've worked all their lives. Veterans who've sacrificed for this country. Students who are out there trying to hopefully advance their own dreams, but also this country's dreams. Soldiers who are overseas fighting for us right now. People who are working hard every day, paying payroll tax, gas taxes, but don't make enough income.

And I want to fight for them. That's what I've been doing for the last four years. Because if they succeed, I believe the country succeeds.

When my grandfather fought in World War II and he came back and he got a G.I. Bill and that allowed him to go to college, that wasn't a handout. That was something that advanced the entire country. And I want to make sure that the next generation has those same opportunities. That's why I'm asking for your vote and that's why I'm asking for another four years.

Crowley: President Obama, Governor Romney, thank you for being here tonight. On that note we have come to an end of this town hall debate. Our thanks to the participants for their time and to the people of Hofstra University for their hospitality. The next and final debate takes place Monday night at Lynn (ph) University in Boca Raton, Florida. Don't forget to watch. Election Day is three weeks from today. Don't forget to vote.

Good night.

Hofstra University, Hemspstead, New York, October, 16, 2012

这是本次选举中最为关键的一点。我们对于如何推动国家发展，有着从根本上不同的愿景。我相信罗姆尼州长是一个好人，他爱他的家庭，关心他的信仰。

　　但是我也同样相信，当他私下里说47%的国民认为他们自己是受害者，却拒绝承担个人责任时，想想他所说的人是谁吧：是辛苦了一辈子，却要拿社会保障金的人；是为美国作出巨大牺牲的退伍老兵；是那些希望能够实现自己和国家梦想的莘莘学子；是在国外正在为我们奋战的军人们；是每天兢兢业业，交着工资税、燃油税，却只能养家糊口的人们。

　　而我，要为这些人奋斗。这正是我过去四年任期内所做的事情。因为我相信，如果这些人能够获得成功，我相信我们国家也会成功。

　　当我的外祖父从第二次世界大战的战场上回来，《退伍军人权利法令》让他能有机会去读大学，这不是施舍。而是推动我们整个国家的动力，我要确保我们的下一代同样拥有这些机会。这也是我寻求你们的选票，给我下一个四年任期的原因所在。

　　克劳利：奥巴马总统，罗姆尼州长，感谢你们今晚的出席。本场市政厅辩论已接近尾声。感谢所有的参与者，感谢霍夫斯特拉大学各位的招待。下一场，也是最后一场辩论，将于周一晚上举行。在佛罗里达州博卡拉顿市的林恩大学举行。请届时收看。大选之日离今天还有三个星期，大家别忘了投票。

　　各位，晚安。

（杜梦臻／译　袁婧／校）

The Third Obama – Romney
Presidential Debate

Bob Schieffer: Good evening from the campus of Lynn University here in Boca Raton, Florida. This is the fourth and last debate of the 2012 campaign, brought to you by the Commission on Presidential Debates. This one's on foreign policy. I'm Bob Schieffer of CBS News. The questions are mine, and I have not shared them with the candidates or their aides.

The audience has taken a vow of silence – no applause, no reaction of any kind except right now when we welcome President Barack Obama and Governor Mitt Romney. Gentlemen, your campaigns have agreed to certain rules and they are simple. They have asked me to divide the evening into segments. I'll pose a question at the beginning of each segment. You will each have two minutes to respond, and then we will have a general discussion until we move to the next segment.

Tonight's debate, as both of your know, comes on the 50th anniversary of the night that President Kennedy told the world that the Soviet Union had installed nuclear missiles in Cuba – perhaps the closest we've ever come to nuclear war. And it is a sobering reminder that every president faces at some point an unexpected threat to our national security from abroad. So let's begin.

The first segment is the challenge of a changing Middle East and the new face of terrorism. I'm going to put this into two segments, so you'll have two topic questions within this one segment on that subject. The first question, and it concerns Libya, the controversy over what happened there continues. Four Americans are dead, including an American ambassador. Questions remain.

奥巴马—罗姆尼第三场电视辩论①

鲍伯·西弗： 晚上好，我现在在佛罗里达州博卡拉顿的林恩大学校园，这是2012年总统竞选的第四场也是最后一场辩论，② 由总统辩论委员会组织。这次辩论的主题是外交政策。我是美国哥伦比亚广播公司新闻节目的鲍伯·西弗。今天由我来提问，在这之前，我未向竞选者和幕僚作任何透露。

听众已经承诺要保持安静——不要鼓掌，不作出任何反应，让我们欢迎巴拉克·奥巴马总统和米特·罗姆尼州长。先生们，你们的竞选团队已经就竞选规则达成一致，这些规则很简单。他们请求我将今晚的辩论分为几个部分进行，我会在每个部分开始时，提出一个问题，你们各有两分钟的时间作出回答，然后，在进行下个部分之前，我们会就这个问题进行一个讨论。

众所周知，50年前的今晚，肯尼迪总统向世界发表演说称，苏联已经在古巴部署核导弹——也许，那是我们离核战争最近的时刻。同时，它冷静地提醒着每位总统，说不定什么时候我们国家的安全就会面临外来势力出乎意料的威胁。我们现在开始辩论吧。

第一部分的主题是，多变的中东局势带来的挑战以及恐怖主义的新面孔。我把这个议题再分为两部分，所以，你们两位需要讨论两个的相关问题。第一个问题是关于利比亚的，那里到底发生了什么事情，一直争议不

---

① 2012年10月22日奥巴马和罗姆尼在最后一场辩论中就美国的外交政策展开唇枪舌剑，辩论一共分为六个部分：美国的全球角色；美国最漫长的战争——阿富汗和巴基斯坦；红线——以色列和伊朗；中东变迁与恐怖主义新面孔；中国的崛起。由于这次是最后一场辩论，这也成为两人面对选民最后陈词的机会，因此双方都力求做到更好。

② 总统大选奥巴马和罗姆尼进行三场辩论，副总统拜登和瑞安进行一场辩论。

What happened? What caused it? Was it spontaneous? Was it an intelligence failure? Was it a policy failure? Was there an attempt to mislead people about what really happened?

Governor Romney, you said this was an example of an American policy in the Middle East that is unraveling before our very eyes. I'd like to hear each of you give your thoughts on that.Governor Romney, you won the toss. You go first.

Romney: Thank you, Bob, and thank you for agreeing to moderate this debate this evening. Thank you to Lynn University for welcoming us here, and Mr. President, it's good to be with you again. We were together at a humorous event a little earlier, and it's nice to maybe be funny this time not on purpose. We'll see what happens.

This is obviously an area of great concern to the entire world and to America in particular, which is to see a – a complete change in the – the – the structure and the – the environment in the Middle East. With the Arab Spring came a great deal of hope that there would be a change towards more moderation and opportunity for greater participation on the part of women and – and public life and in economic life in the Middle East. But instead we've seen in nation after nation a number of disturbing events. Of course, we see in Syria 30,000 civilians having been killed by the military there. We see in – in – in Libya an attack apparently by – well, I think we know now by terrorists of some kind against – against our people there, four people dead. Our hearts and minds go to them. Mali has been taken over, the northern part of Mali, by al-Qaida-type individuals. We have in – in Egypt a Muslim Brotherhood president.

And so what we're seeing is a – a – a pretty dramatic reversal in the kind of hopes we had for that region. Of course, the greatest threat of all is Iran, four years closer to a nuclear weapon. And – and we're going to have to recognize that we have to do as the president has done. I congratulate him on – on taking out Osama bin Laden and going after the leadership in al-Qaida. But we can't kill our way out of this mess. We're – we're going to have to put in place a

断。包括一位美国大使在内，有四名美国人丧生，问题悬而未决。到底发生了什么？原因何在？袭击事件是自发的吗？存在情报失误吗？这是政策的失败吗？是否存在误导公众掩盖真相？

罗姆尼州长，您说过这次事件就是美国的中东政策瓦解的例子。我想听听你们对这个问题各自的看法。罗姆尼州长，您赢了抛硬币比赛，您先来谈一下。

罗姆尼：谢谢你，鲍伯。谢谢你担任今晚的辩论主持，感谢林恩大学的邀请。总统先生，很高兴再次见到你。我们之前在一个滑稽的场合相遇，这次我的态度却不一样，但希望气氛依旧轻松，我们看看接下来会发生什么。

对全世界，尤其是对美国来说，这个地区显然引起了广泛的关注，中东地区格局和环境发生了巨大变化，"阿拉伯之春"[①] 以后，人们热切希望中东的气氛会更加缓和，让妇女更多地参与中东地区的公共生活和经济生活。然而我们看到的是一个又一个国家陷入混乱。我们看到三万叙利亚平民遭到军方杀害；在利比亚，某些恐怖分子对我们驻利比亚的人员发动了袭击，导致四名美国人丧生，我们为他们哀悼。马里被占领了，北部地区被类似基地组织的人员控制；在埃及还出现了出身穆斯林兄弟会[②] 的总统。

这个地区眼下局势与我们的期望背道而驰。当然，最大的威胁是伊朗，距他们拥有核武器的时间又缩短了四年。我们必须意识到总统的所作

---

① 指自2010年年底在北非和西亚的阿拉伯国家和其他地区的一些国家发生的一系列以"民主"和"经济"等为主题的反政府社会运动，先后波及突尼斯、埃及、利比亚、也门、叙利亚等国，多名领导人先后下台，其影响之深、范围之广、爆发之突然、来势之迅猛吸引了全世界的高度关注。西方媒体乐观地把"一个新中东即将诞生"预见为这次运动的前景。参见：http://baike.baidu.com。

② 伊斯兰复兴运动的宗教性政治组织。1928年哈桑·巴纳（Hassan al-Banna）于埃及伊斯梅利亚创立，1929年正式成立，最初，他以自己的名字命名"班纳运动"，后改为"穆斯林兄弟会"。严格地说，这个组织并不仅是埃及独有的一个半公开、半非法组织，而是一个起源于埃及、影响力遍布中东乃至全球的穆斯林群众性组织，甚至有人认为，它是近代历史最悠久、规模最大、组织最严密的、在世界范围内最具影响力的伊斯兰政治集团。参见：http://baike.baidu.com。

very comprehensive and robust strategy to help the – the world of Islam and – and other parts of the world reject this radical violent extremism which is – it's really not on the run. It's certainly not hiding. This is a group that is now involved in 10 or 12 countries, and it presents an enormous threat to our friends, to the world, to America long term, and we must have a comprehensive strategy to help reject this kind of extremism.

Schieffer: Mr. President.

Obama: Well, my first job as commander in chief, Bob, is to keep the American people safe, and that's what we've done over the last four years. We ended the war in Iraq, refocused our attention on those who actually killed us on 9/11. And as a consequence, al-Qaida's core leadership has been decimated.

In addition, we're now able to transition out of Afghanistan in a responsible way, making sure that Afghans take responsibility for their own security, and that allows us also to rebuild alliances and make friends around the world to combat future threats. Now, with respect to Libya, as I indicated in the last debate, when we received that phone call, I immediately made sure that, number one, we did everything we could to secure those Americans who were still in harm's way; number two, that we would investigate exactly what happened; and number three, most importantly, that we would go after those who killed Americans, and we would bring them to justice, and that's exactly what we're going to do.

But I think it's important to step back and think about what happened in Libya. Now, keep in mind that I and Americans took leadership in organizing an international coalition that made sure that we were able to – without putting troops on the ground, at the cost of less than what we spent in two weeks in Iraq – liberate a country that had been under the yoke of dictatorship for 40 years, got rid of a despot who had killed Americans.

And as a consequence, despite this tragedy, you had tens of thousands of Libyans after the events in Benghazi marching and saying, America's our friend. We stand with them. Now that represents the opportunity we have to take

所为是必要的。我对他就消灭本·拉登以及追捕基地组织头目作出的成果表示祝贺。但是，这不足以让我们摆脱困境，我们必须采取一个综合的、强硬的战略，来帮助伊斯兰世界和其他国家，对抗这种激进的暴力极端主义——它现在大行其道。这个组织现在已经渗透至10或12个国家，它对我们的盟友、世界和美国构成了长期的、巨大的威胁，我们必须要采取一个全面的战略以对抗这种极端主义。

西弗：总统该您说了。

奥巴马：好的，鲍伯，作为三军总司令，我的首要工作是确保美国人民的安全，这是过去四年我们的所作所为。我们结束了伊拉克战争，将注意力重新集中于那些在"9·11"事件中迫害我们的人身上，最终消灭了基地组织的核心领导层。

另外，我们现在能够以负责任的方式从阿富汗撤军，确保阿富汗人能够担负起自己的安全，这也让我们得以重建同盟，在世界各地结交朋友以战胜未来的威胁。就利比亚而言，我在上次辩论就指出，我们接到电话后，要做的第一件事就是不惜一切代价确保当地美国人的安全；第二件事是，我们将调查事件的真相；第三件事，也就是最重要的，我们将追捕那些杀害我们同胞的人，将他们绳之以法，这才是我们着手要做的事。

但我认为，退一步想想在利比亚发生的事情是十分重要的。现在请记住，我和美国人民在组织国际联盟方面发挥了领导作用，以确保我们能够在不派出地面部队、花费不超过我们在伊拉克两周花销的情况下，解放了曾受独裁者统治40年的国家，除掉了一个曾杀害过美国人的暴君。

advantage of. And you know, Governor Romney, I'm glad that you agree that we have been successful in going after al-Qaida, but I have to tell you that, you know, your strategy previously has been one that has been all over the map and is not designed to keep Americans safe or to build on the opportunities that exist in the Middle East.

Romney: Well, my strategy's pretty straightforward, which is to go after the bad guys, to make sure we do our very best to interrupt them, to – to kill them, to take them out of the picture. But my strategy is broader than – than that. That's – that's important, of course, but the key that we're going to have to pursue is a – is a pathway to – to get the Muslim world to be able to reject extremism on its own. We don't want another Iraq. We don't want another Afghanistan. That's not the right course for us. The right course for us is to make sure that we go after the – the people who are leaders of these various anti-American groups and these – these jihadists, but also help the Muslim world.

And how we do that? A group of Arab scholars came together, organized by the U.N., to look at how we can help the – the world reject these – these terrorists. And the answer they came up was this.

One, more economic development. We should key our foreign aid, our direct foreign investment and that of our friends – we should coordinate it to make sure that we – we push back and give them more economic development.

Number two, better education.

Number three, gender equality.

Number four, the rule of law. We have to help these nations create civil societies.

But what's been happening over the last couple years as we watched this tumult in the Middle East, this rising tide of chaos occur, you see al-Qaida rushing in, you see other jihadist groups rushing in. And – and they're throughout many nations of the Middle East.

It's wonderful that Libya seems to be making some progress, despite this

　　尽管发生了美国驻利比亚领事馆遇袭的悲剧，但您会发现在这之后，成千上万的利比亚人在班加西游行，说美国是我们的朋友，我们和他们在一条战线上，这意味着我们应该抓住这个机会。如您所知，罗姆尼州长，我很高兴您认可我们在打击基地组织方面所取得的成功，但我也要告诉您，您之前的计划天南地北，不着边际，不能确保美国人的安全，也无法抓住中东的机遇。

　　罗姆尼：好的，我的策略直截了当，就是追捕坏人，确保我们竭尽所能阻止他们，消灭他们，把他们铲除。但是我的策略不局限于此，消灭他们当然很重要，不过我们的核心途径是，要让穆斯林世界能够独立抵制极端主义。我们不想要另一个伊拉克，我们不想要另一个阿富汗，对我们来说，那不是正确的道路。正确的道路是，我们得不仅打击各种反美组织的头目和那些圣战分子，我们也要帮助穆斯林世界。

　　我们如何做到呢？一群阿拉伯学者在联合国的组织下聚集起来，研究我们如何来帮助穆斯林世界抵制那些恐怖分子。他们得出的答案是这样的：第一，大力促进经济发展，应重视我们和盟友的对外援助、国外直接投资——我们应组织协调确保我们促进穆斯林世界的经济发展。

　　第二，发展教育。

　　第三，消除性别歧视。

　　第四，树立法治观念，我们要帮助这些国家建立文明社会。

　　在过去几年里，我们看到中东地区起伏动荡，混乱不堪，基地组织和其他圣战分子涌入许多中东国家。

terrible tragedy, but next door, of course, we have Egypt. Libya's 6 million population, Egypt 80 million population. We want – we want to make sure that we're seeing progress throughout the Middle East. With Mali now having North Mali taken over by al-Qaida, with Syria having Assad continuing to – or to kill – to murder his own people, this is a region in tumult. And of course Iran on the path to a nuclear weapon. We've got real gaps in the region.

Schieffer: We'll get to that, but let's give the president a chance.

Obama: Governor Romney, I'm glad that you recognize that al-Qaida's a threat because a few months ago when you were asked, what's the biggest geopolitical threat facing America, you said Russia – not al-Qaida, you said Russia. And the 1980s are now calling to ask for their foreign policy back because, you know, the Cold War's been over for 20 years.

But, Governor, when it comes to our foreign policy, you seem to want to import the foreign policies of the 1980s, just like the social policies of the 1950s and the economic policies of the 1920s. You say that you're not interested in duplicating what happened in Iraq, but just a few weeks ago you said you think we should have more troops in Iraq right now.

And the – the challenge we have – I know you haven't been in a position to actually execute foreign policy, but every time you've offered an opinion, you've been wrong. You said we should have gone into Iraq despite the fact that there were no weapons of mass destruction. You said that we should still have troops in Iraq to this day. You indicated that we shouldn't be passing nuclear treaties with Russia, despite the fact that 71 senators, Democrats and Republicans, voted for it.

You've said that first we should not have a timeline in Afghanistan then you said we should. Now you say maybe or it depends, which means not only were you wrong but you were also confusing and sending mixed messages both to our troops and our allies.

So what – what we need to do with respect to the Middle East is strong,

虽然利比亚发生了惨剧，但仍然有些可喜的进步，但是，它的邻国埃及是个问题。利比亚有600万人口，埃及则有8000万人口，我们希望推动整个中东地区的进步。现在马里的北部受控于基地分子，叙利亚阿萨德总统还在杀戮同胞，这是区域性的动乱。还有，伊朗向核武器之路咄咄逼近，我们看到这个地区的确存在差异。

西弗：我们一会儿再谈那个问题，先给总统一个机会。

奥巴马：罗姆尼州长，很高兴您能意识到基地组织是个威胁，因为几个月前当您被问到这个问题时，您说俄罗斯是美国面临的最大地缘政治挑战——不是基地组织，您说的是俄罗斯。20世纪80年代的外交政策已经过时，因为，您知道距冷战已经结束20年了。

但是州长，当我们讨论外交政策的时候，您似乎还想沿用上世纪80年代那一套，就像您想要引入50年代的社会政策和20年代的经济政策一样。您说，您对重演发生在伊拉克的事情漠不关心，但是仅在几周之前，您又说我们应该在伊拉克增加军力。

而且，我们面临的挑战——我知道您没有实际执行过外交政策，但是，您提出的每一个观点都是错的。您说，尽管那里实际并没有大规模杀伤性武器，我们也应当进军伊拉克。您说，我们应仍在伊拉克驻军。您指

411

steady leadership, not wrong and reckless leadership that is all over the map. And unfortunately, that's the kind of opinions that you've offered throughout this campaign, and it is not a recipe for American strength or keeping America safe over the long term.

Schieffer: I'm going to add a couple of minutes here to give you a chance to respond.

Romney: Well, of course I don't concur with what the president said about my own record and the things that I've said. They don't happen to be accurate. But – but I can say this: that we're talking about the Middle East and how to help the Middle East reject the kind of terrorism we're seeing and the rising tide of tumult and – and confusion. And – and attacking me is not an agenda. Attacking me is not talking about how we're going to deal with the challenges that exist in the Middle East and take advantage of the opportunity there and stem the tide of this violence. But I'll respond to a couple of the things you mentioned. First of all, Russia, I indicated, is a geopolitical foe, not –

Obama: Number one –

Romney: Excuse me. It's a geopolitical foe. And I said in the same – in the same paragraph, I said, and Iran is the greatest national security threat we face. Russia does continue to battle us in the U.N. time and time again. I have clear eyes on this. I'm not going to wear rose-colored glasses when it comes to Russia or Mr. Putin, and I'm certainly not going to say to him, I'll give you more flexibility after the election. After the election he'll get more backbone.

Number two, with regards to Iraq, you and I agreed, I believe, that there should have been a status of forces agreement. Did you –

Obama: That's not true.

Romney: Oh, you didn't – you didn't want a status of forces agreement?

Obama: No, but what I – what I would not have done is left 10,000 troops in Iraq that would tie us down. That certainly would not help us in the Middle East.

出，虽然民主党和共和党中，有71位参议员投票支持，我们也不应该通过和俄罗斯的核条约。

您开始说，不应当设定时间期限从阿富汗撤军，后来，您又说我们应该这样。现在，您又说视情况而定，这就说明您不但观点错误，而且还混淆信息，给我们的军队和我们的盟友发出模棱两可的信息。

在中东问题上，我们需要的是强大、稳健的领导力，而非错误、不计后果、不着边际的领导力。不幸的是，您在整个竞选中所表达的那些观点，无法确保能够长期帮助美国强大，维护美国安全。

西弗：我要增加几分钟，让您（罗姆尼）来作出回应。

罗姆尼：好的，我当然不赞成总统对我言行的看法，那是不准确的。但我可以说，我们讨论的是中东地区和怎样帮助中东地区抵制起伏动荡、混乱不堪的恐怖主义，攻击我也无济于事。攻击我并不涉及我们如何应对中东地区的挑战，如何利用现有的机会抑制那里高涨的暴力。不过我要回应您刚才谈到的几件事情。首先，俄罗斯，我的意思是俄罗斯是一个地缘战略对手，不是——

奥巴马：第一

罗姆尼：抱歉。俄罗斯是一个地缘战略对手，我在同一段话中说到过，伊朗是我们国家面临的最大安全威胁，而俄罗斯继续时不时地在联合国内和我们作对，这一点我看得很清楚。谈到俄罗斯或者普京总统①，我不会抱乐观态度。而且，我也绝对不会对他说，我当选后会给你更多的便利，反而我会更加强硬。

第二，关于伊拉克，我和您的意见一致。我认为，应该有一个《驻军地位协议》。您——

奥巴马：那不对。

罗姆尼：您不想要一个《驻军地位协议》？

奥巴马：我想，但我不会把一万人的军队留驻在伊拉克，造成我方困

---

① 弗拉基米尔·弗拉基米罗维奇·普京，俄罗斯总统。2000年至2008年任总统期间，使俄罗斯在军事与政治实力上均有相当的提升，但在民主方面也存在到一些争议，是一位"铁腕总统"。然而，普京在俄罗斯国内获得了极高的支持率，2012年5月7日举行总统就职典礼，普京再次宣誓就任俄罗斯总统。

Romney: There was an effort on the part of the president to have a status of forces agreement. And I concurred in that and said we should have some number of troops that stayed on. That was something I concurred with.

Obama: Governor –

Romney: That was your posture. That was my posture as well. I thought it should have been 5,000 troops.

Obama: Governor –

Romney: I thought it should have been more troops. But you –

Obama: This is just a few weeks ago.

Romney: The answer was, we got no troop whatsoever.

Obama: This is just a few weeks ago that you indicated that we should still have troops in Iraq.

Romney: No, I didn't. I'm sorry, that's –

Obama: You made a major speech.

Romney: I indicated – I indicated that you failed to put in place a status of forces agreement at the end of the conflict that –

Schieffer: Governor –

Obama: Governor, here's – here's one thing – here's one thing – here's one thing I've learned as commander in chief.

Schieffer: Let him have –

Obama: You've got to be clear, both to our allies and our enemies, about where you stand and what you mean. Now, you just gave a speech a few weeks ago in which you said we should still have troops in Iraq. That is not a recipe for making sure that we are taking advantage of the opportunities and meeting the challenges of the Middle East.

Now, it is absolutely true that we cannot just beat these challenges militarily, and so what I've done throughout my presidency and will continue to do, is, number one, make sure that these countries are supporting our counterterrorism efforts; number two, make sure that they are standing by our

局，那样，当然也不会对我们的中东地区事务有所帮助。

罗姆尼： 总统曾经就《驻军地位协议》作出过努力，也曾说过我们应该仍在那里有一些驻军，这点我赞成，我同意。

奥巴马： 州长——

罗姆尼： 那是您的立场，也是我的立场。我想在伊拉克的驻军应该有5000人。

奥巴马： 州长——

罗姆尼： 我认为该有更多的驻军，但是您——

奥巴马： 仅仅是在几周前。

罗姆尼： 结果我们一兵一卒都没留下。

奥巴马： 仅在几周之前，您还暗示说我们应该在伊拉克仍继续驻军。

罗姆尼： 不，我没有——对不起，那是——

奥巴马： 而且您发表了重要讲话。

罗姆尼： 我是在暗示，您没能在冲突结束时，达成《驻军地位协议》——

西弗： 州长——

奥巴马： 州长——当三军总司令时，我学会了一个道理——

西弗： 让他讲——

奥巴马： 您需要对我们的盟友和敌人明确您的立场和您的意思。您在几周前发表演讲，说我们应该在伊拉克驻扎军队。这不是确保我们利用机遇、应对中东地区挑战的药方。

interests in Israel's security, because it is a true friend and our greatest ally in the region. Number three, we do have to make sure that we're protecting religious minorities and women because these countries can't develop unless all the population – not just half of it – is developing. Number four, we do have to develop their economic – their economic capabilities. But number five, the other thing that we have to do is recognize that we can't continue to do nation building in these regions. Part of American leadership is making sure that we're doing nation building here at home. That will help us maintain the kind of American leadership that we need.

Schieffer: Let me interject the second topic question in this segment about the Middle East and so on, and that is, you both mentioned – alluded to this, and that is Syria. The war in Syria has now spilled over into Lebanon. We have, what, more than a hundred people that were killed there in a bomb. There were demonstrations there, eight people dead.

Mr. President, it's been more than a year since you saw – you told Assad he had to go. Since then 30,000 Syrians have died. We've had 300,000 refugees. The war goes on. He's still there. Should we reassess our policy and see if we can find a better way to influence events there, or is that even possible? And it's you – you go first, sir.

Obama: What we've done is organize the international community, saying Assad has to go. We've mobilized sanctions against that government. We have made sure that they are isolated. We have provided humanitarian assistance, and we are helping the opposition organize, and we're particularly interested in making sure that we're mobilizing the moderate forces inside of Syria. But ultimately, Syrians are going to have to determine their own future. And so everything we're doing, we're doing in consultation with our partners in the region, including Israel, which obviously has a huge interest in seeing what happens in Syria, coordinating with Turkey and other countries in the region that have a great interest in this.

毫无疑问，我们不能只用军事手段去应对这些挑战，我在任期内所采取的措施，我会继续实施下去。那就是，第一，确保这些国家支持我们的反恐行动。第二，确保他们支持我们在以色列安全方面的利益，因为以色列是我们的盟友，是这个地区的大国。第三，我们要确保宗教少数派和妇女受到保护，因为只有所有人得到发展，国家才能发展，而不仅仅是依靠半数人的力量。第四，我们要帮助其发展经济实力。第五，我们必须意识到我们不能继续在那些地区进行国家建设，美国的领导策略之一是，要确保我们在国内进行国家建设，这将有助于我们维持美国必需的领导能力。

西弗：在有关中东问题的辩论中，让我插进第二个辩论话题，即你们都提到的叙利亚问题，叙利亚的战火现已蔓延到黎巴嫩，在一场炸弹袭击中有100多人丧生，还有8人在示威中死亡。

总统先生，叙利亚战争已经持续了一年多的时间，您曾经对阿萨德表示，他必须下台，自那之后，已经有3万叙利亚人死亡，有30万人沦为难民，战争仍然在继续，阿萨德仍然在任。我们是否应该重新评估我们的政策，看看我们是否能够找到一个更理想的方式来影响叙利亚的局势。或者说是否存在这种可能性？总统先生，您先回答。

奥巴马：我们所做的是为了组织国际社会，让阿萨德必须走人。我们已经动员力量，准备制裁该政府，我们确保他们已经被孤立。我们已经提供了人道援助，我们正在帮助反对派，我们尤其想确保我们能够动员叙利亚的中立派。但是最终叙利亚的未来将要由它们自己来决定。因此我们所做的每一件事，都要与这一地区的盟友商量，其中包括以色列，该国显然对叙利亚正在发生的一切非常感兴趣；土耳其和这一地区的其他国家，他们与对此也非常感兴趣。

Now, this – what we're seeing taking place in Syria is heartbreaking, and that's why we are going to do everything we can to make sure that we are helping the opposition. But we also have to recognize that, you know, for us to get more entangled militarily in Syria is a serious step. And we have to do so making absolutely certain that we know who we are helping, that we're not putting arms in the hands of folks who eventually could turn them against us or our allies in the region.

And I am confident that Assad's days are numbered. But what we can't do is to simply suggest that, as Governor Romney at times has suggested, that giving heavy weapons, for example, to the Syrian opposition is a simple proposition that would lead us to be safer over the long term.

Schieffer: Governor.

Romney: Well, let's step back and talk about what's happening in Syria and how important it is. First of all, 30,000 people being killed by their government is a humanitarian disaster.

Secondly, Syria's an opportunity for us because Syria plays an important role in the Middle East, particularly right now. Syria is Iran's only ally in the Arab world. It's their route to the sea. It's the route for them to arm Hezbollah in Lebanon, which threatens, of course, our ally Israel. And so seeing Syria remove Assad is a very high priority for us. Number two, seeing a – a replacement government being responsible people is critical for us. And finally, we don't want to have military involvement there. We don't want to get drawn into a military conflict.

And so the right course for us is working through our partners and with our own resources to identify responsible parties within Syria, organize them, bring them together in a – in a form of – of – if not government, a form of – of council that can take the lead in Syria, and then make sure they have the arms necessary to defend themselves. We do need to make sure that they don't have arms that get into the – the wrong hands. Those arms could be used to hurt us down the road. We need to make sure as well that we coordinate this effort with our allies

现在——我们看到的叙利亚正在发生的一切让人痛心，这也是我们竭尽所能帮助反对派的原因。但是我们也不得不承认，你们知道，对我们来说，让叙利亚陷入军事混乱是非常严肃的一步，我们必须分清利害，我们不能把武器发放给那些最终会调转矛头，反对我们或者反对我们在该地区的盟友的人手里。

我相信，阿萨德已经时日不多。罗姆尼州长曾经提过一个建议，例如把重型武器交给叙利亚反对派就可能让我们长期安全，但我们不能单单依靠这个简单的建议。

西弗： 州长，您的看法呢？

罗姆尼： 让我们回过头来说说在叙利亚发生的事情，以及叙利亚问题的重要性。第一，三万人被他们的政府杀害，这无疑是一场人道主义灾难。

第二，叙利亚对我们来说是一个机会，因为叙利亚在中东扮演着重要的角色，尤其是现在。叙利亚是伊朗在阿拉伯世界的唯一盟友，是伊朗的入海通道，是他们向黎巴嫩的真主党提供武装的路径，因而威胁到我们的盟友以色列。所以，把阿萨德从叙利亚铲除是我们的首选，并且让富有责任心的人组成一个叙利亚新政府，对我们来说至关重要。最后，我们不希望在那里进行军事干预，不希望陷入一场军事冲突。

所以，正确的道路是和我们的伙伴密切合作，利用手头的资源寻找叙利亚国内负责任的党派，把他们组织成为能够领导叙利亚的一不是政府一是委员会，并确保他们拥有能够捍卫自己的武器，并不让这些武器落入敌人的手中，给我们带来伤害。在叙利亚问题上，我们需要扮演一个高效的领导角色，确保武装、正在武装的起义者将成为一个负责任的派别。

and particularly with – with – with Israel. But the Saudis and the Qatari and – and – and the Turks are all very concerned about this. They're willing to work with us. We need to have a very effective leadership effort in Syria, making sure that the – the – the insurgents there are armed and that the insurgents that become armed are people who will be the responsible parties.

Recognize I believe that Assad must go. I believe he will go. But I believe we want to make sure that we have the relationships of friendship with the people that take his place such that in the years to come we see Syria as a – as a friend and Syria as a responsible party in the Middle East. This – this is a critical opportunity for America.

And what I'm afraid of is that we've watched over the past year or so first the president saying, well, we'll let the U.N. deal with it, and Assad – excuse me, Kofi Annan came in and – and said, we're going to try – have a cease-fire. That didn't work. Then it looked to the Russians and said, see if you can do something. we should. We should be playing the leadership role there, not on the ground with military –

Schieffer: All right.

Romney: – by the leadership role.

Obama: We are – we playing the leadership role. We organized the "Friends of Syria." We are mobilizing humanitarian support and support for the opposition. And we are making sure that that those we help are those who will be friends of ours in the long term and friends of our allies in the region over the long term.

But you know, going back to Libya, because this is an example of – of how we make choices, you know, when we went into Libya and we were able to immediately stop the massacre there because of the unique circumstances and the coalition that we had helped to organize, we also had to make sure that Moammar Gadhafi didn't stay there. And to the governor's credit, you supported us going into Libya and the coalition that we organized. But when it came time to making sure that Gadhafi did not stay in power, that he was captured,

我认为阿萨德必须下台，也相信他将会下台。我们需要与新的领导班子建立起友好的合作关系，几年后我将把叙利亚视为我们的，视为中东地区一个负责任的国家，这是美国的重大机遇。

我忧心忡忡，因为前几年我们也看到了，总统说，让联合国来处理他——阿萨德——抱歉，科菲·安南站出来说，我们要停息战火，但无济于事。然后，俄罗斯又参与其中，说看你们是否能有所作为。我们应该在叙利亚问题上扮演领导者的角色，不是在军事干预的基础上——

西弗：好的。

罗姆尼：——要扮演领导者的角色。

奥巴马：我们是正在扮演领导者的角色。我们组织了"叙利亚之友"。我们正动员人道主义支援，支持反对派，我们要确保我们帮助的人，是我们长期的盟友和我们区域联盟的长期盟友。

不过，让我们回到利比亚话题，大家知道，利比亚就是证明我们如何做选择的一个生动的范例，由于特殊的环境以及我们组建起来的联盟，我们进入利比亚后，能够立刻终止那里的大屠杀，我们也要确保奥马尔·卡扎菲[①]倒台。值得肯定的是，州长，您当时是支持我们进入利比亚组织联盟的，但是当我们确保卡扎菲不当权并且被捕的时候，您暗示这偏离并混淆了我们的任务目标。

---

① 卡扎菲（1942—2011），利比亚革命警卫队上校，利比亚前最高领导人，曾领导"自由军官组织"，为利比亚1969年9月1日革命的精神领袖，推翻了亲西方的伊德里斯王朝，并建立了阿拉伯利比亚共和国。长达42年的统治使他成为阿拉伯国家中执政时间最长的领导者。卡扎菲是一个富有争议的人物，世人对他的评价毁誉参半。即便在被西方制裁长达十年的过程中，凭借丰富的石油资源，卡扎菲控制的利比亚成为非洲最富裕的国家之一。参见：http://baike.baidu.com。

Governor, your suggestion was that this was mission creep, that this was mission muddle.

Imagine if we had pulled out at that point. That – Moammar Gadhafi had more American blood on his hands than any individual other than Osama bin Laden. And so we were going to make sure that we finished the job. That's part of the reason why the Libyans stand with us. But we did so in a careful, thoughtful way, making certain that we knew who we were dealing with, that those forces of moderation on the ground were ones that we could work with. And we have to take the same kind of steady, thoughtful leadership when it comes to Syria. That's exactly what we're doing.

Schieffer: Governor, can I just ask you, would you go beyond what the administration would do? Like, for example, would you put in no-fly zones over Syria?

Romney: I don't – I don't want to have our military involved in – in Syria. I don't think there's a necessity to put our military in Syria at – at this stage.I don't anticipate that in the future.

As I indicated, our objectives are to replace Assad and to have in place a new government which is friendly to us – a responsible government, if possible. And I want to make sure the get armed and they have the arms necessary to defend themselves but also to remove – to remove Assad. But I do not want to see a military involvement on the part of – of our – of our troops.

And this isn't – this isn't going to be necessary. We have – with our partners in the region, we have sufficient resources to support those groups. But look, this has been going on for a year. This is a time – this should have been a time for American leadership. We should have taken a leading role – not militarily, but a leading role organizationally, governmentally, to bring together the parties there to find responsible parties.

As you hear from intelligence sources even today, the insurgents are highly disparate. They haven't come together. They haven't formed a unity group, a

想象一下，如果在那时我们撤离，卡扎菲的双手会沾染比本拉·丹还多的美国人的鲜血。所以我们必须要确保我们已经完成任务。这就是为什么利比亚人和我们站在同一条战线上的部分原因。不过，我们当时那样做是经过深思熟虑的，用一种非常小心谨慎的方式，确定我们自己知道我们的敌人是谁，知道战场上的温和派是我们可以合作的对象。针对叙利亚问题，我们需要采取同样稳定、深思熟虑的领导方式，这就是我们的所作所为。

西弗： 州长，请您回答一下，如果您当选，您是否会作出比当前政府更多的举措？比如，您是否会在叙利亚设立禁飞区？

罗姆尼： 我不希望我们的军队卷入到叙利亚问题，我并不觉得现阶段，有必要将军队派驻到叙利亚，将来也是如此。

正如我提到的，我们的目标是让阿萨德下台，如果可能的话，协助组建一个对我们更友好、也更负责任的新政府。而且，我希望他们能够全副武装起来并拥有必要的军力来捍卫自己，将阿萨德赶下台。但是我不希望我们的军队也参与进来。

也没有这个必要。不过，我们在这个地区拥有盟友，具备充分的资源来支持反对力量。但是，看吧，叙利亚战争已经持续了一年，已经到了美国扮演领导者角色的时候了。我们应该从组织上、政治上扮演领导角色，而从非军事上，从而团结反对力量来找到负责任的党派。

情报指出，直至今日，反对派差别很大，他们并没有团结一致，形成一种统一的组织和委员会。他们需要这样做，美国能够帮助他们实现这个目标。我们需要确保他们拥有必要的武器来发挥重要作用除掉阿萨德。

council of some kind. That needs to happen. America can help that happen. And we need to make sure they have the arms they need to carry out the very important role, which is getting rid of Assad.

Schieffer: Could we get a quick response, Mr. President, because I want to ask –

Obama: Well, I'll – I'll – I'll be – I'll be very quick. What you just heard Governor Romney said is he doesn't have different ideas, and that's because we're doing exactly what we should be doing to try to promote a moderate, Syrian leadership and a – an effective transition so that we get Assad out. That's the kind of leadership we've shown. That's the kind of leadership we'll continue to show.

Schieffer: May I ask you, you know, during the Egyptian turmoil, there came a point when you said it was time for President Mubarak to go.

Obama: Right.

Schieffer: Some in your administration thought perhaps we should have waited a while on that. Do you have any regrets about that?

Obama: No, I don't because I think that America has to stand with democracy. The notion that we would have tanks run over those young people who were in Tahrir Square, that is not the kind of American leadership that John F. Kennedy talked about 50 years ago.

But what I've also said is that now that you have a democratically elected government in Egypt, that they have to make sure that they take responsibility for protecting religious minorities – and we have put significant pressure on them to make sure they're doing that – to recognize the rights of women, which is critical throughout the region. These countries can't develop if young women are not given the kind of education that they need.

They have to abide by their treaty with Israel. That is a red line for us, because not only is Israel's security at stake, but our security is at stake if that unravels.

They have to make sure that they're cooperating with us when it comes to

西弗： 您能快速回答一下吗，总统先生，因为我想问——

奥巴马： 好的，我会很快说完，你们刚刚听罗姆尼州长说他并没有不同看法，这是因为我们当前采取的举措都是必要的，即培养一个温和派叙利亚领导层，实现一个有效的过渡，以便将阿萨德赶下台。这就是我们所展现的领导力，而且在将来，我们仍将如此。

西弗： 请回答，埃及发生动乱期间，您说是时候要把穆巴拉克总统赶下台了。

奥巴马： 是的。

西弗： 您政府中的有一些人可能会认为您有些操之过急，您现在后悔吗？

奥巴马： 我不后悔，因为我认为美国必须与民主联系在一起。有人认为，我们应该用坦克镇压解放广场上抗议示威的年轻人，但这不是美国的领导方式，约翰·肯尼迪[①]早在50年前就说过。

我也曾说过，既然埃及有了民主政府，他们必须确保自己担负起保护宗教少数派的责任——我们对他们施压，保证他们做到这些——让他们承认女性的权利，这对这个地区至关重要，如果年轻女性不能接受所需要的教育，这些国家就不能发展壮大。

他们必须遵守和以色列的条约，这对我们来说是一条底线，因为一旦这个条约废止，不但以色列岌岌可危，我们的安全也会受到威胁。

---

① 1960年当选为美国总统，成为美国历史上最年轻的当选总统，也是美国历史上唯一信奉罗马天主教的总统和唯一获得普利策奖的总统。参见：http://baike.baidu.com。

counterterrorism. And we will help them with respect to developing their own economy, because ultimately, what's going to make the Egyptian revolution successful for the people of Egypt but also for the world is if those young people who gathered there are seeing opportunities. Their aspirations are similar to young people's here. They want jobs. They want to be able to make sure their kids are going to a good school. They want to make sure that they have a roof over their heads and that they have a – the prospects of a better life in the future.

And so one of the things that we've been doing is – is, for example, organizing entrepreneurship conferences with these Egyptians to – to give them a sense of how they can start rebuilding their economy in a way that's noncorrupt, that's transparent.

But what is also important for us to understand is – is that for America to be successful in this region, there are some things that we're going to have to do here at home as well. You know, one of the challenges over the last decade is we've done experiments in nation building in places like Iraq and Afghanistan. And we've neglected, for example, developing our own economy, our own energy sectors, our own education system. And it's very hard for us to project leadership around the world when we're not doing what we need to do here.

Schieffer: Governor Romney, I want to hear your response to that, but I would just ask you, would you have stuck with Mubarak?

Romney: No, I believe, as the president indicated and said at the time, that I supported his – his action there. I felt that – I wish we'd have had a better vision of the future. I wish that, looking back at the beginning of the president's term and even further back than that, that we'd have recognized that there was a growing energy and passion for freedom in that part of the world and that we would have worked more aggressively with our – our friend and with other friends in the region to have them make the transition towards a more representative form of government such that it didn't explode in the way it did. But once it exploded, I felt the same as the president did, which is these –

他们应与我们通力合作应对反恐，我们也会协助他们发展自己的经济，因为最终埃及革命能在国内国际取得成功的原因是，那里的年轻人能够发现机遇，他们的渴望和这里的年轻人一样，他们想要一份工作，他们想确保他们的孩子将来能上一所学校，希望有一个能够遮风挡雨的地方，希望能有一个更好的未来。

我们所做事情之一就是，例如，为埃及人召开创业会议，教他们通过廉洁透明的方式来重建他们的经济。

但是我们也必须知道，美国要想在那个地区取得成功，我们必须努力发展自己。你们知道，在过去10年我们面临的一个挑战就是，在诸如伊拉克、阿富汗等国家进行了国家重建试验，但我们却忽视了发展我们自己的经济，发展我们自己的能源，发展我们自己的教育体系。如果自身发展不利，那么我们就很难领导世界。

西弗： 罗姆尼州长，我想听听您对此问题的意见，但我只让您回答，您会一直纠结于穆巴拉克吗？

罗姆尼： 我认为不会，我同意总统的观点，也支持他的做法。我希望我们有个更加美好的未来。我希望，回顾奥巴马总统刚上任时，甚至更早的时候，我们都得承认，在那个地区，对自由的渴求正在高涨，我希望更加热情地和我们的盟友以及那个地区的其他盟友一道，帮助他们过渡到一个代表人民的政府，就不会像上届政府那样分崩离析。但是一旦政府倒台，我和奥巴马总统的感受一样，那就是埃及的大街小巷都充斥了自由的欢呼声，人们纷纷谈论我们的原则，说穆巴拉克的所作所为难以想象，我们绝对不支持他镇压人民。

these freedom voices in the – the streets of Egypt where the people who were speaking of our principles and the – the – President Mubarak had done things which were unimaginable, and the idea of him crushing his people was not something that we could possibly support.

Let me – let me step back and talk about what I think our mission has to be in the Middle East, and even more broadly, because our purpose is to make sure the world is more – is peaceful. We want a peaceful planet. We want people to be able to enjoy their lives and know they're going to have a bright and prosperous future and not be at war. That's our purpose. And the mantle of – of leadership for promoting the principles of peace has fallen to America. We didn't ask for it, but it's an honor that we have it.

But for us to be able to promote those principles of peace requires us to be strong, and that begins with a strong economy here at home, and unfortunately, the economy is not stronger. When the – when the – the president of Iraq – excuse me – of Iran, Ahmadinejad, says that our debt makes us not a great country, that's a frightening thing. The former chief of – chief of the Joints Chief of Staff said that – Admiral Mullen – said that our debt is the biggest national security threat we face. This – we have weakened our economy.

We need a strong economy. We need to have as well a strong military. Our military is second to none in the world. We're blessed with terrific soldiers and extraordinary technology and intelligence. But the idea of a trillion dollars in cuts through sequestration and budget cuts to the military would change that.

We need to have strong allies. Our association and – and connection with our allies is essential to America's strength. We're the – the great nation that has allies, 42 allies and friends around the world.

And finally, we have to stand by our principles. And if we're strong in each of those things, American influence will grow. But unfortunately, in nowhere in the world is America's influence greater today than it was four years ago.

Schieffer: All right.

让我回过头来，谈谈我们在中东乃至更广阔地域上的使命，因为我们的目标是保卫世界和平，我们想让世界更加和平，希望人们能够享受生活并且知道他们将会拥有一个更加光明、更加繁荣的未来，而不是战火连连的未来，这是我们的目的。领导促进和平的使命已经降临在美国身上，我们从未要求，但是我们深感荣幸。

我们想要推进那些和平原则，就必须变得强大，首当其冲的就是国内经济强盛，然而不幸的是，经济并没有变得更加强盛。当伊朗总统内贾德说我们的债务使我们不再强大时，那是一件可怕的事情。前参谋长联席会议主席马伦上将说，我们的债务是我们国家面临的最大安全威胁，债务问题已经削弱了我们的经济。

我们需要强盛的经济、强大的军队，我们的军队是举世无双的，拥有出色的士兵，领先的科技和情报。但是，扣押削减万亿美元、削减军事预算将会改变现状。

我们需要强大的盟友关系，和盟友的关系对美国来讲非常重要。我们在世界范围内有42个盟友，是一个广泛交友的大国。

最后，我们必须坚持我们的原则。如果我们方方面面都强大，美国的影响力就会攀升。但不幸的是，美国在世界各地的影响力都大不如四年前——

西弗：好的。

罗姆尼：那是因为我们在上述四个方面实力都减弱了。

Romney: And that's because we've become weaker on each of those four dimensions.

Schieffer: All right – perfect. You're going to get a chance to respond to that because that's a perfect segue into our next segment, and that is what is America's role in the world. And that is the question. What do each of you see as our role in the world? And I believe, Governor Romney, it's your turn to go first.

Romney: Well, I – I absolutely believe that America has a – a responsibility and the privilege of helping defend freedom and promote the principles that – that make the world more peaceful. And those principles include human rights, human dignity, free enterprise, freedom of expression, elections, because when there are elections, people tend to vote for peace. They don't vote for war. So we want to – to promote those principles around the world. We recognize that there are places of conflict in the world. We want to end those conflicts to the extent humanly possible. But in order to be able to fulfill our role in the world, America must be strong. America must lead.

And for that to happen, we have to strengthen our economy here at home. You can't have 23 million people struggling to get a job. You – you can't have an economy that over the last three years keeps slowing down its growth rate. You can't have kids coming out of college, half of whom can't find a job today, or a job that's commensurate with their college degree. We have to get our economy going.

And our military – we've got to strengthen our military long- term. We don't know what the world is going to throw at us down the road. We – we make decisions today in a military that – that will confront challenges we can't imagine.

In the 2000 debates there was no mention of terrorism, for instance. And a year later, 9/11 happened. So we have to make decisions based upon uncertainty. And that means a strong military. I will not cut our military budget.

We have to also stand by our allies. I think the tension that existed between Israel and the United States was very unfortunate. I think also that pulling our

430

西弗：好的——很好。您将有机会反驳，因为这个问题刚好可以进入下个部分，那就是美国在世界中扮演的角色。您们两个如何看待这个问题？我想罗姆尼州长，您先回答这个问题。

罗姆尼：好的，我完全同意美国有责任和特权帮助保卫自由，以及推广一些原则，从而让世界更加和平，这些原则包括人权、人的尊严、自由企业制度、言论自由、选举自由，因为当选举存在的时候，人们倾向于为和平投票，而非战争，所以我们想在全世界推广这些原则。世界上还存在有冲突的地区，我们想要尽可能人道地去结束这些战争。为了能够实现我们在世界上的角色，美国必须变得强大，必须起领导作用。

要实现这一点，得强化国内经济，您不能让2300万人在为就业挣扎——不能让经济在过去的三年里持续下滑，不能让半数大学毕业生找不到工作或找不到与他们学历匹配的工作，必须设法让经济运转起来。

必须从长远角度去强化我们的军力，我们无法预知国家将来会遇到什么困难。我们今天在军事策略方面所作的决定，是为了帮助我们去应对无法预知的挑战。

比如，2000年的总统辩论没有提到恐怖主义，仅在一年之后，就发生了"9·11"恐怖袭击事件。所以我们要未雨绸缪，而这意味着要有强大的军力，所以我不会削减军费开支。

我们也要支持我们的盟国，我认为以色列和美国之间的紧张局面实在令人唏嘘，我们的导弹防御项目撤出波兰非常可惜，这在某种程度上破坏了我们之间的友好关系。

missile defense program out of Poland in the way we was also unfortunate in terms of, if you will, disrupting the relationship in some ways that existed between us.

And then of course, with regards to standing for our principles, when – when the students took to the streets in Tehran and the people there protested, the Green Revolution occurred. For the president to be silent I thought was an enormous mistake. We have to stand for our principles, stand for our allies, stand for a strong military and stand for a stronger economy.

Schieffer: Mr. President.

Obama: America remains the one indispensable nation. And the world needs a strong America. And it is stronger now then when I came into office. Because we ended the war in Iraq, we were able to refocus our attention on not only the terrorist threat but also beginning a transition process in Afghanistan. It also allowed us to refocus on alliances and relationships that had been neglected for a decade.

And, Governor Romney, our alliances have never been stronger. In Asia, in Europe, in Africa, with Israel where we have unprecedented military and intelligence cooperation, including dealing with the Iranian threat. But what we also have been able to do is position ourselves so we can start rebuilding America.

And that's what my plan does: Making sure that we're bringing manufacturing back to our shores so that we're creating jobs here, as we've done with the auto industry, not rewarding companies that are shipping jobs overseas; making sure that we've got the best education system in the world, including retraining our workers for the jobs of tomorrow; doing everything we can to control our energy.

We've cut our oil imports to the lowest level in two decades because we've developed oil and natural gas, but we also have to develop clean energy technologies that will allow us to cut our exports in half by 2020. That's the kind of leadership that we need to show.

就捍卫我们的原则而言，当学生走上德黑兰街头，人们进行抗议示威，伊朗绿色革命爆发，总统却保持沉默，我认为这是一个极大的错误，我们应该站出来支持我们的原则、我们的盟友、一个强有力的军队、一个强健的经济。

西弗：总统先生，您的意见？

奥巴马：美国是一个不可或缺的国家，世界需要一个强大的美国。美国现在比我四年前就职时更加强大，因为我们结束了伊拉克战争，我们不仅能将注意力重新放在恐怖分子的威胁上，并且也开始了阿富汗的过渡进程，这也使得我们将重点重新放到我们忽视了10年之久的联盟和与其他国家的关系上来。

罗姆尼州长，现在我们的联盟比任何时候都要牢固。在亚洲、欧洲、非洲和以色列，我们进行了前所未有的军事和情报合作，包括应对伊朗的威胁。但我们也能够正确定位自己从而开始重建美国。

我的计划是：确保制造业岗位回流到美国，在美国创造制造业工作岗位，效仿汽车工业，而不是奖励那些把工作岗位输往海外的公司；确保我们的教育体制世界一流，包括重新培训我们员工，使之能够应对未来的工作；采取一切措施掌控我们自己的能源。

我们已经将石油的进口量降至20年来的最低点，因为我们开发了自己的石油和天然气，我们也要发展清洁能源技术，那将使得我们能够在2020年将进口量减少一半，这就是我们需要展现的领导力。

And we've got to make sure that we reduce our deficit. Unfortunately, Governor Romney's plan doesn't do it. We've got to do it in a responsible way, by cutting out spending we don't need but also asking the wealthiest to pay a little bit more. That way we can invest in the research and technology that's always kept us at the cutting edge.

Now Governor Romney has taken a different approach throughout this campaign. You know, both at home and abroad, he has proposed wrong and reckless policies. He's praised George Bush as good economic steward and Dick Cheney as somebody who shows great wisdom and judgment. And taking us back to those kinds of strategies that got us into this mess are not the way that we are going to maintain leadership in the 21st century.

Schieffer: Governor Romney, wrong and reckless policies?

Romney: I've got a policy for the future and agenda for the future. And when it comes to our economy here at home, I know what it takes to create 12 million new jobs and rising take- home pay. And what we've seen over the last four years is something I don't want to see over the next four years. The – the president said by now we'd be at 5.4 percent unemployment. We're 9 million jobs short of that. I will get America working again and see rising take- home pay again. And I'll do it with five simple steps.

Number one, were going to have North American energy independence. We're going to do it by taking full advantage of oil, coal, gas, nuclear and our renewables.

Number two, we're going to increase our trade. Trade grows about 12 percent per year. It doubles about every – every five or – or so years. We can do better than that, particularly in Latin America. The opportunities for us in Latin America we have just not taken advantage of fully.

As a matter of fact, Latin America's economy is almost as big as the economy of China. We're all focused on China. Latin America is a huge opportunity for us: time zone, language opportunities.

同时，我们已经采取措施以确保我们减少赤字。不幸的是，罗姆尼州长的计划并不奏效，我们要以一种负责任的方式来实现这一点，通过削减不必要的开支，让更富人多支付一点税款，那样我们就可以投资于研究和技术，让我们时刻走在时代的前沿。

罗姆尼州长在竞选期间，则采取了截然不同的方法，你们知道，就国内外议题提出了错误的、不计后果的政策。他赞扬小布什[①] 是一个很好的经济管理者，迪克·切尼[②] 是非明断，智慧过人，他让我们重新回到那些让我们陷入混乱的策略，这不是我们在21世纪保持领导能力的方法。

西弗：罗姆尼州长，您对错误和不计后果的政策的回应是什么？

罗姆尼：我有应对未来的政策和议程。就国内的经济而言，我知道要采取什么措施来创造1200万个就业岗位，提高实际收入。我不想在未来四年看到四年前的老样子。奥巴马总统曾说到目前为止失业率达到5.4%，但是我们现在距离这个目标还缺900万个就业岗位。我将重振美国的工作机会，提高实际收入，我们将用五个简单的步骤来实现这个目标：

第一，实现北美能源独立，充分利用石油、煤炭、天然气、核能和可再生能源。

第二，增加贸易，让贸易年增长率达到12%，每隔五年翻一倍，我们可以做得比这个更好，尤其是在拉美地区，我们并没有充分利用好拉美的机遇。

实际上，拉美国家的经济总量与中国的经济总量相当，我们太过于把重点放在中国了，拉美对我们来说是一个巨大的机遇：时区和语言的便利。

---

① 乔治·沃克·布什为美国第43任总统。
② 迪克·切尼是乔治·沃克·布什任内的美国副总统。

Number three, we're going to have to have training programs that work for our workers and schools that finally put the parents and the teachers and the kids first, and the teachers union's going to have to go behind.

And then we're going to have to get to a balanced budget. We can't expect entrepreneurs and businesses large and small to take their life savings or their companies' money and invest in America if they think we're headed to the road to Greece. And that's where we're going right now unless we finally get off this spending and borrowing binge. And I'll get us on track to a balanced budget.

And finally, number five, we've got to champion small business. Small business is where – where jobs come from. Two-thirds of our jobs come from small businesses. New business formation is down to the lowest level in 30 years under this administration. I want to bring it back and get back good jobs and rising take-home pay.

Obama: Well, let's talk about what we need to compete. First of all, Governor Romney talks about small businesses, but Governor, when you were in Massachusetts, small businesses' development ranked about 48, I think, out of 50 states, in Massachusetts, because the policies that you're promoting actually don't help small businesses. And the way you define small businesses include folks at the very top. They include you and me. That's not the kind of small business promotion we need.

But – but let's take an example that we know is going to make a difference 21st century, and that's our education policy. We didn't have a lot of chance to talk about this in the last debate. You know, under my leadership, what we've done is reformed education, working with governors, 46 states. We've seen progress and gains in schools that were having a terrible time, and they're starting to finally make progress. And what I now want to do is to hire more teachers, especially in math and science, because we know that we've fallen behind when it comes to math and science. And those teachers can make a difference.

Now, Governor Romney, when you were asked by teachers whether or

第三，设置对工人有利的培训项目，我们的学校要将家长、教师、孩子放在首位，教师工会其次。

然后，要实现预算平衡。我们不能期待企

业家和大小型企业主们把毕生的积蓄和公司财产拿出来投资于美国，因为他们认为我们可能会重蹈希腊的路子，除非我们现在实现预算平衡，否则我们正在走向希腊之路。而我将使我们走向预算平衡的路径。

第五点，我们将辅助小型企业，小型企业是就业的来源，我们三分之二的工作岗位来自于小企业。在奥巴马政府的领导下，创业数量已经降至30年来的最低点。我想提高这一数字，让好的工作岗位，提高实际收入。

奥巴马：好吧，让我们来谈谈竞争之处。首先，罗姆尼州长谈到小企业，但是州长，当您在马萨诸塞州时，由于您推动的政策事实上并没有帮助小企业，小企业的发展在50个州中排名第48位。当您定义小企业时，也包括了那些收入最高层的人士，也许还包括了像我和您这样的人，而这不是我们需要扶持的那种小企业。

让我举个例子，一个确信能在21世纪给美国带来变革的例子——教育政策。在上一次的辩论中，我们没有过多地谈论这个话题。大家知道，在我的领导下，我们对46个州进行了改革，已经看到那些曾经落后的学校取得了一些进步和收获。现在我想要雇佣更多的老师，特别是数学、科学领域的老师，这些老师能够起到一些积极作用。

not this would help the economy grow, you said, this isn't going to help the economy grow. When you were asked about reduced class sizes, you said class sizes don't make a difference. But I tell you, if you talk to teachers, they will tell you it does make a difference.

And if we've got math teachers who are able to provide the kind of support that they need for our kids, that's what's going to determine whether or not the new businesses are created here. Companies are going to locate here depending on whether we've got the most highly skilled workforce. And the kinds of budget proposals that you've put forward – when we don't ask either you or me to pay a dime more in terms of reducing the deficit, but instead we slash support for education, that's undermining our long-term competitiveness. That is not good for America's position in the world. And the world notices.

Schieffer: Let me get back to foreign policy.

Romney: Well —

Schieffer: Can I just get back —

Romney: Well, I need to speak a moment if you'll let me, Bob —

Schieffer: OK.

Romney: – just about education, because I'm – I'm so proud of the state that I had the chance to be governor of. We have, every two years, tests that look at how well our kids are doing. Fourth graders and eighth graders are tested in English and math. While I was governor, I was proud that our fourth graders came out number one of all 50 states in English and then also in math, and our eighth graders number one in English and also in math – first time one state had been number one in all four measures. How did we do that?

Well, Republicans and Democrats came together on a bipartisan basis to put in place education that focused on having great teachers in the classroom. And that was –

Obama: Ten years earlier –

Romney: That was – that was what allowed us to become the number one

罗姆尼州长，当您被老师们问及，这能否帮助实现经济的增长，您说，这不能。当您被问及减少班级规模的问题，您说班级规模的大小不会有什么差别。但是我告诉您，如果您和老师交谈过，他们会告诉您确实是有差别的。

如果数学老师能够提供给学生一些必要的支持，这将对新企业能否在这里创建起到决定性作用，因为它取决于我们是否具有高素质的劳动力。另外，您所提出的那种预算——你我都不会因为削减赤字而多付一个子儿——，相反，我们却要削减对教育的支出，那会破坏我们的长期竞争力，对美国的国际地位也十分不利，世界各国都将注意到这一点。

西弗： 让我们回到外交政策。

罗姆尼： 好的——

西弗： 我们能回到——

罗姆尼： 好的，我需要说一下，如你允许，鲍伯——

西弗： 好的。

罗姆尼： ——就谈一下教育，能够成为马萨诸塞州的州长，我引以为傲。我们每两年会对学生的表现进行一次测试，并对四年级和八年级的学生进行英语和数学测试。当我担任职州长时，在英语和数学考试中，我们州四年级学生的成绩在50个州中名列第一，我引以为傲。八年级的学生也是———个州能独占四科鳌头这还是第一次，我们如何做到这一点的呢？

好，共和党人、民主党人团结起来，抛开党派分歧，落实教育问题，重点就是要请好老师上课。那就是——

奥巴马： 十年前——

罗姆尼： 那就是我们学生的成绩名列前茅的原因。

439

state in the nation. And this is – and we were –

Obama: But that was 10 years before you took office.

Romney: And we – absolutely.

Schieffer: Gentlemen –

Obama: And then you cut education spending when you came into office.

Romney: The first – the first – and we kept our schools number one in the nation. They're still number one today. And the principles that we've put in place – we also gave kids not just a graduation exam that – that determined whether they were up to the skills needed to – to be able to compete, but also, if they graduated in the top quarter of their class, they got a four-year tuition-free ride at any Massachusetts public institution of higher learning.

Obama: That happened – that happened before you came into office.

Schieffer: Governor –

Romney: That was actually mine, actually, Mr. President. You got that fact wrong.

Schieffer: Let me – I want to try to shift it, because we have heard some of this in the other debates. Governor, you say you want a bigger military. You want a bigger Navy. You don't want to cut defense spending. What I want to ask you, we're talking about financial problems in this country. Where are you going to get the money?

Romney: Well, let's – let's come back and talk about the military, but all the way – all the way through. First of all, I'm going through, from the very beginning, we're going to cut about 5 percent of the discretionary budget excluding military. That's number one. All right?

Schieffer: But can you do this without driving us deeper into debt?

Romney: The good news is, I'll be happy to have you take a look. Come on our website, you'll look at how we get to a balanced budget within eight to 10 years. We do it by getting - by reducing spending in a whole series of programs. By the way, number one I get rid of is "Obamacare." There are a

440

奥巴马：但是，那是您出任州长10年之前发生的事。

罗姆尼：我们——的确。

西弗：先生们——

奥巴马：您就任后还削减了教育经费。

罗姆尼：首先，我们的学校一直在全国名列前茅，现在也是如此。我们引入的原则——不仅仅是让学生参加毕业考试，以便衡量他们是否具备所需要的技能以进程竞争。同时，如果他们以全年级前四分之一的成绩毕业，他们将获得马萨诸塞州任何一所公立高等学府四年的免费大学教育。

奥巴马：这是您上任之前的事了。

西弗：州长——

罗姆尼：这的确是我任期内发生的事情，总统先生，您搞错了事实。

西弗：请允许我转换一下话题，因为我们已经在别的讨论中了听到这个观点。州长，您说您希望有一支规模更大的军队，一支更强大的海军，不希望削减国防开支。我们现在讨论国家的财政问题，请您回答，我们从哪里得到这笔费用？

罗姆尼：好，那就让我们回过头来，讨论军队问题，详细地谈一谈，首先，我要从最开始的部分谈起，我们将削减大约5%的弹性预算，但不包括军费在内。这是第一位的，好吗？

西弗：但是您能保证做到这点而不使我们陷入更多的债务吗？

罗姆尼：好消息是，我很乐意让你们看看，登录我们的网站，你可以看到我们将如何在8到10年内实现预算平衡，我们通过削减许多开支项目来做到这一点。顺便说一句，首先就是废除"奥巴马医改"。奥巴马医改在很多方面听起来不错，但开诚布公地说，我们无力承担。这种方案并非一个理想的政策，不具有经济可承受性，当选之后，我会取消这个政策；尽可能以人道的方式，取消它。我们会逐步取消没有必要的政策。

number of things that sound good but, frankly, we just can't afford them. And that one doesn't sound good, and it's not affordable, so I get rid of that one from day one; to the extent humanly possible, we get that out. We take program after program that we don't absolutely have to have and we get rid of them.

Number two, we take some programs that we are going to keep, like Medicaid, which is a program for the poor. We're – take that health care program for the poor, and we give it to the states to run because states run these programs more efficiently. As a governor, I thought, please, give me this program.

I can run this more efficiently than the federal government. And states, by the way, are proving it. States like Arizona, Rhode Island have taken these Medicaid dollars, have shown they can run these programs more cost effectively.

Obama: Bob —

Romney: So I want to do those two things that gets us – it gets us to a balanced budget with eight in – eight to 10 years.

Obama: Bob —

Romney: Let's go back to the military, though.

Schieffer: Well, that's what I'm trying to find out about.

Romney: Let's talk about the military.

Obama: You should have answered the first question. Look, Governor Romney's called for $5 trillion of tax cuts that he says he's going to pay for by closing deductions. Now, the math doesn't work but he continues to claim that he's going to do it. He then wants to spend another $2 trillion on military spending that our military's not asking for.

Now, keep in mind that our military spending has gone up every single year that I've been in office. We spend more on our military than the next 10 countries combined – China, Russia, France, the United – United Kingdom, you name it, next 10. And what I did was work with our Joint Chiefs of Staff to think about what are we going to need in the future to make sure that we are safe? And that's the budget that we've put forward.

第二，但我们还会继续有些项目，比如面向穷人的医疗补助。我们会把这个针对穷人的医疗计划，交给州政府负责，因为州政府能够更加有效地运行这些计划。作为一名州长，我当时就想，拜托把这个项目交给我吧。

我能够比联邦政府更有效地推行这项计划，顺便说一下，州政府正在证明这一点，一些州，比如亚利桑那州、罗德岛州拿到了医疗补助的资金，已经证明他们在推行类似的项目时更具有成本效益。

奥巴马： 鲍伯——

罗姆尼： 做到这两件事，我们就能在8到10年内实现预算平衡。

奥巴马： 鲍伯——

罗姆尼： 让我们谈一下军费问题。

西弗： 好的，那也是我想说的。

罗姆尼： 让我们谈谈军费问题。

奥巴马： 您应该先回答第一个问题。大家看，罗姆尼州长要求减税5万亿美元，他声称将通过结束课税减免对此进行弥补。现在这在数学上是行不通的，但是他仍然声称他会这样做。随后，他将额外增加2万亿美元的不必要的军费支出。

现在要谨记，在我执政期间，军费开支每年都在上涨，我们的军费开支比中国、俄罗斯、法国、英国等其他10个国家加起来还要多。我所做的是和参谋长联席会议考虑我们将来需要采取什么措施来确保我们的安全。

But what you can't do is spend $2 trillion in additional military spending that the military is not asking for, $5 trillion on tax cuts, you say that you're going to pay for it by closing loopholes and deductions without naming what those loopholes and deductions are, and then somehow you're also going to deal with the deficit that we've already got. The math simply doesn't work.

But when it comes to our military, what we have to think about is not, you know, just budgets, we got to think about capabilities. We need to be thinking about cybersecurity. We need to be thinking about space. That's exactly what our budget does, but it's driven by strategy. It's not driven by politics. It's not driven by members of Congress and what they would like to see. It's driven by what are we going to need to keep the American people safe.

That's exactly what our budget does. And it also then allows us to reduce our deficit, which is a significant national security concern because we've got to make sure that our economy is strong at home so that we can project military power overseas.

Romney: Bob, I'm pleased that I've balanced budgets. I was in the world of business for 25 years.

If you didn't balance your budget, you went out of business. I went to the Olympics that was out of balance, and we got it on balance and made a success there. I had the chance to be governor of a state. Four years in a row, Democrats and Republicans came together to balance the budget. We cut taxes 19 times, balanced our budget. The president hasn't balanced a budget yet. I expect to have the opportunity to do so myself.

Schieffer: All right.

Romney: I – I'm going to be able to balance the budget. Let's talk about military spending, and that's this. Our Navy –

Schieffer: About 30 seconds.

Romney: Our Navy is older – excuse me – our Navy is smaller now than any time since 1917. The Navy said they needed 313 ships to carry out their

但是，我们不能增加额外的2万亿美元的不必要的军费开支，也不能把5万亿美元用于减税，您说会通过消除漏洞和课税减免来弥补，但是您并未例举出这些漏洞和课税减免的名目，然后您还要处理财政赤字的问题，这在数学上行不通。

说到军队，大家知道，我们应该考虑的不只是预算，我们还应该考虑自身的承受能力。我们需要考虑网络安全问题，有关太空探索的问题。这才是实际的预算，但这要靠策略驱使，而非政治、国会议员以及他们的愿望的驱使，驱使这些政策的出发点是希望确保美国人民的安全。

这才是实际的预算，它将促使我们减少赤字，赤字的确是一个重要的国家安全问题，因为我们必须确保国内经济的强大，以便我们可以向海外部署军事力量。

罗姆尼： 鲍伯，我很高兴我曾实现过预算平衡，我曾在商界打拼25年。

如果不能做到预算平衡，就无法做生意。那届奥运会预算失衡，我帮助他们实现平衡并且取得成功。后来我当上了州长，连续4年民主党和共和党都通力合作，努力实现预算平衡。我们曾经19次减税，平衡预算，但总统尚且还没有平衡预算，我希望给我这样一个机会来实现它。

西弗： 好的。

罗姆尼： 我有能力平衡预算。让我们讨论一下军费，那就是，我们的海军——

西弗： 您有30秒的时间。

罗姆尼： 我们的海军已经老化——抱歉——规模小于1917年。海军方面表示，他们需要313艘军舰来执行任务，而我们当前的数量不到285艘。如果我们继续削减军费开支，军舰的数量不足200艘，这简直无法接受，我想确保我们的海军能有足够的军舰。

mission. We're now down to 285. We're headed down to the – to the low 200s if we go through with sequestration. That's unacceptable to me. I want to make sure that we have the ships that are required by our Navy.

Our Air Force is older and smaller than any time since it was founded in 1947. We've changed for the first time since FDR[①]. We – since FDR we had the – we've always had the strategy of saying we could fight in two conflicts at once. Now we're changing to one conflict.

Look, this, in my view, is the highest responsibility of the president of the United States, which is to maintain the safety of the American people. And I will not cut our military budget by a trillion dollars, which is the combination of the budget cuts that the president has as well as the sequestration cuts. That, in my view, is – is – is making our future less certain and less secure. I won't do it.

Obama: Bob, I just need to comment on this. First of all, the sequester is not something that I proposed. It's something that Congress has proposed. It will not happen. The budget that we're talking about is not reducing our military spending. It's maintaining it.

But I think Governor Romney maybe hasn't spent enough time looking at how our military works. You – you mentioned the Navy, for example, and that we have fewer ships than we did in 1916. Well, Governor, we also have fewer horses and bayonets – because the nature of our military's changed. We have these things called aircraft carriers where planes land on them. We have these ships that go underwater, nuclear submarines.

And so the question is not a game of Battleship where we're counting ships. It's – it's what are our capabilities. And so when I sit down with the secretary of the Navy and the Joint Chiefs of Staff, we determine how are we going to be best able to meet all of our defense needs in a way that also keeps

---

① Franklin Delano Roosevelt，富兰克林·德拉诺·罗斯福的简称。美国第32位总统，美国历史上唯一蝉联四届（第四届未任满）的总统。

我们的空军也是自1947年建军以来最老化而且规模最小的一届。这是我们自富兰克林·德拉诺·罗斯福以后的第一次政策调整。罗斯福之后，我们的政策一直是保证两地同时开战，现在军力则只能处理一桩战事。

看吧，我认为美国总统的最大职责就是确保美国人的安全，我不会通过像总统那样削减预算加上扣押预算，以此来削减1万亿美元军费预算，在我看来，这会让我们的未来更加不确定，更加不安，我不会那样做。

奥巴马：鲍伯，我需要对此作出评论。首先，扣押预算并不是我提出的，是国会提议的，这并不会变成现实。我们讨论的不是减少军队的开支，而是要确保它的开支。

但我认为，罗姆尼州长，您可能没有时间仔细研究我们的军队的运作情况。比如，您提到了海军，以及军舰数量不及1916年。好，州长先生，我们的军马和刺刀的数量同样也不及过去——因为我们军队的性质发生了变化。我们现在拥有可以停飞机的航空母舰，有可以潜水的舰艇，核潜艇。

所以，问题在于我们不是在进行战舰游戏，只依靠船只的数量，关键问题是——我们的战斗力。当我和海军部长及参谋长联席会议坐下来谈话时，我们讨论的是如何最大程度地满足国防需要，让军队士气不灭，讨论的是在退役老兵返乡时，如何给他们提供所需要的帮助。您所提出的预算并没有反映这一点，因为它并不奏效。

faith with our troops, that also makes sure that our veterans have the kind of support that they need when they come home. And that is not reflected in the kind of budget that you're putting forward, because it just don't work.

Schieffer: All right.

Obama: And you know, we've visited the website quite a bit. And it still doesn't work.

Schieffer: A lot to cover. I'd like – I'd like to move to the next segment: red lines, Israel and Iran. Would either of you – and you'll have two minutes, and President Obama, you have the first go at this one. Would either of you be willing to declare that an attack on Israel is an attack on the United States, which of course is the same promise that we give to our close allies like Japan? And if you made such a declaration, would not that deter Iran? It's certainly deterred the Soviet Union for a long, long time when we made that – when we made that promise to our allies.

Mr. President.

Obama: Well, first of all, Israel is a true friend. It is our greatest ally in the region. And if Israel is attacked, America will stand with Israel. I've made that clear throughout my presidency. And –

Schieffer: So you're saying we've already made that declaration?

Obama: I will stand with Israel if they are attacked. And this is the reason why, working with Israel, we have created the strongest military and intelligence cooperation between our two countries in history. In fact, this week we'll be carrying out the largest military exercise with Israel in history, this very week.

But to the issue of Iran, as long as I'm president of the United States, Iran will not get a nuclear weapon.

I've made that clear when I came into office. We then organized the strongest coalition and the strongest sanctions against Iran in history, and it is crippling their economy. Their currency has dropped 80 percent. Their oil production has plunged to the lowest level since they were fighting a war with

西弗：好的。

奥巴马：大家知道，我们经常访问您的网站，但您的预算并不起任何作用。

西弗：要讨论的东西太多了，我想进入下一部分，那就是："红线"之争、以色列和伊朗。你们各有两分钟的时间，奥巴马总统您先来，您是否愿意宣布对以色列的袭击就是对美国的袭击？就如同我们对盟国日本的承诺一样？如果你们发表了那样的声明，不就恰好威慑到伊朗了吗？多年前，我们对盟友作出了那样的承诺，威慑了苏联很长时间。

奥巴马：好的，首先，以色列是一个挚友，也是我们在那个地区最伟大的盟友。如果以色列遭到袭击，美国会同以色列并肩作战，在我的任期内，已很清晰地表明了这一点。而且——

西弗：您的意思是说，我们已经发表了那样的声明？

奥巴马：如果以色列遭到袭击，我会同以色列并肩作战，因为从历史上看，我们与以色列已经建立了两国之间最强大的军事和情报合作。实际上，这周我们将和以色列进行历史上最大规模的军事演习，就在本周。

关于伊朗问题，只要我是美国的总统，伊朗就不会获得核武器。

我在就任伊始就说明了这一点，之后我们建立了有史以来反对伊朗的最强大的联盟和对伊朗最严厉的制裁，这正在摧毁他们的经济，他们的货币已经跌了80%，他们的石油生产量已经降至20年前两伊战争以来的最低点，他们的经济已经破败不堪。

Iraq 20 years ago. So their economy is in a shambles.

And the reason we did this is because a nuclear Iran is a threat to our national security and it's threat to Israel's national security. We cannot afford to have a nuclear arms race in the most volatile region of the world. Iran's a state sponsor of terrorism, and for them to be able to provide nuclear technology to nonstate actors – that's unacceptable. And they have said that they want to see Israel wiped off the map.

So the work that we've done with respect to sanctions now offers Iran a choice. They can take the diplomatic route and end their nuclear program or they will have to face a united world and a United States president, me, who said we're not going to take any options off the table.

The disagreement I have with Governor Romney is that during the course of this campaign he's often talked as if we should take premature military action. I think that would be a mistake because when I've sent young men and women into harm's way, I always understand that that is the last rest, not the first resort.

Schieffer: Two minutes.

Romney: Well, first of all, I – I want to underscore the – the same point the president made, which is that if I'm president of the United States, when I'm president of the United States, we will stand with Israel. And – and if Israel is attacked, we have their back, not just diplomatically, not just culturally, but militarily. That's number one.

Number two, with regards to – to Iran and the threat of Iran, there's no question but that a nuclear Iran, a nuclear-capable Iran, is unacceptable to America.

It presents a threat not only to our friends, but ultimately a threat to us to have Iran have nuclear material, nuclear weapons that could be used against us or used to be threatening to us.

It's also essential for us to understand what our mission is in Iran, and that is to dissuade Iran from having a nuclear weapon through peaceful and diplomatic means. And crippling sanctions are something I'd called for five

我们这么做，是因为一个拥有核武器的伊朗对我们的国家安全来说是一个威胁，对以色列的国家安全也是威胁，若在世界上最不稳定的地区，来一场核军备竞赛，我们承受不起。伊朗是恐怖主义的赞助国，如果他们能够向非国家人员提供核技术，那是无法接受的。伊朗还说，希望以色列从地图上消失。

所以现在我们的制裁给伊朗提供了一次选择的机会，他们可以采取外交措施并终止核武器计划。否则，他们要面对的是一个团结起来的世界和一个美国总统，也就是我，我曾经说过没有讨价还价的余地。

我和罗姆尼州长的分歧在于，在这次竞选期间，他经常说，我们应该提前发起军事行动，我认为这是错误的，因为我把青年男女送上战场，那是不得已而为之，绝非首选。

西弗：您有两分钟时间作出回应。

罗姆尼：好的，第一，我想强调刚才总统的观点，如果我是美国总统，如果我当上了美国总统，以色列受袭时我们将与它并肩作战，不仅是在外交上，也在文化上，军事上，这是第一点。

第二，关于伊朗及其对美国的威胁。毫无疑问，一个拥有核武器的伊朗，具有核能力的伊朗，美国是无法接受的。

如果伊朗拥有用来对付我们或对我们构成威胁的核材料、核武器，那将不仅威胁到我们的盟友，也会威胁到我们自身。

理解我们在伊朗的使命十分重要，即用和平和外交手段去劝阻伊朗拥有核武器。我五年前在以色列的海尔兹利亚会议上的讲话中就呼吁对伊朗进行严厉制裁，当时我列出了七个步骤。

years ago when I was in Israel speaking at the Herzliya Conference. I laid out seven steps.

Crippling sanctions were number one. And they do work. You're seeing it right now in the economy. It's absolutely the right thing to do to have crippling sanctions. I'd have put them in place earlier, but it's good that we have them.

Number two, something I would add today is I would tighten those sanctions. I would say that ships that carry Iranian oil can't come into our ports. I imagine the EU would agree with us as well. Not only ships couldn't, I'd say companies that are moving their oil can't, people who are trading in their oil can't. I would tighten those sanctions further.

Secondly, I'd take on diplomatic isolation efforts. I'd make sure that Ahmadinejad is indicted under the Genocide Convention. His words amount to genocide incitation. I would indict him for it. I would also make sure that their diplomats are treated like the pariah they are around the world, the same way we treated the apartheid diplomats of South Africa.

We need to increase pressure time and time again on Iran because anything other than a – a – a solution to this which says – which stops this nuclear folly of theirs is unacceptable to America. And of course, a military action is the last resort. It is something one would only, only consider if all of the other avenues had been – had been tried to their full extent.

Schieffer: Let me ask both of you, there – as you know, there are reports that Iran and the United States, as part of an international group, have agreed in principle to talks about Iran's nuclear program. What is the deal if there are such talks? What is the deal that you would accept? Mr. President.

Obama: Well, first of all, those were reports in the newspaper. They are not true. But our goal is to get Iran to recognize it needs to give up its nuclear program and abide by the U.N. resolutions that have been in place, because they have the opportunity to re-enter the community of nations, and we would welcome that. There are – there are people in Iran who have the same

严厉制裁是第一步，这的确起到作用了，经济上的影响你们也看到了，严厉制裁是完全正确的。如果是我，我会更早一点对伊朗实施制裁，效果会更加明显。

第二步，我想补充的是加紧制裁。首先，让那些运载伊朗石油的船只，不得进入我们的港口，我想欧盟也会同意这么做，不仅船只不能进港，那些运输他们石油的公司，与他们做石油贸易的人，也都不允许进入港口。我会实施更加严厉的制裁。

其次，我会采取外交孤立，我要确保内贾德因《防止及惩治灭绝种族罪公约》① 而受到起诉，他的言辞已经是在煽动种族屠杀，我会起诉他这一条。同时，我也会让他们的外交官在全球受到次等待遇，就像我们处理种族隔离时期的南非外交官那样。

我需要不断对伊朗施压，因为除了这个解决方法之外，其他阻止他们的核闹剧的方法美国都无法接受。当然，军事行动是最后的选择，只有当所有途径都尝试无效之后，才会采取军事行动这一步。

西弗： 请你们来回答一下——大家知道，有报道称，伊朗和美国进行了小范围的国际接触，已经同意就伊朗核项目举行会谈，若有此事，你们会达成什么样的协议呢？你们会接受怎样的协议？总统先生，您先来谈一下。

奥巴马： 好的，首先，这些报纸上的报道并不属实。但是我们的目标，是让伊朗意识到，必须放弃核项目并遵守一致通过的联合国决议，因为这样他们才有重新进入国际社会的机会，我们对此也表示欢迎。伊朗地区的人民也和世界上的其他人民一样，渴望更好的生活。我们希望他们的领导人作出正确的决策，但我们能够接受的协议是他们终止核项目，这非常的直截了当。

---

① 指 Convention on the Prevention and Punishment of the Crime of Genocide，意为《防止及惩治灭绝种族罪公约》，已经在1951年1月12日正式生效。

aspirations as people all around the world, for a better life. And we hope that their leadership takes the right decision. But the deal we'll accept is, they end their nuclear program. It's very straightforward.

And you know, I'm glad that Governor Romney agrees with the steps that we're taking. You know, there have been times, Governor, frankly, during the course of this campaign, where it sounded like you thought that you'd do the some things we did, but you'd say them louder and somehow that that would make a difference, and it turns out that the work involved in setting up these crippling sanctions is painstaking; it's meticulous. We started from the day we got into office.

And the reason it was so important – and this is a testament to how we've restored American credibility and strength around the world – is we had to make sure that all the countries participated, even countries like Russia and China, because if it's just us that are imposing sanctions, we've had sanctions in place for a long time. It's because we got everybody to agree that Iran is seeing so much pressure. And we've got to maintain that pressure.

There is a deal to be had, and that is that they abide by the rules that have already been established; they convince the international community they are not pursuing a nuclear program; there are inspections that are very intrusive. But over time, what they can do is regain credibility. In the meantime, though, we're not going to let up the pressure until we have clear evidence that that takes place.

And one last thing. I'm – just to make this point: The clock is ticking. We're not going to allow Iran to perpetually engage in negotiations that lead nowhere. And I've been very clear to them, you know, because of the intelligence coordination that we do with a range of countries, including Israel, we have a sense of when they would get breakout capacity, which means that we would not be able to intervene in time to stop their nuclear program, and that clock is ticking.

Schieffer: All right.

Obama: And we're going to make sure that if they do not meet the demands of the international community, then we are going to take all options

你们知道，我也很高兴，罗姆尼州长同意我们所采取的措施。大家知道，州长，坦白地说，在这次竞选期间，您和我们做的事情分明一样，但您会喊得更响亮，好像有所不同。但事实是，针对伊朗的严厉制裁措施实施起来是十分艰苦、严谨的。从我上任伊始，就开始采取措施。

因为这非常重要，对我们如何恢复美国在世界各地的可信度和力量而言，非常重要。我们要确保所有的国家都参与其中，甚至包括俄罗斯、中国这样的国家，因为如果只是我们单方面采取制裁措施，我们早就开始落实制裁措施了，这是因为我们想让所有人都同意制裁，让伊朗面临更多的压力，我们需要保持这样的压力。

我们要达成的协议就是，伊朗必须遵守已经建立的规则；他们必须说服国际社会，他们不再打算实施核计划；他们要经历非常严格的审查。不过随着时间的流逝，他们能做的是重新恢复信誉，同时，我们也不会放松施压，直到我们拥有非常确凿的证据说明他们已经放弃了核项目。

最后一点，我只想说明一下，时间紧迫，我们不会允许伊朗无休止地参与毫无结果的谈判，在这一点上我的立场非常明确，大家知道，由于我们和包括以色列在内的一些国家进行情报协调，我们能够知道他们何时取得突破，这意味着那时我们将不能及时干涉以制止他们的核计划，并且时间紧迫。

西弗：好的。

奥巴马：如果他们不服从国际社会的要求，我们将采取所有必要措施以确保他们不拥有核武器。

necessary to make sure they don't have a nuclear weapon.

Schieffer: Governor.

Romney: I think from the very beginning, one of the challenges we've had with Iran is that they have looked at this administration and – and felt that the administration was not as strong as it needed to be. I think they saw weakness where they had expected to find American strength.

And I say that because from the very beginning, the president, in his campaign some four years ago, said he'd meet with all the world's worst actors in his first year. He'd – he'd sit down with Chavez and – and Kim Jong-Il, with Castro and with – with President Ahmadinejad of – of Iran. And – and I think they looked and thought, well, that's an unusual honor to receive from the president of the United States.

And then the president began what I've called an apology tour of going to – to various nations in the Middle East and – and criticizing America. I think they looked at that and saw weakness. Then when there were dissidents in the streets of Tehran, the Green Revolution, holding signs saying, is America with us, the president was silent. I think they noticed that as well. And I think that when the president said he was going to create daylight between ourselves and Israel that – that they noticed that as well.

All of these things suggested, I think, to the Iranian mullahs that, hey, you know, we can keep on pushing along here; we can keep talks going on, but we're just going to keep on spinning centrifuges. Now there are some 10,000 centrifuges spinning uranium, preparing to – to create a – a – a – a nuclear threat to the United States and to the world.

That's unacceptable for us, and – and – and it's essential for a president to show strength from the very beginning to make it very clear what is acceptable and not acceptable. And an Iranian nuclear program is not acceptable to us. They must not develop nuclear capability. And the way to make sure they understand that is by having from the very beginning the tightest sanctions possible. They

西弗: 州长,您的意见。

罗姆尼: 我认为,一开始伊朗对我们造成的一个挑战是,他们打量了一下奥巴马政府的策略,并认为这个政府不够强大,我想他们看到了美国实力的弱点,这正是他们曾经的期望。

我之所以这么说是因为总统在四年前参加竞选的时候,就说他将在就任的一年时间内,会见世界上表现最糟的领导人,他将与查韦斯①、金正日②、卡斯特罗③、伊朗总统内贾德进行会谈。我想这些人看到这一切之后会想,这是来自美国总统的特别荣誉。

随后总统开始前往中东各国,发表批评美国的言论,我称其为道歉之旅。我想他们从中看到了美国的脆弱之处。德黑兰发生绿色革命,抗议者手上举着标语,美国和我们同心协力吗?总统保持了沉默,我想他们也注意到了这一点。我认为总统曾宣称他将在我们和以色列之间创造曙光,我想他们也注意到了这一点。

我认为所有的这一切都向伊朗的毛拉④们表明,你们知道,我们可以继续沿着这条路前进;继续进行会谈,继续运转离心机,目前伊朗已经有近一万台离心机在加工铀,准备威胁美国和全世界。

这是我们无法接受的,总统有必要一开始就对伊朗非常明确地表明,什么是可以接受的,什么是不可以接受的。并且说明我们不接受伊朗进行核项目,他们不能发展核实力,确保他们明白这一点的方式,就是从一开始就尽可能实施严厉的制裁措施。我们应该强化制裁,必须让我们的外交孤立措施更加严厉。当我们起诉内贾德时,我们需要尽可能地向他们施加最大的压力,因为这样的话,我们就不需要采取军事行动了。

---

① 乌戈·查韦斯,全名乌戈·拉斐尔·查韦斯·弗里亚斯,是第53任委内瑞拉总统。

② 金正日是朝鲜前领导人金日成的长子,是朝鲜民主主义人民共和国的第二代最高领导人。

③ 菲德尔·亚历杭德罗·卡斯特罗·鲁斯,古巴前最高领导人,杰出的马克思主义者,享誉世界的无产阶级革命家、政治家、思想家、军事家,是当今国际共产主义运动中德高望重的领导人。参见:http://baike.baidu.com。

④ 伊斯兰教内用于学者或宗教领袖的称号,特别是在中东和印度次大陆。现称毛拉者,多为宗教领袖。

need to be tightened. Our diplomatic isolation needs to be tougher. We need to indict Ahmadinejad. We need to put the pressure on them as hard as we possibly can, because if we do that, we won't have to take the military action.

Obama: Bob, let me just respond. Nothing Governor Romney just said is true, starting with this notion of me apologizing. This has been probably the biggest whopper that's been told during the course of this campaign, and every fact-checker and every reporter's looked at it. The governor has said this is not true.

And when it comes to tightening sanctions, look, as I said before, we've put in the toughest, most crippling sanctions ever. And the fact is while we were coordinating an international coalition to make sure these sanctions were effective, you were still invested in a Chinese state oil company that was doing business with the Iranian oil sector. So I'll let the American people decide, judge who's going to be more effective and more credible when it comes to imposing crippling sanctions.

And with respect to our attitude about the Iranian revolution, I was very clear about the murderous activities that had taken place, and that was contrary to international law and everything that civilized people stand for. And – and so the strength that we have shown in Iran is shown by the fact that we've been able to mobilize the world. When I came into office, the world was divided. Iran was resurgent. Iran is at its weakest point economically, strategically, militarily than since – than in many years.

Romney: We're four years closer to a nuclear Iran. We're four years closer to a nuclear Iran. And – and we should not have wasted these four years to the extent they've – they continue to be able to spin these centrifuges and get that much closer. That's number one.

Number two, Mr. President, the reason I call it an apology tour is because you went to the Middle East and you flew to – to Egypt and to Saudi Arabia and to – to Turkey and Iraq. And – and by way, you skipped Israel, our closest friend in the region, but you went to the other nations. And by the way, they

奥巴马：鲍伯，让我来回应一下，罗姆尼所言并不属实。从我"道歉"的说法开始，我想这是本次竞选活动的最大谎言，所有核查过事实的人和对此进行研究过的记者都目睹了这一切，州长所言并不属实。

就强化制裁措施而言，看吧，正如我之前说过的，我们已经对伊朗采取了最严厉、最有破坏力的制裁措施，实际上，当我们协调国际联盟来确保这些措施生效时，您却仍投资于一家与伊朗石油部门有生意往来的中国国有石油公司。所以，让美国人民来判断，在实施严厉制裁方面，谁能处理得更有效、更可信？

就我们对伊朗革命的态度而言，我很清楚谋杀活动已经发生，我也很清楚这与国际法、文明人类的利益背道而驰。我们在伊朗议题上所展现的力量体现在我们能够动员全世界。在我就任总统时，世界四分五裂，伊朗正在复苏，而现在伊朗目前处于经济、战略、军事上多年来的最衰落的时候。

罗姆尼：我们距伊朗拥有核武器又近了四年。我们不能再浪费四年，让他们的离心机不断运转，离我们越来越近，这是第一点。

第二点，总统先生，我之所以将这次访问说成是道歉之旅，那是因为，当您访问中东地区，您飞往埃及、沙特、土耳其、伊拉克。顺便说一下，您漏掉了以色列——我们在中东地区关系最密切的朋友，但是您去了

noticed that you skipped Israel. And then in those nations and on Arabic TV you said that America had been dismissive and derisive. You said that on occasion America had dictated to other nations. Mr. President, America has not dictated to other nations. We have freed other nations from dictators.

Obama: Bob, let me – let me respond. You know, if we're going to talk about trips that we've taken, you know, when I was a candidate for office, first trip I took was to visit our troops.

And when I went to Israel as a candidate, I didn't take donors, I didn't attend fundraisers, I went to Yad Vashem, the – the Holocaust museum there, to remind myself the – the nature of evil and why our bond with Israel will be unbreakable.

And then I went down to the border towns of Sderot, which had experienced missiles raining down from Hamas. And I saw families there who showed me where missiles had come down near their children's bedrooms, and I was reminded of – of what that would mean if those were my kids, which is why, as president, we funded an Iron Dome program to stop those missiles.

So that's how I've used my travels when I travel to Israel and when I travel to the region.

And the central question at this point is going to be, who's going to be credible to all parties involved?

And they can look at my track record – whether it's Iran sanctions, whether it's dealing with counterterrorism, whether it's supporting democracy, whether it's supporting women's rights, whether it's supporting religious minorities – and they can say that the president of the United States and the United States of America has stood on the right side of history. And – and that kind of credibility is precisely why we've been able to show leadership on a wide range of issues facing the world right now.

Schieffer: What if – what if the prime minister of Israel called you on the phone and said: Our bombers are on the way. We're going to bomb Iran. What do you say?

其他国家，顺便说一下，他们也注意到您忽略了以色列。您曾先后在这些国家、在阿拉伯电视上说美国向来傲慢，一直嘲笑他们。您说，美国曾经对其他国家发号施令，总统先生，美国并没有发号施令，我们是把其他国家从独裁者的统治下解放出来。

奥巴马：鲍伯，让我回应一下。你们知道，如果我们要谈及我的访问，大家都知道，当我还是总统竞选候选人的时候，我的首个行程就是访问我们的军队。

当我以候选人的身份，访问以色列的时候，我没有接受捐助，没有参加筹款活动。我去了以色列犹太大屠杀纪念馆[①]，来提醒自己人类邪恶的本性，以及为什么我们和以色列的联系是不可打破的。

然后我去了边境城镇斯德洛，这里曾遭到了来自哈马斯导弹的袭击。随后我看望了当地的居民，他们向我展示，落在他们孩子房间附近的导弹。那提醒我，如果他们是我的孩子，这意味着什么。作为总统，这也是为什么我资助反导弹来袭的铁穹项目的原因。

这就是我在以色列和中东地区的访问旅程。

现在的核心问题是，对于所有的参与的党派来说，谁足够可信？

他们可以考察我的记录，不管是对伊朗的制裁措施，还是处理反恐问题，还是支持民主、女性权利和宗教少数派，他们都可以说，美国总统和美国站在历史的正确一方。这种可信度正是我们在处理一系列国际议题上展现出的领导能力。

西弗：如果以色列首相打电话给您说，我们的轰炸机上路了，我们将要轰炸伊朗，您会采取什么措施？

---

① 以色列犹太大屠杀纪念馆是以色列官方设立的犹太人大屠杀纪念馆，位于以色列耶路撒冷，1953年根据以色列国通过的纪念法令成立。

Romney: Bob, let's not go into hypotheticals of that nature. Our relationship with Israel, my relationship with the prime minister of Israel is such that we would not get a call saying our bombers are on the way or their fighters are on the way. This is the kind of thing that would have been discussed and thoroughly evaluated well before that kind of action.

Schieffer: So you're saying just what –

Romney: I'm – that's – that's –

Schieffer: OK. But let's see what –

Romney: Yes, but let me – let me – let me come back – let's come back – let's come back and go back to what the president was speaking about, which is what's happening in the world and – and – and the president's statement that things are going so well.

Look, I – I look at what's happening around the world and I see Iran four years closer to a bomb. I see the Middle East with a rising tide of violence, chaos, tumult. I see jihadists continuing to spread. Whether they're rising or just about the same level hard to – hard to precisely measure, but it's clear they're there. They're very, very strong.

I see Syria with 30,000 civilians dead, Assad still in power. I see our trade deficit with China larger than it's – growing larger every year as a matter of fact. I look around the world and I don't feel that – you see North Korea continuing to export their nuclear technology.

Russia's said they're not going to follow Nunn-Lugar anymore; they're away from their nuclear proliferation treaty that we had with them. I look around the world, I don't see our influence growing around the world. I see our influence receding, in part because of the failure of the president to deal with our economic challenges at home, in part because of our withdrawal from our commitment to our military and the way I think it ought to be, in part because of the – the – the turmoil with Israel. I mean, the president received a letter from 38 Democrat senators saying the tensions with Israel were a real problem.

罗姆尼：鲍伯，让我们不要讨论那种假设性的问题。我们和以色列的关系，我们和以色列首相的关系是如此密切，我们不会接到这样的电话称他们的轰炸机上路了，或者说，他们的战斗机已经出发。这种事情是会事先进行讨论和充分评估的。

西弗：所以您说这——

罗姆尼：我认为——那是——那是

西弗：好吧，但让我们来看一下——

罗姆尼：好的，但是让我回到刚刚总统正在谈论的问题，看看世界正在发生什么，以及总统那些关于事态良好的声明。

看吧，让我来看一下世界上发生的事情，我看到伊朗又向核弹走近了四年，我看到中东地区不断高涨的暴力、动乱和骚动，我看到圣战分子仍然在继续蔓延。现在要准确地判断他们是正在发展还是维持现在的水平，还比较困难。但是，显而易见，他们非常强大。

我看到叙利亚已经有三万平民丧生，阿萨德继续掌权。我看到我们和中国的贸易逆差实际上每年都在扩大。看看世界，我没有感觉到——你们会发现朝鲜正在继续出口其核技术。

俄罗斯宣称他们将不再遵守《纳恩—卢格武器消减和安全条约》；撤销了我们与其达成的核扩散条约。环顾世界，我并没有看到我们的影响力在全球扩大，而是正在衰退，部分原因是奥巴马总统无法应对国内经济的挑战，部分原因是我们撤回了对军方的承诺，部分原因是我们和以色列不稳定的关系，我的意思是说，总统曾收到38位民主党参议员的联名信件，称美国与以色列的紧张关系是一个实实在在的问题。

Obama: No.

Romney: They asked him, please repair the tension – Democrat senators – please repair the damage in his – in his own party.

Schieffer: All right.

Obama: Governor, the problem is, is that on a whole range of issues, whether it's the Middle East, whether it's Afghanistan, whether it's Iraq, whether it's now Iran, you've been all over the map. I mean, I'm pleased that you now are endorsing our policy of applying diplomatic pressure and potentially having bilateral discussions with the Iranians to end their nuclear program. But just a few years ago you said that's something you'd never do, in the same way that you initially opposed a time table in Afghanistan, now you're for it, although it depends; in the same way that you say you would have ended the war in Iraq, but recently gave a speech saying that we should have 20,000 more folks in there; the same way that you said that it was mission creep to go after Gadhafi.

When it comes to going after Osama bin Laden, you said, well, any president would make that call. But when you were a candidate in 2008 – as I was – and I said, if I got bin Laden in our sights, I would take that shot, you said we shouldn't move heaven and earth to get one man, and you said we should ask Pakistan for permission.

And if we had asked Pakistan for permission, we would not have gotten him. And it was worth moving heaven and earth to get him.

You know, after we killed bin Laden, I was at Ground Zero[①] for a memorial and talked to a – a – a young woman who was 4 years old when 9/11 happened. And the last conversation she had with her father was him calling from the twin towers, saying, Peyton, I love you, and I will always watch over you. And for the

---

① 也称为"零地带"或"原爆点",原为军事术语,狭义指原子弹爆炸时投影至地面的中心点,广义指大规模爆炸的中心点。而"9·11"恐怖袭击后很长一段时间,这个词被用来专指世贸双子楼遗址那片废墟。

奥巴马：不是这样的。

罗姆尼：他们向总统发出请求，修复紧张关系——民主党参议员——请修复民主党内的关系。

西弗：好的。

奥巴马：州长，问题是，在一系列问题上，不管是在中东还是在阿富汗，不管是伊拉克还是伊朗，您一直天南地北，不着边际。我的意思是，我很高兴您现在支持我们对伊朗采取外交施压，支持我们有可能和伊朗人举行双边会谈以终结核项目。但是就在几年前，您还称这是您绝对不会做的事情。同样，您起初反对制定阿富汗撤军时间期限，现在您又提出表示支持，尽管这要根据情况而定；同样，您曾表示支持结束伊拉克战争，但是在您最近的一次演讲中提到，我们应该向那里再派遣2万人；还有，您在捉拿卡扎菲的问题上也是一样。

当我们捉拿了本·拉登时，您说，好的，任何总统都会这么做的。但是当2008年你和我一样都是候选人的时候，我说如果我们将本·拉登定为我们的打击目标，我会采取行动，而您说我们不应当为了一个人在那里大动干戈，应该请求获得巴基斯坦的批准。

如果当时我们请求巴基斯坦的批准，我们就无法捉拿他。而他也确实值得我们大动干戈去捉拿他。

你们知道，在我们击毙本·拉登之后，我在世贸遗址参加一个纪念仪式并和一位青年女子交谈，"9·11"事件发生时，她只有四岁。她和他父亲的最后一次谈话，是她父亲从双子塔打来的电话，说"皮伊顿，我爱你，我将永远守护你"。在随后的10年里，这段话一直在她心里萦绕不去。她对我说，您知道，终于干掉了本·拉登了，也算了了我一桩心事。

next decade she was haunted by that conversation. And she said to me, you know, by finally getting bin Laden, that brought some closure to me.

And when we do things like that, when we bring those who have harmed us to justice, that sends a message to the world, and it tells Peyton that we did not forget her father.

Schieffer: All right.

Obama: And – and I make that point because that's the kind of clarity of leadership – and those decisions are not always popular. Those decisions generally are not poll-tested. And even some in my own party, including my current vice president, had the same critique as you did. But what the American people understand is, is that I look at what we need to get done to keep the American people safe and to move our interests forward, and I make those decisions.

Schieffer: All right. Let's go – and that leads us – this takes us right to the next segment, Governor, America's longest war, Afghanistan and Pakistan.

Romney: Bob –

Schieffer: Governor, you get to go first.

Romney: You can't – you can't – well, OK, but you can't have the president just lay out a whole series of items without giving me a chance to respond.

Schieffer: With respect, sir, you had laid out quite a program there.

Romney: Well, that's probably true.

Schieffer: And we'll – we'll give you –

Obama: We'll agree–

Schieffer: We'll catch you up. The United States is scheduled to turn over responsibility for security in Afghanistan to the Afghans.

At that point we will withdraw our combat troops, leave a smaller force of Americans, if I understand our policy, in Afghanistan for training purposes. It seems to me the key question here is what do you do if the deadline arrives and

　　我们采取那样的行动，我们把那些伤害我们的人绳之以法，这就是向全世界发出一个信息，让皮伊顿知道，我们没有忘记她的父亲。

　　西弗：好的。

　　奥巴马：我想说明一点，是因为领导能力的透明度——这些决策并不总是受到青睐，它们没有经过民意调查，甚至一些党内人士，包括我的现任副总统，都像您那样曾对我提出过批评意见。但是美国人民能够理解，我知道我们需要采取怎样的措施，来确保美国人民的安全，推动我们的利益，于是我作出了那些决策。

　　西弗：好的，这正好让我们讨论下一个话题，即美国参与的时间最长的战争，阿富汗和巴基斯坦战争。州长，您先来。

　　罗姆尼：鲍伯——

　　西弗：州长，您先发言。

　　罗姆尼：您不能——您不能——好的，好吧，但您不能总让总统进行完整的阐述，而不给我机会作出回应。

　　西弗：恕我冒昧，您已经阐述很多了。

　　罗姆尼：好的，可能是这样。

　　西弗：我们将——我们将给您——

it is obvious the Afghans are unable to handle their security? Do we still leave? And I believe Governor Romney, it – you go first.

Romney: Well, we're going to be finished by 2014. And when I'm president, we'll make sure we bring our troops out by the end of 2014. The commanders and the generals there are on track to do so. We've seen progress over the past several years. The surge has been successful, and the training program is proceeding at pace. There are now a large number of Afghan security forces, 350,000, that are – are ready to step in to provide security. And – and we're going to be able to make that transition by the end of – of 2014. So our troops'll come home at that point.

I – I can tell you, at the same time, that – that we will make sure that we – we look at what's happening in Pakistan and recognize that what's happening in Pakistan is going to have a major impact on the success in Afghanistan. And – and I say that because I know a lot of people just feel like we should just brush our hands and walk away. And I don't mean you, Mr. President, but some people in the – in our nation feel that Pakistan doesn't – being nice to us and that we should just walk away from them.

But Pakistan is important to the region, to the world and to us, because Pakistan has 100 nuclear warheads, and they're rushing to build a lot more. They'll have more than Great Britain sometime in the – in the relatively near future. They also have the Haqqani network and – and the Taliban existent within their country. And so a – a Pakistan that falls apart, becomes a failed state would be of extraordinary danger to Afghanistan and us. And so we're going to have to remain helpful in encouraging Pakistan to move towards a – a more stable government and – and rebuild a relationship with us. And that means that – that – that our aid that we provide to Pakistan is going to have to be conditioned upon certain benchmarks being met.

So for me, I look at this as both a – a – a need to help move Pakistan in the right direction and also to get Afghanistan to be ready. And they will be ready

奥巴马：我们都同意——

西弗：我们需要抓紧时间。美国计划将阿富汗安全的职责转交给阿富汗政府。

那时，我们将撤走作战部队，只为培训目的留下少许美国部队，如果我对政策没有理解错的话。关键的问题是，期限一到，而阿富汗人显然不具备安全能力的话，您会怎么做？在这种情况下，我们依然会撤军吗？罗姆尼州长，我认为您应该先回答。

罗姆尼：好的，我们一定会在2014年之前完成撤军。如果我当选，我们将确保在2014年年底之前，撤走我们的军队。指挥官和将军们正在着手撤军行动，过去几年，我们取得了不错的进展，训练计划也在推进，阿富汗的安全力量规模已经达到了大概35万人，他们已经作好接管安全事务的准备，我们能够在2014年完成这种过渡，所以我们的士兵将在那时回国。

同时，我也想让你们知道，我们将密切关注巴基斯坦的局势，并意识到巴基斯坦的局势对我们在阿富汗取得的成功能够产生重大影响。并且，我想说，因为我知道很多人认为我们应该拂袖而去，总统先生，我不是针对您，但是我们国家有些人认为巴基斯坦对我们并不友好，我们应该拂袖而去。

但是，巴基斯坦对其所在地区、整个世界和我们来说都非常重要，因为巴基斯坦拥有100枚核弹头并且他们仍然在不断地制造着更多的核弹头，在不久的将来，他们的核弹头数量将超过英国，他们还面临着"哈卡尼网络"和塔利班武装问题。因此，一个分裂的巴基斯坦将成为一个失败的国家，这将对阿富汗和我们构成威胁，因此，我们要继续提供帮助，鼓励巴基斯坦朝着更稳定的政府这条路前进，并重建与我们的关系。那意味着，我们给他们提供的帮助不得不建立在某些基准之上。

所以，对我来说，我既把这看成是巴基斯坦走向正轨的必由之路，也把这看成是让阿富汗作好准备的措施，他们将为2014年底做好准备。

by the end of 2014.

Schieffer: Mr. President.

Obama: You know, when I came into office, we were still bogged down in Iraq, and Afghanistan had been drifting for a decade. We ended the war in Iraq, refocused our attention on Afghanistan. And we did deliver a surge of troops. That was facilitated in part because we had ended the war in Iraq.

And we are now in a position where we have met many of the objectives that got us there in the first place. Part of what had happened is we'd forgotten why we'd gone. We went because there were people who were responsible for 3,000 American deaths. And so we decimated al-Qaida's core leadership in the border regions between Afghanistan and Pakistan. We then started to build up Afghan forces. And we're now in a position where we can transition out, because there's no reason why Americans should die when Afghans are perfectly capable of defending their own country.

Now, that transition's – has to take place in a responsible fashion. We've been there a long time, and we've got to make sure that we and our coalition partners are pulling out responsibly and giving Afghans the capabilities that they need.

But what I think the American people recognize is after a decade of war, it's time to do some nation-building here at home. And what we can now do is free up some resources to, for example, put Americans back to work, especially our veterans, rebuilding our roads, our bridges, our schools, making sure that, you know, our veterans are getting the care that they need when it comes to post-traumatic stress disorder and traumatic brain injury, making sure that the certifications that they need for good jobs of the future are in place.

You know, I was having lunch with some – a veteran in Minnesota who had been a medic dealing with the most extreme circumstances. When he came home and he wanted to become a nurse, he had to start from scratch. And what we've said is, let's change those certifications.

The first lady has done great work with an organization called Joining

西弗：总统，该您了。

奥巴马：你们知道，当我就任总统时，我们深陷于伊拉克和阿富汗战争已经有10年之久。我们结束了伊拉克战争，重新将目光聚焦到阿富汗。我们采取了增兵行动，之所以进展顺利，在一定程度上归功于我们结束了伊拉克战争。

现在我们的情况是，我们已经完成了最初的很多目标，但部分情况是我们可能已经忘记了自己的初衷。我们这么做是因为那里有人要为3000名美国人的死亡负责。所以，我们铲除了阿富汗和巴基斯坦边界地区基地组织的核心领导人物。之后，我们开始组建阿富汗军队，现在已经有能力完成这种过渡，因为如果阿富汗人已经具有保卫自己国家安全的能力，就没有理由还让美国人继续为此牺牲。

现在，这种过渡必须以一种负责任的方式进行。我们已经在阿富汗驻军很长时间了，我们要确保我们自己以及我们的盟友担负起责任，赋予阿富汗人他们需要的能力。

但是，我认为美国人已经意识到，在持续了10年的战争之后，现在是我们建设美国的时候了。我们现在能做的是拿出一些资源，比如，让失业的美国人重新回到工作岗位，尤其是退伍老兵，重建我们的公路、桥梁和学校。你们知道，当退伍老兵出现创伤后的应激障碍和创伤性脑损伤时，我们要确保他们能够获得必要的照顾，确保他们获得相应资格证书以适应未来工作的需要。

我曾经与明尼苏达州的一名老兵一起吃过午饭，他是一名军医，处理过最严重的伤情，退役返乡后，他希望成为一名护理人员，因此不得不重新开始。我想说的是，我们有责任改

Forces putting our veterans back to work. And as a consequence, veterans' unemployment is actually now lower than general population, it was higher when I came into office. So those are the kinds of things that we can now do because we're making that transition in Afghanistan.

Schieffer: All right. Let me go to Governor Romney because you talked about Pakistan and what needs to be done there. General Allen, our commander in Afghanistan, says that Americans continue to die at the hands of groups who are supported by Pakistan. We know that Pakistan has arrested the doctor who helped us catch Obama's – bin Laden. It still provides safe haven for terrorists, yet we continue to give Pakistan billions of dollars. Is it time for us to divorce Pakistan?

Romney: No, it's not time to divorce a nation on earth that has a hundred nuclear weapons and is on the way to double that at some point, a nation that has serious threats from terrorist groups within its nation – as I indicated before, the Taliban, Haqqani network. It's a nation that's not like – like others and that does not have a civilian leadership that is calling the shots there.

You've got the ISI, their intelligence organization is probably the most powerful of the – of the three branches there. Then you have the military and then you have the – the civilian government. This is a nation which if it falls apart – if it becomes a failed state, there are nuclear weapons there and you've got – you've got terrorists there who could grab their – their hands onto those nuclear weapons.

This is – this is an important part of the world for us. Pakistan is – is technically an ally, and they're not acting very much like an ally right now, but we have some work to do.

And I – I don't blame the administration for the fact that the relationship with Pakistan is strained. We had to go into Pakistan; we had to go in there to get Osama bin Laden. That was the right thing to do. And that upset them, but there was obviously a great deal of anger even before that. But we're going to have to work with the – with the people in Pakistan to try and help them move

变这种资格证书要求。

第一夫人与"支持军队"组织配合，做了大量工作，让我们的老兵重返工作岗位，其结果是老兵的失业率低于普通民众，情况比我刚就任总统时要好得多。所以这就是我们现在的所作所为，因为我们在阿富汗过渡时期，作了同样的转变。

西弗： 好的，罗姆尼州长，您提到了巴基斯坦以及所需要采取的举措。驻阿富汗指挥官艾伦将军表示，仍有美国人死于巴基斯坦支持的武装分子之手，我们知道，巴基斯坦已经抓捕了曾帮助我们找到奥萨马·本·拉登的医生，但巴基斯坦仍是恐怖分子的安全天堂，而我们仍然一直在给巴基斯坦提供数十亿美元的资金援助。现在到了我们和巴基斯坦划清界限的时候了吗？

罗姆尼： 不，现在还不是划清界限的时候，他们拥有100枚核弹头，我们反而应该在某些方面加强合作。正如我之前提到的，从国内恐怖组织到塔利班到"哈卡尼网络"，巴基斯坦已经面临严峻的威胁，它不像其他国家一样，有文明领导层作决策。

你们知道，他们的情报机构在巴基斯坦国家机构中是最有权力的，然后才是军队和平民政府。如果国家陷入分裂，如果国家破败，他们的核武器很可能会落入恐怖分子之手。

对我们来说，这是世界的重要组成部分，从技术层面讲，巴基斯坦是我们的盟友，虽然他们现在的所作所为不太像一个盟友，但是我们可以采取一些行动来弥补——

我不会指责当前政府把巴基斯坦与美国的关系搞僵。我们不得不进入巴基斯坦；不得不去那里把本·拉登揪出来。做这些事情没错，这令他们心烦意乱，但是在这之前，他们显然积聚了大量怒火。我们必须和

 The Third Obama – Romney Presidential Debate

to a more responsible course than the one that they're on. And it's important for them, it's important for the nuclear weapons, it's important for the success of Afghanistan, because inside Pakistan you have a large group of Pashtuns that are – that are Taliban, that they're going to come rushing back into Afghanistan when we go. And that's one of the reasons the Afghan security forces have so much work to do to be able to fight against that. But it's important for us to recognize that we can't just walk away from Pakistan. But we do need to make sure that as we – as we send support for them, that this is tied to them making progress on – on matters that would lead them to becoming a civil society.

Schieffer: Let me ask you, Governor, because we know President Obama's position on this, what is – what is your position on the use of drones?

Romney: Well, I believe that we should use any and all means necessary to take out people who pose a threat to us and our friends around the world. And it's widely reported that drones are being used in drone strikes, and I support that entirely and feel the president was right to up the usage of that technology and believe that we should continue to use it to continue to go after the people who represent a threat to this nation and to our friends.

Let me also note that, as I said earlier, we're going to have to do more than just going after leaders and – and killing bad guys, important as that is. We're also going to have to have a far more effective and comprehensive strategy to help move the world away from terror and Islamic extremism.

We haven't done that yet. We talk a lot about these things, but you look at the – the record. You look at the record of the last four years and say, is Iran closer to a bomb? Yes. Is the Middle East in tumult? Yes. Is – is al-Qaida on the run, on its heels? No. Is – are Israel and the Palestinians closer to – to reaching a peace agreement? No, they haven't had talks in two years. We have not seen the progress we need to have, and I'm convinced that with strong leadership and an effort to build a strategy based upon helping these nations reject extremism, we can see the kind of peace and prosperity the world demands.

474

巴基斯坦的人民团结起来，努力帮助他们走上更好的发展轨道。这对他们很重要，这对核武器也很重要，这也关系到阿富汗的成败，因为在巴基斯坦内部有很多普什图人①，他们是塔利班，我们走后，他们会重返阿富汗，这就是为什么阿富汗安全部队要对抗塔利班还须作出很多努力的原因。但对我们来说，重要的是，认清我们不能只是简单地从巴基斯坦撤军，我们需要给他们支持，让他们取得进步，成为一个文明的社会。

西弗：州长，由于我们已经知道奥巴马总统的立场，请您来回答，您对使用无人驾驶飞机的立场是什么？

罗姆尼：好的，我想我们应该利用各种手段铲除对我们和对我们世界各地的朋友构成威胁的人。很多报道称，无人机被正用来进行空袭，我完全赞成这一做法，也认为总统采用这项技术是正确的，我们应当继续利用它来追赶对我们国家和我们盟友构成威胁的人。

我要强调一点，如我早先所说的，我们不能仅仅只是抓捕头目，消灭恶人也同样重要，我们需要有一个更有效、更全面的策略，让世界远离恐怖分子和伊斯兰极端分子。

我们至今还没有完成这项任务。我们对此谈论了很多，但是，查看一下记录。如果您查看一下过去四年的记录，您就会问道，伊朗现在是否离研制出原子弹更近一步？是的。中东是否动荡不安？是的。基地分子正在忙于逃命、时日不多吗？不是的。以色列和巴勒斯坦是否距离达成和平协议更近了一步？不是的，他们两年都没有进行会谈了。我们没有看到需要的进展，我相信，通过强有力的领导和建立一个以帮助这些国家对抗极端主义为基础的策略，我们就能看到一个和平发展、欣欣向荣的世界。

---

① 普什图人是阿富汗东南部和巴基斯坦西部的主要穆斯林民族。

Obama: Well, keep in mind our strategy wasn't just going after bin Laden. We've created partnerships throughout the region to deal with extremism – in Somalia, in Yemen, in Pakistan. And what we've also done is engage these governments in the kind of reforms that are actually going to make a difference in people's lives day to day, to make sure that their government aren't corrupt, to make sure that they are treating women with the kind of respect and dignity that every nation that succeeds has shown, and to make sure that they've got a free market system that works.

So across the board, we are engaging them in building capacity in these countries and we have stood on the side of democracy. One thing I think Americans should be proud of – when Tunisians began to protest, this nation, me, my administration stood with them earlier than just about any other country. In Egypt we stood on the side of democracy. In Libya we stood on the side of the people. And as a consequence there is no doubt that attitudes about Americans have changed.

But there are always going to be elements in these countries that potentially threaten the United States. And we want to shrink those groups and those networks, and we can do that, but we're always also going to have to maintain vigilance when it comes to terrorist activities. The truth, though, is that al-Qaida is much weaker than it was when I came into office, and they don't have the same capacities to attack the U.S. homeland and our allies as they did four years ago.

Schieffer: Let's go to the next segment because it's a very important one. It is the rise of China and future challenges for America. I want to just begin this by asking both of you – and Mr. President, you go first this time – what do you believe is the greatest future threat to the national security of this country?

Obama: Well, I think it will continue to be terrorist networks. We have to remain vigilant, as I just said. But with respect to China, China's both an adversary but also a potential partner in the international community if it's following the rules. So my attitude coming into office was that we are going to

奥巴马：记住，我们的策略不是仅仅追捕本·拉登。我们已经在中东建立起伙伴关系，来应对在索马里、也门、巴基斯坦等地的极端主义。我们还敦促这些政府实施一些改革，以此逐步改善当地人的生活，并确保他们的政府不腐败，确保他们像其他成功的国家那样尊重妇女，确保他们拥有正常运作的自由市场体系。

纵观全局，我们一直在敦促他们提高国家能力，而且我们站在民主的立场。有一点我想美国人应该感到自豪——当突尼斯人开始抗议这个国家时，我和我的政府先于其他国家和他们站在一起；在埃及，我们站在民主的一边；在利比亚，我们站在人民的一边。因而，毫无疑问，他们对美国人的态度已经发生改变。

但是，这些国家总是存在某些因素对美国构成潜在的威胁。我们希望缩小这些群体和这些网络，我们有能力做到这一点，不过，提及恐怖分子，我们得始终保持警惕。事实上，与我刚上任时相比，基地组织的力量已经削弱了很多，他们现在不具备四年前的能力来袭击我们和我们的盟友。

西弗：进入下个部分，这很重要，那就是中国的崛起和美国未来面临的挑战。我想通过提问你们两位来开始这个话题，奥巴马总统，这次您先回答，您觉得对美国国家安全而言，未来最大的威胁是什么？

奥巴马：好的，我想最大的威胁仍旧是恐怖分子网络，就像我刚才所说的，我们必须继续保持警惕。关于中国，中国既是一个对手，但是如果它遵守规则的话，它同时也是国际社会中一个潜在的合作伙伴。我任职的态度是，我们会继续坚持中国遵循与其他国家一样的规则。

insist that China plays by the same rules as everybody else.

And I know Americans had – had seen jobs being shipped overseas, businesses and workers not getting a level playing field when it came to trade. And that's the reason why I set up a trade task force to go after cheaters when it came to international trade. That's the reason why we have brought more cases against China for violating trade rules than the other – the previous administration had done in two terms. And we've won just about every case that we've filed, that – that has been decided. In fact, just recently, steelworkers in Ohio and throughout the Midwest, Pennsylvania, are in a position now to sell steel to China because we won that case.

We had a tire case in which they were flooding us with cheap domestic tires – or – or – or cheap Chinese tires. And we put a stop to it and, as a consequence, saved jobs throughout America. I have to say that Governor Romney criticized me for being too tough in that tire case, said this wouldn't be good for American workers and that it would be protectionist. But I tell you, those workers don't feel that way. They feel as if they had finally an administration who was going to take this issue seriously.

Over the long term, in order for us to compete with China, we've also got to make sure, though, that we're taking – taking care of business here at home. If we don't have the best education system in the world, if we don't continue to put money into research and technology that will allow us to – to create great businesses here in the United States, that's how we lose the competition. And unfortunately, Governor Romney's budget and his proposals would not allow us to make those investments.

Schieffer: All right. Governor.

Romney: Well, first of all, it's not government that makes business successful. It's not government investments that make businesses grow and hire people.

Let me also note that the greatest threat that the world faces, the greatest

我知道美国人已经察觉到工作机会正在不断地流向海外，当涉及贸易问题时，企业和工人不能获得公平的竞争环境，这就是为什么我组建了一支贸易工作小组来打击国际贸易中的不守规矩的人，这就是为什么我们提起了更多的反对中国违反贸易规则的案子，比前两任政府加起来的还多。我们几乎打赢了每一场官司。其实，就在最近，俄亥俄州和中西部、宾夕法尼亚州的钢铁工人终于能向中国出口钢铁了，因为我们打赢了那场官司。

我们还有一个轮胎案，我们控告他们向我们倾销廉价国内轮胎或者说廉价的中国轮胎，我们成功地制止了他们，因此保全了全美国的工作机会。我得说，罗姆尼州长批评我在轮胎案中的措施过于强硬，说这对美国工人没有好处，说这是贸易保护主义，但我告诉您，那些工人并不这样认为，他们觉得，终于有了一个严肃对待这个问题的政府。

尽管长期以来，为了使我们能够和中国竞争，我们已经开始关注国内的企业。如果我们不再具备世界上最好的教育系统，如果我们不继续向研究和技术领域投资，以保证我们创造美国的伟大事业，那样我们就会输掉这场竞争。然而不幸的是，罗姆尼州长的预算和提议将无法让我们实现这些投资。

西弗：好的，州长，到您了。

罗姆尼：好的，首先，不是政府使企业获得成功，不是政府的投资使得企业获得发展、雇佣员工。

我还要强调一下，世界面临的最大挑战、最大的国家安全威胁是伊朗的核武器。

national security threat, is a nuclear Iran.

Let's talk about China. China has an interest that's very much like ours in one respect, and that is they want a stable world. They don't want war. They don't want to see protectionism. They don't want to see the – the world break out into – into various forms of chaos, because they have to – they have to manufacture goods and put people to work. And they have about 20,000 – 20 million, rather, people coming out of the farms every year, coming into the cities, needing jobs. So they want the economy to work and the world to be free and open.

And so we can be a partner with China. We don't have to be an adversary in any way, shape or form. We can work with them. We can collaborate with them if they're willing to be responsible.

Now, they look at us and say, is it a good idea to be with America?

How strong are we going to be? How strong is our economy?

They look at the fact that we owe them a trillion dollars and owe other people 16 trillion (dollars) in total, including them. They – they look at our – our decision to – to cut back on our military capabilities – a trillion dollars. The secretary of defense called these trillion dollars of cuts to our military devastating. It's not my term. It's the president's own secretary of defense called them devastating. They look at America's commitments around the world and they see what's happening and they say, well, OK, is America going to be strong? And the answer is yes. If I'm president, America will be very strong.

We'll also make sure that we have trade relations with China that work for us. I've watched year in and year out as companies have shut down and people have lost their jobs because China has not played by the same rules, in part by holding down artificially the value of their currency. It holds down the prices of their goods. It means our goods aren't as competitive and we lose jobs. That's got to end.

They're making some progress; they need to make more. That's why on

让我们讨论一下中国，从某个方面讲，中国和我们的利益基本一致，那就是他们想要一个稳定的世界。他们不想要战争，他们不想看到贸易保护主义，他们不想看到世界四分五裂、混乱不堪，因为，他们必须制造商品，让人们工作。他们每年有大概2000万人从农村来到城市，他们需要工作。所以，他们希望经济运行良好，世界自由开放。

因此，我们可以成为中国的一个伙伴，我们没有必要处处和中国以各种形式作对，我们可以和他们一起合作。如果他们愿意承担责任，我们愿意与之合作。

现在，他们看着我们，然后说，和美国合作是好事吗？

我们将会变得多么强大？我们经济有多强劲？

他们现在看到一个事实，我们欠他们一万亿美元，算上他们的话，我们一共欠所有国家共16万亿美元。他们看到我们决定削弱军力，要削减一万亿美元。国防部长称，这一万亿美元的削减，对我们的军队具有毁灭性。这不是我的说法，是总统的国防部长的说法。他们还看到美国在全世界的行动，看到所发生的一切，他们会说，好的，美国将会变得强大吗？回答是肯定的。如果我是总统，美国会变得强大无比。

我们也要确保对我们有利的中国贸易关系。我看到年复一年，因为中国没能遵守同样的规则，很多公司倒闭，人们失业，部分原因是通过人为地压低他们的货币币值，这就降低了他们商品的价格，也意味着我们的商品不像他们的商品那样具有竞争力，因此我们丢掉了工作，必须结束这一切。

day one I will label them a currency manipulator which allows us to apply tariffs where they're taking jobs. They're stealing our intellectual property, our patents, our designs, our technology, hacking into our computers, counterfeiting our goods. They have to understand, we want to trade with them, we want a world that's stable, we like free enterprise, but you got to play by the rules.

Schieffer: Well, Governor, let me just ask you, if you declare them a currency manipulator on day one, some people are saying you're just going to start a trade war with China on day one. Is that – isn't there a risk that that could happen?

Romney: Well, they sell us about this much stuff every year. And we sell them about this much stuff every year. So it's pretty clear who doesn't want a trade war. And there's one going on right now that we don't know about. It's a silent one and they're winning. We have an enormous trade imbalance with China. And it's worse this year than last year. And it was worse last year than the year before.

And – and so we have to understand that we can't just surrender and – and lose jobs year in and year out. We have to say to our friends in China, look, you guys are playing aggressively, we understand it, but – but this can't keep on going. You can't keep on holding down the value of your currency, stealing our intellectual property, counterfeiting our products, selling them around the world, even into the United States.

I was with one company that makes valves in – in process industries. And they said, look, we were – we were having some valves coming in that – that were broken, and we had to repair them under warranty. And we looked them up, and – and they had our serial number on them. And then we noticed that – that there was more than one with that same serial number. They were counterfeit products being made overseas with the same serial number as a U.S. company, the same packaging. These were being sold into our market and around the world as if they were made by the U.S. competitor.

482

他们逐渐蒸蒸日上；他们需要更加进步。这就是为什么我上任的第一天，我将把他们归为汇率操纵国，对他们抢走我们工作的行业征收关税。他们正在窃取我们的知识产权、我们的专利、我们的设计、我们的技术，非法闯进我们的电脑，仿造我们的产品。他们必须明白，我们想和他们做贸易，我们想要一个稳定的世界，我们喜欢自由企业，但是您必须按照规则行事。

西弗：好，州长，让我问一下您，如果您在上任的第一天就宣布中国是一个汇率操纵国，有人会说您在上任的第一天就会对中国发起贸易战，这不就有可能冒风险吗？

罗姆尼：好的，他们每年都卖给我们很多东西，而我们卖给他们的东西要少得多，所以显而易见，是哪方不想打这场贸易战。现在就进行着一场战争，只是我们不知道而已，这是一场悄无声息的贸易战，而且他们正在取胜。我们和中国的贸易存在非常大的不平衡，而且，今年的状况比去年更糟，去年的状况又要比前年更糟。

我们必须知道我们不能只是屈服，不能年复一年地丢掉工作。我们不得不对我们的中国朋友说，你们不能太咄咄逼人了，我们表示理解，但是这不能够再这样下去了。你们不能继续压低你们的货币面值，窃取我们的知识产权、山寨我们的产品，然后卖给全世界，甚至在美国销售。

我曾经去过一家制造阀门的加工企业，他们说，看，我们买进的一些阀门受损了，我们必须在保修期内把它修好。我们看着这些阀门，然后发现上面有我们的序列号，接着我们发现具有相同序列号的阀门不止一个。他们是在海外制造的仿造产品，和美国的公司有着一样的序列号，同样的包装。他们在我们的市场和全世界的市场销售，就好似美国竞争者制造的一样。

This can't go on. I want a great relationship with China. China can be our partner. But – but that doesn't mean they can just roll all over us and steal our jobs on an unfair basis.

Obama: Well, Governor Romney's right. You are familiar with jobs being shipped overseas, because you invested in companies that were shipping jobs overseas. And, you know, that's your right. I mean, that's how our free market works.

But I've made a different bet on American workers. You know, if we had taken your advice, Governor Romney, about our auto industry, we'd be buying cars from China instead of selling cars to China. If we take your advice with respect to how we change our tax codes so that companies that are in profits overseas don't pay U.S. taxes compared to companies here that are paying taxes, now, that's estimated to create 800,000 jobs. The problem is they won't be here; they'll be in places like China. And if we're not making investments in education and basic research, which is not something that the private sector is doing at a sufficient pace right now and has never done, then we will lose the lead in things like clean energy technology.

Now, with respect to what we've done with China already, U.S. exports have doubled, since I came into office, to China. And actually, currencies are at their most advantageous point for U.S. exporters since 1993. We absolutely have to make more progress, and that's why we're going to keep on pressing.

And when it comes to our military and Chinese security, part of the reason that we were able to pivot to the Asia-Pacific region after having ended the war in Iraq and transitioning out of Afghanistan, is precisely because this is going to be a massive growth area in the future. And we believe China can be a partner, but we're also sending a very clear signal that America is a Pacific power, that we are going to have a presence there. We are working with countries in the region to make sure, for example, that ships can pass through, that commerce continues. And we're organizing trade relations with countries other than China

这种情况不能够再持续下去了。我想和中国保持一个友好的关系，中国可以成为我们的伙伴，但是这不意味着他们可以凌驾于我们之上，不公平地偷走我们的工作。

奥巴马：罗姆尼州长此言有理，您对我们流失在海外的工作比较熟悉，是因为您投资的一些公司当时正在往海外转移工作机会。大家知道，那是您的权利，我的意思是说，那就是自由市场运转的机制。

但是，关于美国的工人，我有不同的看法。您知道，如果我们采纳了您对汽车行业的建议，我们恐怕正在从中国购买汽车，而不是向中国销售汽车。如果我们采纳了您变更税收法规方面的建议，让从海外盈利的公司不必像美国公司一样按照美国标准缴税，估计现在那些公司能够创造80万个工作岗位，问题是这些工作岗位不会在美国；他们会在像中国这样的地方。私营部门对教育和基础研究做得不够，也从未到位，如果我们再不投资这两项的话，我们将失去许多项目的领导地位，比如清洁能源技术。

现在，由于我们已经对中国方面采取措施，自我就任以来，美国对中国的出口已经翻倍。实际上，目前双方的汇率处在自1993年以来对美国最有利的位置。我们必须取得更多的进展，那就是为什么我们要对中国持续施压。

至于我们的军队和中国的安全，结束伊拉克战争、撤出阿富汗之后，我们能够在亚太地区成为轴心，部分是因为这一地区经济未来将大规模增长。我们相信中国是一个伙伴，同时我们也发出非常明确的信号，即美国是太平洋地区的一个大国，我们将会在那里存在。我们正在与这个地区的国家一道努力，比如，确保船只能够通行，商业得以继续。除了中国，我

so that China starts feeling more pressure about meeting basic international standards. That's the kind of leadership we've shown in the region. That's the kind of leadership that we'll continue to show.

Romney: I just want to take one of those points. Again, attacking me is not talking about an agenda for getting more trade and opening up more jobs in this country. But the president mentioned the auto industry and that somehow I would be in favor of jobs being elsewhere. Nothing could be further from the truth. I'm a son of Detroit. I was born in Detroit. My dad was head of a car company. I like American cars. And I would do nothing to hurt the U.S. auto industry. My plan to get the industry on its feet when it was in real trouble was not to start writing checks. It was President Bush that wrote the first checks. I disagree with that. I said they need – these companies need to go through a managed bankruptcy, and in that process they can get government help and government guarantees, but they need to go through bankruptcy to get rid of excess cost and the debt burden that they'd – they'd built up.

And fortunately the president picked –

Obama: Governor Romney, that's not what you said.

Romney: Fortunately, the president – you can take – you can take a look at the op-ed.

Obama: Governor, you did not –

Romney: You can take a look at the op-ed.

Obama: You did not say that you would provide, Governor, help.

Romney: You know, I'm – I'm still speaking. I said that we would provide guarantees and – and that was what was able to allow these companies to go through bankruptcy, to come out of bankruptcy. Under no circumstances would I do anything other than to help this industry get on its feet. And the idea that has been suggested that I would liquidate the industry – of course not. Of course not.

Obama: Let's check the record.

Romney: That's the height of silliness.

们还和其他国家建立起贸易关系，以便中国开始意识到更多的压力，从而遵循基本的国际准则。这就是我们在这个地区展示的领导力，这也是我们将继续展示的领导力。

罗姆尼：我只是想说明一点。再次说明一点，攻击我并不能获得更多的贸易、创造更多的工作机会。但总统提到了汽车行业，还说我有些赞成工作机会流失。这严重扭曲了事实。我是底特律的孩子，我出生在底特律。我的父亲是一个汽车公司的领导，我喜欢美国汽车，我不会做任何有损美国汽车行业的事情。要让这个行业在真正困难的时候能够站稳脚跟，我的计划不是动手开支票。布什总统开了第一批支票，我不同意他的做法。我说这些公司要经历可管控的破产，在那个过程中，他们可以获得政府的帮助和政府的担保，但是，他们必须经历破产这一过程，来摆脱积累的额外成本和债务负担。

但幸运的是，总统——

奥巴马：罗姆尼州长，您不是那么说的。

罗姆尼：庆幸的是，总统——您可以去看一下我的专栏。

奥巴马：州长，您没有——

罗姆尼：您可以看一下专栏。

奥巴马：您没说过您会提供帮助，州长。

罗姆尼：您知道，我一直在说，我说我们会提供担保——能够让这些公司经历破产，从破产中重生。无论如何，我都会帮助这个行业站稳脚跟。而暗示我会清算变卖这个行业的想法是不对的，当然是不对的。

奥巴马：让我们看下记录。

罗姆尼：真是愚蠢至极。

Obama: Let's – let's check the record.

Romney: I have never said I would – I would liquidate the industry. I want to keep the industry growing and thriving.

Obama: Governor, the people in Detroit don't forget.

Romney: And – and that's I have the kind of commitment to make sure that our industries in this country can compete and be successful. We in this country can compete successfully with anyone in the world. And we're going to. We're going to have to have a president, however, that doesn't think that somehow the government investing in – in car companies like Tesla and – and Fisker, making electric battery cars – this is not research, Mr. President. These are the government investing in companies, investing in Solyndra. This is a company. This isn't basic research. I – I want to invest in research. Research is great. Providing funding to universities and think tanks – great. But investing in companies? Absolutely not. That's the wrong way to go.

Obama: Governor, the fact of the matter is –

Romney: I'm still speaking.

Obama: Well –

Romney: So I want to make sure that we make – we make America more competitive –

Obama: Yeah.

Romney: – and that we do those things that make America the most attractive place in the world for entrepreneurs, innovators, businesses to grow. But your investing in companies doesn't do that. In fact it makes it less likely for them to come here –

Obama: All right, Governor –

Romney: – because the private sector's not going to invest in a – in a – in a solar company if –

Obama: I'm happy – I'm – I'm – I'm happy to respond –

Romney: – if you're investing government money and someone else's.

奥巴马：让我们——让我们看下记录。

罗姆尼：我从未说过——我会清算变卖这个行业，我想要这个行业发展壮大。

奥巴马：州长，底特律人民是不会忘记的。

罗姆尼：这是为什么我致力于确保我们的行业有竞争力、取得成功的原因。我们这个国家能够和世界上其他任何一个国家成功竞争，而且我们是会成功的。然而，我们还必须有这样一位总统，他认为不应该向诸如特斯拉、菲斯克这样的电动汽车公司投资，这不是研究，总统先生。这是政府投资公司，向索伦德拉投资，这是一个公司，这并不是基础研究。我想投资研究，研究很伟大，给大学和智囊团提供资金很好，但是投资公司呢？当然不行，那是错误的途径。

奥巴马：州长，这一问题的事实是——

罗姆尼：我还没说完呢。

奥巴马：好的——

罗姆尼：所以我想确保我们使美国更具竞争力——

奥巴马：好的。

罗姆尼：——我们的所作所为就是要让美国成为对企业家、发明家、商人来说是世界上最具吸引力的地方。但是，您投资公司并不会实现它，相反，这会使得那些人更不愿意过来——

奥巴马：好吧，州长——

罗姆尼：——因为私营部门不会投资一个太阳能公司，如果——

奥巴马：我很乐意作出回应——

罗姆尼：——如果您用政府资金或其他人的钱的话。

Obama: You've held the floor for a while. The – look, I think anybody out there can check the record. Governor Romney, you keep on trying to, you know, airbrush history here.

You were very clear that you would not provide government assistance to the U.S. auto companies even if they went through bankruptcy. You said that they could get it in the private marketplace. That wasn't true. They would have gone through a –

Romney: You're wrong. You're wrong, Mr. President.

Obama: I – no, I am not wrong.

Romney: People can look it up. You're right.

Obama: People will look it up.

Romney: Good.

Obama: But more importantly, it is true that in order for us to be competitive, we're going to have to make some smart choices right now. Cutting our education budget – that's not a smart choice. That will not help us compete with China. Cutting our investments in research and technology – that's not a smart choice. That will not help us compete with China. Bringing down (sic) our deficit by adding $7 trillion of tax cuts and military spending that our military's not asking for before we even get to the debt that we currently have – that is not going to make us more competitive. Those are the kinds of choices that the American people face right now. Having a tax code that rewards companies that are shipping jobs overseas instead of companies that are investing here in the United States – that will not make us more competitive.

And – and the one thing that I'm absolutely clear about is that after a decade in which we saw drift, jobs being shipped overseas, nobody championing American workers and American businesses, we've now begun to make some real progress. What we can't do is go back to the same policies that got us into such difficulty in the first place. And that's why we have to move forward and not go back.

奥巴马：请您稍等一会儿——我认为大家都可以查看一下记录。罗姆尼州长，大家知道，您一直在试图美化历史。

您很清楚，您不会向美国汽车公司提供政府帮助，即使它们经历破产，您说他们可以从私人交易市场得到帮助，那是不对的，它们会经历一个——

罗姆尼：您错了，您错了，总统。

奥巴马：我——不，我没错。

罗姆尼：人们可以去查证，这点是对的。

奥巴马：人们将会查证。

罗姆尼：好的。

奥巴马：但是，更重要的是，的确，为了使我们更具有竞争力，我们要立刻做出一些更明智的决定，削减教育预算并非一种明智的选择，那不会帮助我们和中国竞争，削减我们对研究和技术的投资，也不是一个聪明的选择，那也不会帮助我们和中国竞争。通过增加7万亿税收、增加军队并没有要求的军费开支，在我们还没有达到现有的负债水平之前，减少我们的赤字，那不会让我们更具有竞争力。这些就是美国人民现在必须要面临的选择，制定税收制度去奖励那些将工作机会转移到海外的公司，而不是投资于美国本土的公司，那也不会使我们更有竞争力。

有件事情，我非常地清楚。在经历了漂泊、工作机会转移到海外，没有人捍卫美国工人和美国企业的10年之后，我们现在开始取得实实在在的进步。我们不能做的是重新回到之前让我们陷入困境的那些政策，这就是为什么我们要前进，而不是后退。

Romney: I couldn't agree more about going forward, but I certainly don't want to go back to the policies of the last four years. The policies of the last four years have seen incomes in America decline every year for middle-income families, now down $4,300 during your term, 23 million Americans still struggling to find a good job. When you came into office, 32 million people on food stamps – today 47 million people on food stamps.

When you came to office, just over $10 trillion in debt – now $16 trillion in debt. It hasn't worked. You said by now we'd be at 5.4 percent unemployment. We're 9 million jobs short of that. I've met some of those people. I've met them in Appleton, Wisconsin. I – I met a young woman in – in – in Philadelphia who's coming out of – out of college, can't find work. I've been – Ann was with someone just the other day that was just weeping about not being able to get work. It's just a tragedy in a nation so prosperous as ours that these last four years have been so hard.

And that – and that's why it's so critical that we make America once again the most attractive place in the world to start businesses, to build jobs, to grow the economy. And that's not going to happen by – by just hiring teachers. Look, I – I love to – I love teachers, and I'm happy to have states and communities that want to hire teachers, do that. I – by the way, I don't like to have the federal government start pushing its way deeper and deeper into – into our schools. Let the states and localities do that. I was a governor. The federal government didn't hire our teachers.

Schieffer: Governor –

Romney: But I love teachers. But I want to get our private sector growing, and I know how to do it.

Schieffer: I think we all love teachers. Gentlemen, thank you so much for a very vigorous debate. We have come to the end. It is time for closing statements. I believe you're first, Mr. President.

Obama: Well, thank you very much Bob, Governor Romney, and to Lynn

罗姆尼：我绝对同意前进，但是我当然不想重新回到过去4年的政策。过去4年的政策使得美国中等收入家庭的收入每年都在下降，在您的任期内，下降了4300美元。2300万美国人还在苦苦地寻找一个好的工作。您就任时，有3200万人靠领取食品券为生，现在却增加到4700万人。

您就任时，只有10万亿美元的债务，现在我们有16万亿的债务，你的那些政策无济于事。您曾说到现在为止，我们只有5.4%的失业率，但是现在距离这个目标，还有900万个工作职位短缺。我曾经见过这些人，我在威斯康星州的阿普尔顿遇到了他们，我在费城遇到了一位年轻女性，她刚大学毕业就找不到工作。我的夫人安前天就遇到一位正在为找不到工作而哭泣的人。在我们这样一个繁荣昌盛的国度，过去4年却如此艰难，这真是一个悲剧。

这就是使得美国再次成为全球最具有吸引力的经商、创业、经济发展之地的重要所在。仅仅靠雇佣教师无法实现这一点。看吧，我热爱教师，也很乐意让州和社区聘请教师来实现这一点。顺便提一下，我不想让联邦政府无休止地插手教育，让各州和地方政府做这件事情吧。我当过州长，联邦政府不会替我们雇佣教师。

西弗：州长——

罗姆尼：我热爱教师，但我想让私营部门发展，我懂得如何去实现这一点。

西弗：我认为我们都热爱教师。先生们，感谢你们精彩的辩论。现在已经接近尾声，是总结陈词的时候了，我想请总统先生先开始。

奥巴马：好的，非常谢谢你，鲍伯，也感谢罗姆尼州长和林恩大学。

University.

You know, you've now heard three debates, months of campaigning and way too many TVcommercials. And now you've got a choice. You know, over the last four years, we've made real progress digging our way out of policies that gave us two prolonged wars, record deficits and the worst economic crisis since the Great Depression.

And Governor Romney wants to take us back to those policies: a foreign policy that's wrong and reckless; economic policies that won't create jobs, won't reduce our deficit, but will make sure that folks at the very top don't have to play by the same rules that you do.

And I've got a different vision for America. I want to build on our strengths. And I put forward a plan to make sure that we're bringing manufacturing jobs back to our shores by rewarding companies and small businesses that are investing here not overseas. I want to make sure we've got the best education system in the world and we're retraining our workers for the jobs of tomorrow.

I want to control our own energy by developing oil and natural gas, but also the energy sources of the future. Yes, I want to reduce our deficit by cutting spending that we don't need, but also by asking the wealthy to do a little bit more so that we can invest in things like research and technology that are the key to a 21st century economy.

As commander in chief, I will maintain the strongest military in the world, keep faith with our troops and go after those who would do us harm. But after a decade of war, I think we all recognize we got to do some nation building here at home, rebuilding our roads, our bridges and especially caring for our veterans who've sacrificed so much for our freedom.

You know, we've been through tough times, but we always bounce back because of our character, because we pull together. And if I have the privilege of being your president for another four years, I promise you I will always listen

大家知道，你们已经看了三场辩论，几个月的竞选活动，和太多的电视竞选广告。现在你们必须要作出选择。大家知道，在过去的四年，我们取得了实质性的进展，从过去政策的淤泥中爬了出来，那些政策让我们经历了两场漫长的战争，破纪录的赤字，自大萧条以来最严峻的经济危机。

罗姆尼州长想带领我们走过去的老路：一个错误和不计后果的外交政策；一个不会创造就业、不会减少赤字，但会让享受特殊待遇的上层人士获益的经济政策。

我为美国制定不同的愿景规划，我想发展我们的优势，我已经提出了一项计划，通过给那些投资于美国而非海外的公司提供奖励以确保制造业的工作岗位回流美国，我想确保我们拥有世界上最好的教育制度，并且重新培训我们的工人，为未来的工作作好准备。

我想我们要通过开发石油和天然气，开发未来的能源，来掌控自己的能源。是的，我想通过削减不必要的开支来减少赤字，但同时也要求富人多缴纳一点税收，以便我们能投资于研究和科技之类的项目，它们对于21世纪的经济至关重要。

作为三军总司令，我将确保我们拥有世界上最强大的军事力量，坚守我们部队的信念，追捕那些对我们构成伤害的人。但是，在经过10年的

to your voices, I will fight for your families and I will work every single day to make sure that America continues to be the greatest nation on earth. Thank you.

Schieffer: Governor.

Romney: Thank you, Bob, Mr. President, folks at Lynn University – good to be with you. I'm optimistic about the future. I'm excited about our prospects as a nation. I want to see peace. I want to see growing peace in this country, it's our objective. We have an opportunity to have real leadership. America's going to have that kind of leadership and continue to promote principles of peace that'll make a world the safer place and make people in this country more confident that their future is secure.

I also want to make sure that we get this economy going. And there are two very different paths the country can take. One is a path represented by the president, which, at the end of four years, would mean we'd have $20 trillion in debt, heading towards Greece. I'll get us on track to a balanced budget. The president's path will mean continuing declining in take-home pay. I want to make sure our take-home pay turns around and starts to grow. The president's path means 20 million people out of work struggling for a good job. I'll get people back to work with 12 million new jobs. I'm going to make sure that we get people off of food stamps not by cutting the program but by getting them good jobs.

America's going to come back. And for that to happen, we're going to have to have a president who can work across the aisle. I was in a state where my legislature was 87 percent Democrat. I learned how to get along on the other side of the aisle. We've got to do that in Washington. Washington is broken. I know what it takes to get this country back. And we'll work with good Democrats and good Republicans to do that.

This nation is the hope of the earth. We've been blessed by having a nation that's free and prosperous thanks to the contributions of the Greatest Generation. They've held a torch for the world to see, the torch of freedom and hope and

战争之后，我想我们都认识到，我们应该在国内进行一些国家建设活动，重新修建我们的道路、我们的桥梁，尤其是要安顿好我们的退役老兵，他们为了我们的自由，作出了很多的牺牲。

大家知道，我们经历过艰难时刻，但是我们总是能够重新振作，靠的就是我们的品格与齐心协力。如果我有幸能够在未来的四年继续做你们的总统，我向你们承诺，我会永远倾听你们的声音，为你们的家庭而战斗，每天努力工作以确保美国继续成为地球上最伟大的国家。谢谢你们。

西弗：州长，到您了。

罗姆尼：谢谢你，鲍伯，总统先生，林恩大学的师生们，很高兴与你们相聚。我对未来十分乐观，一想到我们国家的前景，我就感到兴奋。我希望看到和平，我希望我们国家越来越和平、安宁，这是我们的目标。我们有机会拥有真正的领导力，美国将需要那样的领导力，继续推进和平原则，让世界更加安全，让美国人民对他们未来的安全更有信心。

我还想确保我们的经济再次运转起来，我国可以走上两条截然不同的道路，一条道路是以总统为代表，那就是在4年之后，我们将会有20万亿美元的债务，准备向希腊看齐，而我将带领我们走上预算平衡之路。总统的道路将意味着实际工资继续减少，我想扭转这种情况，让收入增加。总统的道路意味着2000万人处于失业状态，大家挣扎着寻找一份好工作。而我将创造1200万个新的工作岗位，让人们重返工作岗位。我将确保人们不再靠领取食物券过活，不是通过削减该项目，而是通过让他们获得好的工作。

美国将会东山再起，为了实现这一目标，我们需要一位能够取得两党支持的总统。在我所任职的州，我的立法机构里87%都是民主党人，我学会了如何与民主党人共事，我们将在华盛顿实现这一点，华盛顿正四分五裂，我知道如何使美国东山再起，我将与杰出的民主党人、共和党人通力合作，共同实现这一目标。

opportunity. Now it's our turn to take that torch. I'm convinced we'll do it. We need strong leadership. I'd like to be that leader, with your support. I'll work with you. I'll lead you in an open and honest way. And I ask for your vote. I'd like to be the next president of the United States to support and help this great nation, and to make sure that we all together maintain America as the hope of the earth. Thank you so much.

Schieffer: Gentlemen, thank you both so much. That brings an end to this year's debates. And we want to thank Lynn University and its students for having us. As I always do at the end of these debates, I leave you with the words of my mom who said, go vote. It makes you feel big and strong.

Obama: That's great.

Schieffer: Good night.

Obama: Thank you.

Lynn University, Boca Raton, Florida, October, 22, 2012

　　这个国家是世界的希望。多亏了最伟大的一代人①做出的贡献，我们有幸能够拥有一个自由和繁荣的国家。他们举起自由、希望和机遇的火把照亮了整个世界，现在是我们接手这个火把的时候了，我相信我们能够做到这一点。我们需要强有力的领导能力，有了你们的支持，我希望能够成为这个领导者。我将与你们通力合作，我将以一种开诚布公的方式来领导你们，我请求你们投票给我，我希望成为美国的下一任总统，来支持和帮助这个伟大的国家，以保证我们团结起来，共同维护美国作为世界希望的地位，非常感谢你们。

　　西弗： 先生们，非常感谢你们两位，今年的辩论到此结束。非常谢谢林恩大学和这里的学生邀请我们。辩论结束时，我经常说一句话，今年我也将这句话送给大家，那就是我母亲曾经说过的，去投票吧，你会感到自己无比强大。

　　奥巴马： 那很好。

　　西弗： 晚安。

　　奥巴马： 谢谢大家。

（袁婧／译　杜梦臻／校）

---

① 1914—1924年出生的美国人。

The Second Inaugural Address
by President Barack Obama

Vice President Biden, Mr. Chief Justice, Members of the United States Congress, distinguished guests, and fellow citizens:

Each time we gather to inaugurate a president, we bear witness to the enduring strength of our Constitution. We affirm the promise of our democracy. We recall that what binds this nation together is not the colors of our skin or the tenets of our faith or the origins of our names. What makes us exceptional – what makes us American – is our allegiance to an idea, articulated in a declaration made more than two centuries ago:

> *"We hold these truths to be self-evident, that all men are created equal, that they are endowed by their Creator with certain unalienable rights, that among these are Life, Liberty, and the pursuit of Happiness."*

Today we continue a never-ending journey, to bridge the meaning of those words with the realities of our time. For history tells us that while these truths may be self-evident, they have never been self-executing; that while freedom is a gift from God, it must be secured by His people here on Earth. The patriots of 1776 did not fight to replace the tyranny of a king with the privileges of a few or the rule of a mob. They gave to us a Republic, a government of, and by, and for the people, entrusting each generation to keep safe our founding creed.

For more than two hundred years, we have.

奥巴马总统连任就职演讲

拜登副总统、首席大法官先生、国会议员们、尊敬的各位嘉宾、亲爱的朋友们，大家好：

每一次我们相聚在此，共庆总统就职，实则在见证美国宪法的恒久力量，在践行美国民主的诺言。我们重申，将国家紧密相连的并非肤色，并非信仰的教条，更非姓氏来源。让我们与众不同，让我们成为美国人的，是我们对于一种信念的恪守。200多年前，独立宣言将这一理念告知世人：

> "人人生而平等，造物主赋予他们不可剥夺的权利，包括生存、自由和追求幸福的权利，我们认为这一真理是不言而喻的。"

今天，我们继续着这一未竟的征程，架起教义与现实之间的桥梁。历

501

Through blood drawn by lash and blood drawn by sword, we learned that no union founded on the principles of liberty and equality could survive half-slave and half-free. We made ourselves anew, and vowed to move forward together.

Together, we determined that a modern economy requires railroads and highways to speed travel and commerce; schools and colleges to train our workers.

Together, we discovered that a free market only thrives when there are rules to ensure competition and fair play.

Together, we resolved that a great nation must care for the vulnerable, and protect its people from life's worst hazards and misfortune. Through it all, we have never relinquished our skepticism of central authority, nor have we succumbed to the fiction that all society's ills can be cured through government alone. Our celebration of initiative and enterprise; our insistence on hard work and personal responsibility, these are constants in our character.

But we have always understood that when times change, so must we; that fidelity to our founding principles requires new responses to new challenges; that preserving our individual freedoms ultimately requires collective action. For the American people can no more meet the demands of today's world by acting alone than American soldiers could have met the forces of fascism or communism with muskets and militias. No single person can train all the math and science teachers we'll need to equip our children for the future, or build the roads and networks and research labs that will bring new jobs and businesses to our shores. Now, more than ever, we must do these things together, as one nation, and one people.

This generation of Americans has been tested by crises that steeled our resolve and proved our resilience. A decade of war is now ending. An economic recovery has begun. America's possibilities are limitless, for we possess all the qualities that this world without boundaries demands: youth and drive; diversity and openness; an endless capacity for risk and a gift for reinvention. My fellow Americans, we are made for this moment, and we will seize it – so long as we

502

史告诉我们，即使真理不言而喻，也从不会自动生效。因为，自由，虽为上帝之恩赐，却仍需世间子民去捍卫。1776年，美国的爱国先驱，英勇奋战，不是为了推翻国王的暴政，也不是为了赢得少数人的特权。他们为世人创立了共和国，一个民有、民治、民享的政府，这成为世代美国人民捍卫至终的建国信条。

过去的200年，我们做到了。

从奴役的血腥枷锁和刀光剑影中，我们懂得了，建立在自由与平等原则之上的联邦不能再继续维持半奴隶和半自由的状态。我们重获新生，立下誓言，共同前进。

我们齐心协力，架设铁路与高速公路，促进旅游与商业交流；建设学校与大学，培训技术工人，这些均是现代经济之必需。

我们一起探索，发现只有以竞争与公平为原则，自由市场才会生机勃勃。

我们共下决心，在这个伟大的国度中，贫弱者必享关怀，民众远离灾祸。一路走来，我们从未放弃对集权的质疑，从未对"一切社会弊端均可为政府一己之力解决"这样的荒诞之言屈膝投降。我们崇尚积极向上、奋发有为，坚持兢兢业业、恪尽职守，这些都是美国精神的基本要义。

我们也明白，时代在变化，我们也需要与时俱进。对建国信条的忠诚，需要我们肩负起新的责任，迎接新的挑战；需要我们捍卫个人自由，最终我们同舟共济。因为美国人不可能再单枪匹马迎接当今世界的挑战，正如美国士兵们不可能再像先辈一样，用步枪和自卫队同敌人作战。凭一己之力无法培训我们所需要的所有数学老师和科学老师，为我们的孩子打造未来；凭一己之力无法建设道路、铺设网络、建立实验室，为国内带来新的工作岗位和商业机遇。如今，与以往任何时候相比，我们更应该同心同德。作为一个国家，一个民族，更应该紧密团结。

我们这代美国人，经历了危机的考验，力挽狂澜，证明了自身的恢复能力。长达十年的战争就要偃旗息鼓，经济的复苏也逐步展开。美国的潜力无法估量，因为我们拥有人类社会普遍需要的全部品质：年轻与活力、多样与开放、无穷的冒险精神以及创造的天赋才能。亲爱的同胞们，我们为此刻而生，我们更应当同舟共济，抓住当下的机遇。

seize it together.

For we, the people, understand that our country cannot succeed when a shrinking few do very well and a growing many barely make it. We believe that America's prosperity must rest upon the broad shoulders of a rising middle class. We know that America thrives when every person can find independence and pride in their work; when the wages of honest labor liberate families from the brink of hardship. We are true to our creed when a little girl born into the bleakest poverty knows that she has the same chance to succeed as anybody else, because she is an American, she is free, and she is equal, not just in the eyes of God but also in our own.

We understand that outworn programs are inadequate to the needs of our time. We must harness new ideas and technology to remake our government, revamp our tax code, reform our schools, and empower our citizens with the skills they need to work harder, learn more, and reach higher. But while the means will change, our purpose endures: a nation that rewards the effort and determination of every single American. That is what this moment requires. That is what will give real meaning to our creed.

We, the people, still believe that every citizen deserves a basic measure of security and dignity. We must make the hard choices to reduce the cost of health care and the size of our deficit. But we reject the belief that America must choose between caring for the generation that built this country and investing in the generation that will build its future. For we remember the lessons of our past, when twilight years were spent in poverty, and parents of a child with a disability had nowhere to turn. We do not believe that in this country, freedom is reserved for the lucky, or happiness for the few. We recognize that no matter how responsibly we live our lives, any one of us, at any time, may face a job loss, or a sudden illness, or a home swept away in a terrible storm. The commitments we make to each other – through Medicare, and Medicaid, and Social Security – these things do not sap our initiative; they strengthen us. They do not make us a

因为，我们，美国同胞们，很清楚，如果收获成功的人愈来愈少，且芸芸众生皆难以企及，那么，我们的国家便无法成功。我们相信，美国的繁荣必须建立在正在崛起的中产阶级的宽阔臂膀之中，我们知道，只有当人人都能在自己工作岗位中感到独立和自豪，只有当诚实劳动获得的收入足以让家庭摆脱贫困的威胁时，美国才会真正发展。只有当一个出生时一贫如洗的小女孩能够意识到，她同其他所有人一样拥有获得成功的同等机遇，因为她是一个美国人，是自由的、平等的，这份自由与平等不仅由上帝来见证，更由我们亲手呵护，只有此时，我们才真正践行了我们的建国纲领。

我们知道，陈旧的程序早已不能满足时代的需求。我们必须应用新的理念和新的技术，重塑政府，改进税法，改革教育制度。让我们的公民拥有他们所需要的技能，更加努力地工作，学到更多的知识，向更高的目标攀登。虽然方式有所变化，但我们的目标是很明确的：国家将为每位公民的努力和果敢提供奖励。这是我们这个时代所要求的，这也将为我们的建国纲领赋予真正的意义。

我们，美国同胞们，依旧相信，每个公民都应当获得基本的安全和尊严。我们必须作出艰难的抉择，降低医疗成本，缩减赤字规模。是为那些曾经效力国家建设的老一代人提供照顾，还是为那些将要成为国之栋梁的新一代人进行投资，我们拒绝在这二者中间只选择其一。因为，我们没有忘记过去的教训：老者暮年却身处贫寒；家有残童却无处求救。我们相信，在这个国度，自由不只是那些幸运儿的专属，换句话说，幸福不应只属于少数人。我们知道，不管我们怎样负责任地生活，我们中的任何人在某些时候都可能面临失业、突发疾病或住房被骇人的飓风摧毁的风险。我们通过医疗保险、联邦医疗补助计划、社会保障项目向每个人作出承诺，这些非但不会枯竭我们的创造力，反而会让我们变的更加坚强；非但不会使我们沦为不劳而获的国度，反而会让我们自主地承担风险，让国家变的更加强大。

我们，美国同胞们，仍然相信，作为美国人，我们所尽的义务并非只为我们自己，子孙后代也在考虑之中。我们将对气候变化的威胁作出回应，我们知道，对气候变化的无视，便是对子子孙孙的背叛。或许依旧有

nation of takers; they free us to take the risks that make this country great.

We, the people, still believe that our obligations as Americans are not just to ourselves, but to all posterity. We will respond to the threat of climate change, knowing that the failure to do so would betray our children and future generations. Some may still deny the overwhelming judgment of science, but none can avoid the devastating impact of raging fires, and crippling drought, and more powerful storms. The path towards sustainable energy sources will be long and sometimes difficult. But America cannot resist this transition; we must lead it. We cannot cede to other nations the technology that will power new jobs and new industries – we must claim its promise. That is how we will maintain our economic vitality and our national treasure – our forests and waterways; our croplands and snowcapped peaks. That is how we will preserve our planet, commanded to our care by God. That's what will lend meaning to the creed our fathers once declared.

We, the people, still believe that enduring security and lasting peace do not require perpetual war. Our brave men and women in uniform, tempered by the flames of battle, are unmatched in skill and courage. Our citizens, seared by the memory of those we have lost, know too well the price that is paid for liberty. The knowledge of their sacrifice will keep us forever vigilant against those who would do us harm. But we are also heirs to those who won the peace and not just the war, who turned sworn enemies into the surest of friends, and we must carry those lessons into this time as well.

We will defend our people and uphold our values through strength of arms and rule of law. We will show the courage to try and resolve our differences with other nations peacefully – not because we are naïve about the dangers we face, but because engagement can more durably lift suspicion and fear. America will remain the anchor of strong alliances in every corner of the globe; and we will renew those institutions that extend our capacity to manage crisis abroad, for no one has a greater stake in a peaceful world than its most powerful nation. We will

人对至高无上的科学论断心存质疑，但是，面对熊熊火灾、暴虐干旱、凶猛飓风所带来的灾难性打击，没有人可以幸免。可再生能源的利用之路漫长而艰巨。但是，面对这一趋势，美国非但不应抵制，反而应当起带头作用。我们许下承诺——绝不能把创造新岗位和新产业的技术拱手相让给他国。这就是保持经济活力，保护森林和航道、农田和雪山等国家财富的方法。我们也将用这种方法保护我们的地球家园，既然造物主将这个星球托付给我们。通过这些努力，我们也将为前辈们曾经宣布的纲领信条赋予新的涵义。

我们，美国同胞们，仍然相信，持久的安定与和平并不需要旷日的战争。我们英勇的男女军人，经受了战火的考验，他们的技能和勇气无可匹敌。那些阵亡志士，美国同胞们将铭记在心，异常清楚我们为自由付出的代价，明白他们的牺牲将让我们对那些试图伤害我们的势力永远保持警惕。我们的前辈，不仅赢得了战争，也赢得了和平，他们化敌为友。我们作为他们的后代，必须把这些经验带入这个时代。

我们将通过强大的军力和法治来保护我们的民众，并捍卫我们的价值观。我们将鼓起勇气，尝试以和平的方式解决我们与他国的分歧，这并非

support democracy from Asia to Africa; from the Americas to the Middle East, because our interests and our conscience compel us to act on behalf of those who long for freedom. And we must be a source of hope to the poor, the sick, the marginalized, the victims of prejudice – not out of mere charity, but because peace in our time requires the constant advance of those principles that our common creed describes: tolerance and opportunity; human dignity and justice.

We, the people, declare today that the most evident of truths – that all of us are created equal – is the star that guides us still; just as it guided our forebears through Seneca Falls, and Selma, and Stonewall; just as it guided all those men and women, sung and unsung, who left footprints along this great Mall, to hear a preacher say that we cannot walk alone; to hear a King proclaim that our individual freedom is inextricably bound to the freedom of every soul on Earth.

It is now our generation's task to carry on what those pioneers began. For our journey is not complete until our wives, our mothers, and daughters can earn a living equal to their efforts. Our journey is not complete until our gay brothers and sisters are treated like anyone else under the law – for if we are truly created equal, then surely the love we commit to one another must be equal as well. Our journey is not complete until no citizen is forced to wait for hours to exercise the right to vote. Our journey is not complete until we find a better way to welcome the striving, hopeful immigrants who still see America as a land of opportunity; until bright young students and engineers are enlisted in our workforce rather than expelled from our country. Our journey is not complete until all our children, from the streets of Detroit to the hills of Appalachia to the quiet lanes of Newtown, know that they are cared for, and cherished, and always safe from harm.

That is our generation's task – to make these words, these rights, these values – of Life, and Liberty, and the Pursuit of Happiness – real for every American. Being true to our founding documents does not require us to agree on every contour of life; it does not mean we will all define liberty in exactly the same way, or follow the same precise path to happiness. Progress does not

因为我们对面临的危机认识浮浅，而是因为接触能够更持久地化解疑虑和恐惧。美国将在全球各个角落保持强大的联盟阵营；我们将更新现有的机制，以拓展我们应对海外危机的能力，这是因为，世界上最强大的国家也能从世界和平中获取最大的利益。我们将支持从亚洲到非洲、从美洲至中东的民主运动，因为我们的利益和良心驱使我们代表那些渴望获得自由的人们采取行动。我们必须成为贫困者、病患者、被边缘化者、异见受害者的希望源泉，不仅仅是出于慈善，而是因为，这个时代的和平需要不断地推进我们共同信念中所包含的原则：宽容和机遇，人类的尊严与正义。

我们，美国同胞们，今天再次宣示：人人生而平等——这一颠扑不破的真理依然是引领我们的恒星。它曾引领我们的先辈穿越纽约塞尼卡瀑布城（女权抗议事件）、塞尔马（黑人权力事件）和石墙骚乱（同性恋与警察发生的暴力事件），曾引领着众多男男女女——或垂名青史或隐名于世，在伟大的征程中，一路走来，留下足迹——去倾听一位牧师的祷告："我们不能孤独前行"，去聆听马丁·路德·金先生的宣言："我们个人的自由与地球上任何灵魂的自由不可分割。"

继承先辈们开创的事业，是我们这代人的责任。我们的征程不会终结，直到我们的妻子、母亲和女儿的付出能够得到同等的回报。我们的征程不会终结，直到让同性恋的兄弟姐妹在法律中享受与其他人同样的待遇——倘若人真是生而平等，那么彼此间的爱也应该是平等的。我们的征程不会结束，直到没有公民被迫要等数个小时才能行使投票权。我们的征途不会结束，直到我们可以找到更好的方法去迎接那些艰难拼搏、心怀梦想的移民，他们仍旧将美国视为一片充满机遇的热土；直到聪慧过人的莘莘学子和工程师们均可人尽其才，而不是被驱逐出境。我们的征程不会结束，直到所有的孩子，从底特律的街道到阿巴拉契亚的山岭，再到康涅狄格州纽恩镇安静的小巷，都能感知到自身所享有的关心与珍爱，而且永远远离伤害。

这就是我们这一代人的任务——让有关生命、自由和追求幸福的言语、权力和价值观，在每个美国人的身上都得到体现。我们的建国纲领不曾要求将每个人的生活方式完全一致；不曾示意，我们需要以完全一样的方式来定义自由，沿着一样的道路奔向幸福。进步，不会强迫我们去终止

compel us to settle centuries-long debates about the role of government for all time – but it does require us to act in our time.

For now decisions are upon us, and we cannot afford delay. We cannot mistake absolutism for principle, or substitute spectacle for politics, or treat name-calling as reasoned debate. We must act, knowing that our work will be imperfect. We must act, knowing that today's victories will be only partial, and that it will be up to those who stand here in four years, and forty years, and four hundred years hence to advance the timeless spirit once conferred to us in a spare Philadelphia hall.

My fellow Americans, the oath I have sworn before you today, like the one recited by others who serve in this Capitol, was an oath to God and country, not party or faction – and we must faithfully execute that pledge during the duration of our service. But the words I spoke today are not so different from the oath that is taken each time a soldier signs up for duty, or an immigrant realizes her dream. My oath is not so different from the pledge we all make to the flag that waves above and that fills our hearts with pride.

They are the words of citizens, and they represent our greatest hope.

You and I, as citizens, have the power to set this country's course.

You and I, as citizens, have the obligation to shape the debates of our time – not only with the votes we cast, but with the voices we lift in defense of our most ancient values and enduring ideals.

Let us, each of us, now embrace with solemn duty and awesome joy what is our lasting birthright. With common effort and common purpose, with passion and dedication, let us answer the call of history and carry into an uncertain future that precious light of freedom.

Thank you, God Bless you, and may He forever bless these United States of America.

Capitol Hill, Washington D. C., January 21, 2013

几个世纪以来对于政府角色的争论，但进步要求我们从现在做起，付诸行动。

时至今日，决策者是我们自己，我们不能再拖延下去。但绝对标准不能成为行事原则，幻想也不能取代政治，或把辱骂行为放在理性辩论的高度。我们必须采取行动，同时要认识到我们的工作并不会十分完美。我们必须采取行动，同时要意识到今天的胜利只是一个开始。仍将有赖于人们在未来4年、40年或是400年去推进当年在费城制宪会议大厅传承给我们的永恒精神。

美国同胞们，我今天在各位面前宣读的誓词，同在国会上曾经宣誓的其他人的誓词一样，是对上帝和国家的起誓，不针对党派，不纠结派别，我们一定在任期内忠实地践行这些承诺。但是，我今天所宣读的誓词，与入伍参军的士兵、与怀揣梦想的移民所宣读的誓词并无多大差别；我的誓词，与众人在这面随风飘扬、激荡人心的国旗下所立下的誓言，并无多大差别。

这些誓词是民众的誓言，代表着我们最伟大的希望。

你和我，作为美国公民，都有权利为祖国绘制路线。

你和我，作为美国公民，有义务确定我们时代辩论的主题，不仅仅是通过一张张选票，还要通过对我们悠久的价值观的捍卫和对理想的锲而不舍的追求。

此时此刻，让我们每个人相互拥抱，心怀庄严的责任和无与伦比的快乐，这些是我们永恒的、与生俱来的权利。有共同的努力和共同的目标，用热情与奉献，让我们回应历史的召唤，将珍贵的自由之光带入未知的未来。

感谢你们，上帝保佑你们，愿上帝永远保佑美利坚合众国。

（杜梦臻／译　王晓娟／校）

Acknowledgements

鸣　谢

　　本书采用了奥巴马总统和罗姆尼州长的竞选演讲和辩论，首先谨向总统本人和州长本人表示诚挚的感谢！并向双方的竞选班底表示衷心的感谢！

　　编译者杜梦臻小姐和袁婧小姐在接到选题任务后，昼夜加班，保质保量完成了编译任务，付出了极大的努力。

　　本书由世界知识出版社图书中心集体策划，并得到了总编辑和社领导的大力支持，是集体劳动和智慧的结晶，具体人名恕不在此一一列举。

　　本书全面反映了美国总统竞选的整个过程，对于学习和了解美国的内政外交政策、政治制度有很大的帮助。同时，对于学习当代英语语言和文化也有极大的助益，衷心地希望本书能够得到读者朋友的喜爱。

编　者

2013 年 1 月 28 日